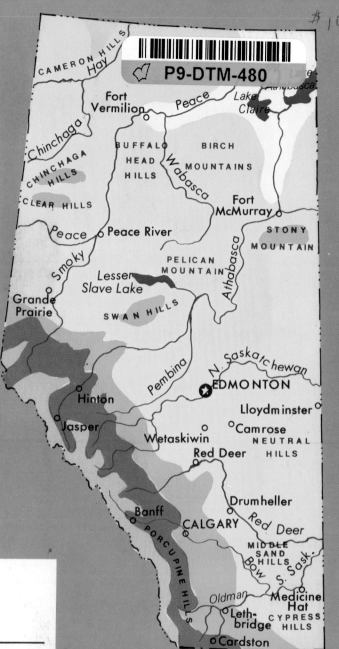

# population of Alberta's cities

Edmonton — 435,503

Calgary — 398,034

Lethbridge — 40,856

Red Deer — 27,431

Medicine Hat — 25,713

Grande Prairie — 12,054

Camrose — 8,903

Lloydminster — 7,817

Wetaskiwin — 6,586

Drumheller — 5,240

# the growth of Edmonton and Calgary

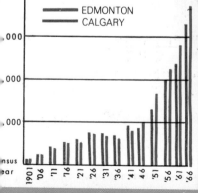

- EDMONTON
- CALGARY

Census Year: 1901, '06, '11, '16, '21, '26, '31, '36, '41, '46, '51, '56, '61, '66

# ALBERTA

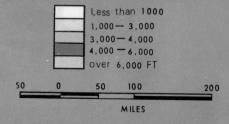

Less than 1000

1,000 — 3,000

3,000 — 4,000

4,000 — 6,000

over 6,000 FT

50   0   50   100   200

MILES

Jim MacGregor has enlivened the history of the West and illuminated the lives of some of its outstanding figures throughout a twenty-five year career as a popular historian. His familiarity with Alberta springs from a life's work and travel in every part of the province.

A past president of the Historical Society of Alberta and presently a governor of the Glenbow-Alberta Institute, Mr. MacGregor is the recipient of numerous awards for his outstanding contributions to the preservation of western Canadian history. Among his ten previously published works are *North-West of Sixteen, Pack Saddles to Tete Jaune Cache, Edmonton: A History, Vilni Zemli; The Ukrainian Settlement of Alberta,* and *The Klondike Rush Through Edmonton.*

In professional life Mr. MacGregor has held a number of important positions as an engineer. A graduate of the University of Alberta, he joined Canadian Utilities Limited in 1929 and left as general manager to become chairman of the Alberta Power Commission in 1952. Prior to his retirement in 1970, he was appointed chairman of the Royal Commission on the Development of Northern Alberta.

In 1971 Mr. MacGregor was granted an honourary Doctor of Laws degree by the University of Alberta.

# A History of Alberta

# James G. MacGregor

Hurtig Publishers

# A History of Alberta

Edmonton, Alberta

Hurtig Publishers
225 Birks Building
Edmonton, Alberta

ISBN 0-88830-063-8

Printed and bound in Canada

# Contents

# Illustrations

# Maps

The maps for *A History of Alberta* were drawn by Lillian (Mrs. W. C.) Wonders.

To the fur traders, farmers
and financiers who have made Alberta
what it is

# Preface

My Alberta is a magnificent land—a magic land. The seasons transform spring's new leaves to fall's blaze of gold, always ending in the sheltered silences of winter's pine forests. For me, no other land can match its rugged grandeur or rival its hold on the heartstrings.

Not only is it beautiful, from the sage-scented Cypress Hills to the redolent spruce-forested Caribou Mountain, but each of its valleys, hills and mountain passes is steeped in history, the history of men following their fortunes to Alberta. For at least ten thousand years, many men—even as you and I—have lived in these valleys and camped beside these lakes and all the while, in elation or despair, toiled to feed their families.

Over these hills have tramped Anthony Henday and David Thompson. Into the valleys came the wolfers and hide hunters and the whisky traders. Crisscrossing the billowing prairies rambled the Crees and Assiniboines, ever watchful of the mighty Blackfoot who during their century of power brooked no interlopers. Then in their thousands came settlers to peer across this flat or to peek into that valley in search of their homesteads. To the land's mastery, in hardship but happiness, they devoted the toil of the rest of their lives. Politicians and prohibition came and went. Good times succeeded hard as pioneers extracted sustenance and fulfillment from the rich soils. Then up and down these same valleys and over these same swelling hills came men with the courage to gamble their all in the pursuit of elusive petroleum pools hidden beneath the beautiful fields or locked away below the lonesome forests. They brought oil and wealth, skyscrapers, paved highways and farm electrification: all the luxuries demanded by a rich, consumer-minded populace.

To me the paved road was once a trail chopped out of the forest by homesteaders heading for their land. The mall of a vast shopping centre where shoppers choose between merchandise from all over the world—this mall was once a field where a pioneer sighted between his horses' heads to lay out his opening furrow. Where huge combines snuffle along so easily, filling their great maws with amber wheat, peasants from Europe with scythe and cradle once bent their aching backs to garner their first pitiful crop, grinding it in hand mills to feed their hungry brood.

A History of Alberta

Unfortunately, in a history which must gallop along to cover the centuries, we have time to tell of but a few individuals' achievements and space to paint mere fragments of Alberta's magnificent wilderness. Moreover, histories can be written from a number of viewpoints, all of them valid and yet each varying from the others as their authors deal with different political and sociological phases, and trace the interaction of selected causes and effects.

I have tried to cast this history against Alberta's riches and its beauty. This book confines itself to how the players who have trod its stage gradually perceived and utilized its resources from the days when these resources supported but ten thousand worthy Indians until today when they have made 1,600,000 Albertans rich beyond the dreams of their fathers.

These players—the first primitive people from Asia; their descendants, the Indians; the fur traders and explorers; the gold panners, railroad builders and homesteaders—all of them held the stage for a while and then vanished into the wings and into history. Sodbusters and pioneers developed into modern farmers and city folk, experiencing all the ups and downs of an agricultural economy. Then came a new breed, the oilmen. They made a dramatic contribution, dwarfing the puny buildings of a generation previous with skyscrapers. Paved highways, with overpasses and complicated grade separation devices ran where once only pack horses in single file could wind their way.

Throughout its development, the hard determination of Alberta's earliest inhabitants and immigrants is evident as each generation, including the most recent crop of university graduates, erects its own signposts to the future.

JAMES G. MACGREGOR
P.ENG., LL.D.

# Acknowledgements

Anyone undertaking to compile a history soon finds himself deeply in debt to scores of authors, individuals and institutions without whose writings, well-stored minds or well-stocked shelves, the job could not be done. To all the many I am grateful for letting me borrow their ideas. To all the people of this rich land of Alberta I am also grateful that over the decades they have funnelled so much of their effort into supporting the province's many and varied libraries and photographic collections —some publicly endowed and some private.

Although it is unfair to mention only one of the many scholars who have helped, nevertheless, while saying a heartfelt thank you to all of them, I must single out one for help in an aspect of our history about which all too little has been written. That individual is Hugh Dempsey, archivist of the Glenbow-Alberta Institute, whose kindness in letting me study the manuscript of his forthcoming book on Chief Crowfoot made possible what little insight I have gained into the way of life of our fascinating prairie predecessors.

Sheilagh Jameson, also of the Glenbow-Alberta Institute, Mrs. H. Kreisel of the Public Archives of Alberta, and my long-time friend Mrs. Shirlee Smith of the Hudson's Bay Company at Winnipeg, ferreted out the bulk of the photographs used in the text—God bless them. I am also grateful to Mrs. W. Wonders for her great ability in suggesting and compiling the many maps.

Finally, while my name appears as author, a major share of the credit goes to my wife Frances, who by her typing, research, helpful criticism and her oiling of the gears of the authorship machine, keeps the partnership pen producing.

# 1
# The First Albertans

Eleven thousand years ago on the banks of the Oldman River near modern Taber, a primitive hunter butchered a buffalo. He crushed the animal's skull with a crudely fashioned hammer which, when found recently, was still embedded in the bone. It may well have been that as he looked around after cutting up the carcass this early wanderer on Alberta's soil blinked at the glare of the vast field of glacial ice on the Blackspring Ridge some thirty miles to the north and west.

This hunter and his associates were among the forerunners of our modern Indians. How long before that time his ancestors had roamed Alberta's southern prairies we have not yet discovered. Modern archaeologists, while admitting that they have just begun to uncover a few clues to the long story, are in general agreement that the first immigrants may have entered Alaska some thirty thousand years ago. Crossing from Siberia over the land bridge, which, although covered now by the Bering Sea, could have been thirteen hundred miles wide during the time of major glaciation, they advanced slowly with spears at the ready for any of the plentiful game animals of the day. If indeed they moved south into the heart of North America at that time, they must have worked their way through an ice-free corridor along Alberta's western side.

Many scholars, however, think that they arrived later and passed through Alberta during a minor recession of the last glacier. In any event, it is known that Indians were living in much of the United States south of the uttermost edge of the last ice sheet while practically all of Alberta and some of northern Montana was still covered with ice. Their movement from Siberia was not a migration in the sense that a group of people intending to reach a certain destination marches forward consistently. It was in fact a gradual drifting through Alaska and the Yukon and down the Alberta corridor in the process of hunting for their daily food, which included mammoths and giant bison. Each day's hunting might send them out in any direction from their night's camp and sometimes they ventured into unexplored ice-rimmed valleys leading south. During the passage of centuries their descendants would move south through Alberta until they reached the southern edge of the glacier and

13

were in what is now the United States. It is thought that over eleven thousand years ago they were relatively numerous in all parts of the United States, far enough south of the Canadian border to be free of ice.

While it is almost certain that thousands of years ago these first immigrants roamed through Alberta, the earliest demonstrable evidence of early man found so far in Alberta is the discovery of the skull crushed by our hunter. The find was made by Dr. L. A. Bayrock of the Research Council of Alberta. Whoever the hunter was, he was of a race which for some centuries had lived on the Great Plains well south of the ice sheet and of a band which was moving north into the wooded lands well watered by the run-off from the receding southern fringe of the glacier. By that time Indians were migrating north toward Alberta from their sometime homeland extending from Wyoming south.

North of the scene of this discovery most of the land we know as Alberta was covered with ice. If our early native had ventured on to the glacier, he would have found the present-day sites of Calgary, Edmonton and Fort Chipewyan covered by ice respectively two thousand feet, five thousand feet and eight thousand feet deep. Subsequently melting away at its southern edge, it receded north uncovering Edmonton about ten thousand years ago and Fort Chipewyan some eight thousand years ago. In its wake it left a desolate moraine of high precipitation covered with immense lakes and marshes. On the firmer soil between the lakes coniferous forests sprang up, while from the ice and the resultant huge glacial lake great streams of meltwater made their way south and east, carving the deep channels which wind across our prairies and parklands: the Gwynne, Rosebud, Etzikom and other coulees carrying water to the Missouri River.

Century by century, as the ice retreated to Calgary, Edmonton and Fort Chipewyan, the earliest pioneers, keeping pace with the glacier's withdrawal and engaging in a nomadic hunting existence, began peopling the future province. As the edge of the ice drew back ever farther north, the damp climate at its former margin gave way to warmer conditions. Finally, extending from about seventy-five hundred to forty-five hundred years ago, a warm, dry climatic phase known to archaeologists as the Altithermal spread north to the Northwest Territories. Before many centuries the weather in America's Great Plains and in Canada's prairie provinces became too hot and dry for any significant populations to remain in them.

Then, about forty-five hundred years ago when the heat began to moderate, central and northern Alberta once more grew up to forests. Better soil had developed and once more hunting nomads moved in to pursue the increasingly numerous big game animals. Alberta's landscape and climate became much like it is in our day. In the north, moose, caribou and deer fed in the marshes and forests, fish teemed in the lakes,

A History of Alberta

and all was well with the rather sparse human population of the northern forests. On the southern prairies and throughout the parklands, and even into the northern forests, a new species of bison, our buffalo, found an ideal environment. And hard on their heels came the prairie Indians to enjoy the good climate, to feast on the buffalo and to have enough time on their hands to develop a somewhat more complex society.

In time, the prairie tribes perfected their effective buffalo hunting techniques and devised methods of killing these shaggy beasts in pounds fashioned of logs or brush, or in jumps where the buffalo were driven to their deaths over cliffs. Sporadic warfare must have been a condition of life as new peoples tried to encroach on this prairie paradise and either were turned back or displaced the natives who fought bitterly for the land they loved.

On the prairies a long era of plenty, relative stability and contentment ensued. Dr. R. G. Forbis's infinitely rewarding excavations at the Old Women's Buffalo Jump near Cayley indicate a long period of prosperity extending back to the time of Christ. Undoubtedly during that period tribe succeeded tribe in the possession of the prairies. During that period too the excavations indicate changing patterns in artifacts as these peoples came and went. One striking change which the digging confirmed was the switch to smaller projectile points about A.D. 600, marking the addition of the bow and arrow to the spear-throwing armoury. The Indians had begun to improve and refine their armaments.

During the long life of the Old Women's Buffalo Jump, the generations of Indians that hunted the buffalo on the endless prairies led a happy existence, and they dotted the plains with other souvenirs of their way of life. These included stone teepee rings, stone cairns, buffalo effigies, medicine wheels, ribstones, pictographs and petroglyphs, all dating from this era. Formed of the stones with which the nomads held down the bases of their buffalo skin lodges, teepee rings are commonly found. Medicine wheels, such as the one a dozen or so miles east of Carmangay, were large circles of boulders from which lines of stones radiated for a hundred feet, usually to the cardinal points of the compass. In the Neutral Hills north of Consort several boulder effigies depicting bison, turtles and snakes, lie on the grassy ground. Stone cairns, such as the one near the junction of the Bow and Oldman rivers, probably commemorate some significant event. Ribstones, like those found about a mile south of Highway 14 near Phillips, are boulders on which, using stone hammers, the Indians pecked out grooves apparently depicting the spinal column and the ribs of buffalo. All are memorials to a way of life now gone forever. These, as well as the pictographs and the petroglyphs painted or scratched on the sandstone cliffs at Writing-On-Stone Provincial Park, indicate a magical religious motivation of the roving men who trod every square foot of our prairies. Probably such monuments were fashioned before the arrival of the white men, even though long after that the Indians continued to respect them.

Over the centuries, as the natives learned the technique of the buffalo drive which had made their food supply more dependable, the population of the prairies increased. Moreover, as their provisions became easier to come by the Indians found that they had more leisure time. They used it to good advantage to decorate their clothing, weapons and teepees and to elaborate their social, ceremonial and religious life. Lack of mobility was a drawback; because all their travelling had to be done on foot, they lived in small bands each occupying its own specific territory and each circumscribed within the limited social circle of its restricted community. The natives of the vast northern wooded areas also supported themselves in small family groups by fishing the lakes and killing adjacent animals. The numerous lakes and rivers of the north, the highways of the forest, carrying their birchbark canoes, gave them all the mobility they needed.

According to Diamond Jenness, four broad linguistic stocks of Indians lived within its present borders just before white men reached Alberta: Athapaskan, Algonkian, Kootenayan and some Siouan stock. The forests, extending from the North Saskatchewan River to the northern boundary of the province, were the home of the Athapaskan people—with the Beaver Indians occupying the heart of that territory from the present site of Edmonton to beyond the Peace River. Surrounding them on the east, north and west respectively were their relatives, the Chipewyan, the Slaves and the Sekani, while in the area between the upper Athabasca and the upper North Saskatchewan rivers lived the Sarcee. The Sarcee were in the process of abandoning their way of life in the woods and of moving out to the prairies, where they allied themselves with the totally unrelated Blackfoot, and thenceforth were in effect prairie Indians.

The Algonkian were represented by the Bloods, Piegans and Blackfoot of the Blackfoot Confederacy which occupied most of the parkland and prairies south of the North Saskatchewan River. Sometimes they grudgingly shared the southeast corner of the province with men of their own linguistic stock, the Gros Ventres. Working in from the east, and also of the same stock, came the Crees, who were beginning to take over the area north of the North Saskatchewan River from Edmonton downstream and extending nearly as far north as Fort McMurray.

The Assiniboines were the sole representatives of the Siouan stock and they began encroaching on the lower Battle River valley.

All by themselves along the foothills south of Banff were the Kootenay. Having already been pushed off the prairies, they were now almost through the passes of the Rocky Mountains. But the Kootenay were not the only tribe which was being driven out of Alberta. At one time the Shoshoni, whom the earlier writers called Snakes, had laid claim to southwestern Alberta as far north as the Red Deer valley.

These were the areas occupied by Alberta's Indians about 1725. Their boundaries were subject to constant change, however, and during the following fifty years, after the white man's presence began to be felt and as the more aggressive tribes wrested lands from the weaker ones, their distribution was considerably different.

Ultimately the existence of the white man in eastern Canada created a pressure which, transmitted from tribe to tribe, began to bear on Alberta's Indians. Long before they had seen a white man this pressure was felt. In the long run, of course, it destroyed the Indian way of life. But for a few decades on the Canadian plains the introduction of some of the white man's goods set the prairie Indians, and particularly the Blackfoot Confederacy, off into a new orbit. For a few vivid decades Blackfoot culture, based upon horses, guns and unlimited buffalo, rose rapidly to the zenith of the rich, colourful and glamorous life which many regard as the apogee of plains culture. Prior to 1730, during the long era which the Blackfoot called the dog-days they travelled on foot and used dogs for transport. About that year the acquisition of horses and guns swept them rapidly onward and upward until slightly over a century later they were at the peak of their spectacular horse-based culture. At its height they were the most powerful, the most warlike, and the most dreaded raiders of the Canadian and Montana plains.

The introduction of white man's goods also wrought changes in the culture of the woods Indians, the various Athapaskan people living north of the North Saskatchewan River, but for a couple of centuries these changes were not so marked as to make much material difference in their way of life. For that reason we can leave them for the present and concentrate on the far more colourful lives of those prairie dwellers whose ancestors came walking west into the Saskatchewan and Alberta prairies well before the white man showed up and of whom the Blackfoot were typical.

They came on foot—stone-age pedestrians plodding about after game, mostly buffalo, and skirmishing with enemy tribesmen. Their primitive weapons were of their own manufacture and they had neither guns, canoes nor horses. Their only domesticated animals were dogs; it was the dog that became their beast of burden in the constant movement from one camp to another. Migrating gradually west into Alberta along courses parallel to and south of the North Saskatchewan River and in a country of grassy slopes, park-like copses and timbered river valleys, they found the land filled with life's necessities: game, wild plant foods, ample water and firewood.

The First Albertans

Travelling over flat plains and along dozens of leafy valleys, they made their way up the big gully north of Lloydminster into the rich Marwayne basin bounded on the south by the blue ridge of the Blackfoot Hills; through the maple brush along the somnolent breeze-scented Battle River into the rolling hills of the Ribstone and Wainwright areas; up Eyehill Creek to Sounding Lake and the dominating Neutral Hills.

And ever they kept moving—moving as the wild herds moved—four or five miles at a time, camping perhaps a whole week if the buffalo lingered, and then with the women and dogs shouldering the household gear, moving again as the buffalo headed north or south or west.

The buffalo were their food, and in some sense were one of their gods. And always as the bison sought new pastures the Blackfoot followed, making a large erratic circuit over the prairie meadows dotted with crocus, wild rose, shooting star and tiger lily. To a modern office worker this life during spring and fall would have seemed a perpetual summer holiday. In truth, much of the time was filled with the grinding labour of moving camp, bringing in the meat and drying and shredding it for winter's use. When buffalo abounded, the Blackfoot shared their food and feasted; when the buffalo were scarce, all shared in tightening their belts. No one was richer than his neighbour, no one was poorer. Accumulating wealth or even a well-stocked larder was impractical. They wrested their living almost day by day from the prairie hills and valleys. Doing so and leading little better than a marginal existence, they had no time for any of the higher flights of philosophy or ceremonial life which have always gone hand in hand with the culture of sedentary farmers.

For no matter how halcyon the green grass months might be, winter with its drifts, biting cold and blizzards was never far from their thoughts. In winter the buffalo deserted the exposed plains and headed for the wooded river valleys and the copse-studded Neutral, Blackfoot and Beaver hills. Carrying their winter provisions, the Blackfoot gratefully followed to the shelter of the woods or the foothills where dead trees afforded firewood and the hills helped break the wind. But even then, although perhaps not so frequently, they had to move as the game animals in their immediate vicinity were killed off.

Most of the time two or three men hunting together could not keep up with the heavy demand for meat. The buffalo, grazing onward, formed herds, large or small, and to fill their larder successfully the Blackfoot families had to cooperate with others in the hunt. This led to sorting themselves into separate hunting bands with perhaps twenty or thirty families in each. Such a band could encircle a small herd more effectively. Moreover, such a band was large enough to defend itself from enemies.

Each family assumed responsibility for moving its own lodge and possessions. The cover of the teepee, limited to about fourteen feet in diameter so as to be easily hauled by dogs, was the heaviest piece and the teepee poles perhaps the most awkward, although they were tied to the dogs as travois.

Such a camp on the march was a picturesque sight. Scouts some distance ahead led the way. The other men fell in alongside and behind the main convoy to act as flank and rear guards. The men bore little but their weapons. Upon the women carrying their infants and other burdens on their backs fell the brunt of the move—on them and on the dogs. At the end of five or six miles both women and dogs were glad to camp. Such short stages limited the area in which any one band roamed.

Time after time they traversed the same small region; within that area every man, woman and child knew every hill and valley and hummock and they camped beside every pond or pool or creek until each knew every acre of his homeland. Although they may never have expressed the idea in words, each came to love the little piece of the beautiful parklands or prairies which he called his home.

And indeed it was a magnificent land, Alberta's parklands and prairies. A vast land over three hundred miles from north to south and rippling away beyond the province's borders, it was an ocean of grass bounded on the north by the boreal forest and in the west lapping at the edge of the pine-clad foothills. A never ending meadow, it was decked with blue and pink and gold, with crocuses, roses and marigolds, and dotted with azure lakes reflecting the blueness of the boundless sky. For with the ever changing clouds, the sky, too, was part of the Indians' paradise.

By and large, the Indian was content to take his place in this pristine ecology without upsetting its equilibrium. Once in a while his campfire got away from him and burned a bit of forest and now and then he deliberately set the prairies on fire, but generally speaking, he rarely tampered with the world as he found it. For weeks and months a woods Indian might paddle along forest-girt streams, and, except for the ashes of a campfire kindled from dead branches, he left no mark of his passing. Out on the prairies a Blackfoot might wander all summer, leaving as a sign of his visit a few well-picked buffalo bones to bleach in the sun for a few years, and then to be absorbed by the soil. Just as during his life he had not disfigured the beautiful countryside, so also when death came and took the world from him, his son did not deface it with a tombstone. Neither the forest nor the prairie was marred by the use he made of it.

Regardless of that, the pressure of the white men jostling each other thousands of miles away on the Atlantic coast was on its way to change his life. Along the coast these interlopers invaded and occupied the natives' land and forced the former owners farther west. In their turn, they pushed others farther inland and started a general movement west.

In addition, those tribes in actual contact with white men secured guns from them and then had a tremendous advantage over the tribes to the west. They soon expanded their territory, forcing the natives who were armed only with bows and arrows to fall back before them.

The Crees of northwestern Ontario and northern Manitoba, for instance, found it much to their interest to maintain friendly relations with the intruding French from Montreal and the interloping English from Hudson Bay. Arming themselves, they rapidly extended their territory westward toward the parkland. Not only did they push the Athapaskans, Beavers, Slaves and Sarcees before them, but they bore down on the Blackfoot. Before long the Blackfoot, forced farther south and west into Alberta, found themselves thrust against the Shoshoni group known as the Snakes. Squeezed in a pincers movement between Crees shooting at them from the east and the Shoshoni charging at them from the south and west, the Blackfoot had begun to feel the pressure generated by the far-off white men. They were soon to experience much more of it.

First came a few benign trinkets, products of the white men's magic —copper pots, iron axes and steel sewing needles, all brought in by the Cree middlemen and traded at an enormous profit to the foot-slogging prairie Indians. Hard on their heels, perhaps twenty years before the first white man saw the parklands, one of the deadly products of the strangers' pressure came down upon the Blackfoot—smallpox. From far to the south, leaping from tribe to tribe, it swept away half the prairie Indians. Before it they fell like autumn leaves; against the white men's diseases they had built up no immunity.

About the same time two more of the white men's gifts reached Alberta's parklands and the Blackfoot. Horses and guns trebled the Indians' mobility and striking power, and the plains tribes welcomed them avidly. Strangely enough, these two gifts arrived from different directions; horses from the Indian tribes to the south and west, and guns from the Crees to the north and east. The Crees had acquired their guns from the French and English fur traders. Before long these Crees, perhaps the most venturesome merchants of all the tribes, were using guns on the one hand to push the Blackfoot west and at the same time selling a few to the same people.

The Spanish invaders, of course, introduced horses to Mexico. On the great plains of the United States the animals thrived, and in one way or another the Indians very soon acquired them and bred large herds. Gradually, by differing routes, horses spread from tribe to tribe, and finally the Shoshoni and Snakes of Nevada and southern Idaho rejoiced in the new mobility these steeds gave them. About the same time, the Mandans of South Dakota acquired horses, so that they entered the Canadian prairies from both the southwest and the southeast.

According to David Thompson's *Narrative,* Saukamappee, a one-time

Cree who had been adopted by the Piegans, reported that somewhere between the Eagle Hills south of Battleford, Saskatchewan, and the Red Deer River, he and his friends actually saw their first horse, possibly in the Neutral Hills. That would be about 1730. It could not have been many years after that before the Piegans themselves had a few of these useful beasts, and by 1754 they owned scores of them.

Saukamappee also related another story about the first use of guns by the Piegans. These weapons were in Cree hands about 1730 when he was still a member of a Cree band. The story illustrates the Piegans' amazement and fear at the Snakes' new steeds, and also indicates the telling effect of the Crees' guns. Here the two white men's gifts, coming from diametrically opposite directions, were first arrayed against each other; the horses from the southwest and the guns from the northeast.

As Saukamappee said, speaking not so much of his own surprise as that of the other combatants: "By this time the affairs of both parties had much changed; we had more guns and iron headed arrows than before; but our enemies the Snake Indians and their allies had Misstutim [big dogs, that is horses] on which they rode, swift as the deer, on which they dashed at the Peeagans, and with their stone Pukamoggan knocked them on the head, and they had thus lost several of their best men. This news we did not well comprehend and it alarmed us, for we had no idea of horses and could not make out what they were. Only three of us went . . . and between us and the Stone Indians we had ten guns and each of us about thirty balls, and powder for the war, and we were considered the strength of the battle. . . . We Prepared for the Battle the best we could. Those of us who had guns stood in the front line, and each of us [had] two balls in his mouth, and a load of powder in his left hand to reload. . . . The War Chief was close to us, anxious to see the effect of our guns. The lines were too far asunder for us to make a sure shot, and we requested him to close the line to about sixty yards, which was gradually done, and lying flat on the ground behind the shields, we watched our opportunity when they drew their bows to shoot at us, their bodies were then exposed and each of us, as opportunity offered, fired with deadly aim, and either killed or severely wounded every one we aimed at." Within a couple of hours the Snakes retired with heavy losses.

It was seldom, however, that the Crees came to assist the Blackfoot; usually they came in the role of attackers. For a generation the Blackfoot were caught between horses ridden by Snake enemies to the southwest and by guns brandished by pedestrian Crees to the northeast. Recoiling from the smoking guns of the Crees they collided with the snorting horses of the Snakes.

Never lacking in mettle they fought on, conquering guns with courage and chargers with cunning, until within the span of one generation they were chasing the Crees with the very guns they had wrested from them and putting the Snakes to rout astride the very horses they had captured from them. The combination of guns and horses lifted all prairie Indians to a new plane of civilization. Mounted on horses, they could range freely; armed with guns and their innate daring they could drive every other tribe before them. Though it became a long and a hard struggle, the Blackfoot triumphed until over the length and the breadth of the prairies their fearsome notoriety struck terror in the enemy lodges.

The horses which transformed them from foot-sloggers to freebooting cavalrymen had the greatest effect. Horses multiplied their mobility: whereas a normal day's march on foot had covered perhaps five miles, now with horses moving the camp they covered ten to fifteen miles. A horse packing two hundred pounds on his back or three hundred on a travois could move four times as much as a dog and could easily go twice as far. Because a Blackfoot could now transport several times the gear he could have with dogs and women as the sole bearers, he could accumulate possessions he could never take with him before.

With horses, buffalo hunting could be carried out over a wider range, with more success and by larger aggregations of Indians. Whereas formerly they had camped and hunted in small bands, now they could gather several of their bands into one ever-moving but large camp, and as a result, a hundred or more hunters could concentrate on a large herd of buffalo. Now there was little difficulty providing plenteous food for all, and the men at least had more leisure time to develop new facets of social life in the much larger arena of the expanded camp community.

Consequently, the Blackfoot's lives became easier and infinitely richer than the plodding existence of their grandfathers. Improved tools and utensils obtainable from the white traders added to that ease and richness. Metal files, awls and knives enabled them not only to fabricate better wares but to do so in less time. Now with more than enough in their larders and more time on their hands, even the women had more time to laugh and to sew and to decorate, and their native artistry came to the fore. They painted their teepees and decorated their clothing, using imported beads or indigenous porcupine quills. During this era, which commenced about 1775, they designed, produced and decorated the rich raiment which we regard as Indian dress, some of the most handsome costumes the world has ever seen. They had entered a new and glamorous era.

Horses, its foundation, became status symbols. Like modern Albertans with their late model cars, these Indians, without saying a word, could advertise their wealth by the number of horses they owned. Horses became a fetish and many a Blackfoot, counting one or two hundred in his herd, had accumulated these animals far beyond any practical use he could make of them. More horses led to more leisure time and more time led to more forays against hostile tribes, and more forays led to more horses in a constantly growing spiral that took in more territory—a spiral whose viciousness was inflicted upon neighbours. Horses enabled the Blackfoot to travel vast distances in pursuit of the pleasure and glories of skirmishing. Success in their forays, and successful the Blackfoot usually were, added to the community's wealth and extended the area to which they began to lay claim.

Within the next few decades the Blackfoot, who as dog Indians had straddled the east boundary of Alberta from the North Saskatchewan River to the Red Deer River, as far west as the Beaver and Hand hills, virtually dominated the prairies of Alberta, Saskatchewan and Montana. To the south for as much as three hundred miles no tribe was safe from their attacks. David Thompson reported a Piegan raid which, starting from the vicinity of Edmonton, went south "about thirty-two degrees of latitude." (Perhaps if Thompson were not mistaken, to the northern edge of Mexico.) Members of that party returned with spoils captured directly from the Spanish. Normally they raided far south beyond the Yellowstone River, westward as far as Sandpoint in Idaho, and fought the Kootenays on the Tobacco Plains west of the Rockies.

By 1800 the Blackfoot had become masters of the northwestern plains from the North Saskatchewan River to the upper branches of the Missouri and from the mouth of the Battle River to the Rockies. Their three tribes, the Blackfoot, Bloods and Piegans, leagued into the Blackfoot Confederacy, roamed Alberta's magnificent prairies in their buffalo expeditions. Camping now in the Neutral Hills and then in the Hand Hills, and skirting the Great Sand Hills between the lower Red Deer River and the South Saskatchewan, they wandered on into the far-flung blue Cypress Hills and the distant haze of the three Sweet Grass Hills. Swinging back during the bright yellow days of fall, they wintered in the Wintering Hills, around Antler Hill south of modern Red Deer, or in the Medicine Lodge Hills west of Sylvan Lake, or the Wildcat ridges west of Calgary, or indeed, in their beautiful and favourite Porcupine Hills. Ever on the move, they were always ready for enemy bands and for the vast buffalo herds which pastured everywhere—around Buffalo Lake, Sullivan Lake and Pakowki Lake, and all over. Camping during sodden, rainy periods, bowing before infrequent hailstorms, riding on with the fresh breeze in their faces and the scent of sage in their nostrils, laughing as they watched the nimble antelope flee before them like cloud shadows sweeping across coulees, they owned and occupied Alberta's wide prairies.

Not that they did not have their problems, their illnesses and misfortunes, their hates and jealousies, and even occasional starvation. Like you and I, they were people enjoying what they could of nature's bounty and governing themselves by their own codes in a loose and democratic organization in which public opinion was the main force. They had their chiefs, usually a civil chief renowned for his eloquence and a war chief, for his leadership on their raids. As such, they were advisors but did not give orders. David Thompson reported that the chiefs "had no power beyond their influence, which would immediately cease by any act of authority and they were careful not to arrogate any superiority over others." In their domestic affairs the Indians maintained a discipline that met the needs of their social life. In larger matters, including warfare, their discipline was lax. Within limits, each man was a law unto himself. Centuries of civilization had drummed discipline and patience into the white man and instilled the notion of deferring the revenge of the moment or the immediate gratification of pleasure so as to attain some later and larger reward. Of this concept the average Indian had little idea. Brave, generous, daring, intelligent and infinitely patient in the chase he was, but rarely would he submit to authority long enough to gain some distant goal.

All civilizations have their codes of good conduct and their own chivalry, and none can comprehend fully the intricacies of another's code. The Indians too had their code of what was honourable and glorious and what was not. Stealing horses was a particularly honourable pursuit. Killing an enemy was both a necessary and a glorious achievement which invested the victor with prestige and respect. But it had to be done according to the code. Shooting a man from ambush might be practical but it brought little glory. Touching an enemy with a bare hand or stick, or subduing him in personal encounter, snatching a gun or bow from him, or stealing his picketed horses were much higher achievements than merely potting him off. All prairie Indians took scalps, but while bringing back a dripping headpiece was a significant accomplishment, it ranked low in the hierarchy of honours.

Though horses and guns had made the Blackfoot aggressive, they also provided the leisure which led to the flowering of their social life. Increasing wealth induced an elaboration of the old religious ceremonies; superimposed on their primitive religion came many new poetic and philosophical elements. Moreover, in the same way that the wealth of modern Albertans has done, it allowed an expansion of social and cultural pursuits. Great public rituals began to mark their civilization: war and scalp dances, ceremonies designed to bring the buffalo, and the great and solemn sun dances.

How it might have developed, how this great upsurge of culture, which had flared up as a by-product of the white man's coming, might have progressed, destiny did not wait to see. Within a century, as the white man's person followed his products to the Alberta plains and parklands, his presence cut the foundations from under the evolving Blackfoot culture. All of us, Indians and whites, are left to speculate sadly on what might have been.

# 2
# Alberta's Earliest White Men

On a sunny September 11 in 1754, near the modern village of Chauvin, the first white man strode into Alberta. Sent out by the Hudson's Bay Company to make friends with the natives and to report on the kind of people they were and what manner of land they enjoyed, Anthony Henday travelled as a paying guest of a band of Cree Indians. That night as he wrote up his journal he set down his first impressions of the land we know as Alberta: "Level land, few woods, & plenty of good water. . . . Indians killed 8 Waskesew."

Henday was a fur trader, not a farmer. Nevertheless, his first impressions on this trip, a journey which was to take him hundreds of miles through some of the best of Alberta's millions of arable acres, might well have been written by a farmer—level land, some woods, plenty of good water and an abundant food supply. Now, after a lapse of two centuries, this entry in Henday's diary, the almost incidental comment of a fur trader concerned with the more pressing matter of meeting prospective customers, assumes an almost prophetic aspect.

When he entered Alberta Henday was on his way to meet the Blackfoot, who, though they had never seen any white man, were already familiar with the white man's tools. They had obtained these from Cree merchants who made their living by buying furs from the prairie Indians and taking them down to sell to the white traders at Hudson Bay. For decades the English had been satisfied to restrict their trading posts to the shores of Hudson Bay and to let these native merchants suffer the hardship of freighting the furs hundreds of miles. Meanwhile, the French from Montreal, driven by different economic pressures, had gradually worked west establishing trading posts on the Great Lakes and on Lake Winnipeg. In doing so, they intercepted Indians who formerly had taken their furs to the Hudson's Bay Company. Finding this profitable, the French continued the practice until they had built posts on the Saskatchewan River, the main traffic artery leading from the prairies to Hudson Bay. When that happened the Hudson's Bay Company's profits suffered and its traders began to consider ways to counter this opposition which threatened to strangle them.

As a preliminary move they had sent Anthony Henday off on his famous venture into Alberta. Three years before this first white man came to call on Alberta's Blackfoot, the French had built the strictly temporary Fort La Jonquière in Saskatchewan, somewhere below the junction of the North and South Saskatchewan rivers, and in 1753 a permanent, well-organized Fort St. Louis on the main river north of modern Kinistino. The time had come when Alberta's Indians, instead of merely feeling the effects of the white man's goods, were soon to see trading posts erected in their midst.

Henday left us an interesting and informative journal of his travels and observations. Not only does it describe the country as he saw it in its beautiful, wild magnificence, but it gives us an insight into the lives of the Indians at this stage in their civilization, when horses and guns were opening its most interesting phase.

Like the Crees of those days who ventured onto the prairies on foot, so did Henday. Like many other so-called discoverers and explorers, his explorations consisted of going where the natives led him and having them show him the routes and the parts of the country he wished to see. He entered Alberta by first ascending the Saskatchewan River, which even then was the great pipeline funneling Alberta's first resources to the east. He came under the protection of Attickasish, a Cree merchant who dealt with the Blackfoot.

He entered the province while Alberta's hillsides were a blaze of red and gold, and then spent all autumn wandering slowly west over the hills and valleys drained by the Battle River. Somewhere near Irma Henday visited an Assiniboine camp and, as he expected, saw a few horses grazing nearby. Seizing the opportunity, he exchanged a gun for a horse, and thus became Alberta's first white horse trader. After he had passed near Stettler, crossed the Red Deer River and moved on to Pine Lake, a small band of Blackfoot met him and escorted him to their main camp. Evidently these tribesmen had known for some time that a strange white man was seeking them out.

All summer long this great concourse of nearly two thousand Black-foot, who had gathered together to see Henday, had followed the buffalo over the prairies and now, about the middle of October, were about to break up into smaller groups and seek the shelter of the woods and foothills. Before dispersing, they were as curious to see the white man as he was to see them. Henday's curiosity turned to amazement when he found "200 tents of Archithinue Natives, pitched in two rows, and an opening in the middle; where we were conducted to the Leader's tent; which was at one end, large enough to contain fifty persons. . . ." The bedraggled, untidy Crees' tents had not prepared him for the majesty of these two rows of white teepees, striking in their simplicity as they lined the broad avenue three-quarters of a mile long.

He was taken to the chief's tent: "he [the chief] received us seated on a clear [white] Buffalo skin, attended by twenty elderly men. He made signs for me to sit down on his right hand; which I did. Our Leader set on several grand-pipes, and smoked all round, according to their usual custom: not a word was yet spoke on either side." Henday's journal continues: "Smoking being over, Buffalo flesh boiled was served round in baskets of a species of bent, and I was presented with ten Buffalo tongues."

After that "Attickasish my Guide, informed him I was sent by the Great Leader who lives down at the great waters, to invite his young men down to see him and to bring with them Beaver skins & Wolves skins: & they would get in return Powder, Shot, Guns, Cloth, Beads, &c." To this the great chief, perhaps suppressing a smile, returned a vague indifferent answer.

On the second day the white man reiterated his request that the Blackfoot come down to Hudson Bay to trade, but the plains chief "made little answer; only said that it was far off, & they could not paddle"—an answer polite, indifferent and noncommittal but tantamount to no.

Although as a commercial venture Henday's visit came to nothing, this first meeting of a white man and a group of Blackfoot chiefs was made on an amicable basis. For the first time a white man had seen one of the great Blackfoot camps and witnessed a way of life which, although he may not have realized it, was in its infancy. A mere twenty years had elapsed since his hosts had obtained horses, and in that remarkably short span of time these animals had transformed their masters from the foot-slogging Indians of the dog-days to the mobile cavalrymen he had seen in this great camp, feasting in the midst of an abundant and beautiful land.

The very first meeting between white man and Blackfoot was over. It had been conducted on a most friendly level. Each, with some minor reservations, had met the other as an equal. Each had been glad to see the other. Henday had wanted something from the Blackfoot and had been politely turned down. The Blackfoot wanted nothing from the white man.

Shortly after the meeting, the great camp broke up into smaller groups which headed west for the winter. Similarly, Henday's Crees travelled westward, crossed the Red Deer River west of Innisfail, and from there until the end of January wandered over a small area near our Rocky Mountain House and Gull Lake. After leaving the Blackfoot, Henday became the first white man to see the main chain of the Rocky Mountains. Later in the winter, moving slowly north and passing a few miles east of modern Edmonton, the band headed for a favourite camping ground near the mouth of the Sturgeon River.

During most of March and April Henday's party remained along

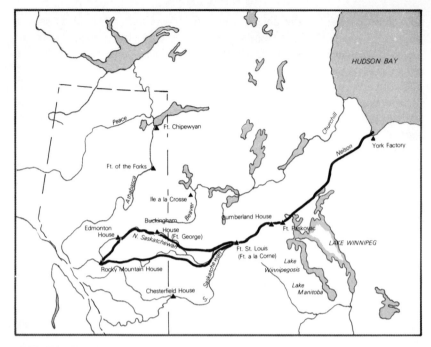

ANTHONY HENDAY

In 1754 Anthony Henday journeyed from Hudson Bay to Rocky Mountain House and became the first white man to arrive in Alberta.

the banks of the North Saskatchewan River, while the Crees, as had been their practice for some decades, made canoes and waited for the ice to go out so that their strong men might embark on the long trip to take the furs to Hudson Bay. April 23, St. George's Day, fell during that interval and Henday became the first white man in Alberta to celebrate it. "Displayed my Flag in Honour of St. George; & the Leaders did the same, after acquainting them & explaining my reason: In the afternoon the ice in the River broke up: a great many Geese and Swans were seen flying to the Northward: In the Evening we had a grand feast with Dancing, Drumming, Talking &c."

Five days later he reported: "Embarked on board my Canoe, & paddled down the river thirty-four Miles, in company with twenty Canoes of Assinipoet Natives: The River large, with several Islands, & high banks & tall woods." Every day or so as Henday's flotilla swept rapidly down the spring spate, it was augmented by other Crees and Assiniboines who waited to join it as it came along. Then, somewhere in western Saskatchewan, awaiting the arrival of his flotilla, was the great chief of the Blackfoot whom he had met in October.

From his second meeting he learned further facts of the fur trade.

A History of Alberta

He discovered that the Blackfoot had brought along several loads of furs, "wolves, Beaver & Foxes etc." Each year when the Crees reached Hudson Bay they allowed the traders there to believe that they had toiled all winter tending their traps. For this they were suitably commended, but the traders, having learned from them that out on the plains there was another tribe, the Blackfoot, asked the Crees to induce this unknown tribe to trap also and to bring their furs down to the Bay. This the Crees promised to do, but each year returned to report that the Blackfoot would not trap. As a result, the company had sent Henday out to try to woo the Blackfoot into trapping.

And now, somewhere in the vicinity of modern Battleford or Saskatoon he found the Blackfoot waiting to shower the Crees with furs. Anxious to obtain the white man's goods, they were quite willing to trap but refused to paddle canoes on the back-breaking trip to Hudson Bay. So they sold their furs to the Crees, who made a good profit on the deal, and who at Hudson Bay passed off the furs as the fruits of their own trapping. Henday discovered that this band of Crees at least were primarily merchants and traders and only incidental trappers. Naturally the Crees had never tried to induce the Blackfoot to take their own furs to the Bay, for had they done so they would have lost their trading profits.

But Henday was to learn even more of the logistics of the trade. The Blackfoot, waiting for the Cree flotilla to come along, were loaded down with dried meat and pemmican which they also sold to the Crees. A brigade of canoes hurrying to make the long trip to the Bay and back during the short summer season had no time to hunt for food. Consequently, long before white men had given the matter any thought, the Crees had worked out this arrangement whereby the Blackfoot sold them pemmican. When later on white men came to build posts in the West and to take out the furs they merely adopted this very logical arrangement. While furs, of course, were the first of Alberta's resources to be exported, the method of exporting them led to the export of this ancillary product, meat from the great prairie pastures. Before the Blackfoot had even seen a white man, they had set their women to work preparing meat for export.

By May 21, 1755, Henday's Crees had traded away every article they could spare for Blackfoot furs and pemmican and set off once more down the Saskatchewan. As Henday said: "We are above sixty Canoes and there are scarce a Gun, Kettle, Hatchet, or Knife amongst us, having traded them with the Archithinue Natives."

Then two or three days later, the flotilla came to the French Fort St. Louis and Henday learned more facts of fur trade life. While the master of the post entertained his fellow white man, his staff were busy taking care of the Indians' needs. According to Henday's journal, "The

Natives received from the Master ten Gallons of Brandy half adulterated with water; and when intoxicated they traded Cased Cats, Martens, & good parchment Beaver skins, refusing Wolves & dressed Beaver. In short he received from the Natives nothing but what were prime Winter furs." By means of liquor the French trader had obtained all the valuable furs but allowed the second-rate stuff to go downstream to his rivals.

After Henday returned to headquarters at York Factory on Hudson Bay the company continued to send men into the West on similar missions. Some of them turned back before reaching Alberta, but Anthony Henday and Joseph Smith spent the winter of 1759–60 near Rocky Mountain House and were able to bring sixty-one canoe loads of furs back to the Bay. As a result of this journey, some Alberta Blood Indians began making regular trips to York Factory. In 1761 Henry Pressick wintered with the Blackfoot in southern Alberta, and he was followed in 1766 by James Deering and by William Pink the following year.

Originally these men had been sent out to try to counter the French traders at The Pas and at Fort St. Louis, but by 1760 the fortunes of war removed these competitors from the western scene and their posts were abandoned. For the next ten years or so the Hudson's Bay Company had the Alberta trade all to itself.

But not for long. The Seven Years' War, which had seen the capture of Quebec and had put an end to French competition on the Saskatchewan River, merely substituted another set of competitors in the shape of new traders from Montreal—the men who by 1779 had coalesced into the North West Company. To counter them the Hudson's Bay Company built in 1774 Cumberland House on the Saskatchewan River near the present east boundary of that province. As traders flocked into the area, the Indians welcomed the resultant competition, and by 1780 the North West Company with its head office in Montreal and the English company working out of Hudson Bay had posts as far up the river as the stretch between modern Prince Albert and Battleford. In the advance up the Saskatchewan the North West Company was always the more aggressive, but within weeks of the time it built a new post its rival followed and built beside it. Despite a raging epidemic of smallpox, which in 1780 devastated the Indians, the companies did a fair business.

Because of the fierce competition both firms supplied the Indians with the one commodity they demanded above all others—liquor. Moreover, each winter both companies sent some of their men out to live with the Indians so that they might become familiar with the various native languages and at the same time return to the fort in the spring laden with fur. For several years such traders wandered all over our Alberta prairies until its geography became well known.

One of the more important of these wandering white men was the

Hudson's Bay Company's James Gaddy. From Manchester House near modern Maidstone, Saskatchewan, he set out in the fall of 1785 with a band of Piegans and spent the winter in their home area in Alberta's southwestern corner. His relations with his customers were so friendly that he returned to spend the next two winters with them. During the fall of 1787 Gaddy, an experienced trader, led a group of men which he scattered about amongst the Piegans. One of these was the relatively inexperienced David Thompson, who was destined to become one of Canada's greatest surveyors and one of the men whose observations, gathered during the next twenty-five years, have given us an invaluable insight into conditions in the early West and into the lives of the Indians at that stage of their culture.

In 1787 Thompson was a lad of seventeen who had arrived on the prairies about a year earlier. Two years later he was selected to be trained as a surveyor, but on this first trip with Gaddy he was merely a very junior member of the party. Fortunately the Piegans reciprocated his friendly interest and by exercising his careful powers of observation he learned much of their recent history, which in his old age he included in his famous *Narrative*.

In 1792, five years after David Thompson followed Gaddy out to visit the Piegans, the next move of the competing companies brought about the building of the rival posts Fort George (North West Company) and Buckingham House (Hudson's Bay Company) near modern Elk Point on the north bank of the Saskatchewan in Alberta. The line of posts that stretched along the Saskatchewan River had reached Alberta.

Almost immediately after the fur traders arrived, the Crees from the wooded lands to the north and the various plains Indians came in to sell their furs. That winter several Northwesters and an occasional Hudson's Bay man, taking a supply of trade goods, fanned out from the posts to live with bands of Indians well back in their home territories. The most interesting of these was Peter Fidler, who, although he could not speak a word of their language at the start, set forth with a band of Piegans who were returning to their homeland in the foothills south of modern Calgary.

For many reasons, Fidler's trip is of especial importance. Like David Thompson who had lived with the Piegans five years earlier, he was a close observer of Indian customs and fortunately all through the winter he kept a fascinating journal which has come down to us. On top of that, he was a trained surveyor and took his instruments along. On this trip he became the first surveyor to practise his profession in what we now regard as the settled portions of Alberta and to locate accurately the Battle, Red Deer, Bow and Highwood rivers, to pinpoint the Rocky Mountains and to record all this information on a map.

Travelling with his Piegan friends Fidler set out early in November

1792 and, after crossing the Red Deer River a few miles east of the modern city, he "first got sight of the Rocky Mountains." By that time, of course, several other white men had seen them, but Fidler was the first to take compass bearings on them. On November 27, for instance, he got a bearing on "a remarkable High Cliff of the Rocky Mountain called by our People the Devils head & by the Muddy river Indians *O mock cow wat che mooks as sin* or the Swans bill. . . ." This is our Devil's Head mountain whose unique dome near the eastern end of Lake Minnewanka is such a distinctive landmark. Then veering slightly east he entered the open prairies and crossed Rosebud Creek. In that vicinity he witnessed the operation of what may have been his first buffalo jump, for the Piegans led him to "a creek a little above a high steep face of rocks on the East Bank of the Creek, which the Indians uses as the purpose of a Buffalo Pound, by driving whole heards [*sic*] before them & breaking their legs, necks, &c. in the fall, which is perpendicular about twenty feet. Vast quantities of Bones are laying there, that had been drove before the rock."

During the mild winter which he spent along the Highwood River and Willow Creek, he visited the site of what we know as the Old Women's Buffalo Jump. Somewhat later, by travelling south in the valley between the Porcupine Hills and the Livingstone Range, he took a bearing on Chief Mountain, whose summit lies across the line in Montana. It, he said, was "called by these Indians *Nin nase tok que* or the King, & by the Southern Indians the Governor of the Mountain, being the highest known place they know off [*sic*]. . . ." In the same locality he met a small band of Kootenay Indians and they had their first sight of a white man.

Finally, on his way back to Buckingham House, on February 12, 1793, on the Red Deer River near the mouth of Threehills Creek he made the first discovery of coal on the Canadian prairies. Then passing near Gopher Head Hill (east of Rumsey) and noting the blue Hand Hills in the distance, he went north past modern Stettler, Donalda and Mannville and reached Buckingham House in March. Both from his employer's standpoint and from that of the modern historian, his trip and the journal he kept were highly successful.

For two years after Fidler's return from his visit to the Piegans, the rival trading organizations were content to make Fort George and Buckingham House their most westerly bases of operation. Then as Duncan McGillivray, the Northwester, explained in his journal, his company decided to build another post much farther up the Saskatchewan River. It was to be located in an area which he described as "a rich and plentiful Country, abounding with all kinds of animals especially Beavers & Otters, which are said to be so numerous that the Women and children kill them with Sticks and hatchets." The fur traders had decided to tap the first of the Edmonton area's many resources.

So in the summer of 1795 John MacDonald, James Hughes, and perhaps twenty other men, travelled upstream to build the North West Company's Fort Augustus on the west bank of the river, on NE 9-55-22-w. 4th and about two miles due north of the heart of modern Fort Saskatchewan. By doing so they caught the Hudson's Bay Company napping. When, however, the dour Scotsman, William Tomison, returned from the Bay that fall, he dashed on to the mouth of the Sturgeon River, and on October 5, 1795, set his men to building Edmonton House within a musket shot of his rivals. From then on Edmonton was a name on a map.

The traders at the mouth of the Sturgeon enjoyed a good business. Not even the presence of two additional fur trading companies from Montreal who had come in to share in the rich pickings seriously affected them. These two new companies, the X Y Company, in which Alexander Mackenzie had a hand, and the Ogilvie Company, built posts nearby and sent men to open other outposts in the general area. To meet their competition and to try to make the newcomers overextend themselves, both the Hudson's Bay Company and the North West Company built posts farther up the Saskatchewan: Pembina House (H.B.CO.) and Boggy Hall (N.W. CO.), both near modern Lodgepole, and Nelson House (H.B.CO.) and Whitemud House (N.W.CO.) both near the mouth of Wabamun Creek. With so many traders competing, the fur bearing animals of the Edmonton region were decimated.

Then in 1799, in a final leap of over a hundred miles towards the southwest but very much farther around the great semicircular course taken by the Saskatchewan River, the North West Company went on to build its Rocky Mountain House, while the Hudson's Bay Company built Acton House nearby. They were located in the region to which in 1790 Peter Pangman of the North West Company had travelled. Hopefully these posts right in the Piegans' back yard would keep them away from the older posts farther east along the Saskatchewan. Moreover, the traders were anxious to deal with the Kootenays, who by this time had been shoved off the prairies into British Columbia by the Piegans and who, when they dared creep through the passes, camped on the tiny area of level flat some seventy miles farther up the river, an area which the white men called the Kootenay Plains. As things turned out, the Piegans held Rocky Mountain House in little esteem, continued to trade where they liked, and continued to make life difficult for the poor Kootenays.

Although Rocky Mountain House was not a marked success, nevertheless, being the post built at the highest practical point along the Saskatchewan, it was the last in the 800-mile-long string of posts which white men had used as stepping stones on their way towards the mountains. This long chain of posts running west curved like a sickle with its sharp edge turned towards the prairies of Saskatchewan and Alberta and drew

Alberta's Earliest White Men

the trade of all the Indians south of it. Still not satisfied that their line of posts was getting all the business possible, both companies loaded some of their bravest men into canoes and sent them up the South Saskatchewan River into the very heart of the prairies. There, in 1800 at the junction of the Red Deer River and the South Saskatchewan, they built their Chesterfield Houses, just across the Saskatchewan border from Empress, Alberta. All around for scores of miles, except on some of the timbered bottoms of the two rivers, there was neither stick nor bush. All around, stretching for hundreds of miles, the prairie ridges and hollows continued in apparent endless monotony. And all over those ridges or through those hollows for a radius of hundreds of miles the intractable plains Indians lived their free, nomadic lives.

For two winters before abandoning the area the rival traders matched their wits with these undisciplined wanderers and faced the natives' anger and distrust with little but sheer daring. They were aware that for the time being the turbulent Indians were content to let their posts exist because there they could exchange pemmican for guns. With these, the Blackfoot in particular could drive back the Crows and Snakes to prevent them from getting firearms. And while Gros Ventres and Blackfoot dealt eagerly for guns, each was jealous of the other, and in the eyes of each, the white man, because he was impartial in selling firearms to both, was construed as an ally of the other tribe and thus an enemy. But for the companies the game was not worth the candle.

Once more Peter Fidler, who was in charge for the Hudson's Bay Company, used his surveying instruments and kept entering in his journal. It throws considerable light on the lives of the plains Indians and mentions an influx of Iroquois, those foreigners from the east, who, like the white men, were invading the natives' lands. About the year 1800 when there was a general westward movement of Indians, several Chippewas, Nipissings and Iroquois migrated to Alberta to trap and make their living. While there was a special concentration of the Iroquois in the Peace River country and along the east slope of the Rocky Mountains, according to Fidler's journal a large band of them went up the South Saskatchewan to the Chesterfield House area and the Cypress Hills. The Blackfoot despised these interlopers but left it to the Gros Ventres to kill many of them and to drive the others out. Incidentally, while Fidler never saw the Cypress Hills, his journal is the first to mention them when in 1801 he sent some of his staff there to collect gum from the pine trees to caulk his canoes.

Chesterfield House, like all the other posts dotted along the north edge of the prairies, had been reached by ascending the Saskatchewan River from Cumberland House near the Manitoba border. This route, however, was only one fork of the two-pronged attack which the traders used to invade Alberta. The two forks diverged at Cumberland House where the northerly one crossed over to the Churchill River to ascend it to its head-waters. These headwaters offered the traders two other choices: by bearing left they could ascend the Beaver River to the vicinity of Lac La Biche in Alberta; by edging to the right up through Ile-à-la-Crosse and over Peter Pond Lake and then across the Methy Portage the traders could descend the Clearwater to its junction with the Athabasca River at our Fort McMurray. Since far more of Alberta lies north of the North Saskatchewan River than south of it, the rival companies' approach by the Churchill River and the Methy Portage opened up a vast area of the province. Moreover, during the Hudson's Bay Company's early days, the Chipewyan Indians had used this route to reach the Bay.

When the first traders set up shop at Hudson Bay, these Indians had lived along the Churchill River until the Crees with their new guns drove them away from it and pushed them and the Beaver Indians back into the dark recesses of northern Alberta and the Northwest Territories. When Governor Knight of the Hudson's Bay Company arrived to take command at the Bay, he began hearing of the Chipewyans and of the havoc the Crees were wreaking on them. In 1715 he sent William Stewart out to try to patch up a peace between the warring tribes.

In the course of his remarkable trip, partly over the barren lands of northern Saskatchewan, Stewart became the first white man to travel in the Mackenzie watershed and to see Great Slave Lake and the Slave River. While he must have passed close to Alberta's extreme northeast corner, it is unlikely that he actually set foot inside the modern province's boundaries, thereby missing the distinction claimed thirty-eight years later by Anthony Henday, Alberta's first white visitor.

When a few months prior to Stewart's departure, Governor Knight held a council with the aggressive Crees and tried to dissuade them from persecuting the Beaver and Chipewyan tribes, they gave him a rough idea of the geography of the land beyond the headwaters of the Churchill River. They told him of the great Athabasca River and of the sea-like Lake Athabasca. The most promising Cree convert to Knight's peaceful policy was an Indian by the name of Swan. He was one of the many merchant types among the Crees whose interests were served better by peace than war, so he undertook to try to bring about a peace, and disappeared up the Churchill River.

Ultimately Swan returned to the Bay and reported that the natives of the lower Athabasca valley (doubtless Beaver Indians) had welcomed his peace overtures. Almost immediately he set off on his second trip and two years later, after wintering on the Athabasca River, possibly near our Fort McMurray, he returned to Fort Churchill. He brought not only the first report of the Athabasca Oil Sands ever to reach white man's ears but true to his merchandising proclivities brought back a sample of "that

Gum or pitch that flows out of the Banks of that River." After that Swan the merchant, putting tribal passions second to the pursuit of profit, continued to trade with the Beaver Indians. Having Swan and several other native traders like him to bring northeastern Alberta's furs down the Churchill River and later on when the Chipewyans themselves came to the Bay, it was many years before the company had occasion to send any other men into the area.

But a day finally came when the Northwesters began ascending the Churchill and crossing into the Athabasca watershed. By 1775 they were established on the Churchill River preparing to cut off its flow of furs down to Hudson Bay. Then in 1776, the year of the American Revolution, when Peter Pond was at his post near modern Prince Albert, he too heard of the rich fur land drained by the Athabasca. In 1778 he crossed the Methy Portage to the Clearwater and Athabasca rivers and about forty river miles up the Athabasca from its mouth, Pond built the first white man's house in Alberta. Some eight years later he and his associates found it advisable for Archibald N. McLeod to build Alberta's second house at the mouth of the Clearwater River at our Fort McMurray.

At Alberta's first white man's residence, Peter Pond, a man of high intelligence, strong character and tremendous geographical curiosity, carried on a most successful trade. During quieter periods he dreamed of the possibility of establishing a trading route down the mighty river of which the Indians had told him, the river which would later bear the name Mackenzie. From what they said, he formed the opinion that it flowed into the Pacific Ocean and he thought that it might afford his company a means of trade with the Orient. Even then Alberta's atmosphere was conducive to hatching great schemes. Unfortunately, though he spent about ten years at his post, it did not fall to Peter Pond to carry out this plan.

After Pond's departure, Alexander Mackenzie, to whom he had communicated his great idea, took charge of the Athabasca area, and in 1788 sent his cousin Roderick Mackenzie downstream to build the first Fort Chipewyan on the south shore of Lake Athabasca. Then, having removed the North West Company's headquarters to that post, Alexander Mackenzie set out in 1789 on the trip that was to take him to the Arctic Ocean, down the river which was so justly named after him.

At Cumberland House in 1790, on his way back from his Mackenzie River trip, he met the two Hudson's Bay Company surveyors, Philip Turnor and Peter Fidler, who that fall set out for Lake Athabasca. On this trip Turnor and Fidler between them made the first survey of the Churchill River, the lower Athabasca, Lake Athabasca and the Slave River to its mouth at Great Slave Lake. On the route Fidler took he made a note of the oil sands and of the fact that the North West Company had already established a post on Great Slave Lake.

## ALEXANDER MACKENZIE

In July 1789 Alexander Mackenzie left Fort Chipewyan with three canoes and descended to the mouth of the Mackenzie River, making the return trip of 2,990 miles in 102 days. In the spring of 1793 he ascended the Peace River, crossed the mountainous terrain of British Columbia and reached the Pacific to become the first man ever to cross the continent north of Mexico.

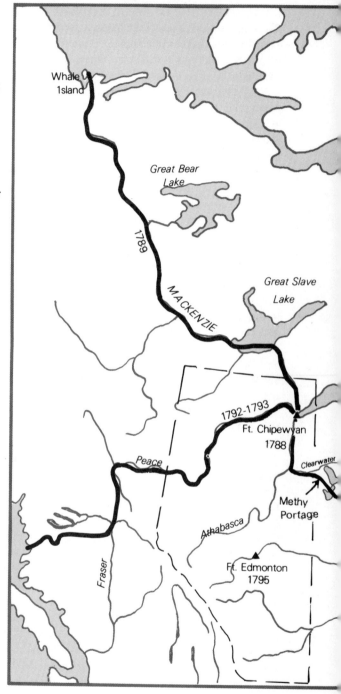

Whale Island

Great Bear Lake

1789

MACKENZIE

Great Slave Lake

1792-1793

Ft. Chipewyan 1788

Peace

Clearwater

Methy Portage

Athabasca

Fraser

Ft. Edmonton 1795

Alberta's Earliest White Men

About 1782, some seventy-five miles above the mouth of the Peace River at the spot ever since known as Peace Point, the Beavers and the Cree Indians, both somewhat exhausted from their decades of hostilities, made another treaty of peace. When in 1787 Alexander Mackenzie sent Archibald McLeod and Charles Boyer north to try to find the Peace River Indians, the two returned about a month later with some of these natives. About the same time Boyer built a post on the north bank of the river just downstream from our Fort Vermilion and near the mouth of the stream which still bears his name. While McLeod and Boyer were undoubtedly the first all-white men to see the mighty Peace River, they had likely been preceded a few years earlier by the Métis, Jacques Beaulieu, the founder of a northern dynasty, who about that time established his family on the Salt River.

During the next few years the North West Company, operating out of Fort Chipewyan on the south shore of the lake, advanced some four or five hundred miles up the Peace River. In 1791 John Finlay built Fort De Tremble about forty miles above our Fort Vermilion, while Archibald McLeod went much farther and built at the mouth of modern Whitemud Creek, some thirty miles below present-day Peace River town.

In October 1792, Alexander Mackenzie wrote, "Having made every necessary preparation, I left Fort Chipewyan, to proceed up the Peace River." He planned to winter at the forks of the Peace and Smoky rivers, and, as soon as the ice went out in the spring, to begin his second great voyage of discovery. With him he took Alexander MacKay, a fellow Scot, who was second in command of the expedition; the rest of the men were: "Joseph Landry, Charles Ducette, Francois Beaulieux, Baptist Bisson, Francois Courtois, and Jaques Beauchamp with two Indians, as hunters and interpreters."

In due course the party reached the site of Fork Fort, some twelve miles above the mouth of the Smoky River. Here he found the two men who had been sent in some weeks earlier busily erecting the first fort to be built in the vicinity of our Peace River town. The next spring he made his way from this point to the Pacific Ocean.

The story of Mackenzie's leadership, nearly incredible fortitude and of his many difficulties and disappointments has been told so often that it needs no repetition here. Suffice it to say that he reached the Pacific coast on July 22, 1793—the first man to cross the continent anywhere north of Mexico.

Since the fall of 1792 when Mackenzie arrived at Fork Fort, the heart of the Peace River country, the stretch of the river from Dunvegan to Peace River town has been occupied continuously at one point or other by white men. In building Fork Fort, Mackenzie and his colleagues had penetrated far west into Alberta. While one of his associates in the

North West Company, Angus Shaw, was busy building Fort George on the Saskatchewan River in eastern Alberta, Mackenzie was erecting his Fork Fort some 270 miles farther west and 150 miles farther north.

When the Northwesters, working their way west up the Churchill River, came to Lac Ile-à-la-Crosse, the tortuous Beaver River eventually led them to the vicinity of Lac La Biche. On the headwaters of the Beaver, at Moose Lake, in 1789, the year Alexander Mackenzie set out down the Mackenzie River, Angus Shaw built his Lac d'Orignal post near Bonny-ville. Within three more years, during which time the Northwesters built Fort George, white men had breached Alberta's eastern defences in three places: along the Clearwater River, the Beaver and the Saskatchewan.

Before eight more years had elapsed, by the turn of the century, white men were not only familiar with most of Alberta's rivers and lakes, but had actually surveyed and mapped the skeleton of its water routes. In addition to the work Peter Fidler had done, David Thompson returned to Alberta in the fall of 1798 to carry out further surveying. He was on his way to Lac La Biche, where he soon built Greenwich House. From there in the spring, surveying as he went, he rode over to Fort Augustus and north to the Pembina River, whence by canoe he floated down to the Athabasca. He descended it and noted the North West Company's outpost at the mouth of Lesser Slave Lake River, and followed the beautiful but wearying windings of that stream to put Lesser Slave Lake on his map. Then returning to the Athabasca and hurrying down it as far as Fort McMurray, in the summer of 1799 he passed east out of the province by the Clearwater River and Methy Portage.

By that time even the run of mill fur trade employees had a general idea of Alberta's geography. Thinking in terms of rivers, they knew how the gigantic Slave River crossed its northern boundary, carrying with it the run-off of the Peace, Athabasca and other streams along which they had travelled. This system alone drained some 123,000 square miles out of the province's 255,285. In the Saskatchewan River watershed, which drains nearly all of the southern half of the province, they knew most of the windings of the Battle, Red Deer, Bow, Belly and Oldman rivers. Among them they had not only seen the great hills of the province, the Cypress and Porcupine, the Hand and Neutral hills and the Swan Hills, as well as the so-called Pelican and Birch mountains of the north, and Caribou Mountain, whose northern slopes slip off into the Northwest Territories, but here and there had gazed longingly at the Rocky Mountains. In short, they knew Alberta.

But more important to them, they knew its Indians, the Crees, Chipewyans, Beavers, Slaves and Sekanis—the Indians of the northern forests —as well as the Sarcees, who even then were beginning to associate with the Blackfoot, and the Assiniboines of the areas adjoining the North

Alberta's Earliest White Men

Saskatchewan River. They also knew the Kootenays, Snakes, Gros Ventres and the intractable Blackfoot.

The Indians of the forested lands, living on the fish of northern Alberta's lakes and on moose and wood buffalo, and moving about in small bands within a limited compass, experienced little change by their contact with the white man and his goods. The white man's guns, of course, smoking in Cree hands, had driven the Beaver and the Slaves farther west, so that by 1800 the western fringe of Cree lands had been extended as far west as Edmonton House. Some Assiniboines, usually on good terms with the Crees, had worked into the woods and into the parklands immediately south of the North Saskatchewan River at least as far west as Edmonton House and were pressing on west. Moreover, partly as employees of the traders and partly coming of their own accord to trap, a number of interloping eastern Indians, Iroquois, Nipissing and Ojibway, had worked their way into the Lac La Biche and Swan Hills area and farther west into the foothills between the Athabasca and North Saskatchewan rivers. The genuine native Indians were most unhappy about this invasion, but, since that area was underpopulated anyway, rarely lifted a hand to stop it.

The white man's goods, axes, steel traps, guns, pots and blankets, had raised the standard of living of all these northern Indians compared to that of previous centuries and had made their lives easier. To obtain these luxuries they had but to trap and trade their furs, and they buckled down to do that. Since generally speaking only one company, the North West Company, exploited the area north of the North Saskatchewan, there was no competition, and, therefore, no need to introduce liquor as a staple of the trade. Moreover, the white man found it good business to encourage peace between the tribes. In general, in the vast forested region of northern Alberta, a spirit of cooperation and even friendship, existed between the red man and the white. They found it mutually beneficial to go out of their way to adjust to each other's peculiar customs.

Conditions on the parklands and plains south of the North Saskatchewan River were vastly different. The plains Indians also wanted the added leisure the white man's wares and metal tools could bring them, and they were willing to go to limited lengths to get them. But with a certain and plentiful food supply ever at hand in the vast herds of buffalo, they had less need for what the white man could offer. Independent, truculent and touchy of temper, they led the traders a never ceasing and harassing dance. As elsewhere, the plains Indians were sharp bargainers, enjoying the competition between rival traders in a seller's market. But in the longer term and by 1800, using an outpouring of liquor, the traders turned the tables and jerked the Indians from their commanding bargaining position as reluctant sellers to the status of eager, thirsty buyers. And yet, though the two races dealt at arm's length, the white and red men needed each other. Or thought they did.

By that year, with guns and ammunition, the Blackfoot were well on their way to dominating southern Alberta. Sixty years earlier, at the close of their dog-days, they had been sorely squeezed between the gun-toting Crees on the northeast and the horse-riding Snakes on the southwest. By 1754 when Henday had seen the first great Blackfoot camp, they had acquired horses and their affairs were on the mend. Now, half a century later, their star was in the ascendant. Now, possessing guns and horses, they were advancing at full gallop towards animosity with Snake and Sioux, Cree and Crow, Kootenay and Assiniboine, Nez Percé and Gros Ventres. From then on for some seventy-five years they were lords of the prairie. Any trader foolish enough to venture too far from his well-armed post rarely returned to tell of his adventures. The prairies were Blackfoot territory and the Blackfoot planned to keep them so.

# 3
# Two Competitive Decades

For two-thirds of the nineteenth century the Blackfoot took care that the Alberta plains remained their territory. In the spring of 1802, finding the bleak prairies and the belligerent Blackfoot too much of a mouthful to digest, the fur traders withdrew from Chesterfield House. For decades thereafter the handful of traders along the North Saskatchewan rarely strayed far into the plains.

Along the North Saskatchewan and the Peace rivers, however, they began consolidating their positions and looking west across the mountains towards the Pacific. In that push towards the coast the more aggressive North West Company, which had been in the van of the drive into Alberta, also led the way. For the time being, the Hudson's Bay Company had its hands full trying to compete in northern Alberta without expanding into unknown territory. Its interests were well represented along the Saskatchewan, but failed to hold their own in the Athabasca-Peace-Mackenzie river watershed. During the four-year period from 1802 to 1806 the Hudson's Bay Company had sent a weak force under Peter Fidler to try to compete with the North West Company at Chipewyan, but was forced to withdraw.

For the next decade the North West Company had the North to itself and concentrated its efforts at Fort Chipewyan, its headquarters for all of the North, and at Fort Dunvegan, which Archibald McLeod built in 1805. From time to time the company maintained lesser posts, such as Fort Vermilion, which over the years changed its location several times.

Along the North Saskatchewan during the first decade of the nineteenth century both companies maintained pairs of opposing posts: Fort George and Buckingham House near the Saskatchewan border; Fort Augustus and Edmonton House; and Rocky Mountain House and Acton House far up the Saskatchewan within sight of the mountains. Of these, Fort Augustus and Edmonton House, although relocated several times to accommodate their customers, became the most important. In 1802 this peregrinating pair, built originally in 1795 near modern Fort Saskatchewan, moved to a site within the modern city of Edmonton and they remained there until 1810. That year both of them went back down the river to the mouth of Whitearth Creek, not far from modern Smoky Lake, for a sojourn of only two years. Then by 1813 they came back to the former location within what is now the city of Edmonton. From that time onward white men have maintained a continuous residence in Edmonton, so that in this respect Edmonton is the oldest occupied spot in the arable portion of Alberta. Thinking in terms of the whole province, however, it takes second place to modern Fort Chipewyan, whose continuous white settlement goes back to 1803.

Whereas the trading posts in the forested areas of the Mackenzie watershed were establishments confined strictly to trading furs, the posts along the North Saskatchewan played a dual role. They did a good trade in furs, but that was secondary to their dealings in pemmican; indeed the main export of the prairies was meat. It was dried and pounded and mixed with grease to form bags of pemmican. Because the canoe trip to Hudson Bay or Montreal had to be made as speedily as possible, the brigades had no time to hunt as they went along. It was necessary, therefore, for both the North West Company's French voyageurs bound for Montreal and the Hudson's Bay Company's Orkney boatmen to carry food with them, and no other concentrated food packed the punch that pemmican did. Moreover, with the North West Company operating another large transport route from central Saskatchewan north to beyond Lake Athabasca, the boats from Edmonton took down extra pemmican to supply the voyageurs on that route. Before long, Fort Augustus and Edmonton House were buying tons of pemmican from the temperamental plains Indians.

When in 1804 the North West Company absorbed the rival x y Company and when about the same time the Ogilvie traders disappeared, the North West Company emerged stronger and more aggressive than ever. By a devious route the absorption of its rivals drove that company into a westward expansion over the mountains. Taking care of the employees of the x y Company forced it into the position of finding jobs for them and this could be done best by opening new posts in hitherto unexplored regions. Fortunately such a move fitted into the company's needs to try to find a shorter route by which it could export its furs.

Along the Peace River this expansion followed Alexander Mackenzie's steps. While a casual look at Mackenzie's *Voyages* leaves the impression that he was mainly concerned with exploring for the sheer satisfaction it brought, his trip to the Pacific had a far more practical motive. The Mackenzie watershed produced a fabulously rich fur harvest, but the expense of taking it to market in faraway Montreal threatened to eat up all the profits. Mackenzie, concerned with rising costs, felt it imperative to find a shorter and cheaper route to the world's markets, and his trip to tidewater was made primarily for that purpose.

In any event, in the fall of 1805 Simon Fraser ascended the Peace

River and within a few years not only followed the Fraser River to its mouth but established several posts in British Columbia. Serving that region made the Peace River into an important route of commerce across Alberta and one which was to remain in use for decades.

But of far more importance to Alberta's destiny were the efforts made by the North West Company to reach the Columbia River from the North Saskatchewan. In the spring of 1807 David Thompson crossed the mountains to the Columbia River, which he ascended as far as Windermere Lake, where he built his Kootenae House. Going on from there in the spring of 1808 he crossed the low divide to the Kootenay River and descended it into Montana, but returned to winter at Kootenae House. On the Kootenay Plains of Alberta in the spring of 1809, on his way to visit Rocky Mountain House, Thompson met the Hudson's Bay Company's Joseph Howse, who in due course built a post on Pend d'Oreille Lake in modern Idaho. Thompson also spent much of 1809 exploring parts of Idaho and Montana and passed that winter at a post he built in what is now Sanders County, Montana, called Saleesh House. In the spring of 1810 he returned to Rocky Mountain House for further supplies which he intended to take back to the Columbia that fall by his usual route. While both the Hudson's Bay Company and the North West Company were fairly familiar by this time with all the territory in the eastern Rocky Mountains for some distance south of the 49th parallel, and while they both operated in this area out of Edmonton, the Montreal-based company had the greater number of posts and men in the region.

Unfortunately David Thompson's dealings with the Kootenay Indians had aroused the ire of his former friends the Piegans. Once more, by carrying goods beyond Piegan territory and supplying their former customers—in this case the Kootenays—a white man had flouted one of the unwritten laws of any tribe of Indians. By a paradox applicable to Indians and white men alike, some of the Piegans profited by trading with the Kootenays while generally the tribe as a whole was at war with them. On the one hand Thompson had transgressed by trading directly with the Kootenays and on the other he had erred by supplying them with guns which they turned on their Piegan enemies.

By the fall of 1810 the Piegans had resolved to stop any more of this nonsense and told Thompson that they would not allow him to cross the mountains through their territory as he had been accustomed to doing. Caught between his impatient employers who wanted him to hurry and the angry Piegans who dared him to try, Thompson was in a bad way. All he could do was make a long end run and try some other pass over the mountains. Returning downstream from Rocky Mountain House to a point near modern Lodgepole, he set off northwesterly, and after a terrific struggle through fallen timber and muskeg, he reached the Athabasca

A History of Alberta

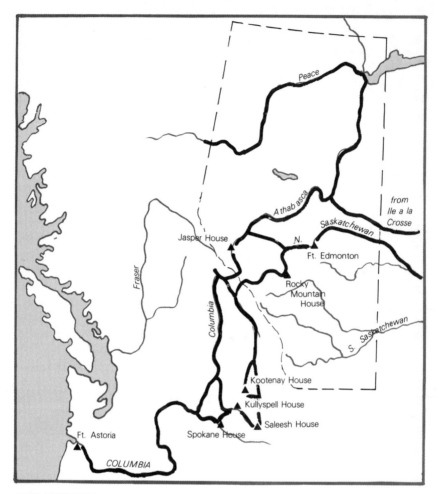

DAVID THOMPSON

Commencing in 1793 David Thompson, one of western Canada's early surveyors, travelled most of Alberta's rivers. During the years 1807 to 1812 he surveyed the Kootenay and Columbia rivers, established several posts south of the 49th parallel and finally made his way to the mouth of the Columbia.

River in the vicinity of Hinton. Working his way up as far as present-day Jasper, he set off over the Athabasca Pass during the first week of January 1811. That pass took him to the Canoe River, which he descended to its mouth at Boat Encampment on the Big Bend of the Columbia. From there he descended the mighty river to its mouth, only to discover that instead of his company being the first to reach that point, John Jacob Astor's Americans had already done so and were building their Astoria post.

Two Competitive Decades

Regardless of that and of any disappointment he may have felt, he had found the key to a new route across Alberta and the Rocky Mountains. Led to the pass by an Iroquois named Thomas, Thompson was the first white man to cross the Athabasca Pass and to map it. For the next several years the North West Company was to use this route, and during succeeding decades it was to become part of the first trans-Canada highway, that highway which transported fur by canoe and pack horse.

By that time Fort Augustus and Edmonton House, the rival posts enclosed by a common stockade on the north bank of the Saskatchewan River, had become the headquarters of all fur trade activity on the western prairies. And that trade covered a vast area. To these posts or to their subsidiary posts tucked safely into the valleys west of the main chain of the Rocky Mountains but serving customers who roamed the plateaus and the river valleys of Idaho, Montana and Wyoming, came all of the trade of the northern Great Plains. For many a year after the hot reception accorded the rival traders at Chesterfield House neither company dared to establish any more posts on the Blackfoot-dominated prairies.

If, however, neither company dared start posts in the short grass country, they still felt safe in sending some of their men out to live with the plains Indians. One of these was big Donald MacDonald, who was to have a long and interesting career in the foothills country. Another was Hugh Munro, who as a youth of eighteen years of age, came to serve the Hudson's Bay Company about 1802 and who married an Indian girl. Munro and MacDonald had many adventures, and took part in an 1808 battle between the Piegans and their enemies the Crows, Snakes and others, which took place near the Old Man's Bowling Green on the headwaters of the Oldman River. Munro later went to live and trade in Montana, where he became the first white man to see one of the most beautiful lakes of the American Rocky Mountains. Overlooking the lake he erected a cross and named the body of water St. Mary's. This early, men from the Edmonton posts were playing a part in Montana.

About this time a husky lad by the name of John Rowand began his career along the upper North Saskatchewan River. The son of an Irish-born Montreal surgeon, he entered the service of the North West Company in 1803. When he was about twenty he wed in the fashion of the country. Years later when travelling through Edmonton, Colonel Lefroy entered into his journal all the details we have of the Rowands' interesting romance, a life-long attachment that was terminated only by the death of Rowand's wife in 1848.

"I was received by Mr. Rowand, widely known among the plains Indians as the 'Big Mountain'; he was a powerful but not very tall man of rough determined aspect and very near lame from an early accident. Hunting alone as a young man he had been thrown from his horse and

A History of Alberta

had broken his leg. By some means intelligence reached the fort of what had occurred and before the whites could do anything an Indian girl had mounted and galloped off in the direction indicated. She found him, nursed him, and saved his life and he married her."

In 1813, shortly after Rowand's marriage, Fort Augustus and Edmonton House moved again, to come to rest once more and for the last time within Edmonton's present city limits. Both forts were rebuilt on the same site which they had left three years earlier and the site which at least as early as 1810 had grown a fair crop of barley.

Gardens and such grain crops as could be ground into flour by hand were an essential part of the economy of any trading post and the management of both companies advocated growing such food. Hence, at all the Saskatchewan posts gardens were tilled. While we have no direct references to such at Fort George on the river near Alberta's east boundary, it is extremely likely that as early as 1793 a garden formed part of the post's economy. Before that, however, at least as early as 1787, Peter Pond was growing a garden at his post on the lower Athabasca. Of it Alexander Mackenzie wrote that he "had formed as fine a kitchen garden as I ever saw in Canada."

Though we may be a bit hazy about the first garden grown, we are on safer ground about the first white child born in Alberta, the offspring of Jean-Baptiste Lagimodière, one of the Hudson's Bay Company's French Canadian employees. Besides being an exceptionally capable frontiersman, he is of particular interest to us because he was the father of the first all white child born in wedlock in the West. Within two or three years of the birth of that baby, who was named René, at Pembina in January 1808, the Lagimodières moved to the Edmonton area where they lived for four years. During that time the couple were blessed with one or two other children and these would be the first all white children born in Alberta. What is also most interesting is that later on, after the Lagimodières settled down in Selkirk's Red River Settlement, their sixth child, Julie, arrived; she was destined to become the mother of Louis Riel.

As usual, as a defence against Indian attack, the new Edmonton trading posts built in 1813 were contained within a common stockade. But by this time friction between the two companies was rising to a dangerous level and it soon began to look as if they were to need defence against each other. The strong rivalry of former years began to grow into a bitterness that in many other parts of the West brought on bloodshed. The Northwesters' belligerence reached its maximum about 1815 after the appearance of Lord Selkirk's colony at what is now Winnipeg. However even then the houses on the upper Saskatchewan were spared its worst extremes.

A year or so before the troubles in Selkirk's colony, the Hudson's

Bay Company, in its battle with the Northwesters, began changing its previous defensive tactics to a more offensive attitude. Until 1814 the English company had made no serious attempt to compete with its rivals in the Peace River country. It stepped up that rivalry, however, in the fall of 1815 when John Clarke led a force of nearly one hundred Hudson's Bay men to Lake Athabasca. The war was on. There, in October, he started to build Fort Wedderburn right in front of his rival's Fort Chipewyan on Potato Island.

Clarke's party was desperately short of food. So, dividing his men, he sent some down the Slave River, others back up the Athabasca, and kept some at Fort Wedderburn. And now at this juncture, the full force of the North West Company's tactics struck him. Open bloodshed ill-suited that company's policy; starvation was a better weapon. The machinery needed to bring this about was all prepared. It lay awaiting the signal to touch it off. John McGillivray of the North West Company at Dunvegan, who happened to be at Chipewyan at the time, gave the word. Clarke decided to lead the remainder of his men up the Peace River—into the far-famed country of plenty. A few days prior to this McGillivray had sent out his instructions bidding the Indians to keep ahead of the Hudson's Bay Company's men and to drive all game back from the river, and, on no account, to have anything to do with Clarke's expedition or to feed its members.

On October 9, 1815, Clarke led his party of some fifty men, in eight canoes, up the Peace River towards the land of moose and buffalo. "On 9 October we embarked without a single ounce of provisions," he reported, "our sole dependence being on a Cree Indian to hunt for us." Judged by the outcome, this was a most foolish undertaking. Yet Clarke was no fool. Well he knew by experience what hunger was and what cold was and the devastating effects of hunger and cold combined. He was aware, as was each of his men, what a slim chance there was of killing game enough to support fifty men while they travelled. Their main dependence lay in their falling in with some Indians who would trade with them and hunt for them.

While Clarke rushed on ahead to Fort Vermilion, most of his men struggled up the river far behind him and reached the mouth of Loon River. The Indians there were anxious to help them, but were mauled by Canadian servants from that fort into holding back provisions from the starving Englishmen. Sixteen men left in canoes for Lake Athabasca, but the river froze and they were forced to take to foot. One by one, individuals fell out along the way. Only three men reached Fort Wedderburn; the rest perished from starvation. Eventually Clarke made his way back to Lake Athabasca.

How simply these calamities are stated in histories: "Sixteen men left in canoes . . . but the river froze . . . three only reached Ft. Wedderburn." Once more the North West Company had won.

But the Hudson's Bay Company tried again, and during the winter of 1816–17 sent Clarke and a number of employees to man Fort Wedderburn again. In opposing fronts the two forces glared at each other all winter until an open conflict broke out before the spring. While no one was killed, the Northwesters captured the Hudson's Bay men and John Clarke was not released until late in 1817.

The Hudson's Bay Company's plans went so far awry that it was not possible to reorganize in time to compete with its rivals the following winter. In the winter of 1818–19, however, they staged a successful counterattack. This time Colin Robertson was in charge at Chipewyan. Clarke went up to the mouth of the Smoky near the site of present-day Peace River town, where he established St. Mary's House, the first Hudson's Bay Company post to be built that far up the river. From it the company even began looking up the Smoky River with the view of ascending it as a route to British Columbia.

By this time the tide of war had started to turn in the Hudson's Bay Company's favour. That winter the company did a good trade and Colin Robertson returned in the fall of 1819. One of his staff whom he left at Fort Chipewyan for the winter was Dr. William Todd, the first physician ever to practice in what is now Alberta.

Then in the fall of 1820 Robertson was succeeded by a man as yet untried in the fierce rivalry of the fur trade, a man who, in the course of years, became its greatest figure—George Simpson. His cunning and adroitness completely turned the tables on the North West Company at Chipewyan and indeed all over the Peace River country. Under his hand, the Hudson's Bay Company's business and influence expanded immensely.

In fact the North West Company's end was near. Its rival was becoming more active. The warfare and outrages all over the north country were having their effect upon public opinion. The massacre of Seven Oaks near Winnipeg had told against it. Even by the end of 1816 the company passed its peak and due to its heavy expenditure on the campaign and its overexpansion in western Canada, bankruptcy began to stare it in the face.

In the spring of 1821, before George Simpson emerged from Fort Chipewyan, the North West Company and the Hudson's Bay Company amalgamated, and the former passed out of existence. Actually, the agreement came as a great relief to the English company, which, though still paying dividends, had its back to the wall. After the pact, the Hudson's Bay Company, utilizing the best of the North West Company's many good men, and employing George Simpson—a genius of its own finding—to manage the whole, operated as a monopoly. Simpson's efforts immediately after the union were directed towards the sorely needed rehabilitation of the fur trade so badly crippled by the preceding strife.

Thus the North West Company passed from the scene. It had been a great company. During the brief span of twenty years, three of its outstanding men, Alexander Mackenzie, David Thompson and Simon Fraser, had mapped the framework of a quarter of a continent and then took steps to occupy it.

In that time Mackenzie had gone down to the Arctic and up the Peace to its headwaters and thence to the Pacific. Fraser, by tracing the river later named after him from its headwaters to its mouth, had made the second crossing of the continent in Canada only three years after the famous Lewis and Clark Expedition in the United States. As well as doing a tremendous amount of other surveying, David Thompson had travelled every foot of the Columbia River. Seldom has history seen the bold outlines of so immense an area sketched out in such a short time.

By 1821 the North West Company had organized its trade over a territory which extended from Tadoussac, Quebec, where Atlantic tides ebb and flow in the mighty St. Lawrence River to where Pacific swells break on the beach near Astoria, Oregon. By the time of the company's demise the work started by the French traders and explorers and continued by the British, who built upon the French footings, was complete. Compounded of the work of the French voyageur, the contribution of the Indians' canoe, rice and pemmican and the organizing ability of the Anglo-Saxon, the North West Company was the forerunner of Confederation. It had laid the foundations of the Dominion of Canada.

Fortunately its empire fell into the capable hands of George Simpson, the dapper little snip of a man who at Fort Chipewyan had cut his fur trade teeth by opposing the North West Company. At the time of the amalgamation neither Simpson nor the dour old Scottish traders with whom he came to associate and to command could possibly have foreseen that Simpson was to rise rapidly and that for some thirty-four years he was to govern all the company's business spread over a vast area of the continent, including much of the western United States.

When he assumed the role of governor of the northern department of the new company, the department which included the Alberta area, Simpson faced many problems. On every front he had them: the wasteful methods of competitive trading had to be revised; better relations had to be established with the plains Indians; the previous heavy expenditure of liquor had to be cut to a minimum; the routes of travel had to be studied and altered; the rival posts standing side by side had to be coalesced or abandoned; the strong men of each company who had fought each other so bitterly had somehow to be reconciled, and finally, he had to find some way of re-deploying or getting rid of the heavy surplus of men who in the days of competition had been such a terrific drain on each company's purse. All of these problems he faced, and in a remarkably short time and with remarkably few errors, he overcame them.

One of his first moves tried to solve two problems with one stroke; an attempt to improve relations with the Blackfoot and use surplus staff. He set on foot a plan that came to be called the Bow River Expedition, which it was hoped would absorb some of the "superfluity of men" and open up trade with the upper Missouri. In other words, it was to be a mission which would try once more to set up posts in the heart of the Blackfoot country. It was to employ "eighty engaged Servants exclusive of Officers" on the south branch of the Saskatchewan River.

Since Peter Fidler's sojourn amongst the Blackfoot at Chesterfield House twenty years earlier, these independent Indian nomads had increasingly taxed the traders' patience. The pemmican they brought in was vital to the transportation system; the goods they purchased had become necessities to their rising standard of living. Even though the trading between the white men and the lords of the prairies was conducted at arm's length with trepidation on the part of the whites and apparent disdain on the part of the Indians, both parties needed the goods the other had to offer.

But two barriers stood between the two races. With their star in the ascendant, the Blackfoot would countenance no interlopers, neither white men nor Crees, Assiniboines or Kootenays, into the rich larder of the prairies and parklands which they had arrogated to themselves. An occasional company trader might come to dwell amongst them, but only on their own terms, and they would trade with the whites only when they felt like it. Moreover, they could not forgive the white man for selling guns to their enemies, the Crees and Assiniboines, who for so long had been pressing on their eastern flank, and to their harried victims, the Kootenays, whom they had driven through the Alberta passes.

The Kootenays did not matter so much, but the Plains Crees and Assiniboines, who had long been loosely allied and who had been friends of the traders for a generation or two, were a different matter. The Blackfoot might claim to be masters of southern Alberta, but every now and then the Crees, sometimes alone and sometimes with the Assiniboines, mocked that claim. On occasions they too ranged far into southern Alberta, as for instance in 1815 when on the Belly River a Cree and Assiniboine party attacked a camp of Blood and Sarcee lodges, killing four men and a woman. These northern Indians had ready access to guns, and after each skirmish Blackfoot anger mounted against the traders who had supplied them.

Moreover, far to the south, along the Yellowstone River, they had recently met another breed of white men, "the Big Knives," the Americans, and that contact did nothing to sweeten their disposition. With the

Big Knives supplying guns to the tribes along their southern flank and the Canadian traders, whom they thenceforth called the "Northern White Men" supplying the Kootenays, their ire mounted. To maintain their position as raiders of the northwestern plains in the face of these added handicaps they had to redouble their efforts and doing so doubled their ferocity and deepened their distrust of white men.

From 1805 on, the North West Company and the Hudson's Bay Company traders along the North Saskatchewan River had watched the development of the Blackfoot's increasing ferocity and aloofness. Prior to that year American traders had merely started up the Missouri River, and the Blackfoot and other plains tribes had no white men to trade with except the Canadians at their posts along the north edge of the prairies. If the Blackfoot had ever heard of Americans, they certainly had never seen any. Then, the fall of 1806 brought news to Edmonton House of the possibility of American competitors in the region of the Yellowstone and Missouri rivers and of the passage of the Lewis and Clark Expedition, the first American group to go down the Columbia River to reach the Pacific. The chief factors of both Fort Augustus and Edmonton House listened attentively, particularly when they heard of the fight between Meriwether Lewis and the Blackfoot on the Marias River of northern Montana—only four hundred miles away—too close for comfort.

In the fall of 1810 the Blackfoot brought the news that American traders in the wake of Lewis and Clark were at last working their way up the Missouri River and indeed had built a fort at the Three Forks of that river. Near this point, about five hundred miles due south of Edmonton, the Indians reported catching some American traders off their guard, killing them and making off with a rich booty in furs and trading goods. At Edmonton House, James Bird worried about the Americans' invasion of the area now known as Montana, Wyoming and Idaho, which up till then had marketed its furs at Edmonton. The news the Blackfoot brought bothered him, but the furs they had captured and now sold at Fort Augustus and Edmonton House rested lightly on his conscience.

About this time, of course, due to the efforts of David Thompson and of Joseph Howse of the Hudson's Bay Company, British traders had crossed the mountains and were also building posts in Montana and Idaho, and mingling with American traders and trappers who had worked their way up the Missouri or the Yellowstone. Before the Blackfoot realized it, white men's posts had circumscribed them and were selling guns to all their enemies. Even at that, for the next decade the Blackfoot made their own area too hot for interloping whites.

This then was the situation when George Simpson of the Hudson's Bay Company dispatched the Bow River Expedition. It went on its way in 1822 with Chief Factor Donald McKenzie in charge and with Chief

Trader John Rowand as second in command. Since in effect it was to be an invasion of the Blackfoot heartland, it was considered a very risky venture which needed a large body of well-armed men. Included were many Iroquois, half-breeds and freemen, who were to trap along the headwaters of the Missouri.

The first move was to take the whole force to the junction of the Red Deer and South Saskatchewan rivers and, in the vicinity of the long abandoned Chesterfield House, to build a new post. When that had been accomplished, enough men were to be left there to receive the Indians' trade and to defend themselves. The remainder of the party then ascended the South Saskatchewan River to the general Lethbridge area, where it was intended to build an outpost from which trade could be carried on with the Piegans while the trappers scoured the headwaters of the Missouri.

The whole expedition was a failure. The new Chesterfield House was occupied for the winter and then abandoned. The Blackfoot were incensed by the introduction of trappers to their homelands, and while Donald McKenzie and John Rowand came home with a handful of furs, they did so with their tails between their legs.

Perhaps the only man who enjoyed his trip to the Blackfoot country was Pierre Bungo, probably the first Negro to come to Alberta to work. On this trip he evidently was a favourite with the Indians, for George Simpson, writing of him some years later, said: "These unsophisticated savages, however, had their curiosity most strongly excited by a negro of the name of Pierre Bungo. This man they inspected in every possible way, twisting him about and pulling his hair, which was so different from their own flowing locks; and at length they came to the conclusion that Pierre Bungo was the oddest specimen of a white man that they had ever seen. These negroes, of whom there were formerly several in the company's service, were universal favourites with the fair sex of the red race; and, at the present day we saw many an Indian that appeared to have a dash of the gentleman in black about him. . . ."

Expeditions into Blackfoot territory were not the sole prerogative of the Hudson's Bay Company. The Bow River Expedition had been sent partly to counter an influx of Americans into its southern edges. In 1821 the Missouri Fur Company began to wonder if it could not build a post much farther north, but its speculations and trial were ended by Blackfoot rifles and knives. During 1822, the same year that Donald McKenzie had made his unsuccessful attempt to penetrate the territory, the Rocky Mountain Fur Company entered the American fur trade. That year Andrew Henry led a party of its trappers up the Missouri to the vicinity of the great falls. He should have known better, for the Blackfoot fell upon them, killing four and driving the rest down the river, and then took the furs they had captured to Alberta's Rocky Mountain House. The Americans found any transfer of furs between the two races invariably going the wrong way. To the accompaniment of gunfire and skull-cracking hand axes, furs owned by the Americans flew off on Blackfoot horses.

And so the situation remained until 1828. In that year Kenneth McKenzie, a Scot who had formerly worked for one of the Canadian companies, built a post for the American Fur Company at the mouth of the Yellowstone River in Assiniboine territory. Then he sent Jacob Berger, who for many years had served the Hudson's Bay Company and who spoke the Blackfoot's language, to see what he could do with the Blackfoot. In the fall of 1830 Berger headed a party of men with the hope of meeting the Blackfoot and inducing them to come to McKenzie's post to trade. Berger's gamble was as desperate as his courage was great, but by some miracle he led about a hundred Piegans in to meet McKenzie.

McKenzie's magic was as great as Berger's; he made friends with the Piegans, and they even agreed to him sending James Kipp up the Missouri to build a post at the mouth of the Marias (near modern Fort Benton)—the first American post in Blackfoot territory. Behind this hitherto unheard of attitude on the part of the Piegans lay McKenzie's understanding of what was irking them most—not Americans as such, but American trappers. The Indians had been accustomed to trading at Canadian posts, but they insisted on bringing in their own furs when the mood took them and they persisted in their stand that no interlopers should enter their lands to trap their animals. When McKenzie adopted the Canadian system to which they were accustomed, the system of a post to which the Blackfoot Confederacy could bring their furs, they agreed to it. As, later on, one of the Blackfoot chiefs told Major Sanford, a United States Indian agent: "If you will send Traders into our Country we will protect them and treat them well; but for Trappers—Never." They needed to trade, they were willing to trade, they were anxious to trade, but as for trappers on their lands, no.

And therein lies one of the keys—only one and perhaps a minor one—that helps to unlock the riddle of why relations between Indians and whites were so bitter in the United States and so relatively peaceful in Canada. In general, before the Canadian fur traders reached Alberta the days of independent, small traders were over and those men who made up either the x y or the North West Company had formed companies. Companies plan to stay in business over a span of years and, therefore, tend to take a longer view of their resources and their customers. Short-sighted, fly-by-night operations aimed at reaping a quick profit and vanishing do not fit into their more moderate approach. On the Canadian side of the 49th parallel the Blackfoot dealt with the large North West Company and the still more conservative Hudson's Bay Company, whereas, during the early decades of that tribe's association with Americans their contact was with more ruthless, independent individuals. Consequently, during the period the Blackfoot preferred to trade with the more stable Canadian concerns. They did not like the Canadian traders, they could never have learned to love them, but they had grown accustomed to them.

Not long after John Rowand came back from the Bow River Expedition in 1823 he took charge of Edmonton House and began making improvements in the route by which the brigades travelled back and forth to Oregon. He persuaded George Simpson to have a post built at Fort Assiniboine on the Athabasca River some eighty miles north and west of Edmonton. This post, which would serve as a stopping place for brigades going up or down the Athabasca on their way to or from the Pacific coast, would also serve as a halfway house for traffic between Edmonton and Lesser Slave Lake and the Peace River country in general. Simpson, on his part, gave orders to have Alberta's first deliberately cut pack trail cleared out from the new post to Edmonton. Of it he wrote: "Sept. 21st, 1824. With Cardinal the Freeman I made an agreement that he should in the course of this ensuing Winter and Spring get a Horse track or road cut from Fort Assiniboine to Edmonton House. . . ."

In the same way that Simpson was taking hold of the Hudson's Bay Company domain as a whole and reducing its affairs to some sort of order, John Rowand took hold of Edmonton House. He realized that not only was it the headquarters of the western prairies and the most important post west of York Factory, but being at the head of practical navigation on the North Saskatchewan River, it was a main depot along the transcontinental route to the coast. Moreover, once the seventy-mile portage to Fort Assiniboine was put into effective operation with relays of horses stationed along it, the trail could also be the main link with the Peace River country. Having all these advantages, Rowand insisted that Edmonton House should be built up to meet the demands likely to be made of it. Under his prideful eye, aided at times by his forceful fists, Edmonton House prospered.

The amalgamation of the two companies revolutionized the fur trade. Prior to 1821 competition had kept the West turbulent. The Indians, foolish indeed in the matter of liquor but otherwise shrewd traders, took advantage of the split in the white men's ranks. The fur trade required a far-flung, expensive organization and economics dictated that its successful exploitation could be carried out only by a monopoly. In the year 1822, before the benefits of amalgamation had had time to take effect, the Hudson's Bay Company's loss on the Saskatchewan River operations was £4,000.

With Governor Simpson's finesse guiding the new monopolistic Canadian fur trade chariot, that situation was about to change. First of all, many of the old competing posts were closed down, and those which were left, such as Edmonton House, rose in importance. Next, as soon as possible, the number of men employed during the days of competition was reduced to the bare minimum.

Having a monopoly the Hudson's Bay Company was now in a position to exploit western Canada's resource of furs to the mutual benefit of the company and the Indians. Once more it could begin to conserve the fur-bearing animals and their long-suffering hunters. It became the company's policy, dictated by humanitarian as well as good business motives, to look to the welfare of its customers and to see that, as far as possible, they kept peace amongst themselves, that they were virtually denied the devastating delights of liquor, and that, if a bad season befell them, they were fed. In the matter of liquor, the London Committee wrote Simpson, saying: "In the course of two or three years at farthest we think the use of spirits among the Indians of all the best fur countries may be entirely given up, and that the quantities given to them may safely be reduced immediately to one-third."

While these instructions applied all over Canada, conditions along the Saskatchewan River made it impractical to enforce them fully there. For the Indians could go some five hundred miles south to the Americans on the Missouri River. And when a roaring thirst parched Blackfoot or Gros Ventres, five hundred miles was regarded as a mere jaunt if a skinful of firewater lay at the end of it. So, though liquor was kept from Indians in the regions where the Hudson's Bay Company had no competition, it could not be cut out entirely at Edmonton House.

The company's paternalistic attitude towards its Indians was, of course, as good for business as it was for the natives; it cut costs. But the company's injunction to its traders to treat Indians as if they were human beings and to deny them grog was not founded solely on the matter of profit. At that time a wave of humanitarian sympathy had swept over Britain to such an extent that it made it politic, if nothing else, for the Bay officials in London to lay down this course. Whatever may have been its motive, however, the regulations prevailing during Simpson's regime mark a great contrast to the period of violence that preceded the amalgamation. The repeated injunction that the Indians must be treated with civility goes far towards explaining the control the company exercised over them. The consequent comparative orderliness of life in Rupert's Land was in marked contrast to the era of hatred and bloodshed which reigned south of the international boundary.

Keeping all these matters in mind, Rowand set to work to make conditions at Edmonton House more livable. For one thing, he had to get more land under cultivation, and soon, as Alexander Ross, who passed there in 1825, said, there were "two large parks for raising grain, and, the soil being good, it produces large crops of barley and potatoes; but the spring and fall frosts prove injurious to wheat, which, in consequence seldom comes to maturity."

As Rowand carried out Simpson's able policies and improvised some of his own, prosperity returned to Edmonton House. Its expenses fell and its profits rose. The once risky Saskatchewan district was now back on the even keel which only a monopoly could ensure. So much was Simpson impressed with Rowand's merit that in 1826 he promoted him to chief factor of the whole Saskatchewan district with his headquarters in Edmonton. This district, as well as including Jasper House, Fort Assiniboine and Lesser Slave Lake, extended from Rocky Mountain House far into Saskatchewan. Between them, Simpson and Rowand had set Edmonton on its course and from it brought what order they could into the fur trade of the western prairies.

But a vast area of Alberta did not come under John Rowand's jurisdiction: the Peace River country and all the huge region from the Hay Lakes to the Caribou Mountains; and the territory down the Athabasca beyond Fort McMurray to Lake Athabasca and down the mighty Slave River. It was governed either from Fort Chipewyan or Dunvegan. To these two centres and a few subsidiary outposts came the furs of the Woods Crees, the Chipewyans and the Beavers. To the traders none of these natives presented the prickly problems posed by the irascible Blackfoot. Except for an occasional clash between a lodge or two of contiguous tribes, these relatively docile Indians rarely disturbed the peace of the area. Trading was a routine, even a friendly matter carried on between traders who could be trusted and Indians who rarely broke faith.

To these posts came all the furs of the canoe folk of the forests who were already dependent upon the white man's goods. Thinly scattered over the whole area, averaging perhaps one soul to every thirty square miles, they and their dogs led a precarious existence on the fish of the lakes and the beasts of the forests. While family by family they dispersed into the corners of the forest to hunt, they congregated from time to time at fishing lakes or at the mouths of rivers to carry on their tribal life or to obtain what goods their pelts would bring from the traders.

Then once more they headed back into their home regions in the hundreds of square miles of primitive forests. Though their lives were as different from those of their remote prairie kinfolk as the woodland caribou is different from the parkland antelope, they enjoyed their homeland. They too lived in a land magnificent and beautiful—a land blessed with the soothing silences and the muffled murmurings of great forests of spruce and poplar, varied here and there with willow-fringed streams and balm-ringed lakes. With them deer and moose, buffalo and caribou, lynx, rabbits and squirrels shared this forest. Bush partridges drummed in its glades. Prairie chicken danced on its sandy, piny knolls, and in winter's powdery snow mazy traces marked the passing of the ptarmigan's feathered foot.

Thus, between forts Chipewyan and Dunvegan in the North and Edmonton House and Rocky Mountain House along the Saskatchewan River, the Hudson's Bay Company maintained contact with all the natives of Alberta. Those in the North whose ready access to white men's goods had alleviated many of their hardships otherwise found little change in their way of life. Those in the south, mainly the Blackfoot, with their increasing herds of horses had almost reached the peak of their wealth and power. For the next twenty or thirty years the white men found them a force to reckon with.

A History of Alberta

# 4
# John Rowand's Regime
# 1830-1854

The expanding activity at Edmonton House, the fur trade headquarters for all the western prairies, kept John Rowand busy. Since the amalgamation of the companies, the Hudson's Bay Company had made use of the buildings of both Fort Augustus and Edmonton House. They were showing signs of aging and when, in 1830 during one of its recurring floods, the North Saskatchewan River flowed over the flat, Rowand decided that it was time to rebuild on the higher ground immediately below today's Legislative Building. At the same time, he resolved to create an establishment worthy of Edmonton's growing importance.

The new post was not completed until 1832 when John Rowand was able to move into his "Big House." It was about thirty by eighty feet, having three stories in addition to a basement. Along the front and back galleries ran the full length of the building. The Big House, by far the largest west of York Factory, was well provided with windows, each made up of panes of glass about seven inches by eight inches. To the Indians, this glass, the first to be used in the West, was a wonder. With his unrivalled grasp of Indian psychology, Rowand saw how this mansion would impress them. It also impressed all of the passing fur traders who called it Rowand's Folly.

George Simpson, who came in 1841, wrote of it: "This fort, both inside and outside, is decorated with paintings and devices to suit the taste of the savages that frequent it. Over the gateway are a most fanciful variety of vanes; but the hall, of which both the ceiling and the walls present the grandest colors and the most fantastic sculpture, absolutely rivets the astonished natives to the spot with wonder and admiration. The buildings are smeared with a red earth, found in the neighborhood which, when mixed with oil, produces a durable brown."

The Indians may well have found the fort's combination of rugged strength and interior decorating somewhat awesome.

Radiating out from it, however, John Rowand, like a corpulent spider, constructed a web whose threads kept him in touch with well over a quarter of a continent. Because it was one of the company's important depots and because it was on the trans-Canada route, Edmonton House was a busy spot. The Hudson's Bay Company supplied its posts along the Pacific coast from San Francisco to Alaska by sea, but, when messages had to be sent rapidly, they sped through Edmonton. So did the personnel for these posts, which were ever changing as new recruits went west and time-expired men came back across the mountains. And all these, when they reached Edmonton House, had some news to tell John Rowand.

Early in October each year some ten boats, manned by fifty men, arrived from York Factory. Immediately the goods were carried into the store and everything wet was set out to dry. As soon as possible the goods were repacked for transport over the portage to Fort Assiniboine. In one typical year seventy-eight pack horses were needed to take the supplies across the portage. Twenty-eight of them took goods which had to go up the Athabasca to the mountains, forty-three carried goods which went downstream to modern Smith and thence across to the Peace River country, and finally, seven loaded with supplies left for Fort Assiniboine itself. For this transport, the company kept two horse-guards where it pastured its herds. A large one lay beyond the Sturgeon River north of St. Albert, while another was located at Lac La Nonne. It says much for the company's relations with the Indians that while it was not wise to flaunt its wealth in horses by pasturing them within sight of the fort, nevertheless some four hundred horses could be kept safely at these distances from the fort, guarded only by a man or two.

After the pack trains had been sent on their way, the chief factor at Edmonton would then turn his attention to the Indians, who, in anticipation of the arrival of a fresh supply of goods, had come in to trade. When they arrived in a band they too observed due ceremony. As they saluted those in the fort with a friendly discharge of firearms, the old guns in the bastions of Edmonton House burst forth with a salvo perhaps more potentially dangerous to those who fired than to any enemy against whom they may ever have been directed. Following these salutes, which echoed and re-echoed from the wooded banks of the valley, the Indians marched in procession through the widely thrown gate and up to the great hall, where the chief factor met them. One band after another would be given goods and ammunition on credit and allowed to go north, south, east or west to hunt furs or prepare pemmican to bring in later to pay off the credit given them.

While all this was going on several servants had their hands full bringing in the crop. Barley and oats were not too much of a problem, but since the wheat of that era took about 135 days to ripen, and therefore usually froze, it was rarely sown. It appeared quite certain that the Edmonton area would never be a wheat growing country. But potatoes were another matter, and each year, to feed the staff during the coming season, hundreds of bushels were dug and stored.

A History of Alberta

Spring too was a busy time, with its heavy trade in pemmican, dried meat, grease, and furs, and the packing and pressing of the furs for the long journey to the sea. The staff hastily ploughed and seeded the farm. The trains of horses began to come in with the furs from Fort Assiniboine and the boats arrived from Rocky Mountain House. All the incoming furs were inspected, packed, and loaded into the boats, while some of the staff were selected and additional help, usually half-breeds, were hired for the long trip to York Factory. About the middle of May the brigade set off down the river with most of the men of the fort. Now that the busy season was over, the long summer's quiet settled down on the post, to be broken only by occasional visits of the Blackfoot.

Frequently these visits threatened to break the threads of Rowand's web. For the Americans on the Missouri kept encroaching on territory and dealing with plains Indians which the Hudson's Bay Company regarded as in its bailiwick. To try to counter them, Rowand sent men out to live with the Piegans in southern Alberta. In 1826 and again in 1827, William McGillivray, a half-breed, led these men. Then in 1831 Rowand sent out a colourful character called Jamey Jock, a half-breed son of James Bird. Jamey was given a large quantity of goods and told to oppose the Americans well out towards the Missouri River in Montana. Alas for Rowand's hopes, the American Fur Company, which was busy setting up a post where the Yellowstone River joins the Missouri, near Williston, North Dakota, proved able to buy Jamey Jock lock, stock and barrel, including some three or four thousand beaver pelts which really belonged to Edmonton House.

Rowand's next move was to send out a strong force in 1832, under J. E. Harriott, to build what was called Piegan Post on the north side of the Bow River, not far east of our Canmore. The Piegans regarded it as an unwelcome intrusion into their territory, and after struggling along for two years, Harriott closed it. He then assumed charge of Rocky Mountain House, and the company had to content itself with what trade the Piegans and other plains Indians would bring there. As a rule, though Harriott remained in charge there until 1841, Rocky Mountain House was closed each summer.

Meantime, with the characteristic enthusiasm Americans bring to any venture, they started developing the Missouri River, and in 1832 brought the first steamboat up as far as Fort Union, near today's Williston, a point as far west as the forks of the North and South Saskatchewan rivers near Prince Albert. Whereas for decades after that Canadian traders continued to get their supplies by York boats dragged laboriously across the hundreds of miles of their long line of communication, the Americans now had the advantage of steamboats puffing their way into the midst of the American plains. Steamboats not only provided less costly supplies and

John Rowand's Regime 1830-1854

trade goods, but made it possible for American traders to buy and ship to eastern markets buffalo hides and robes from the Blackfoot—heavy items which the Hudson's Bay traders could not send to market. The turbulent plains Indians, watching these developments, found themselves in a seller's market, and made the most of playing one set of traders against another. During the fall of 1833, when Prince Maximilian zu Wied from Europe was visiting the Americans' Fort McKenzie near modern Fort Benton, all three tribes of the Blackfoot Confederacy, the Bloods, Piegans and Blackfoot, came in to trade.

Worrying about this state of affairs, John Rowand wrote in 1840: "But I am sorry to say we are losing ground with the Slave [Blackfoot] tribes who laugh at the poverty of our shops and who do not hesitate to remind one of the old times before they got introduced to the American traders when they had but one shop to go to. . . . What they speak most of is about the presents the Indians receive from the Americans twice a year. . . . The Piegans who are the worst of all the Slave tribes to please expect a great many things for nothing. They are all Chiefs who must be dressed as such, Gratis of course. If not, off they go back to the Americans where they say they are sure of being well received for their few furs, Buffalo Robes, Wolves and their Horses. [These] form one of their principal articles of trade with the Americans and us too, to enable us to keep up the number of Horses so much required for the Company's work and for the sales to our men and Indians, etc. . . ."

And yet the Piegans who were causing him all this anguish had their own problems, principally in the shape of Cree and Assiniboine enemies. While the Blackfoot claimed the prairies as their territory, the Crees and Assiniboines, and sometimes lesser groups, such as the Saulteaux, failed to respect their claim. Minor skirmishes between these hostile tribes were always taking place when here and there the Crees slapped the Blackfoot in the face, and then, perhaps a month later, the Bloods or Piegans returned the compliment by pulling off their scalps. Not only did they harry the Blackfoot along their eastern flank in Alberta and Saskatchewan, but they carried their raids as far south as the Missouri River. During Prince Maximilian's visit to Fort McKenzie, he witnessed a rather large scale battle in which the Crees and Assiniboines, having attacked a Piegan camp, found that tribe's reinforcements too numerous and lost many of their warriors before they escaped from the scene of their rash attack.

About 1840 John Rowand cited another example of the difficulty of dealing with the plains people. When on their way to Edmonton, some thirty-eight tents of Gros Ventres and Blackfoot who had been induced to "turn their backs on the Americans" were slaughtered by some Crees and Saulteaux. "Only six Crees and two Soteaux remained upon the place of bloodshed. The others after taking the scalps of more than one hundred men, women and children got off with upwards of two hundred horses and everything else they found worth carrying with them. Not very long ago another small camp of Cercees was attacked by some plain Crees and Stone Indians who killed a few of them and also took their horses. For all these misfortunes we are the ones who get blamed for it for inviting them back to us."

Such skirmishes between the Blackfoot on the one hand and the Cree and Assiniboine on the other were the normal state of affairs on Alberta's prairies and parklands. As one season flowed into another, almost every one of the province's hundreds of square miles of billowing hills or winding valleys must have witnessed a minor fray or a major battle. From Eagletail Hill overlooking the North Saskatchewan to the Sweet Grass Hills straddling Alberta's south boundary, and from the Blackfoot and Cypress hills in the east to the Medicine Lodge and Porcupine hills in the shadow of the mountains, few indeed must be the creek sides or pond margins that have not echoed to the screams of fleeing widows or the exultant shouts of victorious warriors. On the whole the Blackfoot more than held their own against their native foes.

Against the white man's diseases, however, neither bravery nor cunning availed. Periodically when these plagues stalked the land they exacted a heavy toll. During the winter of 1819–20 the traders at Edmonton House reported a measles epidemic which wiped out a third of the Blackfoot and Gros Ventres tribes. Then in 1836 many children strangled in the throes of the mysterious and fearful diphtheria. Neither of these visited such awful devastation on the plains Indians as the smallpox epidemic which began in June 1837. It travelled up the Missouri on the American Fur Company's steamboat *St. Peter's*, and at Fort Union transferred to a keel boat bound for Fort McKenzie. A number of Piegans and Blood Indians were there and Alexander Culbertson, the trader, tried to keep them from mingling and trading with the passengers, but they could not understand his motive and insisted on doing so. Ten days after they left the fort smallpox began to break out and spread wildly.

When after two months no more Piegans or Bloods came in to trade, Culbertson went out to look for them. Heading north and west, he came upon a Piegan camp of about sixty lodges in which two women, too feeble to travel, were the sole survivors. Amidst the eerie silence and the horrible stench, he found that "hundreds of decaying forms of human beings, horses and dogs lay scattered everywhere among the lodges." Somewhat farther north, close to the mouths of the Belly and St. Mary rivers, near modern Lethbridge, the death rate had been so high amongst the Bloods and the Blackfoot that ever after they have called the campground the Grave Yard. From there the loathsome disease swept on northward until two-thirds of the Blackfoot Confederacy had perished—some six thousand out of nine thousand.

Among the survivors was a lad about eight years old who had been

John Rowand's Regime 1830-1854

born a Blood but by this time had been adopted into the Blackfoot tribe—
a lad later to be known alike to white men and Indians as a great chief
who earned the name Crowfoot. The other natives of the plains also suffered severe losses so that numerically the Blackfoot were left in about
the same relative position as they had been before the onset of the disease.
For a while the devastation took the heart out of all the prairie Indians,
but in due course they rallied, and within two or three years resumed their
intertribal raiding and killing. Within a few years the combination of a
salubrious climate, a plentiful food supply and a healthful heredity enabled
the Blackfoot to increase in numbers. It is doubtful, however, if they and
the other Alberta Indians ever again regained the population they had
prior to the epidemic. Led by several prominent men, such as Old Swan,
Old Sun and Three Swans, the Blackfoot tribe made a remarkable come-
back until within fifteen years they reached the height of their power.
From the North Saskatchewan River south past the Neutral and the Hand
hills to the Belly Buttes and far into Montana, buffalo ribs sizzled on their
, campfires and all was well.

About the time the epidemic had subsided, in September 1838, the
first two missionaries ever to enter Alberta visited John Rowand. For five
days Fathers Francois Blanchet and Modeste Demers, acting under orders
from Bishop Provencher of St. Boniface on the Red River, rested at Edmonton on their way to open a mission at the Hudson's Bay Company's
Fort Vancouver on the Columbia River. They gave Rowand fresh food
for thought. Hitherto no one not directly connected with the fur trade had
ever visited the Edmonton area, and now these priests, the narrow edge
of the wedge of civilization, had put in an appearance. The visit of these
two priests gave Edmonton its first official service with candle and book.

Around Edmonton and the other posts along the river, the tally of
half-breed children of voyageurs and of Hudson's Bay Company labourers
and traders was growing apace. Some lived and traded with the Indians,
and some had already moved out to support themselves by fishing at Lac
Ste. Anne and Lac La Nonne, but since they were increasing far more
rapidly than the company could employ them, they were a growing problem. Perhaps if missionaries came out they could settle these people into
some semblance of agrarian life.

But the winds of change continued to blow and about two years later,
on October 18, 1840, the Reverend Robert Terrill Rundle, representing
the Wesleyan Society of London, became the first missionary to reside in
Edmonton. A man of great zeal and fortitude, he crossed the sea to face
conditions of which he had only a vague conception. Though he arrived
under the handicap of being a greenhorn, he remained until the spring of
1848, and during that interval proved to be a man of rare courage. Going
out to find and to tend his flock, he ranged from modern Saskatoon on

the east to Jasper on the west, and from Banff in the south, where now the impressive mountain bears his name, to Lesser Slave Lake in the north. Suffering great hardship at times, and once returning to Edmonton House alone with an arm which had been broken days before, he nevertheless made a mark upon the Cree and Stoney Indians that persisted for generations.

Then on June 19, 1842, the Reverend Father A. Thibault, an Oblate from St. Boniface, arrived at Edmonton. This worthy man, who travelled hither and yon serving the natives and the Métis, covered the same territory as Rundle. A year or so later, after sizing up the situation, he established a mission at Lac Ste. Anne. Here, in a soil that could be cultivated and near the Hudson's Bay Company's old fishery station, he hoped to induce the Métis to settle down to farm. He hoped also that here, back in the bush, far removed from the domain of attacking plains Indians, the Crees could worship in peace.

John Rowand could see little value in missionaries. Writing to a friend in 1843, he expressed the opinion that "the worst thing for the trade is these ministers and priests—the natives will never work half so well now—they like praying and singing. Mr. Thingheaute [Thibault] is allowed to go back again to the Saskatchewan. We shall all be saints after a time. Rundle says that all Catholics will go to . . . for himself he is sure of going straite to heaven when he dies, but he longs to get a wife."

The Hudson's Bay Company also dealt with Russians in Alaska and mandarins in China, and had way stations at Honolulu and the Sandwich Islands. In 1841 Sir George Simpson decided to take a trip around the world. John Rowand met him at Fort Garry and on July 3 they started west towards Edmonton. The party had about thirty horses and one light cart, and planned to change horses at the main posts at Forts Ellice, Carlton, Pitt and Edmonton. Although Simpson rode, he was probably the first to bring a wheeled vehicle all the way from Winnipeg to Edmonton along the trail which came to be known as the Carlton or Edmonton Trail. Covering forty or fifty miles a day, Simpson's party made the trip in twenty-two days.

One interesting episode took place in 1841 while Sir George Simpson was at Edmonton. Though John Rowand may have had his difficulties with the Blackfoot, Bloods and Piegans, they came in to greet Simpson, whom they knew was ruler of all the West. The missionaries who had but recently appeared in the country might talk to them of a Supreme Being or of the Great White Mother overseas, but to the Indians Simpson was an all-powerful Manitou. On this occasion he was here in person, and they did not miss the opportunity to wait on him. Quoting Simpson: "These chiefs were Blackfoot, Piegans, Sarcees and Blood Indians, all dressed in their grandest clothes and decorated with scalp locks. I paid them a visit,

John Rowand's Regime 1830-1854

giving each of them some tobacco. Instead of receiving their presents with the usual indifference of savages, they thanked me in rotation, and, taking my hand in theirs, made long prayers to me as a high and powerful conjuror. They implored me to grant, that their horses might be swift, that the buffalo might constantly abound, and that their wives might live long and look young."

These chiefs were clear-headed. What greater good than these blessings could plains Indians want—or for that matter, their white brothers?

Leaving Edmonton, Simpson's party travelled by pack horses along a new route, which took them south past Gull Lake to Lake Minnewanka and on through what is now Banff and the pass that now bears Simpson's name. From it they went on to Fort Colville, which was a few miles upstream from the Grand Coulee Dam of modern times. Thence Simpson and Rowand floated down the Columbia to Fort Vancouver, which was located on the right bank of the river across from the modern city of Portland. Ultimately the two men crossed the Pacific to Honolulu, and arrived at the Sandwich Islands. Simpson went on to Russia and subsequently returned via London to Canada, while John Rowand turned back towards Edmonton. In spending the winter at Honolulu, Rowand must surely have been the first Albertan to bask under palm trees during January and February.

But Simpson carried his worries with him. England and the United States were competing for possession of the territory which we know as the states of Washington and Oregon. Britain rightly claimed all of the west coast between the limits set by the Russians in Alaska and the Mexicans in California, and based her claim upon the fact that the Hudson's Bay Company traders had occupied the country and traded in it for years. America, however, was casting longing eyes on it. In the fall of 1841 a few American families completed the long trek over the Oregon Trail. In 1842, 114 people reached Oregon by the same route. The rush of Americans to the coast was on, and increased in tempo year after year. Before leaving Fort Garry, Simpson did what he could to fill Oregon with Canadians, and took steps to send twenty-three families of Red River half-breeds out there. He arranged that they be given land, livestock and implements, and that generally the company would take them under its wing. These emigrants set out from Fort Garry, and after leaving Edmonton they too took the same general route Simpson had taken, but instead of following exactly in his steps James Sinclair, their guide, took them through the pass we still know as Sinclair Pass.

Sinclair's party of Canadians was soon swallowed up by the much greater influx of Americans to Oregon, and for the next few years settlers from the eastern United States continued to pour in. By 1844, the year of the presidential election, a great clamour arose to drive the British and the Hudson's Bay Company out. During the whole of the winter of 1844–45 Sir George Simpson remained in London to advise the British government. By spring, the possibility of war was very real.

The threat of war eventually passed away but it aroused sufficient interest in eastern Canada that it set loose a comparative flood of travellers upon Edmonton House. During the next decade, many strangers either not connected with or only remotely related to the fur trade, availed themselves of Edmonton's hospitality.

Of them all Paul Kane has left us the best picture we have of the state of affairs there. Now regarded as one of Canada's greatest early artists, he persuaded Sir George Simpson to let him accompany one of the brigades to Oregon. On this trip he painted innumerable pictures of Indian life in the far West, and later on wrote one of Canada's most interesting travel books, *Wanderings of an Artist.*

In travelling through the country south of modern Willingdon, Kane ran into buffalo, for he wrote: "We had much difficulty that evening in finding a place to encamp away from the immense number of buffaloes that surrounded us, and we found it necessary to fire off our guns during the night to keep them away. . . ."

Kane's description of the fort at Edmonton gives a good idea of the conditions there: "Edmonton is a large establishment . . . with forty or fifty men with their wives and children, amounting altogether to about 130, who all live within the pickets of the fort. Their employment consists chiefly in building boats for the trade, sawing timber, most of which they raft down the river from ninety miles higher up, cutting up the small poplar which abounds on the margin of the river for fire-wood, 800 cords of which are consumed every winter, to supply the numerous fires in the establishment. The employment of the women, who are all, without a single exception, either squaws or half-breeds, consists in making moccasins and clothing for the men, and converting the dried meat into pemmican."

Continuing, he described the storing of meat and the great ice house, a feature common to all the forts which collected meat from the plains. "This is made by digging a square hole, capable of containing 700 or 800 buffalo carcases. As soon as the ice in the river is of sufficient thickness, it is cut into square blocks of uniform size with saws; with these blocks the floor of the pit is regularly paved, and the blocks cemented together by pouring water in between them, and allowing it to freeze solid. In like manner, the walls are solidly built up to the surface of the ground. The head and feet of the buffalo, when killed, are cut off, and the carcase, without being skinned, is divided into quarters, and piled in layers in the pit as brought in, until it is filled up when the whole is covered with a thick coating of straw, which is again protected from the sun and rain by a shed. In this manner the meat keeps perfectly good through the whole summer and eats much better than fresh killed meat, being more tender and better flavoured."

Shortly after Kane's visit, a young Canadian priest sponsored by the Oblate Order came to take Father Thibault's place in the Edmonton area and at Lac Ste Anne. In 1852, Father Albert Lacombe, then twenty-five years old, left St. Boniface with the Hudson's Bay brigade bound for Edmonton. At Cumberland House he met Chief Factor Rowand and travelled with him to their common destination. These two men, the old factor nearing the end of his life, and the young priest just beginning his career were the two outstanding figures along the Saskatchewan, each dominating his field for half of the nineteenth century. The old man represented the best traditions of the Hudson's Bay Company's rule, the young man foreshadowed the life that was to be along the Saskatchewan.

At any time along the trails of the West for the next sixty-five years one might meet Father Lacombe in his tattered robe, or see his red and white banner emerge around the next bend. All the West was his parish, but particularly so were Edmonton and Calgary. All the people of the West were his charge, whites, half-breeds, Crees, Piegans; but, above all, he gave his life to the Blackfoot.

By 1860, under the most severe pioneering conditions, both the Methodists and the Roman Catholics had sown the first seeds of Christianity in southern Alberta—tiny seeds, maybe, scratched into thorny ground, but seeds of great virility which were destined to fulfill their sects' hopes. While their first endeavours were centred in Edmonton, the missionaries were not long in working their way north to the Peace River country and far beyond that to establish missions well down the Mackenzie River.

The first pastor to enter the Peace River area was the Reverend James Evans, the Methodist superintendent of that church's western missions who in 1841 made a reconnaissance of his far-flung territory which took him to Lesser Slave Lake. In due course he also went to Fort Chipewyan, the first missionary to go that far north.

He was followed in February 1842 by his cohort, Rev. R. T. Rundle who accompanied George McDougall, a fur trader, back to his post at the west end of Lesser Slave Lake. Taking dogs, they went by way of Fort Assiniboine and the Lesser Slave Lake River, but travelling conditions were so difficult that they came close to perishing from both starvation and freezing on the ice of the vast, wind-swept lake. Moreover, Rundle's face was swollen and throbbing from the unrelieved pain of an aching tooth. As his diary says, "the men were freezing, although wrapped in their blankets, and also had their nostrils packed with moss. Mr. MacD. overheard them talking of the probability of their being frozen to death. We walked and partook of our only meal of the day—some soup made of flour and part of a buffalo tongue. Dogs starving and eating the ends from the sledges. At dusk we started again. Terribly cold at night, and the men were so fatigued that they were falling asleep on the ice; and Mr. MacD. was afraid they would freeze to death."

Perhaps his throbbing tooth distorted either his faith or his syntax, for his diary strikes an equivocal note of which undoubtedly he was unaware. It reads: "so now we had nothing to do but proceed and put our trust in the Almighty. But what a gloomy prospect was before us. . . ." Fortunately they got through to the Hudson's Bay Company's post. After that Rundle made several trips to Lesser Slave Lake and from one of them he returned to Edmonton in April 1846, in company with Father Bourassa. Ordinarily in the early West, the Protestant and Catholic clerics railed at each other with the religious bitterness of the nineteenth century, but on this occasion, at least when these men of diverse faiths shared in common the hardships of their vocation, the lion lay down with the lamb.

Like Rundle, Father Bourassa, the first priest to visit the Peace River country, did so from his base near Edmonton. During the years 1845 to 1847 he travelled extensively along the Peace River. The main drive towards the North, however, came not from Edmonton but from the long established route which Alexander Mackenzie and his colleagues had used over the Methy Portage. In 1847 Father Taché used it to visit the Indians at Fort Chipewyan, and so did Father Faraud, in 1848, when he started building La Nativity Mission near the Hudson's Bay Company's post. About a decade later, Father Clut reached Fort Chipewyan but continued north to serve the Indians down the Slave and Mackenzie rivers. By 1862 when Father Faraud was created Bishop of Athabasca-Mackenzie with his headquarters at Fort Chipewyan, the Roman Catholics were well established in the remote North.

While the Anglican church was late in settling a missionary along the North Saskatchewan in Alberta, its priests soon followed the Roman Catholics into the Mackenzie River watershed. In 1858 Archdeacon Hunter passed Fort Chipewyan and went on to serve the natives at Fort Simpson. He was followed the next year by the Reverend W. W. Kirkby. From then on the two old church bodies, one French and the other English, competed with each other all over the far North. The culture of civilization was reaching far out.

No part of the world was more difficult of access than the far North. Some of the missions were two thousand miles from the church headquarters at Fort Garry or St. Boniface. Even these communities were a thousand miles from the nearest railway. The two thousand miles had to be travelled in summer by canoe and long portage and in winter on foot by tramping mile after mile of snowy waste behind dog teams.

No part of the world was more difficult to live in, nor in which the

John Rowand's Regime 1830-1854

food supply of the natives was more precarious. Occasionally plenty was the order of the day, only to be followed by starvation. Lucky, indeed, were the missionaries if half-rotten meat or fish could be found. As a last resort, life could be sustained, and often was, by eating one's moccasins or other leather clothing. Sometimes even this recourse did not carry the famished through till a better food supply was found. Nevertheless, because of the missionaries' courage, hardihood and zeal, they exposed Alberta's northern Indians to another facet of the white man's culture. But years were to elapse before anyone found a way to make any religious impression on the Blackfoot.

While the first decade of religious endeavour was carrying the various missionaries hither and yon about Alberta, the old master, John Rowand, remained at Edmonton guiding the Hudson's Bay Company's business. The belligerent Blackfoot bothered him some, the prodding missionaries badgered him, but as a man getting past his prime he worried most about the signs of change which were in the air. The good old days of the fur trade had slipped away and now civilization, however remote, was turning its eyes towards his territory. Whenever it did, trouble broke out, and trouble usually rapped the Hudson's Bay Company's knuckles.

In Oregon, for instance, at the far end of the long line of communication across the continent, Simpson's efforts had met defeat. American settlers had flooded the area, and a militant United States, puffed up with the doctrine of "manifest destiny," threatened war if British interests did not pull out of Oregon. For in the expansive outlook of the rapidly growing republic of the United States of America no idea was more widespread, no slogan more appealing than the one that God had chosen its people for a special mission. Their destiny was manifest. They were to extend their republican salvation over the whole continent.

Canadians were not interested in Oregon; if war came, Britain would have to wage it under a heavy disadvantage and would risk an aroused America gobbling up the Maritimes and Upper and Lower Canada. The gamble was too great, so in June 1846, by the Treaty of Oregon, the Hudson's Bay Company was in effect kicked out and the boundary between Canada and the United States was continued along the 49th parallel from the summit of the Rockies west to the Pacific.

Moreover for the last decade, at the Red River Settlement, rumblings against the company had risen to an outcry. Because it was an agricultural settlement of sorts, and because it was not very far north of the rampaging Americans, the situation there worsened year after year. From the ranks of the Red River half-breeds an occasional trader quite independent of the Hudson's Bay Company—a free trader—popped up his head and other traders from the United States appeared. In 1849, when, at the trial of a free trader named Sayer, open rebellion of the half-breeds was averted

A History of Alberta

only by a narrow squeak, the company's hitherto legal monopoly was in effect broken.

By that time John Rowand was beginning to notice his age. Nevertheless, he carried on at Edmonton, clamping his stiffening fingers all the more tightly on its affairs, until the spring of 1854. Once more he set out in May along the route which after fifty years of journeying was so intimately familiar. Upon arriving at Fort Pitt, where his son John was in charge, his sixty-five years must have felt heavy, because he told the young man that when his time came he wished to be buried among his kin at Montreal. It was a premonition. Next day, when a violent quarrel broke out amongst the boatmen, John Rowand, his ready temper flashing, rushed out to quell the fight, and fell dead.

His death marked the closing of an era—an era that had seen the fur trade as the sole industry of the West. It had witnessed the transition to peaceful and honourable trading between native and immigrant. The Indians north of the North Saskatchewan River had settled down to a routine way of life. South of the river, over the vast rustling parkland and rippling grasslands, the challenging Crees and Assiniboines on the one hand and charging Blackfoot, Gros Ventres and Sarcee on the other, kept activity in the region at such a full rolling boil that routine, even with assistance from John Rowand, had found no place to roost.

But death did not close Rowand's story. A bizarre chapter was still to be written before the chief factor's bones reached their final resting place. He was buried at Fort Pitt, but when his old friend Governor Simpson heard of his request, he had the body disinterred, so that the bones might be buried in Montreal; thereby hangs a true tale, attested by W. E. S. Gladstone, who arrived at Edmonton in 1848. In a letter describing this event, he said: "Well the next spring they tolded to dig up the body and send the bones to St. Boniface on red river so they got an indian to dig it up and boil the flash of, it was sayed that the wemmen of the fort made soap with the fat of the pot . . . the indian was drunk all the time he was boiling it."

Further adventures, however, were to befall the old trader's remains. Sir George Simpson, in a letter to Rowand's doctor son in Montreal, told more of the story.

"I directed that [the package with the bones] should be brought out this summer [1856] to Norway House, from whence I conveyed it this summer in my own canoe to Red River, but some of the crew had discovered the contents of the package, I was afraid they might from a superstitious feeling drop it overboard at some time and therefore had it repacked and sent to York Factory for transmission to England by ship, from whence it will be forwarded to this place [Lachine]."

Finally, on November 10, 1858, over four years after his death,

Rowand's bones were buried in Montreal's Mount Royal Cemetery. Subsequently, a red granite monument, costing some £500, was erected over them. Thus ended the career of one of the great men of the early West, son of a physician and father of another, who gave half a century of his life to Alberta and enjoyed every hour of it.

# 5
# Palliser and Others
# 1855-1869

Even though events originating far to the east and even across the Atlantic were being aimed in its direction, little change took place for fifteen years after Rowand's final burial. Volumes have been written explaining the many vantage points from which the various currents and crosscurrents must be viewed. In the interest of conserving space for history of a more provincial character, it is only possible to glance at these forces of national history in a most limited way.

In 1858 the prairies, which were merely a part of Rupert's Land, which in turn was only that part of British North America belonging to the Hudson's Bay Company, were an empty land still controlled by a few fur traders. With the amalgamation of the companies in 1821, Rupert's Land had come to mean a vast area stretching west from Labrador to include the watershed of the Mackenzie River and practically all the area which is now known as the province of British Columbia and the states of Idaho, Washington, Oregon and part of California. When the Treaty of Oregon had lopped off everything south of the 49th parallel, the Hudson's Bay Company was still left with much of northern Quebec and all of Canada west of Ontario. Now a decade later there was talk of the British government taking away Vancouver Island. Moreover, both in Canada and Britain, there were many advocates of taking over the rest of the company's property.

Generally, however, with a few rare exceptions, Canadians in Upper and Lower Canada were only mildly concerned with the prairies. The British, remembering what had happened in Oregon and therefore ever watchful of the United States, were gravely concerned over them, and hoped to find some way to keep them from falling into American hands. With Washington politicians fervid in their belief in manifest destiny and egging on the thousands of their venturesome land-hungry pioneers who year by year pressed on westward, British fears were justified.

It is not surprising then that the British rather than the Canadians were the first to take any positive action. They did so by instituting two enquiries which took the form of setting up a select committee

73

of the House of Commons on the one hand and of sending out the Palliser expedition on the other. The Hudson's Bay Company charter was due for reconsideration in 1858 and before renewing it the select committee was to find the answer to two questions. Should the ownership and hence the government of Rupert's Land be taken away from the Hudson's Bay Company? If so, who could take it over and govern it? The new duality of Upper and Lower Canada was the logical entity to assume control, but if it did, how could it administer and defend the prairies?

In giving evidence before this committee, Sir George Simpson had said that the prairies and parklands of the West were "not well adapted for settlement." Many modern critics have seized upon his evidence bearing on the agricultural possibilities of the West and have said that with ulterior motive he deliberately beclouded the issue. In this they have been unfair. It is true that even had the Hudson's Bay Company known that the West could be farmed profitably, their spokesmen, anxious not to lose their fur trade business, would not have pushed the truth forward. They honestly believed, however, that due to early frosts grain growing would be too hazardous. And at that time they were right. With our hindsight, we know that within recent years some 200,000 farmers cultivated the three prairie provinces. Very few of us, however, realize that this was only made possible by the improvements plant scientists have made in developing strains of wheat that would ripen in our climate. Wheat used to take from 135 to 155 days to ripen, while our modern wheats take some 105 days.

Fortunately the committee heard from the Canadas' Chief Justice Draper, who in requesting the right for Canada to explore and settle the lands west of Lake Superior, showed vision. For he said: "I hope you will not laugh at me as very visionary, but I hope to live to see the time . . . when there is a railway going all across that country and ending on the Pacific."

Finally the committee recommended that steps be taken to create the colonies of Vancouver Island and British Columbia, and that Canada be given the right to settle and to take over the Red River area. The question of the Hudson's Bay Company's charter was left in the air, and this was tantamount to continuing it.

One of the recommendations in the committee's report read as follows: "the opinion at which your Committee have arrived is founded on the following considerations: 1st. The great importance to the more peopled portions of British North America that law and order should, as far as possible, be maintained in these territories; 2nd. The fatal effects which they believe would infallibly result to the Indian population from a system of open competition in the fur trade, and the consequent

A History of Alberta

introduction of spirits in a far greater degree than is the case at present; and 3rd. The probability of the indiscriminate destruction of the more valuable fur-bearing animals in the course of a few years. . . ." For these reasons the committee felt it desirable that the Hudson's Bay Company should continue to enjoy the privilege of exclusive trade.

Of far more interest to Albertans, however, was another step the British government took even before the select committee had time to act. That was to send out from London the Palliser expedition to gain some factual information about western Canada. Captain John Palliser, a cheerful, adventurous military-minded Irishman, who in 1848 had returned from a hunting trip which had taken him far up the Missouri River, had found the prairies fascinating. During the next decade he dreamed of making a private trip to explore the Canadian West and then by some judicious nudging on March 31, 1857, found himself commissioned to undertake this study. His letter of instructions stressed the importance "of regularly recording the physical features of the country through which you will pass, noting its principal elevations, the nature of its soil, its capability of agriculture, the quantity and quality of its timber, and any indications of coal or other minerals."

At last someone had been delegated to study the prairies with an eye to seeing what resources, other than fur, lay in them. While Palliser performed his duty well, three of his very capable staff were exceptionally well fitted to recognize and report on the bounties which the fur traders had seen but not noticed. The first of these was Dr. James Hector, a physician and a geologist, who proved to be both gifted and versatile. The second was Eugene Bourgeau, a French botanist, who according to Palliser turned out to be a "prince of botanical collectors." The other was Lieutenant Thomas Blakiston, R.A., a bit of a martinet but a careful observer and an accurate surveyor.

For two years the Palliser expedition, in one group or another, roved the prairies, explored the Rockies, wandered through the parklands, and took a look at the edge of the boreal forest. During the winter of 1857–58, Fort Carlton was their base camp, while the next year most of the party wintered at Edmonton.

A little over a hundred years after the first white man came to look at Alberta with a fur trader's eyes, Palliser and his associates came to peer into the possibility that the prairies might be fit for farmers. When, during 1858 the group turned its attention to Alberta and to examining the passes through which a road might be built to link up with British Columbia, its members spared no effort in spying out the land. Sometimes Palliser took most of the party along with him, but frequently he sent the other stalwart of the group, Dr. Hector, on separate trips to study Alberta's geology.

No significant part of the province south of an east and west line through Edmonton escaped the expedition's attention or failed to be recorded on the valuable maps its members compiled. By the time they left Alberta in 1859 they had gathered the information which enabled them to make a painstaking assessment of the worth of the prairies. In spite of the limits of time and money at their disposal and the limitation of having to travel with dogs in the wintertime and with pack horses or carts in summer, they had done a remarkable job. For the expedition's report, mainly the work of three able, conscientious and energetic men, John Palliser, Dr. James Hector and Thomas Blakiston, involved a prodigious amount of effort.

When its various members' memoirs were compiled, they provided much level-headed information about the prospects of agriculture. Palliser singled out the most arid area of the plains, which is still known as Palliser's Triangle. Dr. Hector, perhaps the most valuable member of the group, considered the Triangle to be practically useless, for he said: "The arid district, though there are many fertile spots throughout its extent, can never be of much advantage to us as a possession."

He thought the parkland and the rich soil adjoining the North Saskatchewan River to be eminently fit for cultivation. Turning his attention to Alberta's boreal forest, he was disparaging, calling its spruce timber "coarse and worthless" to the point where it was only good for a "very inferior quality of firewood."

Palliser drew attention to the abundance of coal in Alberta, and, in summing up the expedition's work, provided the first realistic assessment of the prairies. To him the possibility of a railroad across Canada seemed too remote to warrant serious study. He concluded that a wagon road might be worked out through the Vermilion Pass, but felt that any such project lay far in the future.

Not only did the report present a favourable picture of the resources of the prairies, but it also provided us with a wealth of information about the state of civilization in Alberta in 1859. For instance, Palliser remarked that the Neutral Hills were the "recognized boundary between the Cree and Blackfoot tribes." Speaking of the "Flag-Hanging Hill," our Flagstaff or Treaty Hill, some fifteen miles east of modern Galahad, he noted that the Sarcee Indians "use it as a place of assembly, and it is very rarely deserted by that people."

On his great swings out into the prairies, Palliser often encountered large Blackfoot camps and was usually impressed with the high calibre of the chiefs. He found the more responsible of them worried about the future. They could see the writing on the wall and were frustrated. As Blakiston said: "They are aware that the buffalo are rapidly decreasing, and foresee that their descendants will have to take to some other way of living than the lazy yet not luxurious mode followed at present . . . year by year they see the animals decrease, and although they consider that they will last their time, and that by them they will be able to keep themselves in tobacco, ammunition, and other requisites, and have an occasional drinking bout, yet they know too well, as one man expressed himself to me, 'If this continues our children cannot live.' "

During March 1858 Dr. Hector visited Lac Ste. Anne, which he found to be a settlement of what he called two villages of thirty to forty houses each. While Father Lacombe and the other priests had advocated cultivating the land and while some barley, potatoes and turnips were grown, it was obvious that the resident Métis had little heart for farming. At the time of Hector's visit they were out on their annual hunting expedition to the plains around Buffalo Lake. As usual during the fall and winter, Lac Ste. Anne supplied tons of whitefish, averaging about four pounds each, to Edmonton. Two years previously forty thousand had been taken and frozen for this purpose and they had all been caught within five days.

At times the visitors were somewhat dubious of how effective the missionaries were in converting the natives and somewhat doubtful of the value of the whole project. Like all visitors to the West, they felt that because of the clerics' bitter hostility to each other and their varying viewpoints on Christianity, they had raised a doubt in the Indians' minds about whether or not the white man's religion was tenable and about the sincerity of its advocates. At times the leaders of the expedition had dined at Edmonton House when clerics of both sects were present and of one occasion Palliser wrote: "It is great fun to see the black looks of the hostile divines, I understand that sometimes hostilities have proceeded further than mere looks."

As the decades passed, the number of half-breeds around the missions and the Hudson's Bay Company posts had increased to the point where the company could no longer employ them all. Naturally, only the most reliable were hired, while the rest had to fend for themselves in much the same manner as their maternal ancestors had done. The largest group in the West was at the Red River Settlement, where at times they paid lip service to farming small plots. They obtained most of their livelihood, however, by going out on their great buffalo hunts which took them far west and south into the prairies. Before long the annual Red River hunt became one of the famous institutions of the West. As early as 1820 the Métis took 540 Red River carts out into the far-flung grasslands; by 1850 when Father Lacombe went with them, over a thousand men, women and children, taking nearly a thousand carts, formed the great cavalcade which killed eight hundred buffalo. As the years went by, it became necessary for this huge procession to go ever farther west until in Palliser's time the Métis occasionally had to travel from Fort Garry to the Cypress Hills in southwestern Saskatchewan.

In organizing the hunt the Métis had to elect temporary leaders, and had to submit to exacting rules and strict disciplines which were not only vital to the success of the hunt but were necessary to ward off Indian attack. Initially these Métis had invaded Sioux territory, and, as the hunt came to be extended farther west, they reached into the territory of the Gros Ventres and the Blackfoot. Each of these tribes, furious at this horde of invaders killing buffalo on their lands, showed no mercy in attacking them. Because of the excellent discipline they exercised on these expeditions, the Métis became the most feared fighters on the plains. Man for man they out-matched the Indians. Travelling in a body through the lands of the fiercest plains tribes, some of their party often were killed, but invariably they meted out far more punishment than they received.

Eventually a small number of Métis began living along the North Saskatchewan River not far from Fort Carlton, and when the Red River hunt headed out into the plains these people journeyed south to join it. About 1840 the Métis overflow from Edmonton House started a colony near the Hudson's Bay Company's fishery station which Hector had visited at Lac Ste. Anne. It was to help them that Father Thibault opened his mission in 1842. By Palliser's time these Métis had organized a hunt of their own, which as a separate entity went out in the vicinity of the Battle River and Buffalo Lake and even farther if necessary. On occasions some of their relatives from the small but long-standing colony at Lac La Biche joined them in their sally into the prairies for buffalo.

On these sorties the Métis came into frequent conflict with the Blackfoot. With the Crees and Assiniboines never admitting the Blackfoot's exclusive claim to the prairies and pressing them hard along a front that extended from the North Saskatchewan River to beyond the 49th parallel and with the mountain Assiniboines or Stoneys in the foothills, and now these Métis thrusting down from the north to kill their buffalo, the Blackfoot were engaged almost weekly in small skirmishes. Though still the most formidable force on Alberta's prairies and still resisting any white man's encroachments, except on their own terms, the noose of destiny as yet barely perceptible was tightening about them. As Palliser had noted, they had perhaps passed the peak of their power.

As well as recording this and much other incidental information about the Métis and Indians, Palliser's report provided eastern Canada and Britain with a reliable document which showed for the first time that with limitations, the prairies were reasonably well fitted for settlement. It called attention to one of Alberta's greatest resources—almost unlimited square miles of arable land.

But while the report called, few listened. Instead, the few who looked to the West trickled in to trade or to harken to the siren cry of gold— one of Alberta's minute and quite incidental riches. Up to this time Alberta had seen no lay white men who were not associated in some way with the Hudson's Bay Company. As late as 1859 no independent traders had worked that far west along the Saskatchewan River. Hector had found some traders at Fort Carlton a year or so earlier, but they and their generous outpouring of liquor had not yet reached Alberta. Other white men were on their way, however—prospectors. In the spring of 1858 at least two parties of miners, about a dozen strong, left St. Paul, Minnesota, and swinging around by Fort Carlton and Edmonton House, some of them crossed the mountains. The next year parties of gold-seekers continued to cross the Canadian plains on their way to the diggings on the Fraser River. One of these parties, of whom a record remains, consisted of Messrs. Colville, Reid, Dickman, Hind and two or three others. Then in the fall of 1860 some American prospectors discovered gold in what they considered to be paying quantities at Rocky Mountain House.

During the summer of 1860 a party consisting of Timolean Love, D. F. McLaurin, A. Perry and Tom Clover ascended the Fraser, came through the Yellowhead Pass and arrived at Edmonton. Along with Perry, Tom Clover remained to prospect the Saskatchewan from Edmonton House to Rocky Mountain House. His name is perpetuated in Clover Bar, a suburb on Edmonton's eastern outskirts. While Perry and Tom Clover were practical working miners, Love was a talker who basked in the acclaim accorded his exaggerations. At Fort Garry he aroused considerable interest in the gold in the Saskatchewan.

Partly as a result of the efforts of such men as Love, eastern Canada also became interested in the faraway gold fields of British Columbia. One manifestation of this was the organization of several groups of miners who planned to go overland from Fort Garry to the Cariboo. Ultimately these groups more or less coalesced at this fort and became known as the Overlanders of 1862. Timolean Love, with his ready tongue, soon latched onto them and for a while became the leader of one of the groups.

The Overlanders, consisting of about 175 men, set forth in two main parties, which both left Fort Garry early in June 1862. Travelling by carts, they made poor time, but at that reached Edmonton House about the end of July. There they left their carts and, still in two parties, continued their trip west through Lac Ste. Anne and Jasper to Kamloops. At Edmonton House, Timolean Love, who was still with them, met his partner Tom Clover. The latter's report of the prospects along the Saskatchewan was so rosy that over sixty men deserted the Overlanders to try their luck at Edmonton.

The third of Alberta's resources to interest white men began to be exploited. Although it turned out to be barely worth panning, nevertheless for a score of years gold kept a few dozen men busy, and during the decade following its discovery it doubled Alberta's white population. Up till that time the fur trade had paid the wages of possibly eighty or a hundred men. Fur's export value, however, was infinitely above all the gold fished out of all the rivers of Alberta's foothills. Any gold produced was the result of the labour of possibly eighty miners, and although they went pretty hungry at times, it sufficed to keep them in what food they had to buy. Furs on the other hand were merely handled and shipped by various white men. Behind them lay the actual producers, several thousand Indians, who supplemented their incomes by devoting part of their time to trapping and curing pelts.

Regardless of that, immediately after Palliser's visit, gold captured the attention of those who looked to Alberta. The lands Palliser had studied and praised were left to soak in Alberta's June rains or bask in August's heat.

All the while, however, Father Lacombe had been planning the next move in his campaign to help the Métis and Indians. One day he announced that he hoped to obtain the services of three Grey Nuns from Montreal to assist at his mission at Lac Ste. Anne. The old traders shook their heads. This was no place for white women, and particularly for delicately reared convent women.

But they came. In 1859, under the protection of Father Remas, a small train of carts drew up to the fort—twelve horses, six carts, and a wild dog. And stiff and bruised from their long trip from Fort Garry, three Grey Nuns climbed down from a cart. In due course they hastened to Lac Ste. Anne. Their coming marked a milestone in the opening up of the West. Moreover, although as the first white woman to visit Edmonton, Marie-Anne Lagimodière, had preceded them by some fifty years, these three were the first educated women to come to the area. They and a young Scottish bride, Mrs. Robert Campbell who went to Fort Chipewyan that spring, were the only all-white women in Alberta.

Times were indeed changing, and the change coincided with the death of Sir George Simpson in 1860. With his passing an era closed. Forty years earlier, when he had first set foot in Canada, the fur trade was in a chaotic condition, with two great companies battling each other to the brink of bankruptcy. With their amalgamation, he had assumed the reins of power over nearly half a continent. Under his guidance, the trade settled into an orderly and a profitable pattern, and the Hudson's Bay Company's name became synonymous with greatness, order and law. During his regime, but in spite of his best planning and of his mightiest effort, the area of Oregon and Washington had fallen before American expansion. Even then he had regrouped his forces and carried on a most successful business all over his Rupert's Land. Among the men we look upon as builders of Canada, Sir George Simpson ranks high.

Yet by 1860 his old fur trading empire had begun to fray at the edges as miners, missionaries and free traders began to creep into the prairies and as statesmen in America, Canada and Britain began to focus their attention on it. Its most vulnerable area was the Red River valley where the adjacent state of Minnesota had come into being and which by 1858 claimed a population of 170,000. These people, settlers seeking more or fairer lands, or businessmen anxious to turn a profit, began to peer across the 49th parallel—the border which as a mere astronomical abstraction bore no relation to geographical actuality.

The Red River valley on the other hand did, and its river flowing north linked Minnesota's thousands to the Fort Garry settlement's hundreds who turned their eyes south towards the growing city of St. Paul. Taking their Red River carts south, hundreds and hundreds of them, they poured thousands of dollars of Canadian trade into American tills. So lucrative was that trade and so enterprising the American businessmen that by June 1859 when the Palliser expedition was wandering over Alberta's plains, the flailing paddles of the first steamer to descend the Red River, the *Anson Northup,* thrashed down to Fort Garry. American eyes had looked upon Canada's prairies and official American hands, eager in anticipation, were not far behind.

In the Canadas meanwhile, with their embryonic industries, increasing wheat crops and skyrocketing timber export, some politicians and statesmen also began looking towards the prairies. Bedevilled, however, with "two nations warring in the bosom of a single state" their leaders confronted difficulty after difficulty. Their problems, magnified almost beyond recognition by black-robed clerics and orange-draped clergy left them little time to look west across the pre-Cambrian barrier. Fortunately a few future-minded men kept looking west—even though it was to fix their eyes upon the spoils they hoped to get by attacking the Hudson's Bay Company in Rupert's Land.

In Britain, having digested the Palliser and the select committee reports, statesmen scratched their heads. Resenting the righteousness roosting on the banners of the American army which had recently "liberated" many of the subjects of its sister Republic of Mexico and grabbed their territory, and fearing similar liberation of the Red River Settlement and a similar gobbling of territory, the British felt it necessary to create a government on the prairies that could cope with the gobbling.

Then in April 1861, as if fate had decided to help them, the United States plunged into the misery of its Civil War. Even after the war had started the New York *Herald,* filled with the average American's overweening delusion that Canadians would jump at any chance to be liberated from the tyranny exercised by British garrisons, revived the old cry of manifest destiny. Far from achieving its purpose, the paper's campaign only doubled Canadians' fear of the United States and doubled their determination to keep clear of American imperialism. Meanwhile, with increasing bloodiness and bitterness, the Civil War dragged on for four years until May 1865. The United States' misfortune provided Canadians with a last chance to keep the American government out of the prairies.

During that interval, Edward Watkin, a British financier associating himself with Barings, the great bankers, and others, formed the International Finance Company, which in 1863 announced that it had bought the Hudson's Bay Company for £1,500,000. The West and all its people with any degree of white blood in their veins began to buzz. Canada too began to take notice. One of the early unwitting moves towards Confederation had begun.

With the sale of the Hudson's Bay Company, of course, went the 255,285 square miles of the future Alberta, along with the much greater area of the rest of Rupert's Land. The whole far-flung region of mighty rivers, vast lakes, boundless forests and endless grasslands— that empire abounding in beaver and buffalo, moose and elk, whose skies were blackened at times by clouds of swans, cranes and passenger pigeons—all of it was part of the deal. So too were the few thousand Métis who centred in the Red River Settlement. And when they heard that along with the muskrats and the mink they too, together with the lands on which they squatted, had been sold, the seeds of discontent long lying dormant in their breasts started to sprout. They began to look up the Red River valley towards their American friends in Minnesota.

Meanwhile, a few statesmen in the Canadas and in the Maritimes had begun discussing a federation of all the British North American colonies. Foremost of these dreamers was the bold, witty Scot, John A. Macdonald, who by his adroitness and political genius eventually brought the dream to fruition. Few factors aided him as much as the Americans' ill-conceived itch for more territory and the fear of what the huge Union army might do after 1865 when the Civil War ended. As Dr. George Hardy said: "The ownership of the Northwest was soon to become a race between Confederation and the clutching fingers of the United States."

On July 1, 1867, Confederation became a fact, with John A. Macdonald at the zenith of his career as prime minister of Canada. His dominion included the four provinces of Nova Scotia, New Brunswick, Quebec and Ontario. Prince Edward Island and Newfoundland had stayed out. Two thousand miles away to the west, beyond the prairies "of no present value" and beyond the formidable wall of the Rocky Mountains, British Columbia watched the new Dominion with a cool eye. Nevertheless, Canada, with its 3,200,000 people and its 662,148 square miles, had come into being. With luck (and John A., the procrastinator, was as lucky as he was astute), Canada's area could expand six times. Confederation had been achieved.

But the prairies and British Columbia were still out of the fold. At the moment the colony of British Columbia seemed safe enough, but with American expansionism still champing at the bit and planning by various pretexts to strike along the valley towards it, the Red River Settlement was the most vulnerable part of British North America.

With its two maritime provinces and its long, skinny provinces of Ontario and Quebec, mere miniatures of their present-day areas, forming a narrow fringe along the St. Lawrence and the Great Lakes, Canada was a pitifully thin and weak country to hold off the Americans. The Hudson's Bay Company still owned all the vast prairies and much of the rest of British North America, and as owners, they were governing this tremendous, empty region. If Canada took over these prairies, how could it finance their development, and how could it govern them?

On November 1, 1869, in spite of the fact that many influential Canadians, exhibiting a not unusual but nonetheless remarkable generosity toward someone else's property, advocated seizing the Hudson's Bay Company's prairie lands without compensation, Macdonald's government concluded an agreement with the English organization. Under it, the company was to receive a cash payment of £300,000 and be left with some three thousand acres around each of its posts, as well as retain some seven million acres of land which were to be allocated on a systematic basis whenever the prairies should be surveyed. It was naturally permitted to continue its fur business. By this agreement, as John A. said, Canada had "quietly annexed" all the land lying on its western flank as far as the Rocky Mountains.

But when John A. spoke, the marriage had yet to be consummated, and, through an oversight, the consummation was far from quiet. For neither he nor anyone else had consulted the 11,500 British or French half-breed settlers in the Red River colony. Suffering from an inferior status and struggling with an inferiority complex for which there was no cure, they defied Canada and the Hudson's Bay Company. In their just fight, Louis Riel, the grandson of the first white woman ever to live in

83

Alberta, partly a selfless patriot and partly the leader of a riot that got out of his hands, led them.

In 1869, before all the fuss started, the Red River colony had stretched for a few miles up and down the Red River. The old mission settlement of St. Boniface faced a newer hamlet of Winnipeg across the river, a hamlet that was growing by leaps and bounds now that steamboats from the United States were arriving. Many of its new citizens were Americans who naturally had hoped that the Red River Settlement would become a part of the United States. Opposed to them was a Canadian faction with leanings toward the Orange Order. Caught between these were the more staid Selkirk settlers, the British half-breeds, and the French Métis who were soon to be led by Louis Riel. The Red River Settlement was a powder keg to be handled respectfully.

Unfortunately and unwittingly Macdonald ignited the situation. Some months before the deal had actually been confirmed, but acting as if the transfer of the territories to Canada had already been made, his government sent surveyors to Winnipeg to lay out the land into a rectangular system of sections and quarter-sections. When they drove pegs into André Nault's hay privilege, he, brave man that he was and made doubly brave by the justice that sat on his side, ran out to stop them. When the surveyors stretched their steel chain out from that peg, Louis Riel, hitherto an unnoticed settler, a man whose blood was one-eighth Indian, trod on the chain and in so doing stepped into history and into legend.

At one stroke the long-ignored Métis had a cause and a leader. The powder keg went off. It threw a surprised John A. Macdonald back on his heels while its echoes reached London and rejoiced Washington, where impudent bills were introduced to Congress designed to release the prairie from the heels of monarchs and tyrants.

In the end, after a winter of near anarchy at Red River, and after Donald Smith (who was later to become Lord Strathcona) had cut Riel's feet from under him, order was restored. The prairies were legally transferred to Canada, and by the Manitoba Act assented to on May 12, 1870, Manitoba, a pocket-sized province of 11,000 square miles, was created. Canada now stretched from Halifax to the Rockies. At last the large area which was later to be called Alberta was part of Canada. So too was the huge area which formerly had been Rupert's Land, all 1,800,000 square miles of it of which Alberta occupied the southwesterly fringe of some 250,000 square miles.

While all this expansion of boundary lines was going on, Alberta's few white men, except for perhaps a dozen fur trade factors or missionaries, were totally indifferent to political entities. Their thoughts ran to furs and gold and to buffalo wandering in their millions over the vast untilled prairies. For though more than a century had passed since the first white men had tramped through Alberta, neither he nor his successors had laid grasping hands on the province's natural beauty. At each post or mission the incumbents had cleared a little patch for vegetables and perhaps a bit for barley. At Edmonton House, for instance, which with its population of 150 souls had the largest fields, probably no more than thirty acres were under cultivation.

Outside of Edmonton the only evidences of the white man's caress were some missions and ten fur trade posts, of which all but Fort Chipewyan and Fort Vermilion came under the direct supervision of Edmonton House. These posts were: Rocky Mountain House, Jasper House, Fort Assiniboine, Lesser Slave Lake, Fort Vermilion, Fort Chipewyan, Lac Ste. Anne, Lac La Biche, Victoria and Dunvegan. At the last five, missions of either or both the Wesleyan or the Roman Catholic faith had church structures or were more or less in residence. As well as these places, there were four separate mission stations, St. Albert, the headquarters of the Roman Catholics, and Whitefish Lake, Pigeon Lake and Victoria, where the Wesleyans were working. In 1870, then, except for one or two whisky traders' shacks in the extreme southern fringe of the province, Edmonton House, four isolated mission stations and ten outlying fur posts more or less tributary to Edmonton were all that the white man had to show for a century of residence in Alberta.

Along the trails to Fort Garry, carts had been passing and repassing for a few years. Along one of them in 1841 George Simpson and the Oregon-bound settlers had brought carts. More recently the Overlanders had travelled it in 1862 and Father Lacombe had sent the first organized brigade of freighting carts to Fort Garry for his mission's supplies; in 1867 he began annual freight shipments along this thousand-mile trail.

In the whole province the total half-breed and white population would be less than two thousand. Because at times smallpox had done its deadly work and because guns in native hands increased the mortality of intertribal warfare, the Indian population, which may have been ten thousand when the white man came a century before, had been reduced to five or six thousand. As recently as the winter of 1864–65, scarlet fever and measles, for instance, had been on the rampage, and, in what are now the provinces of Alberta and Saskatchewan, killed about twelve hundred of the native population.

Even though the few settlements were tiny and even though the white population was insignificant, the missionaries had gotten away to a good start. As early as September 1862 Alberta's first school was established at Edmonton House when at Father Lacombe's instigation Brother Scollen taught some twenty pupils in a log building within the palisades, a labour he continued until 1871.

The early 1860s were busy years in Father Lacombe's life. In 1861, some ten miles from Edmonton House, he started the mission of St. Albert which down the decades was to contribute so much to the West.

85

Two years later, the three Grey Nuns, who had been stationed at Lac Ste. Anne, moved over to the new establishment, and about the same time the good father got his horse-driven grist mill into operation.

In 1862, two Methodist missionaries, George and John McDougall, father and son, arrived at Edmonton House. After visiting the Reverend Henry Steinhauer's settlement at Whitefish Lake and coming on west, Rev. George McDougall set John to work building a new mission at Victoria, some seventy river-miles downstream from Edmonton. To this mission the older man returned in 1863, bringing his wife and family, and here he made fast friends with Pakan and Maskepatoon, two famous Cree chiefs. In remembrance of one of them, the old settlement of Victoria is today called Pakan.

Like Father Lacombe, the two McDougalls were to leave their mark on Alberta. George, who lost his life in a blizzard, was perhaps the greater man, but because of John McDougall's half-century of devotion to the cause he espoused and his overweening egotism, he became one of the West's great men. Never a shrinking violet, as shown by his auto-biographical books, his constant acknowledgement of his manifest fitness ran hand in hand with his biting criticism of the Lord's enemies. Amongst these he numbered his rival in the race for converts, Father Lacombe, whose long sojourn in the prairies, self-sacrifice and final recognition as one of the West's gigantic figures paralleled his own. For the West, like the rest of the Christian world of the time, was steeped in religious bigotry and bitter intolerance. Nevertheless, during its crucial era what has been called McDougall's muscular Christianity, coupled with his vigour as a frontiersman, served the West well.

In 1864 young John McDougall established the first Protestant schools west of Portage la Prairie, starting one at Victoria and another at Whitefish Lake. The same year, because the mission at Victoria had attracted so many Indians and half-breeds, the Hudson's Bay Company opened an outpost there.

Missionary activity, however, was not confined to the south half of the province. Priests of both the Roman and Anglican persuasion pushed their missions ever farther into the remoteness of the vast northland. Here and there in a small green clearing on the rocky shore of some spruce-girt lake, hundreds of miles from any other, they built their missions. In such a clearing, also used for growing vegetables and grain, stood a little church and sometimes a hospital, while all around spread the dark, endless forest. There, as the sun went down in a glory of red and gold, far out over the water rang the Angelus bell, a signal of peace surpassing even that of the lake's solitude.

Amongst the outstanding clergy of the North was Father Tissier, who in 1867 went to Fort Dunvegan to start the first mission in what is now the settled portion of the Peace River country. Another was Bishop

Faraud, to whom fell the problem of transporting supplies to the faraway missions and who directed the first freight shipments overland from Fort Pitt on the Saskatchewan River to Lac La Biche. This was in 1868, and the next May Faraud sent the missions' freight down the Lac La Biche River in four-ton scows. This route proved successful and was in use for the next twenty years. Then there was Bishop Grouard, probably the most famous of all the northern priests, who first reached Fort Chipewyan in 1862 and through frost, ice and blizzard, hunger and hardship, mosquitoes and muskeg, ministered to his flock over a quarter of a continent. He lived to the great age of ninety-one years, having been sixty-nine years a priest and forty years a bishop. To few of the sons of men is it given to reach ninety-one. To fewer still is it given to fill these years with such beneficent activity.

The first Anglicans to go into the north country did so in 1858. That year Archdeacon Hunter travelled from Fort Garry to Fort Simpson on the Mackenzie. The next year Rev. W. W. Kirkby followed him. In 1865, six months after he left London, England, the Reverend W. C. Bompas arrived at Fort Simpson. For forty-one years he travelled almost continuously up and down his immense diocese. Rev. Bompas kept scanty records of his travels, but he and his colleague, or competitor, Father Grouard, must surely have established records unexcelled in the annals of the missions.

Spending some time at Chipewyan during the winter of 1867, Bompas went up the Peace River to Fort Vermilion the following summer. The country around the fort impressed him very much, but he described the Beaver Indians as "very pitiable and fast dying off." As there was no other religious institution there at the time, he thought it an ideal place for an Anglican mission.

While these heroic Anglican or Catholic priests endured many a hardship in the far North, they did not experience the frustration their confreres had in dealing with the warring tribes south of Edmonton House. The northern half of the province remained almost as it had been since the earliest traders had entered it. At Edmonton, however, around 1860, life was becoming more complex as wandering gold prospectors came in to try their luck along the Saskatchewan River. For they were ever in a state of flux, some coming in from across the mountains, some from Fort Garry, and others from Fort Benton or even from the Peace River, while still others returned to all of these places. By August 1863, many of them and many of the Overlanders who had stayed at Edmonton had decided that the gold in the Saskatchewan was not worthwhile, and for a spell their departure comforted the Hudson's Bay Company's Chief Factor W. J. Christie, another outstanding factor at Edmonton who took charge some five years after Rowand's death.

Amongst these miners were two interesting men who liked Alberta and for the rest of their lives made it their headquarters: Jim Gibbons and Sam Livingstone, both old Forty-niners. Moreover, in 1865 another of these wanderers, John George "Kootenai" Brown and his companion crossed the grasslands to the vicinity of Medicine Hat. There Brown, who was to become one of southern Alberta's most colourful pioneers, had a brush with the Blackfoot and, after pulling an arrow out of his back, rode on north and east for days until he fell in with a band of Métis at Duck Lake, Saskatchewan.

Up to this time the Métis in Alberta were mainly under the Hudson's Bay Company's thumb and brought in furs which they purchased from the Indians. By 1863 the population of the Métis settlements at Lac La Biche, Victoria, St. Albert and Lac Ste. Anne had increased rapidly. Many of the Red River half-breeds, fretting over the increasing encroachment of white adventurers and apprehensive of what might happen when that settlement became part of Canada, decided to move a thousand miles west to join their relatives.

With Indians stirred up by miners, free traders and firewater, and an incursion of Métis, the Hudson's Bay Company maintained its lessening grip on the Alberta area under conditions that were most insecure and unsatisfactory. Its old rule had gone. Moreover, due to the approach of free traders and the resultant heavy expense, Edmonton House began experiencing a deficit of from £2,000 to £6,000 a year. The company would have liked to abandon the heavy liability of Edmonton. Everyone knew, however, that if it did, the American fur traders would come whooping in.

As it was, the Americans did enter Alberta and came as far north as they dared. In 1869 traders from Fort Benton, Montana, came in and built the first Fort Whoop-Up, near modern Lethbridge. That same year, Dave Akers and Liver-Eating Johnston built the Spitzee Post on the Highwood River. Other so-called whisky forts were added during the next year or so, including a post built within the present limits of the city of Calgary. Not content with that advance, however, the American whisky traders brought cartloads of liquor and other trade goods to Tail Creek, near Buffalo Lake, and on occasion even traded in the vicinity of Edmonton.

Then in 1869, Father Lacombe, with three Métis and a cart, set out for Fort Benton to investigate the feasibility of obtaining goods for St. Albert through American channels. Now, on top of the comings and goings of gold miners and the incursion of whisky traders, even Canadian clerics were setting their thoughts towards Montana. For a time, while they experimented with the guns and booze the Montana traders held out to them, the Blackfoot ceased trading at Edmonton. The country was rapidly being oriented towards the Americans.

# 6
# Mounties and Whisky Posts 1870-1874

By 1870 Blackfoot power and prestige were already waning. On all sides adversity had begun to close in on the Confederacy: the Crees and Assiniboines had to hunt the diminishing buffalo herds ever farther south; miners and ranchers were followed ever farther west by American army posts, such as Fort Shaw built near Great Falls in 1867; and independent American traders with their rotgut whisky—all these were wearing them down. Year by year, these pressures gnawed ever deeper, sapping their vitality.

Of all these pressures liquor was the most destructive. So long as the Blackfoot had two large companies to deal with, the Hudson's Bay Company on the North Saskatchewan and the American Fur Company on the Missouri, they could obtain liquor in considerable but not unlimited quantities. Each company recognized the fact that if by unmerciful trading methods or by an unmitigated outpouring of liquor it reduced its native customers to paupers, it would kill the fur-fringed, golden-egged goose.

Then in 1864 the American Fur Company went broke. Pandemonium broke loose on the liquor front as a maniac flock of American free traders gushed over the Blackfoot lands on a flood of whisky. To these traders the future was now. Pour out the whisky, grab the furs and get away. To hell with the consequences.

And such whisky! Tobacco, old tea leaves and molasses brought to a full rolling boil, then cooled, seasoned to taste with Perry's painkiller and alcohol and dolled up to a dubious pink with red ink. There was many a formula, but all of them were fiery to taste and deadly to drink. Horrible scenes followed the broaching of a keg amidst the lodges. Liquor released all an Indian's inhibitions and revealed all his frustrations, and frustration had become his daily lot.

At the peak of liquor's devastation, around 1873, the whisky sellers and the hide hunters with their kegs and rifles walked openly in the light of day where Hudson's Bay Company employees had rarely dared to penetrate. They were fearless men, often unemployed veterans hardened by the cruelties of the Civil War who wandered almost at will in Alberta's Blood, Blackfoot and Piegan territory.

As they crossed back and forth over the 49th parallel, the unmarked boundary between the United States and Canadian territory (a concept which the natives called the medicine line), so did the wandering camps of the Blackfoot Confederacy. A band of the Blackfoot tribe might winter where today the city of Red Deer's main street lies, then in the spring wander south to the site of today's roaring town of Great Falls on the Missouri and, before winter's snows lay too deep, be back in some wooded coulee along our Battle River. The Bloods and Piegans, who, as a rule, thought of Alberta's more southerly regions as their wintering area, were equally, if not more, international in their rovings. Of the three groups which made up the Confederacy, the Blackfoot tribe occupied the most northerly range and came into more frequent contact with the men at Edmonton House.

By 1855, under its three predominant but aging chiefs, Old Sun, Old Swan and Three Suns, the Blackfoot had progressed far along the scale of its changing civilization. In his approach to white men each of these chiefs had been moderate and had always leaned in the direction of peaceful coexistence with them as well as with the often hostile neighbouring tribes. Of the three, Old Swan was the most highly respected. He had long experienced the white men's benefits, and, being a thinking man, felt it preferable for his tribe to be friendly towards them.

During the next five years Old Swan and Old Sun, the more peaceable of the chiefs, died and were succeeded by younger radicals. Almost at once the Hudson's Bay Company officials noticed the effect of these new leaders and Chief Factor Christie at Edmonton House reported that the Blackfoot were becoming increasingly dangerous, destroying their small crops around the post, trying to pick quarrels, thirsting to rid themselves of all white men and eager to burn the fort.

Then in 1864 an epidemic of scarlet fever ravaged Alberta's Blackfoot Confederacy. At the same time, open hostilities broke out between the tribes and the American armies. The raiders of the plains were beginning to feel the pinch of being on bad terms with everyone. The next spring, to fill their cup of sorrow, the last of the trio of moderate chiefs, Three Suns, died. The last voice which had advocated peace was gone.

Unfortunately he was succeeded by a son who took his father's name but whose disposition was vastly dissimilar. An indication of his feelings toward all whites came into the open a couple of years later at what we now call Massacre Butte, two miles north of modern Cowley. There the young Three Suns took a leading part in attacking a small train of westbound American settlers which had formed part of Captain Fiske's rather widely scattered expedition from Minnesota. Waiting until the travellers had camped for the night, Three Suns and his cohorts struck and killed all twelve of the little party of men, women and children.

90 A History of Alberta

Relations between the Confederacy and white men, both American and British, had continued to ferment. Hostilities, however, were not confined to the traders. For instance, in 1860, on the Milk River in southern Alberta, Crees and Assiniboines attacked the Pend d'Oreilles, an American tribe, and killed twenty, wounded twenty-five more and stole 290 horses. Fortunately for the Pend d'Oreilles some Piegans happened along and prevented the Crees and Assiniboines from continuing the slaughter.

When in 1865 Crowfoot (later to succeed Three Suns) and his band were camped in the vicinity of Red Deer Lake some miles farther down the Battle River from Three Suns' camp, eight hundred Crees attacked the upstream camp. During the dark of the night attack, in which their guest Father Lacombe was wounded, the Blackfoot with their eighty men fought back desperately as chaos erupted around their lodges. As soon as he heard the shooting, Crowfoot called his men and rushed to Three Suns' assistance. Their combined efforts averted complete disaster but twelve men, women and children had been killed and scalped, fifteen had been wounded, most of their pemmican had been carried away, and many of their lodges cut to pieces. Moreover, the Crees, who lost twenty in the fray, had made off with about three hundred horses.

If ever there was a time when this fratricidal killing should have been ended it was at this period when the white man's pressure was becoming so manifest and when it would have been desirable for all Indians to make common cause against the intruders. But that was not to be.

Despite the efforts of the remarkable Cree Maskepatoon who devoted much of his energy to bringing about a lasting peace between Cree and Blackfoot, it was not to be. Maskepatoon, who spent his life in the Edmonton area, deserves more attention than he has been given. Most of our information about him comes from the Methodist missionaries whose writings smack of the fondness lavished upon a neophyte, but he appears to have been a great man. Undoubtedly amongst the wide variety of chiefs there were other Indians of his ilk, but they must have been few and far between. Even though we can discount some of his recorded saintliness, he was nevertheless a peacemaker.

Practising that difficult role under dramatic circumstances, he brought about an accord around 1850 which is commemorated in the name of the Peace Hills near modern Wetaskiwin. In April 1869, still following his peace-oriented philosophy, he walked into a treacherous Blackfoot trap where Big Swan, the quarrelsome Blackfoot chief, killed him and horribly mutilated his body.

Shortly after that, smallpox, the dreaded killer, struck tribe after tribe. One of its early victims was Three Suns, chief of the Blackfoot tribe. Like a prairie fire it swept north over the plains, leaving behind bleaching skeletons and stark teepee poles. By the spring of 1870 it had swept on to the Bloods, the Blackfoot and the Assiniboines, and by June it was clutching at the half-breed camp at Tail Creek, where the Métis hunters from St. Albert and Edmonton House were assembled for their buffalo hunt. Chief Factor Christie, in reporting the progress of the plague, said, "it spread through the whole [camp], and in the early part of September their situation was most pitiful, small-pox of the worst form in every tent, with deaths daily. . . ."

About one-half of Alberta's Indians died of the disease. The official figures for the Saskatchewan District show that 2,686 of the plains Indians were swept away, while 485 Crees and 373 half-breeds died.

The smallpox smote St. Albert in its most virulent form. There, six hundred souls out of nine hundred caught the disease, and in spite of the untiring devotion of priests and nuns, 320 died. At Victoria, perhaps because it was a much smaller settlement than St. Albert, and perhaps due to the policies adopted by Rev. George McDougall, the native mortality was proportionately less. All the missionary's family except Mrs. McDougall caught the disease and two of her children, Flora and Georgina, died. So did her adopted Indian daughter Anna. Then, some weeks later, during his absence, John McDougall's wife became another victim.

Like all previous decades, the one that began in 1870 opened with warfare. On January 23 of that year, in a bitterly unjust attack thirty miles south of the Canadian border, the American army fell upon an innocent band of Piegans, killing 173 men, and capturing 140 women and children. The following April, in a fight with the Crees at the northern tip of their territory directly across the river from Fort Edmonton, the Blackfoot lost six of their people.

They got some of their own back, however, towards the end of October 1870 in a massive slaughter at the point where the CPR's long steel trestle now crosses the deep valley within the city of Lethbridge. Between six and eight hundred Crees and Assiniboines made a tragic mistake by attacking a Blood camp a short distance upriver without realizing that a large band of Piegans (armed with the Americans' latest repeating rifles) was in the vicinity. When the Piegans heard the shooting, they rushed over, routed the Crees and Assiniboines and killed between two and three hundred of them. Many of the Crees were mowed down as they waded the river. Jerry Potts, the famous half-breed scout, played an active part in the Blackfoot ranks, and afterwards said: "You could fire with your eyes shut and be sure to kill a Cree." Big Bear, Piapot and Little Pine of the Crees were also participants but they lived to fight another day. Although the Blackfoot were victorious and suffered relatively few casualties, the cumulative effect of having everyone's hand against them was wearing them down. Fortunately, except for minor skirmishes, the year 1870 marked the end of this senseless intertribal slaughter.

But the plains Indians emerged from their long era of warfare only to be plunged into an even more devastating period which woefully reduced their numbers and irretrievably lowered their morale—the four-year reign of the American whisky forts. For some years, at intervals of about fifty miles, independent traders had been scattered all over Montana. When the most southerly Hudson's Bay Company post was over two hundred miles north of the border, it was only to be expected that the Americans should extend their activities into southern Alberta.

The first of the whisky traders to set up shop in Alberta were J. J. Healy and Alfred B. Hamilton, a nephew of I. G. Baker, the prominent Fort Benton merchant. In the fall of 1869 they set off over rolling hills drab in the brassy ripeness of a continuous field of buffalo wool grass and kept on until, after leaving the Sweet Grass Hills behind and to the east and crossing the Milk River, they finally looked down upon the tree-fringed flats at the junction of the St. Mary and the Oldman rivers near modern Lethbridge. There they built the first American traders' post on Alberta's soil. In ironic recollection of I. G. Baker's parting words as they pulled away from Fort Benton, "Don't let the Indians whoop you up," they named the spot Fort Whoop-Up. The first of the so-called whisky posts had come into being.

Whoop-Up's spectacular success soon brought several other traders up to Alberta to build posts. While Fort Whoop-Up was the kingpin of them all, equally stirring times took place at its earliest rival, a post built a few miles away at the confluence of the Belly and Waterton rivers. Not to be overshadowed by Whoop-Up, its owners, Dutch Fred Wachter and Liver-Eating Johnston, selected a colourful name for their establishment. On their way to Alberta a pursuing United States marshall did not over-take them until they stopped at the Milk River, where, being on Canadian soil, they could defy him—where they could safely "stand him off." In hilarity over their success they named their post Standoff.

To complete the roster of colourful names, Mose Solomon built a minor post on the Belly River which came to be called Slide-out. This trio of memorable names, Whoop-Up, Standoff and Slide-out, exemplifies the rough humour of these whisky traders, some of the most courageous, reckless men ever to risk their lives in any borderland. Unfortunately they were as cruel and ruthless as they were brave. Despising the Indians as being of less worth than dogs, they laughed at the demoralization they inflicted on them. As J. J. Healy said: "These men taught the Blackfeet, Piegans, Sarcees and Crees to behave." Their posts have come to typify the worst excesses of the short era of the whisky trade, one of the blackest eras in the history of America's wildest ever frontier. And yet south of the 49th parallel some law, however defective, existed. North of it for two hundred miles there was none. In that area these men's Bowie knives, six-shooters, repeating rifles and ruthlessness ruled.

During the next four years over a dozen other whisky posts moved in to share the wealth in this strip where no law existed. The most northerly was Fred Kanouse's post built in 1871 on the Elbow River within Calgary's present city limits.

The same milieu which supported the whisky posts attracted two other sets of reckless, hard working and hard living men, the wolfers and the hide hunters. Everyone else hated the wolfers, a ghoulish gang which spread poison far and wide. Shooting a buffalo, they opened it, saturated the meat with strychnine and came back for the next few days to skin the carcasses of the wolves, sometimes a hundred of them, which, contorted into frightful shapes by the agonies induced by the hideous poison, lay all about.

The hide hunters swept over the prairies at a time when new factories were springing up in the eastern United States, creating an insatiable demand for leather belts to run their machinery. The hunters with their high-powered rifles fanned out all over the grasslands, and as Dr. W. G. Hardy has so well phrased it: "in the rush for the hides alone, while the meat was left stinking on the plains, in a few years the shaggy carpet of moving beasts was to be practically exterminated."

Inevitably, of course, the Indians hated all these men, the whisky peddlers who debauched and impoverished them, the wolfers who poisoned and killed their dogs, and the hide hunters who decimated the remaining buffalo. Even though these traders had brought them repeating rifles with which they could kill more buffalo more quickly, they still hated them. For these guns availed them little; with them they could bring in more hides to trade for more whisky and ammunition to acquire more robes to trade for more whisky. This vicious circle going round and round always came back to a drunken debauch and poverty.

Supplying the whisky posts, the wolfers and hide hunters with their tons of legitimate trade goods, rolling in the whisky barrels and taking furs and hides back to Fort Benton, soon brought into being a sizable transportation system. The trunk road, winding for 210 miles from the Missouri River to Fort Whoop-Up and well plastered with the offerings of patient oxen, soon burst into fame as the Whoop-Up Trail. In the same manner that far to the east the Americans had worked out a way into Canada down the Red River valley, so they laid out the Whoop-Up Trail —another access road to new territory which by default and with their cynical lawlessness they were rapidly taking over.

The first result, of course, a mere by-product of the process, was to do away with the Indians, and everything indicated that that would not take long. As years later one retired whisky trader put it when talking to one of the early ranchers, Alexander Staveley Hill: "If we had only been allowed to carry on the business in our own way for another two years, there would have been no trouble now as to feeding the Indians, for there would have been none left to feed: whisky, pistols, strychnine, and other like processes would have effectively cleared away these wretched natives." Despite accusations levelled at the Americans, there was no deliberate plot to wipe out the Indians. Nobody planned their destruction, nobody did it deliberately. In fact the whisky traders hoped that their Indians, the basis of their lucrative trade, would last forever. But, with their philosophy of grabbing a quick buck, they persisted in policies which they knew were killing off their customers. But then, of course, they knew that "it could never happen in our time."

Within five years of the start of the whisky forts the Indians, who must also shoulder their share of the responsibility, had become a poverty-stricken rabble. As Father Scollen, the Roman Catholic missionary, wrote: "In the summer of 1874, I was travelling amongst the Blackfeet. It was painful to me to see the state of poverty to which they had been reduced. Formerly, they had been the most opulent Indians in the country, now they were clothed in rags without horses and without guns." Incident after incident recorded by early writers corroborates his observation.

Hudson's Bay Company officials, worried about the situation, warned the Canadian government of what was going on; casual travellers wrote of the debauchery, and officials delegated to visit Alberta spoke in the same vein. During 1872 the federal government, spurred on by the missionaries' pleas and by other reports of conditions in the western prairies, sent out Colonel P. Robertson-Ross to study the situation and to bring back recommendations on how best to establish law and order. He said: "The demoralization of the Indians and injury to the country from this illicit traffic [liquor] is very great. It is stated on good authority that last year eighty-eight of the Blackfeet Indians were murdered in drunken brawls among themselves. . . ." He also noted that Americans from Fort Benton made their way to Edmonton, where they openly sold whisky, declaring that "as there was no force to prevent them, they would do just as they pleased."

At Ottawa cabinet ministers and civil servants alike, confronted with a host of challenges all concerned with setting the new Canada on the road to success, turned their attention to this vexing problem of what to do for the prairies. It was a two-pronged problem; on the one hand it was imperative that the Indians be protected, and on the other, Canada must pinch off this nonmilitary but nonetheless clear-cut American invasion. It seemed wise to adopt Colonel Robertson-Ross's suggestion of stationing a military force in the West and to do so quickly. With that in mind, in the House of Commons on April 28, 1873, Prime Minister John A. Macdonald gave notice of a proposed bill to create a police force for that purpose.

One day later and two thousand miles away in the remote folds of

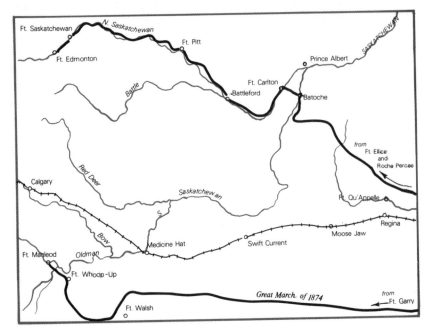

MARCH OF THE MOUNTED POLICE

In 1874 the main body of the North West Mounted Police marched across the plains from Winnipeg and established Fort Macleod. In Saskatchewan a small part of the force diverged to make their way northwest to Fort Edmonton.

Alberta's most southeasterly hills, a band of American wolfers outbound from Fort Benton in pursuit of whichever Indians had stolen several of their horses, opened fire on an innocent Assiniboine camp and killed thirty men, women and children. Within a week the echo of their shots reached Ottawa and provided exactly the impetus needed to speed up John A. Macdonald's police bill and to set the organization of the North West Mounted Police off at a round gallop.

No one has been able to ferret out the details of the massacre, but if the picture of the killings was confused, Canada's reaction to it was clear-cut. Now, an aroused populace was ready to back up any remedial measures and this backing spurred John A. Macdonald's police along so rapidly that the force organized and raised that summer made its way over the Dawson Road and spent the winter at the Hudson's Bay Company's Lower Fort Garry. From there it planned to head west the next spring to settle matters with the whisky peddlers.

Canadians are fortunate that one hundred years ago they had men of the calibre of those who headed the NWMP, selected the recruits, instilled

A History of Alberta

in them their own British ideals of conduct and duties of a police force and disciplined them into the most famous police body in the world. All these—ideals, selection and discipline—were essential to this force, which, inexperienced as it started out, soon rose to surmount all its difficulties and now for a century has merited the unparalleled respect which Canadians repose in it.

After leaving Fort Garry early in June 1874 and assembling at Dufferin near the 49th parallel, the force, a mere handful of men, set out to bring law to 300,000 square miles of near wilderness. Commanded by Lieutenant-Colonel G. A. French, with Major J. F. Macleod as second in command, and with such officers as Inspector W. D. Jarvis, Sévère Gagnon, J. M. Walsh, L. N. F. Crozier, and C. E. Denny, the force comprising 275 men and officers stretched over a column two miles long. With 339 horses, 142 draft oxen, ninety-three cattle for slaughter, 114 Red River carts with twenty Métis drivers, seventy-three wagons, two nine-pounder muzzle loading field guns, two brass mortars, several mowing machines, forges and field kitchens, the exponents of the new era headed west. Late in the afternoon of July 8, ablaze in their scarlet tunics, eager to fulfill the mission which would later become their motto, *maintiens le droit*, they left Dufferin and rode into the setting sun. Never in western history had such a force challenged the great plains.

The red coats had been no capricious choice. For long, Canadian Indians had found the red coats of British regiments to be anti-American. For long, during desperate days, the Sioux and the Blackfoot had found the blue of the American cavalry a stench in their nostrils. Appropriately, this force of which the missionaries had talked, this force which was to protect the Indians on the Canadian side of the border came clad as it should be, in red. South of the medicine line blue prevailed, north of it, red; blue for treachery and broken treaties, red for protection and the straight tongue. And never, as the weeks passing by brought the first tentative contacts between the Mounties and the Indians, never was the dignity of the red uniform more carefully cultivated. Along with their martial discipline the new police exploited every ounce of drama they could extract from the pageant of their military drill or from the ceremonial processes of the law—the law which was to be one law for red men or white.

Their immediate problem was to reach the sore spot; for many a week, under the pitiless blue sky, as these red-breasted soldiers, green as the grass under foot, sweated along, they wondered if they ever would. Suffering severe hardship, much of it caused by inexperience, they pushed on west past Roche Percée where part of the force under Inspector Jarvis split off to head for Edmonton House. The main body crawled west over Wood Mountain, and headed for the Cypress Hills and the flat country beyond. Parched on the sun-beaten plains, sickened by alkali water from stinking sloughs, badgered by mosquitoes and horse flies, despairing of their Métis guides' ability, their procession crept along.

Finally, after unnecessary hardship, the Mounted Police camped for a while on the flank of the west butte of the Sweet Grass Hills while Commissioner French and Major Macleod went south to Fort Benton to procure supplies for the forthcoming winter. The American merchants there, versatile as ever, did a remarkable double shuffle and put themselves out to serve the Canadians. Without any recorded comment on the irony of turning for help to these Americans whom they had come to dislodge from Alberta, Commissioner French contracted with the I. G. Baker Company for the extensive supplies the Mounties would need as soon as they headed north, and knocked the stuffing out of the Fort Benton traders' forts Whoop-Up and Standoff. Having done that, the Commissioner returned to Manitoba to administer the affairs of the force.

At Fort Benton Major Macleod picked up the best bargain the force had found since it left Fort Garry. There he acquired the services of Jerry Potts, the sawed-off half-breed, stooped and twisted from an old injury. Nevertheless, Jerry Potts, the man who four years earlier had exulted in the fight with the Crees, was the very epitome of frontier skill, courage and toughness. In the years ahead, with his loyalty, his infallible judgment of trail conditions and his uncanny wisdom in plains' lore, Jerry Potts proved invaluable as guide, interpreter and general advisor.

Taking the police force under his wing, he led them along the Whoop-Up Trail to the point of its descent into the valley of the St. Mary River. To their left, its great block lording over the pine-clad foothills, stood the peak the Indians had fittingly called Chief Mountain. Beyond the trough that was the valley of the St. Mary River the bare hills rose towards the dark blue of the Porcupine Hills, while behind them the jagged, snowy peaks of the Rockies jutted far into the clear sky.

That way, somewhere below them in the bottom of the valley at the junction of the St. Mary and Oldman rivers, lay Fort Whoop-Up. They had left Winnipeg nine hundred miles ago, expecting to fight for it with cannons and mortars. Jerry Potts shook his head, explaining that the very news of their approach had emptied the fort and the surrounding country of whisky peddlers. But Major Macleod, a good commander, prepared for the worst, and when the high stockades came into view on the flat below, he stopped to size up the situation. Although this grey-visaged stronghold, with the Stars and Stripes flying above it and its great gate flung wide open, looked tranquil enough, Macleod spread out his two nine-pounders and his mortars so as to bear upon it, and assigning his men to their stations, rode up to the fort.

But it was an empty nest; the birds had flown, leaving only one of their number behind—grey-haired and innocent-looking Dave Akers. All smiles, he invited Macleod in and fed him, and with the guile of the robber in the hen roost, in effect declared that there wasn't nobody here but us chickens.

So simply, so utterly, the capture of Fort Whoop-Up fizzled out.

After searching the place and finding no liquor, the police column accepted Jerry Pott's advice and followed the trail which the whisky traders had used when heading farther north. At the brink of a broad tree-lined valley Potts swept his arm around and announced "de Ole Man's River." There, he declared, they should build their headquarters.

Thus it came about on October 13, 1874, as the sun set behind the Porcupine Hills, the tents pitched along the river bank indicated that the NWMP had come home. The very next day, on an island in the Oldman River the men started to build Fort Macleod. Their one-thousand-mile trek across the prairies was ended. So was the infamous Fort Whoop-Up. So, or nearly so, was the whisky trade.

In many ways their march across the prairies had been one of the notable feats of Canada's history. Yet newspapers in the east puffed it up far beyond its very real accomplishment. The glory which easterners ascribed to this column of cavalry crossing the plains raised the hackles of the handful of acclimatized westerners of the time. Included among them was Rev. John McDougall, who in scoffing at the force's greenness and at its near failure to reach the West perhaps revealed some of his own lifelong inferiority complex. For westerners, themselves the green-horns of the previous decade, have never suffered greenhorns gladly, especially since they all came from the East. And if these newcomers spoke with an English accent or dared reveal signs of education, they were doubly suspect. One of Alberta's earliest imports was an intense distrust of the East and of the easterners' motives.

The truth about the Mounties' march lies between these extreme points of view. It is true that from the commander down to the most junior sub-constable the police were inexperienced. It is also true that a handful of Métis or died-in-the-wool westerners could have made the trip in half the time. But this was not a mere handful; and, encumbered by cattle, cannons and mowing machines, it could not progress more rapidly than the slowest link in its necessarily cumbersome make-up.

The Mounties' main achievement, however, lay not in the fact of their long march but in how its hardships, reacting upon their sturdiness of character, transformed them from green recruits to a hardened command capable of meeting the harsh western plains on their own terms. They had been tried in a crucible and had not been found wanting. Their trek created an *esprit de corps* which ever after carried them through. Their journey, acting as a catalyst upon sound material, made men of them.

Mounties and Whisky Posts 1870-1874

# 7
# The End of the Plains Indians' Freedom 1874-1881

The Mounties, expecting the Blackfoot to welcome them with open arms, were disappointed that for some time the natives remained aloof. By this time Crowfoot, who in 1869 had succeeded Three Suns as chief of the Blackfoot tribe, had also become one of the Confederacy's leading chiefs and most of his people relied on him to make the first contact with the new soldiers. His approach was cautious; he delegated one of his band to call on Major Macleod. During the visit the delegate dropped the information that at Pine Coulee some fifty miles to the north a couple of traders were dishing out liquor. When Macleod requested him to show Inspector Crozier the way to the traders' post, the Indian complied and was highly gratified at what ensued. Crozier caught two men named Taylor and Bond with some liquor and a great deal of booty. While the Mounties upended the liquor jugs, Crowfoot's messenger listened as their contents gurgled out and watched, perhaps sadly, as they soaked into the soil. But that was not all. The red coats confiscated more than a hundred buffalo robes, ten guns and sixteen horses, and on top of that fined the men two hundred dollars each. This was the Mounties' first haul—a significant one. Obviously the new soldiers meant business.

When his delegate came back to report, Crowfoot was relieved and soon he and his people found themselves trusting the police. At an early conference at the new post Macleod explained the policy the police hoped to adopt, and Crowfoot shook hands with that officer and all the other white men present. With naturally graceful gestures he bared his right arm and thanked the sun and the queen for sending the police to quell the whisky traders and to protect his people. On a subsequent occasion he is reported to have said: "You are a brave man, *Stamix Otokan* [Bull's Head]; the law of the Great White Mother must be good when she has a son like you. We will obey that law."

So spoke the powerful chief who knew that with a wave of his hand his own Blackfoot tribe alone could wipe out every white man in the West. So spoke the long-headed chief who, seeing the inevitable, knew how little warfare would avail his people's destiny.

From that day, Crowfoot and Macleod, each admiring the other's

A History of Alberta

courage and essential fairness and each bent on peaceful measures, held the other in high respect. Though often uncertain as the next few years rolled by and often angry at the police, Crowfoot kept his promise.

Hardened in warfare and schooled in the councils of his tribe, he was not only a forceful man but a thinking man. Although his mind had veered towards peace, he had been a brave warrior and until his death carried some of the marks of his battles in a limping leg. With the death of Big Swan in 1872, he and Old Sun between them assumed control of the Blackfoot tribe, but more and more he came to be regarded as its leading man. By 1870 he was a rich man at the peak of economic success. He owned some four hundred horses and, to take care of his material possessions, had a number of paid retainers, as well as at least four wives out of the total of some ten women which he had wed over the years.

His family life had been marked by disappointment. He had fathered relatively few children; only two or three of them reached maturity and only one of these was healthy. When in 1873 this son, of whom he was extremely proud, was killed on an expedition against the Crees, Crowfoot was bowed in grief. That grief, superimposed on the loneliness borne by all leaders, filled the rest of his life. Not long after this loss, he met a Cree, a younger man named Poundmaker. Because of his striking resemblance to his dead son, Crowfoot adopted him.

In the same way that he had paid only the necessary minimum of attention to the ceremonies of his fathers, he listened to religion as advocated by Father Lacombe or Rev. John McDougall with a casual ear. He liked both these men, admired their altruism and trusted them, but like all leaders listening to conflicting advice from many quarters, he had to sift out and formulate his own policy. In the main, that policy was that the Blackfoot had no option but to accept the calamity of the white man's takeover and somehow try to skate over the thin ice to a solid, though dismal shore.

During the years of Crowfoot's acquaintance with these missionaries, before the arrival of the NWMP, the Blackfoot power had started its rapid decline. Hounded by American soldiers, increasingly harassed by Crees and Assiniboines, they had also turned to the debauchery induced by whisky. Before long, by selling their horses for liquor and trading their buffalo robes for booze instead of reserving them for domestic uses, they dropped far down the ladder into poverty. Crowfoot railed against the worst of the whisky peddlers and all the while depleted his horses and wealth to help their victims.

During the summer of 1874, at the government's request, Rev. McDougall called on Crowfoot and explained the creation of the Mounted Police and what they hoped to do. When he had done so, the chief, acknowledging that his people were utterly incapable of resisting the

The End of the Plains Indians' Freedom 1874-1881

temptation of liquor and aware of how rapidly it was destroying them, expressed extreme satisfaction at the news. Fortunately these red-coated soldiers turned out to be as Rev. McDougall had said they would be, and almost immediately the sale of whisky stopped. Within two years some measure of the Blackfoot's former prosperity returned to the lodges. By that time the police had built additional posts: Fort Walsh near the site of the Cypress Hills massacre, and Fort Calgary, which had previously been the scene of some of the drunken orgies of Crowfoot's people.

At the same time, however, traders, kept honest by the Mounties, had built villages around all three of these posts, and a few ranchers had followed them in. This injection of white people into the southern prairies began to worry the Blackfoot. By that time white intrusion into spots along the North Saskatchewan River had also begun to irk the Crees and Assiniboines.

Into this worrisome milieu the American Sioux dropped a tantalizing offer. They proposed that all the tribes should forget their mutual hostilities and, before it was too late, unite to drive all whites out of the West. Crowfoot, seeing more virtue in peace than war, could not forget how the police had saved his people from the whisky traders and how different these soldiers' attributes had been from that of the American army. He counseled peace.

At the same time, he told the Mounties what the Sioux were thinking, and remarked: "We all see that the day is coming when the buffalo will all be killed, and we shall have nothing more to live on." While many of his younger men were eager for war with the whites, the older chief could see the writing on the wall. Crowfoot felt his people's well-being would be served best by working with the police and by having the white man's goodwill and help with the transition that was bound to come.

Up north along the North Saskatchewan River, many of the Crees and Assiniboines were also seeing bad days ahead. Various government authorities, hoping to achieve a peaceful accommodation between white settlers and the native owners of the land, felt the time had come to follow precedents set farther east and to make treaties with the Indians. It was taken for granted that when the buffalo were gone the Indians would see the necessity of turning to the soil for a living, and willingly or not, would settle down to an agricultural economy. At that point the government would try to see that they got off to a good start and that from there on they would cultivate the land on a reserve of their own choice. This would throw the rest of the land open to white settlers who were bound to come in and, hopefully, would prevent friction between the newcomers and the natives.

At last, soil, the second of the parklands' great resources, was on the point of being put to use. For a century, and indirectly through the Indians, white men had been using buffalo and beaver, the animal

A History of Alberta

resources of the area. But now the time had come to see what use could be made of this hitherto neglected resource by cultivating it. Prospective immigrants were beginning to express interest. Under cultivation this soil could probably be utilized to provide a living for millions, as well as for the tribes of Indians who now ignored it. If farmed, small patches of it here and there would yield enough to feed the few thousand Indians. If then the natives could be encouraged to select small reserves and to work these, they would have a more stable economy than hunting had ever provided. On the rest of the land tens of thousands of white settlers could also make a good living.

So it looked in theory. On the basis of that theory, which at the time seemed logical, government authorities, with the assistance of the missionaries and the Mounties, approached the Crees with the suggestion that they sign an agreement giving up their lands. As a result, in August 1876, Indian Treaty No. 6 came into being.

By that treaty, negotiated mainly at Fort Carlton, the Indians ceded the area encircled by a line running approximately through the following modern towns: from The Pas in Manitoba west to Athabasca in Alberta and on to Jasper, thence south to Lake Louise and east to Stettler, and on to Empress and Swift Current and Hudson Bay Junction, and thence back to The Pas. It contained one hundred and twenty-one thousand square miles—not acres, but square miles. This large area gives a rough indication of what part of the prairies of Alberta and Saskatchewan the Crees and their allies, the Assiniboines and a few Chippewas, some thirty-six hundred Indians all together, considered their territory. It is also an indication of how far they had crowded the Blackfoot Confederacy into the south and western parts of Saskatchewan and Alberta. Not all the Crees were willing to sign and in this they were led by Big Bear, a strong man who would not knuckle under to the white man. Although he could advance no better solution to his people's problem, and finally signed the treaty six years later, this adversary of the white man stands out as a sincere Indian patriot.

The secretary of the commission, on his return to Fort Garry early in October, reported to Ottawa that of the $60,000 in cash with which he had been entrusted, he was turning back $12,730. The rest, some $47,000, had bought 121,000 square miles of the richest soil in Canada. By this treaty, signed a hundred years after Peter Pond had established his post at Prince Albert and the Hudson's Bay Company had built its first post in the vicinity of Fort Carlton, most of central Alberta passed out of Indian hands. It had taken the fur traders and hide hunters a century to drive most of the buffalo out of these 121,000 square miles. It had taken white settlers only a hundred years to start to follow in the traders' steps and to begin to demand the land.

Once the buffalo should be gone, this vast area would be of little practical value to the Indians. They could ramble over it at will but with rumbling stomachs rambling was a dubious pleasure. Wandering along over some of the best soil in the world, they had never had to think of it in terms of agriculture, and now, left to their own devices, on this soil which could yield food for millions, they would starve.

The $47,000 which the white men had paid meant very little in itself. If they had merely spent that sum to acquire the land and then had let it lie, they would have wasted their money. It was only worth that much provided that by the sweat of their brows they would delve and plough it. The time had come, however, when white settlers were willing to sweat and dig. And when that time came, when men were able to use the soil and were anxious to use it, neither government nor missionaries nor pious precepts could keep them out. All the government of Canada could do, all the genuine concern of missionaries or Mounties could do, was to try to soften the settlers' impact upon a people unprepared, unwilling, or unable to till the land. Sentimentally they or we might deplore this takeover of the Indians' land, but sentiment does not fill bellies, red or white.

Three months before the treaty was signed at Fort Carlton and five hundred miles directly south near the Yellowstone River in Montana, the Sioux, under Sitting Bull, had annihilated General Custer and his military command. Rarely, if ever, had there been such a smashing Indian victory; every one of 265 soldiers was killed. Finally the Sioux had turned on the white men and in one glorious battle had obtained some token measure of revenge for all their suffering.

For two or three days they rejoiced. Then, anticipating the fearful retribution which the white men surely would inflict, they fled to Canada. By the time the Fort Carlton treaty had been signed, many of these Sioux refugees had crossed the border into the Cypress Hills and its eastern neighbour, Wood Mountain. By the end of 1876 several thousand Sioux had sought sanctuary in that area.

Thereby, for three or four years, they added many a vexing complication to the already complex Indian problems north of the border. Crees, Assiniboines and Blackfoot all suffered in consequence. The Dominion government, afraid of the American army's eagerness to use these refugee Sioux as a pretext for invading Canada's prairies, watched and worried. Above all, the threat of the Sioux presence hung most precariously over the heads of the police. A total of 102 men at Fort Walsh had to cope with some four thousand Sioux and had to prevent hostilities from breaking out between the Sioux and the Crees, Assiniboines and Blackfoot. Finally, in one of the greatest tests of courage and in one of the most dramatic demonstrations of competence and worth ever exhibited by any police force, Superintendent J. M. Walsh and his men defused the

A History of Alberta

bomb and gradually pushed its living components across the line to the United States.

The story is too long to tell fully here. With his Irish courage and temper and his profound knowledge of practical psychology, backed by some one hundred men, Walsh kept the lid on the seething cauldron which threatened to scald the Canadian prairies. Typical of many incidents in Walsh's courageous confrontation of the horde of Sioux was the time when, during a heated argument, he threatened to lock up Sitting Bull as a prisoner. The chief flared back, swearing that no man could talk to him like that, and Walsh with his temper pushed to the limit, stood and reviled this powerful leader of a thousand warriors until Sitting Bull reached for his revolver. That did it. Walsh grabbed him, frog-marched him out the door and flung him in the dust. As Sitting Bull scrambled to his feet, Walsh delivered the ultimate offence in the form of a hearty kick to his backside. Then, while dozens of warriors seethed in rage, Walsh stood defying them until, thinking better of it, they moved away.

Three years had elapsed since the Sioux had wiped out Custer's men —three years of hunger and uncertainty during which the Canadian authorities acting through the Mounted Police had subtly and consistently undermined Sitting Bull's authority and humbled the famous Indian leader. Now torn between a man's natural reaction to fight back and his need to mollify these white police, the only military body which had not oppressed his people, the chief was in a mortifying position. It would have been but a moment's work to wipe out Walsh and his few men; instead, at great personal cost, he had the courage to bridle his passion. A great man, facing problems with which neither he nor his followers could cope—impossible, insoluble problems—he deserves the praise and sympathy of posterity.

Crowfoot and the other chiefs of the Blackfoot Confederacy were deeply disturbed when Sitting Bull and his Sioux, their traditional enemies, occupied the Cypress Hills area. For a while the Mounties worried lest the presence of the Sioux would prevent the Blackfoot from signing a treaty similar to that signed by the Crees in 1876.

Fortunately their worries were largely unfounded and, when at Blackfoot Crossing on the Bow River in September 1877 the Blackfoot signed Treaty No. 7, harmony prevailed. There were, of course, problems and jealousies which took time to smooth out. For one thing, the police had made a tactical error in assuming that Crowfoot was the head chief of the Blackfoot Confederacy and not just the main chief of the Blackfoot tribe (which in fact was all he was); they had treated him with a precedence which annoyed some of the others. For a couple of days it appeared that some of the chiefs, including Red Crow, the famous warrior, diplomat and orator of the Blood tribe and a man equally as

The End of the Plains Indians' Freedom 1874-1881

important as Crowfoot, and indeed commanding a larger following, might keep their people out of the treaty. In the end Red Crow and the others more or less gracefully acquiesced in allowing Crowfoot to assume the mantle of leader of all the Confederacy, with which the police had erroneously invested him, and they signed the treaty.

They surrendered the remainder of southern Alberta which had not been included in Treaty No. 6—some 50,000 square miles—under the terms of Treaty No. 7. In exchange, the government contracted to pay $12 to each Indian man, woman and child after the treaty signing, as well as an annuity of $5; to furnish $2,000 worth of ammunition annually, as well as a stipulated number of cattle, agricultural tools, hand tools, and seeds; and in addition to some minor items, each main chief was to receive $25 annually and the lesser chiefs $15. It was pointed out to the Indians that white men were to be allowed to move into the land the Indians were ceding and to make their living on any of it they chose. The plains Indians were to be free to hunt over their old lands as long as the buffalo lasted, but since that animal's extermination was a foregone conclusion, the Indians were to be assigned reserves of their own choosing on which they were to live when the time came. It was expected that then they would support themselves in much the same way as white men did by cultivating the earth.

To try to help them make the transition to a sedentary agricultural economy, the government undertook to furnish them with some cattle, wagons and machinery; provide instructors to teach them to farm; maintain schools for their children and hire teachers; provide a medicine chest for each band, and finally to assure them of aid and food in case of "any pestilence" or "general famine." By assigning to every family of five persons a square mile on the proposed reserves, the treaty gave it four times as much land as the quarter-section granted to a white homesteader who was expected to feed and support his family on one-quarter of a square mile.

The government had taken over Rupert's Land from the Hudson's Bay Company for a driblet, but a realistic driblet. In the same way, it took the Indians' land for a pittance, but a pittance that was designed to help them settle down to farming. The terms of the treaty, of course, were conceived and written by white men, men who, seeing no practical alternative but for the Indians to turn to agriculture, tried to ensure that they got off to a good start in this direction. As it turned out, the Indians were not practical in the white man's sense. Physically they could have tilled the soil or tended cattle; psychologically they could not.

Most of the chiefs were of the same frame of mind as Crowfoot. Knowing that the buffalo could not last many more years, contrasting the treatment the police had meted out to them with that which their

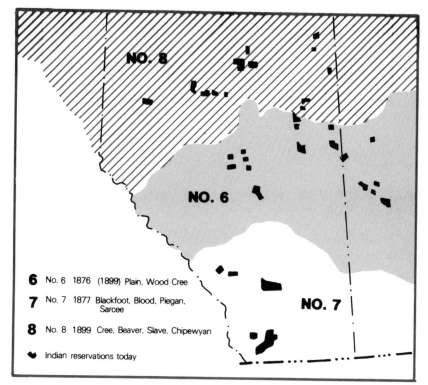

INDIAN TREATIES

Territories in the southern portion of the province ceded by native tribes at the main treaties and the reservations set aside for them.

6  No. 6  1876  (1899) Plain, Wood Cree

7  No. 7  1877  Blackfoot, Blood, Piegan, Sarcee

8  No. 8  1899  Cree, Beaver, Slave, Chipewyan

♥  Indian reservations today

---

relatives across the 49th parallel were receiving, and making the best of the bad bargain which was their lot, they agreed to sign the treaty—reluctantly, of course, and without fully comprehending the changes that lay in store for their people. For weeks the Blackfoot had talked over their problems, looking for possible solutions, and when it was time to sign the treaty they reposed confidence in Crowfoot's judgment. But no man, especially a leader, can stand alone, and Crowfoot had been careful to garner advice from as many men as possible—his Indian colleagues, missionaries and the police. Then, balancing one opinion against another, he made the decision to sign, a decision which under the circumstances was a sensible one.

By his introductory remarks at the signing of the treaty, Crowfoot set the stage for his people's point of view. "While I speak," he began, "be kind and patient. I have to speak for my people. . . . The plains are large and wide; we are the children of the plains; this has long been our

The End of the Plains Indians' Freedom 1874-1881

home and the buffalo have always been our food. . . . If the police had not come to this country, where would we all be now? Bad men and whisky were killing us so fast that very few of us would have been alive today. The Mounted Police have protected us as the feathers of the bird protect it from the frosts of winter. I wish all my people good and trust that all our hearts will increase in goodness from this time forward. I am satisfied. I will sign the treaty."

Finally, with a wave of his hand, Crowfoot gave assent to the X marking his signature to the treaty document, and in a voice ringing with conviction said: "I have been the first to sign; I shall be the last to break."

Other outstanding men to sign the treaty included Old Sun of the Blackfoot, Red Crow and Rainy Chief of the Bloods, Sitting-on-an-Eagle-Tail of the Piegans, Bull's Head of the Sarcees and Bear's Paw of the Stoneys.

In this manner the treaty was signed. In this manner the lands passed to the white men. The Blackfoot reign of over a century on the prairies was ended.

Since that day nearly a hundred years ago, some white men and many Indians have decried the white man's part in Treaties No. 6 and No. 7. They have claimed that the Indians did not understand the treaties and, moreover, that they were not fair to the Indians. Viewed through today's hindsight there was much in the treaties and their application, and in the subsequent neglect of the Indians that we find deplorable. Even though each Indian family had available to it four times the area of land a white homesteader would receive, that allocation of land had little real meaning. The white man knew how to farm or could learn quickly and was eager to do so, whereas it was too much to expect the Indians to make the rapid transition to agriculture. And yet the vision of the time could perceive no other course for the natives to follow.

The treaties themselves or the men who wrote them should not be criticised as harshly as should subsequent generations for passing by on the other side and neglecting the Indians when it became evident that from the native point of view (and from the point of view of modern Canada) the treaties were not working out successfully. But the treaties were not bad in every respect. Under them the Indians were at least saved from extinction, were given some medical care and education and have increased from less than ten thousand in the 1880s to some twenty-nine thousand today.

The fact of life, which both the Indians and the Mounties faced at the time, was that the Indians were going to lose their lands in any event. Losing them in this peaceful manner, where the government stood by and tried to help the natives with their transition, was infinitely better than the alternative, which was bloody fighting. Many a white settler—maybe hundreds of them—would have been killed, but individual whites in their wrath would have wiped out the few natives whom starvation had left alive, and in doing so soon would have insisted on government help with the killing. That much at least Crowfoot and other chiefs of his calibre could see.

Were they—the chiefs, not the thoughtless rank and file—aware of the meaning of the treaty? How could they be? They could understand that they would get a few dollars, some cattle and medicines, all visible items easy to comprehend. None of them, however, not even Crowfoot, could conceive of what it would be like to be cooped up on a reserve, grubbing year after year in a piddling field. Old Indians claim that none of them could comprehend giving up their hills and valleys and the land over which they had roamed, and have said that they might as well have been asked to give up the air and the blue sky and the sunshine— conceptions they could never understand. Undoubtedly this is true, as it is for a young man to apprehend that some day in his old age he will die. Nevertheless, while he may not comprehend thus being deprived of the world he knows so well, inevitably, whether he understands or not, he will have to comply.

The chiefs and the thinking few were not children or men with the minds of children. They were men like the Mounties and the government officials, and seeing the facts of life confronting them, had no other choice. Though none perhaps had the wit to foresee all the implications, the Indians' tragedy was that a stone-age people had no time to adjust to the ruthless new era ahead.

Sad though the prospect was, in one respect the Canadian Blackfoot were lucky they were in Canada. This is not due to the British being any more virtuous or kindly than the Americans; except for the meritorious role of the Hudson's Bay Company, it was mainly due to geography. With respect to the Hudson's Bay Company, it was a large commercial corporation which had controlled the area for decades, and being able to look to a corporate future, it treated the Indians well as compared to the treatment they received from the largely independent type of traders along the Missouri, who were here today and gone tomorrow and were out to make a quick profit. That was one factor.

The other was that in the United States, the frontier had expanded westward without stopping, in a continuous progression and the farther west it went the more cumulatively lawless it became, until by the time it reached Montana the frontier left much to be desired. Both settlers and traders, imbued with the outlook that the only good Indian is a dead one, took the law into their own hands. In Canada, by contrast, the almost uninhabitable area between old Ontario and the prairies saved the grassland region from this continuous progression increasing in lawlessness as it spread west. When, too, the time came that a military force appeared necessary in western Canada, it was a vastly different one than its counterpart in the United States, which had a century of Indian conflict under its belt. The NWMP had no tradition of continually harassing Indians, and moreover, was not egged on by settlers.

Fortunately for the Indians and for Canada's reputation, the police, when they set out, came from Britain and eastern Canada where the mores of the relatively more stable and mature eastern provinces dominated the thinking behind policy decisions affecting the West. In other words, by 1874, when it was time to take control of the western prairies, no frontier civilization growing wilder as it went west was automatically inflicted on the plains. Instead, both settlers and the new military force suddenly leaped the pre-Cambrian gap separating Ontario from the West and brought with them the mores of the East, which taught that after all Indians were human beings. Canada's geographical gap worked towards stability in the West's institutions and peace with the plains Indians.

But neither the Blackfoot, the Mounties nor the government could foresee or prepare for the calamity that lay immediately ahead. For it came like an irresistible wind which as it passed sucked the last of the buffalo off the prairies and scattered the Blackfoot into little broken bands begging at the police posts.

Once glorious, as in their pride and wealth, the Blackfoot had watched their thousands of horses graze far over the prairie hills, and the disappearance of the buffalo brought their crumbling civilization crashing about their ears. By the spring of 1879 when many of Crowfoot's people were on the point of starving, he sent a delegation to the Indian department at Battleford, the white man's recently established capital of the Northwest Territories. By midsummer Edgar Dewdney, the newly appointed commissioner, bringing a temporary supply of flour and meat, visited Crowfoot. He reported finding "1,300 Indians in a very destitute condition, and many on the verge of starvation and young men . . . so weak they could hardly work; the old people and widows . . . had nothing, and many a pitiable tale was told of the misery they had endured."

Two months later they were starving again, creeping about desperately searching for rabbits, gophers and badgers, and Crowfoot had no option but to lead his tribe out after the diminishing herds. In the Judith Basin of Montana they found enough buffalo to get them through the winter. There too they found many Métis assembled, all of them under the thumb of Louis Riel, who frequently talked to Crowfoot about starting an uprising in Canada. There too, unfortunately, they found American whisky traders. In the presence of liquor not even Crowfoot could control his tribesmen. The drunken orgies, fights and killings which had been so disastrous in Alberta six years earlier started all over again and Crowfoot

A History of Alberta

watched sadly as his people slid rapidly down the icy one-way slope towards dissolution. Down the slope too went all but a vestige of the chief's control of the tribe as the younger men, soaked in liquor and listening to the rantings of Riel's emissaries, went their headstrong way to bring down on the tribe the Americans' wrath.

In spite of extreme hunger, complicated by measles and mumps which struck nearly simultaneously, most of the Blackfoot tribe survived the severe winter of 1880–81. By its end of all the millions of buffalo which had ranged the Canadian and Montana plains only a corporal's guard of them in little startled groups of a dozen or so hid here and there in a fold of the hills which so recently had rumbled to the tread of mighty multitudes.

No one will ever know who killed the last of the wild, shaggy beasts, but during the winter of 1881–82 the Blackfoot found a few—two here and four there—between the lower Bow and Red Deer rivers, and returning to camp, rejoicing at their luck, left Alberta forever bereft of its romantic, earliest, wild resource.

By the end of May 1881, though Crowfoot still had a following of about one thousand of the Blackfoot tribe, some five hundred people had returned to Fort Macleod where they welcomed the pitiful rations which were all the hard-pressed police could provide.

In July that year much to the relief of the Mounted Police, Sitting Bull followed the last of the Sioux out of Canada to surrender to the American authorities. About the same time, with heavy steps, Crowfoot turned his face towards Alberta. In both cases, starvation—to some extent a deliberate weapon which the government of Canada had used to get the Sioux out of the country and to get its Canadian Indians to go onto their reserves—had worked.

Crowfoot's followers, cheered on by the aging leader's courage, reserving their few horses for the very old and the very young, packed what they could on their dogs and headed north. For once more, as they had been 150 years earlier, they were dog Indians again. As painfully and slowly, day after day, they made their way north towards Fort Macleod, children and old people sickened and died. Starvation and weariness took their toll and the route of their six-week trek was marked with fresh graves. Day after day, near the rear of the column Crowfoot plodded along exhorting the laggards and lifting the fallen. Crowfoot, once the rich, once the mighty chief of the Blackfoot, but now an aging man ill and in tatters, who had given all his horses and goods to help weaker ones and who during the last three years had seen two thousand people of the Confederacy die, came limping along. A beggar he was now, a beggar in all but the resolute jut of his jaw and the glint in his eye.

Finally, as the official correspondence explains, "Crow Foot arrived here on the 20th ulto [July 1881] with 1,064 followers, all in a most destitute condition. A large proportion of his followers consisted of old men, women and children. They were nearly all on foot."

A mere ten years previously they had been lords of all the prairies. Now, broken, decimated and starving, they had crawled back to cower in a mere corner of the prairies they had ruled. Like the buffalo which a decade earlier they had crowded forward to destruction at the lip of the buffalo jump, hunger had driven the Canadian Blackfoot to their dubious destiny as mendicants on the reserve. Well might even the most sympathetic of the white observers have concluded that the once mighty Blackfoot were on the verge of extinction—a spent force whose embers were greying to ashes.

# 8
# White Progress to 1881

Three days, all falling within the same week in July 1881, marked the end of one era for Alberta and the opening of another. On the nineteenth, Sitting Bull surrendered to the American authorities and Canada's Sioux problem ended. The next day, five hundred miles to the northwest on their way to settle on their reserve, Crowfoot and his starving followers straggled into Fort Macleod; Canada's prairie Indians had come to the end of their freedom. Less than a week later the first CPR train to cross the new bridge over the Red River rolled into Winnipeg to initiate the new era.

White men, busily, and on the whole quietly, had been enlarging the bridgeheads from which by 1881 they were ready to take over the province. Armed with all their agricultural know-how and machinery, they were on their way to occupy the lands vacated by the buffalo and wrested from the Blackfoot. Alberta's most important resource, rich land, was on the verge of exploitation.

Though we have dealt with the arrival of the NWMP at Fort Macleod and their subsequent performance, there were many other facets to the foundations the white race had been laying since 1870. One was the survey of the 49th parallel which treaties made decades earlier had set as the boundary between the Canadian prairies and the United States. In what is now Alberta, the few who gave the border any thought knew that it lay somewhere in the vicinity of the Sweet Grass Hills and generally south of the Milk River Ridge. Now the time had come to mark it with a series of monuments. In 1872, by a joint effort of the two countries, the International Boundary Commission was set up.

Starting from the vicinity of the Red River in May 1873, the surveyors worked west and some fifteen months later they had reached the monument which had been placed at the summit of the Rocky Mountains west of Waterton Lakes in 1861. When all the personnel of the combined British and American parties were added up they formed a formidable force. On one occasion in the fall of 1874 when they all camped together on the west butte of the Sweet Grass Hills, and all of the drivers and drovers, surveyors and scientists, soldiers and supply personnel, converged

113

on one campground, more than five hundred men formed the population of this temporary community.

Shortly after leaving that camp and going down the west side of the hills, the surveyors photographed the scene of a skirmish between some Crows and Piegans. As Captain Anderson of the Royal Engineers wrote, the bodies were "all sun dried and features indistinguishable. Every head had the whole of the hair removed in the Indian process of scalping, and there were empty cartridges and arrowheads lying on all sides." Evidently the Crows had dug pits with their knives in which to make their last stand, but the victors had collected the bodies from them into a small compass so as to perform a war dance around them.

When the surveyors reached the monument at the summit west of Waterton Lakes they were 765 miles from the Red River. Along all of that distance, often struggling through snowstorms or prairie fires, they had erected 388 earth mounds or cairns at intervals of one to three miles. Thenceforth, neither Indians, horse thieves nor whisky peddlers could plead ignorance of where the line lay.

The boundary surveyors had done an excellent job and had done it without fanfare. While their 765-mile expedition west across the barren base of the Palliser Triangle actually ranks as a major feat, they, unlike the much publicized march of the Mounties, did not attract the newspapers' attention. This lack of recognition of the surveyors, who were as hardy plainsmen and woodsmen as any trapper, trader or explorer, has always been the lot of their profession. For they were the sons of Martha, who did their work quietly and whose glory was not acclaim but accuracy.

When in 1870 Canada acquired the Northwest Territories the authorities, anticipating a rush of settlers, had to take three major steps. The first was to decide on a political framework which could take care of the settlers' needs and could adapt as the population increased. The second was to adopt a policy to enable the prospective farmers to obtain possession of parcels of land. The third involved devising a method of dividing the immense region into sections and quarter-sections, and then sending surveyors to carry out that subdivision.

On the political front, the Manitoba Act of 1870 defined the boundaries of a pocket-sized Manitoba (which later on was to be expanded greatly) and created the Northwest Territories. They included all of western Canada except for the colony of British Columbia and the province of Manitoba, and, as well, took in all the territory adjacent to, but at that time not taken into, the colony of Newfoundland or the provinces of Ontario and Quebec.

Pursuant to the Northwest Territories Act of 1875, a separate lieutenant-governor and a council of five were appointed. Moreover, provision was made so that whenever any region not exceeding one thousand square miles attained a population of not less than one thousand men of voting age (excluding Indians) such an area might be proclaimed an electoral district, entitled to send a member to the council. By 1880 under this provision the settlement around Prince Albert qualified to elect a member, but there were too few voters in what we know as Alberta to warrant an elected representative.

This lack of population was a condition which the Dominion government, reserving unto itself the control of resources and the disposition of lands, set about to correct. By 1872 Ottawa had worked out a policy designed to kill two birds with one stone: the settlement of the prairies on the one hand and, on the other, the building of railways to serve the settlers.

For many reasons it was necessary to speed up the building of the railway, the Canadian Pacific Railway across the prairies and mountains to the Pacific coast. The obstacles in the way of financing such a dubious economic venture were as many and as great as the reasons for wanting it. The government solved the financial problem in what everyone at the time agreed was the only possible way—by means of the land through which it had to pass. As a result, under the terms its charter of 1872 the CPR was given twenty-five million acres. A grant so immense as that made an appreciable inroad into even the prairies' seemingly illimitable lands and reduced the amount left for free homesteads.

But the CPR's property was not the only reserve with which the government had to contend. Another was the land belonging to the Hudson's Bay Company. As part of the recompense made to it for ceding its lands, the company was allowed to retain three thousand acres in a block around each of its posts, and, in addition, was to have one-twentieth of the fertile belt reserved to it. As well as these two big slices of land set aside for the CPR and the Hudson's Bay Company there were several smaller reservations such as those for Indians and Métis. In addition to these, the government, with commendable foresight, kept two sections out of every township of thirty-six sections for school lands. The result was that when an immigrant came to select his land he found that in most townships more than one-half of the area was withheld from immediate settlement. Within a few years, of course, the CPR and the Hudson's Bay Company sold many of their sections.

Even though most of the subsequent prairie railways were subsidized by land grants and many millions of acres were thereby taken out of the realm of immediate disposal to farmers—even then the land open for settlement was enough for hundreds of thousands of homesteaders. Eventually they came pouring in at an unprecedented rate; nevertheless, four decades later a considerable amount of land was still open for filing.

The first Dominion Lands Act of 1872 provided for free homesteads

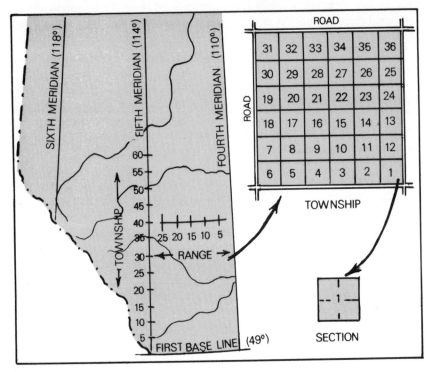

TOWNSHIPS, RANGES AND SECTIONS

When the prairies were subdivided into farms, a series of north and south meridians were laid out. The Fifth Meridian (longitude 114°) passed through Calgary. Between the meridians the land was surveyed into townships which were further divided into sections and quarter-sections.

of 160 acres (a quarter-section) for settlers. After paying a ten dollar filing fee, the homesteader had to comply with a three-year residence clause and another stipulating that within that time he had to break so much land (usually 15 acres) and erect a domicile. When he met these simple requirements, he was given a freehold title to his land. While over the years there were minor modifications to these regulations, on the whole the plan which the government worked out in 1872 served satisfactorily for many decades.

Having devised a method whereby a settler might homestead 160 acres, the authorities had to make haste to parcel out the vast, empty prairies into townships of thirty-six sections and the sections into quarter-sections of 160 acres. About 1871, after the Red River Rebellion had left its stain on Canada's history, the Dominion government set on foot a campaign of surveying on a scale never equalled before or subsequently. It envisioned the eventual subdivision of 183,000,000

A History of Alberta

acres of arable land—some 286,000 sections (square miles) of the Canadian prairies—to be accomplished more rapidly than settlers could rush in to claim them. By the time of Crowfoot's return to his reserve in 1881 some sixteen million acres (100,000 quarter-sections) had been surveyed. But that much work had only whetted the surveyors' appetites. During the following four years over fifty-one million additional acres were done—another 318,794 quarter-sections. Over the decades the process was to go on until in Manitoba, Saskatchewan and Alberta respectively some 210,000, 478,000 and 454,000 sections were surveyed. And no body of men working away through rain or hail, mosquitoes or snow, often far out in the wilderness, ever excelled the fortitude of that generation of rugged surveyors.

The first of the Dominion land surveyors to set up his transit in Alberta was W. S. Gore, who in 1873 laid out the three-thousand-acre reserves to which the Hudson's Bay Company was entitled at Edmonton, Victoria, Fort Assiniboine, Rocky Mountain House, Lac La Nonne, and at six other sites. The next man employed by the Dominion Lands Survey in Alberta was W. F. King, who in 1877 ran the 14th base line in the vicinity of Edmonton. By a strange coincidence, it passed just north of George McDougall's recently built church, and a few years later Edmonton's Jasper Avenue west of First Street was made to conform to it. In 1878 J. S. Dennis, Jr., ran parts of the 4th meridian, which some thirty years later was to form the eastern boundary of Alberta and was to split the Barr colony into two villages, one in Saskatchewan and the other in Alberta, glaring at each other across what had been Lloydminster's main street.

During 1881 the Dominion Lands Survey began the task of sub-dividing several townships in the vicinity of Edmonton and Fort Macleod. At last the task of marking off Alberta's forests and prairies into quarter-sections had begun. At the time, these two, Edmonton, nearly a hundred years old, and Fort Macleod, the recent upstart, were the only significant communities in the province.

Neither the Dominion surveyors nor the boundary commission, however, focussed as much attention on the West as the CPR surveyors. When in 1871 John A. Macdonald swung his Confederation noose and caught British Columbia's head in it, his Canada did indeed stretch from sea to sea. But his neck was also stretched out for he had undertaken to build a railway to the coastal province within ten years.

As a start, Macdonald made Sandford Fleming engineer-in-chief of the visionary CPR. By 1872, sparing neither money nor vigour, Fleming had twenty-five parties of surveyors in the field, six of which were studying various routes through the mountains such as the Yellowhead, Athabasca, Howse and Peace River passes. During 1873–74 they con-

White Progress to 1881

centrated on the Yellowhead Pass as Sandford Fleming tried to compare the merits of seven different routes from Edmonton to the coast. While this survey work continued to be carried on in various parts of the West, by 1875 the route of the line had been determined from the East to the vicinity of Edmonton. Amongst the very few white traders living at Edmonton a new confidence began to reign; before long they hoped to find themselves on the transcontinental railroad enjoying all of its benefits. Edmonton's future appeared excellent.

The arrival of the northern wing of the Mounted Police in the fall of 1874 confirmed that prospect. From Roche Percée in southern Saskatchewan on August 1, 1874, "A" Division under Inspector W. D. Jarvis, Sub-Inspector Gagnon, and Sergeant-Major Sam Steele, split off from the main body and struck out for Edmonton. They took with them twelve half-breeds, twenty-four wagons, fifty-five carts, about fifty-five sick or tired horses, sixty-two oxen, fifty cows and calves, as well as the agricultural implements and general stores (including over 25,000 lbs. of flour) not essential to the main body. Travelling by way of Fort Ellice and Fort Carlton and reaching McDougall's mission at Victoria on October 19 almost in a state of collapse, they struggled on to winter at Edmonton.

The following spring they started to erect their new post, not at Edmonton but at a location some twenty miles farther downstream which they first called Sturgeon Creek Post but soon renamed Fort Saskatchewan. While they were building, the first steamboat ever to ascend the North Saskatchewan River that far puffed by. This was the *Northcote*, which on July 22, 1875, reached Edmonton. Thenceforth the hamlet became the upper terminus of a line of steamboat communication starting at Winnipeg.

Commencing a year later, a small police detachment at Edmonton operated a semi-official post office called Edmonton. It was not until March 1, 1878, however, that a fully official post office was opened under the name of Fort Edmonton, with Richard Hardisty as its properly appointed postmaster.

In 1876, to accommodate the many men who were coming and going, Donald Ross, who had come to Edmonton four years earlier, started its first and famous hotel. Edmonton had begun to acquire some of the amenities of civilization. The transcontinental railway was on its way. Its actual route was still a little vague, but by 1877 the contractors had strung a telegraph line which for the moment terminated near Hay Lakes. It appeared that at last Edmonton's place in the sun was assured.

About 1878 a sprinkling of settlers began to claim land near the hamlet and were able to sustain themselves by agriculture alone if they had to. Bill Cust, an old Forty-niner who had moved to the Sturgeon River from his trading post at Hudson Hope on the Peace River, did more than that. In 1881 he was reported to have sown 130 acres to wheat, thirty-six to barley and twelve to oats.

Out of a handful of curious adventurers who came to Edmonton at this time Frank Oliver stands out. A man of little book learning, he arrived in 1876 and immediately saw possibilities in Edmonton. Paying twenty-five dollars for one of the first lots sold in the town he was to adopt, he tried his luck as a trader for two or three years. Then on December 8, 1880, he put out the first issue of his Edmonton *Bulletin,* the first paper to be published in Alberta and a worthy colleague of the *Saskatchewan Herald,* first paper in the Northwest Territories which Patrick Gammie Laurie printed at Battleford.

The fiery little *Bulletin,* always reflecting Oliver's peppery personality and his Liberal political views, rapidly grew in stature. Its threefold policy, damning John A. Macdonald and the Conservatives, battling for the rights of settlers, and lauding the rich possibilities of the prairies, exerted a great influence. For the student of the early days, its unusual wealth of accurate reporting makes it a gold mine of information.

Starting with the *Northcote* in 1875, steamboats plying the river brought in goods for the Hudson's Bay Company. Then at least as early as 1879, the old pack trail to Athabasca Landing had been cut out to permit the passage of carts hauling freight for the far North. Recently, too, a new trail had come into use to the new Fort Calgary established in 1875. This trail was an extension and a deviation from the one that had been used for decades to reach Rocky Mountain House and Lake Minnewanka. By means of this trail Edmonton hoped to dominate the south country in the same way that for so long it had been the jumping-off place for the far North.

Calgary was conceived in confusion. The building of the fort was delayed, the Mounties sent north from Fort Macleod to man it crossed the river from the north side to reach it, and it had difficulty in deciding what to call itself. Though it quickly recovered and grew from a lusty infant to a busy town and finally to one of the predominant—some say *the* predominant—cities of the plains, it had its problems getting started.

By an order-in-council dated April 10, 1875, the NWMP was authorized to establish a post on the Bow River and Assistant Commissioner Macleod sent Inspector E. Brisbois and fifty men of "F" Troop north to start building. Arriving by a most circuitous route, Brisbois got his first look at the site of Calgary from today's North Hill. Captain C. E. Denny, who was one of the party, never forgot his first view of the valley of Calgary in September 1875, and wrote: "Below us lay a lovely valley, flanked on the south by rolling hills. Thick woods bordered the

119

banks of both streams; to the west towered mountains with their snowy peaks; beyond the Elbow stretched another wide valley, and heavy timber further west along the Bow. Buffalo in large bands grazed in the valley . . . . Our first sight of this enchanting spot was one never to be forgotten, one to which only a poet could do justice."

The party crossed the Bow and in the acute angle between the two rivers chose the site of their future fort. Camped in a tent, with a pile of building logs nearby, were the sole residents of the core of the area which was to become Calgary, Rev. Father Doucet and an Indian boy. In marking out the site of their fortress the police had a free hand for their buildings were the very first to be completed.

Nevertheless, men had not hitherto neglected the area. For centuries the Indians had regarded the forks of these two rivers as a choice campground in a rich and beautiful countryside. Even after whisky traders built posts up the Elbow they continued to frequent the area and their rows with the traders and their fratricidal killings enlivened the brief, bloody era before the police came.

In the course of building their fortress the police found ample evidence of the devastation these traders had wrought. Scattered about not far from their camp and near a death lodge "lay the remains of several Indians mutilated and dismembered by wolves." Farther up the Elbow the charred remnants of Kanouse's post were a reminder of similar debauchery. Here and there human skulls indicated the havoc which whisky had worked.

Before Fort Calgary was built, however, others besides traders had set out to carry on their life's work in the general area of the upper Bow River. In 1872 Father Fourmand and his confrere Father Constantin Scollen, the Irish priest who had started the school in Fort Edmonton, chose a site for a mission on the Elbow River near Bragg Creek. The next year the Methodist McDougalls started their sojourn amongst the Stoney Indians at the spot they called Morley. This venture became a combined ranch and religious institution, for the missionary McDougalls, father George and son John, had found in ranching the only means by which they could support their primary interest, their mission. The other son, David the trader, less interested in souls than in skins and steers, completed the trio which, following in Rev. Rundle's steps, brought Methodism to the Stoneys and the first cattle to the southern foothills.

When taking in these cattle, John McDougall and his brother were the first to cut out the Edmonton–Calgary Trail as far south as the open prairie at Lone Pine, whence their route veered west. They left Edmonton on October 22, 1873, with a double wagon, twenty-nine Red River carts, two other white men and some twenty-five half-breeds, and accompanied

A History of Alberta

by John's wife and family, they led a flock of loose horses and cattle along the crude 200-mile trail. In due course they started their mission.

The next year, perhaps eyeing David McDougall's trade with the Indians, the Hudson's Bay Company sent Angus Fraser from Rocky Mountain House to build a post above the mouth of the Ghost River. At that time everyone referred to the new police post as the Bow Fort and the embryo settlement as the Elbow. When, however, in February 1876 Colonel Macleod, who by this time had been promoted to commissioner of the force, discovered that Inspector Brisbois had issued an order calling the fort after himself, he countermanded it. Writing to the minister of justice at Ottawa, Assistant Commissioner Irvine advanced Colonel Macleod's suggestion that it be called Fort Calgary, a name which according to the colonel meant "clear running water." That name was borne by a castle on the Island of Mull owned by the MacKenzies with whom Macleod was connected by marriage. Although the officials at Ottawa confirmed the name, Gaelic scholars doubt that it has any reference to water. In any event, Colonel Macleod appears to have believed that it did.

Regardless of that, the Mounties' fort did not reign long in solitary glory. While some of I. G. Baker's men were working on the police post, others set to work to build a store for his company. As soon as it was finished, D. W. Davis, who but a few years before had been a whisky trader a short distance up the Elbow River, took charge of it. Father Doucet, who had planned to build at the junction of the two streams, decided to move a mile up the Elbow to the vicinity of today's Holy Cross Hospital. At the same time, on the flat some distance west of the new fort, John McDougall built a log chapel. The Hudson's Bay Company moved one of its buildings to a site east of the Elbow down from the Ghost River. To stock its new store, the company hauled goods from Edmonton by Red River carts. In doing so it inaugurated the Calgary–Edmonton cart trail by continuing south from the Lone Pine, the point to which the McDougall party had cut it two years earlier. Moreover, from time to time several Blackfoot and Sarcees came in to camp on the adjacent flats. By the beginning of 1876 the raw little village had become a bustling centre.

A month later its inhabitants, police, Métis and Blackfoot alike, were to be saddened by the death of Rev. George McDougall. He had been hunting in the vicinity of Nose Creek and evidently died of a stroke or heart attack. At the age of fifty-five, after enduring more than three decades of continual hardship and escaping manifold dangers to promote the cause of his church and to ameliorate the lot of his Indians, George McDougall had passed on to his reward. He had died as he had lived, simply, and still facing forward.

121

After its first burst of activity, Calgary, the crude shack town, marked time. A very few settlers such as John Glenn, who in 1879 broke four and one-half acres at the mouth of Fish Creek, came in to eke out a marginal existence on the flats along nearby rivers. A few ranchers also drove in cattle, but even by 1881 when Crowfoot returned to his reserve fifty miles downstream, Calgary's population was only seventy-five. Perhaps its lack of growth reflected the fact that the NWMP were bringing peace to the area. As fast as new venturers built in the community, the police were withdrawn. Fort Calgary had been established by some fifty of them, but after 1877 when Treaty No. 7 had been signed at Blackfoot Crossing, that number had been reduced to twenty-seven. By 1880 when it had become evident that the action was taking place farther south and that Calgary was a peaceful backwater, only four police were left.

In some ways Calgary's importance paralleled that of the Mounties' post at Tail Creek, the halfway point between Fort Calgary and Fort Saskatchewan. For twenty years or so Tail Creek, which drains Buffalo Lake into Red Deer River, had been a key point in the Métis buffalo running expeditions. Then about 1872 when an early winter caught the hunters far from their home settlements, they had thrown up several shacks along the creek. In 1875 the NWMP had built a log detachment of three buildings and a stockade and for three years stationed a few men there. They were to keep an eye on the Métis and to nab any whisky peddlers who might be expected to come sneaking up from the south. At that time there were perhaps a hundred shacks scattered along the banks of the Red Deer River, as well as on both sides of Tail Creek for some miles from its mouth, or along the shores of Buffalo Lake.

Once the whisky trade was knocked on the head and once it was realized that the few Métis who remained in the vicinity posed no security problem, and, furthermore, once the Calgary–Edmonton Trail by way of Red Deer Crossing came into active life, the number of police at Tail Creek was reduced. In 1878 the detachment was discontinued.

In the fall of 1880, even though affairs at Tail Creek were quiet enough, Calgarians suddenly found themselves astride the powder keg of Chief Bulls Head's rather justifiable anger. Unwilling to move to his recently assigned Sarcee reserve west of Calgary and suffering from the starvation so prevalent in Indian camps, Bulls Head moved his band to the flats surrounding the straggling hamlet and for a few days terrorized everyone there. Shooting off their guns inside the stores, the Indians demanded food and merchandise and made the nights hideous by howling and banging on the walls of buildings. Apparently the police force, then consisting of Sergeant Johnson and three constables, had been too drastically reduced.

When Constable W. Wright made an exhausting, non-stop ride to Fort Macleod, Inspector Crozier there dispatched Captain Denny and about thirty men to the relief of the bedevilled Calgarians. Spurring their horses through the blustery November weather, this force reached Calgary on the second day. Denny insisted that the terrorism stop and that the five hundred or so Sarcees accompany him to Fort Macleod. But Bulls Head refused to move. Finally, when the Sarcees showed no indications of giving in, Denny ordered Sergeant Lauder to begin pulling down the lodges. As they fell, lives dangled in the balance, but the policemen's bold front and bluff succeeded, and the Indians started to pack up and move.

It was not Calgary, however, with its population of seventy-five, which had put Edmonton's nose out of joint but the vibrant village of Fort Macleod far out in the rolling grasslands a hundred miles farther south. Now that the Mounties had driven a stake through the vitals of the whisky trade and by patrolling out from that stake had rubbed out the rule of the six-shooter, ordinarily peaceful folk began to use the fort as a hub about which they could exploit the area's rich resources.

Since they were quick to seize the opportunity Fort Macleod grew into a centre of expanding trade and enterprise. When by December 1874 the crude police post had become habitable, the merchant princes of Fort Benton, the I. G. Baker Company, and the rival T. C. Power & Bro. had erected well stocked stores. Scattered about were two or three other shops, several sod-roofed shacks, the homes of Métis and ox-train drivers, and other establishments. Before long Tony La Chappelle opened his business. Two rectangular billiard tables and two round tables similarly covered with green baize contributed to his support and to the camaraderie of Fort Macleod, for at them, day and night, with their hats shading their eyes, and their black cigars smoking, sat an assortment of frontiersmen pushing in or pulling out red, white or blue poker chips.

In the life of this village, drab to look at but stimulating to live in, the cash spent by the constables supplemented buffalo robes and wolf skins as the medium of exchange. Wagon trains, winding over the long trail to Fort Benton and bringing in the groceries, out-spanned on the gravel flats and then loaded up with robes and hides. Propelled by mules or oxen, urged along by the lurid expletives of bull-whackers and mule-skinners, these wagon trains formed a major industry.

Naturally and without opposition American businessmen had extended their operations into our chinook belt. At that time Alberta had two main communities: Fort Edmonton, supplied with Canadian goods from the East along the Saskatchewan River, and Fort Macleod, supplied from the Missouri. And that supply from the south had helped to establish Alberta's main axis, the Fort Macleod–Fort Edmonton Trail.

But skinners or whackers were not Fort Macleod's only colourful characters. D. W. Davis was such a man. Having been in charge of the notorious Fort Whoop-Up before the police came, he had turned his hand to help build Fort Macleod and Fort Calgary, and then he had gone on to managing Baker's Calgary store. Finally he had returned to manage their emporium at Fort Macleod, and some years later he was to become Alberta's first federal member of Parliament.

Kamoose "Squaw Thief" Taylor was another man worth watching. His varied career, ranging from preacher to whisky trader, finally led to his being one of the Mounties' first captives. Since they had seized his liquor, equipment and robes and fined him as well, he could never bring himself to include them amongst the friends nearest to his heart. Nevertheless, a few years later he built and operated the famous Macleod Hotel, and in due course became a citizen of some esteem.

H. A. Fred Kanouse, bearing a name easily confused with Kamoose, began his Alberta career in a whisky post on the Elbow River. There the Blood Indians wounded him in a skirmish and drove him away. About 1877 he teamed up with Kootenai Brown in a store on the shore of Lower Waterton Lake. After the Indians began to boycott his store, he moved into Fort Macleod and before long brought in some of the south's early cattle.

His partner at Waterton Lake, John George "Kootenai" Brown, was an equally adventurous man. Coming from a genteel Irish family and equipped with a fair education, he served about a year in India as an officer in the First Batallion 8th Regiment before resigning and turning his face towards the new continent. In 1865, on his way east from the gold fields of British Columbia, he got his first view of the Waterton Lakes, continued to what is now Medicine Hat (where in an encounter with a band of Blackfoot he received an arrow in his back), and thence wandered for years as a scout and wolfer south of the 49th parallel. Finally, after killing a man in anger and being acquitted of murder, he returned to the Waterton area in 1877 and teamed up with Fred Kanouse. Thenceforth he was a frequent visitor to Fort Macleod and a character familiar and well-liked by all the ranchers in south-western Alberta.

Long before any ranchers had turned their cows out to fend for themselves in Alberta's chinook belt, however, cattle had found the province's climate tolerable if not always congenial. The first cattle to enter Alberta had been taken to Edmonton House a year or so earlier than 1833, for in that year that post sent "two cows, a heifer and a young bull" to Fort Dunvegan on the Peace River. Moreover, not long after their arrival in the West the Catholic and Methodist missionaries had kept cattle at such places as their Lac Ste. Anne and Victoria stations.

A History of Alberta

It is perhaps not surprising then that the first few cattle taken into southern Alberta were those driven south to the Morley mission in 1873 by Rev. John McDougall. These were augmented during the summer of 1874 when, about the time the Mounted Police column was setting out from Winnipeg, David and John McDougall went to Montana and brought back an additional thirty beasts.

When the police arrived they brought cows with them and almost immediately the I. G. Baker Company, which had contracted to supply the Mounties' needs, drove a further herd to Fort Macleod and slaughtered them there. From then on as individuals such as William Lee at Brockett, Joe McFarland and Harry Olson farther downstream, and others, acquired small herds, cattle became common in the chinook belt.

In 1876 a few men brought other cattle from Montana, and the next year a couple of Mounted Policemen, W. F. Parker and Robert Whitney, both of whom took an early discharge from the force, started ranching in a small way. In a burst of enthusiasm, Sergeant Whitney, while still in the force, had bought twenty-five head which had been trailed in by J. B. Smith of Montana and then faced the problems of having no hay to carry them through the winter. As a result, he simply turned them loose, in spite of the jeers of his companions who predicted that because of Indians, buffalo, unfenced range and storms, he would never see them again. In the spring, two men sent to look for them came back on the second day to report the near miracle of their survival—every one of the beasts was accounted for. This, the first roundup established the fact that cattle could survive and even thrive on Alberta's open range, a fact that other men on their scattered ranches were beginning to realize. Before long other policemen who had completed their three-year service left the force to try their hand at ranching, men like H. Bell, J. D. Murray and Robert Patterson.

With white ranchers and settlers poking around along the Oldman River and the North Saskatchewan River, it was only natural that they should start probing into Alberta's other resources. When they did they were well pleased, for sticking out of the cutbanks they found several seams of good coal, while clothing the foothills and the vast areas north of Edmonton great stands of spruce timber swayed in the breezes. As early as 1875 the police operated a sawmill at Fort Macleod. About the same time but two miles east of Edmonton, the Hudson's Bay Company got its sawmill into operation. Alberta's lumbering, which was to become such an important industry, had already started.

Coal mining got away to an earlier start. For decades, of course, the blacksmiths at Edmonton House had picked some coal out of the river banks to use in their forges. From time to time some of the whisky

125

traders in the chinook belt had pried a few loads of coal out of the southern river banks. It fell to the lot of Nicholas Sheran, however, to mine coal as a commercial venture.

Sheran, a typical Irish adventurer, had fought during the American Civil War's terrible battle of Gettysburg and then, after drifting to Montana, came to Alberta in 1870 looking for gold with J. J. Healy. After fruitlessly panning several streams, he hit his own bonanza at the junction of the St. Mary and Oldman rivers. For there he started a coal mine. In 1872, finding that site unprofitable, he selected a new one in the valley over which later on the CPR trestle was to span the river at modern Lethbridge. Before long he was shipping coal down the Whoop-Up Trail to Fort Benton, and when the police built Fort Macleod he supplied fuel to them. As a consequence of his enterprise, the site of his new mine—the future Lethbridge—was called Coal Banks.

During 1879, to shift the centre of operation of the NWMP farther east where the Sioux were becoming a problem, the authorities decided to make Fort Walsh the headquarters of the force. As a result, the number of men stationed at Fort Macleod was materially reduced. That was the year when for the first time the police lost one of its men by Indian action. In the vicinity of Fort Walsh, while performing an unimportant errand, Constable A. Graburn was shot in the back and killed. A Blood Indian by the name of Star Child was suspected of the murder, but at his trial he was acquitted for lack of evidence.

While white men had been treading softly and all the while creeping in to lay claim to some select spring or water course and looking to a future filled with promise, the natives, such as the Blackfoot, were undergoing their Gethsemane. At the end of 1881 Edgar Dewdney, the Indian commissioner, made an estimate of the number of natives on the plains of Alberta and Saskatchewan; he arrived at the figure of 11,577, without counting the five thousand around Fort Walsh (mainly Sioux) and another four thousand Canadian Indians which he believed to be wandering in the United States. Out of the total, Alberta probably had a larger number than Saskatchewan.

Finally all these Indians had realized that the buffalo were gone. Now and suddenly, they had been obliged to choose the least disastrous of the scanty alternatives before them. That was to live within the confines of their reserves onto which the prospect of starvation, a prospect deliberately manipulated to some extent by the white authorities, had driven them. As independent people their race was run. Although the authorities had undertaken to feed them, provided they resided on their reserves, and had made a valiant attempt to do so, they found it a task beyond their means. The irony of the situation was that the Indians' desperate need for meat provided a market for the very ranchers who

A History of Alberta

were now beginning to occupy the natives' long-time homeland. The authorities had to turn to the ranchers to supply the meat for the Indians. Ironically the needs of the natives, whose lands the ranchers had usurped, turned out to be the means whereby these interlopers gained their foothold.

In 1881 the white men in Alberta—some fifteen hundred including Métis—were a mere handful compared to the thousands of Indians. A census of all those who stood still long enough to be counted indicated that the Métis and whites living in the general vicinity of the North Saskatchewan River—263 at the Edmonton settlement and others at Lac Ste. Anne, Fort Saskatchewan, Lac La Biche, etc.—totalled 766. At or adjacent to Fort Calgary lived another hundred or so, while those in and around Fort Macleod probably added up to five hundred.

Even before the land was surveyed they had come in to spy out the region of the foothills and the chinook belt, and, having looked, found it a land, if not all milk and honey, at least of clear, gravelly streams, upland meadows and hillsides beautiful in their carpet of flowers or knee-deep in succulent grass. As deepening shadows, which were to last a century, began to creep over the Indian reserves, the morning sun had begun to shine for the white man. From the Coal Banks west and from Calgary south—all over Alberta's majestic southwest—up the Elbow and the Belly, the Highwood and the Oldman rivers; up the creeks, the Fish and Sheep, the Willow, Meadow and Mosquito, the Olsen, Oxley and Lyndon creeks, white men with the wind in their faces and the sun on their backs sought out the land and found it glorious.

As a white man's haven Alberta's morning had dawned. The Indians had been elbowed aside. The tide of settlement was starting to lap at its edges. Year after year the scurrying surveyors were coming to know more of Alberta's interior and were marvelling at its soil's richness, while far away in the East, dawdling politicians held out the promise of a railway.

# 9
# Railroad and Rebellion
# 1881-1885

By 1881 nearly a thousand adventurous white men had lifted a corner of the curtain of Alberta's stage and peered in expectantly. What they saw, whether along the North Saskatchewan River or in the chinook belt, was vastly encouraging. North of the coal along the Saskatchewan River lay unlimited forests; south of it, rich parklands. In the chinook belt, coal, timber and rippling grasslands extended all along the foothills, while farther east, grazed only by deer, antelope and gophers, stretched endless flower-strewn, rolling pastures scented by wolf willow or sage. In short, they had peered into a land ready to flow with milk and honey.

All of these pioneers, focussing on the future, averted their eyes from a reality of the present: the natives. Only the Mounties and a few government officials, trying to tuck the Indians into reserves and trying even more desperately to feed them, felt the victor's twinge of conscience at the vanquished's plight. For the Indians, defeated not by the white man's superior force but by starvation, were and continued to be in a pitiable state. For them there appeared to be no future.

By contrast, to a thousand or so white pioneers the future was rosy. The wealth of a vast province lay before them and all that was needed to develop it were settlers, capital and a railway, and all three were on their way. Thus far admittedly these forerunners of the multitudes yet to come had only sketched in the rough outlines of the white man's toehold. All they had established was the bridgehead of three villages, Edmonton, Calgary and Fort Macleod, with a line of communication connecting them. As yet it was but a crude trail coming up from Montana, running north four hundred miles to Edmonton and then stretching sketchily for another hundred miles to the Athabasca River. It was Alberta's tenuous backbone. In the future it would be Alberta's main axis.

Edmonton, the ninety-year-old top knob on Alberta's spine, with its Agricultural Society (organized in 1879) and some seven hundred people in its environs, was the largest community. South of it, two hundred miles through the bush and far out on the open prairies, lay Edmonton's little upstart neighbour, Calgary, a hamlet of seventy-five people around the Mounted Police post. Another hundred miles or so down the trail at the rump of the province, Edmonton's only real rival, Fort Macleod, a brawling brat which, including ranchers, could muster some five hundred adults, would bear watching.

Because of these three centres and because the plains immediately west of Winnipeg were beginning to attract more settlers, it became advisable to divide the prairie portion of the Northwest Territories into four official districts. By an order-in-council on May 8, 1882, these four, Assiniboia, Saskatchewan, Athabasca and Alberta, were established. The first three were logical names to confer on their areas, but the fourth, with Edmonton on the North Saskatchewan River at one end of it and Fort Macleod on the Oldman River at the other, presented more of a problem. Fortunately it came to bear the last name of the Princess Louise, wife of the Marquis of Lorne, Canada's Governor General.

For the time being, in the sense that they had no elected representation, these new districts had no political significance. Representation was extended not to these districts as such but was confined to any areas which had at least one thousand voters. Of these in 1880 the region around Prince Albert had been erected into the electoral district of Lorne and could send a member to the Northwest Territories Council. It was to be 1883 before any other areas reached that status. That year the capital of the Northwest Territories, which for four years had sojourned in Battleford, was transferred to Regina. That year also, because enough settlers had filtered in, five other such electoral districts were set up: Regina, Qu'Appelle, Moose Jaw, Broadview and Edmonton. Frank Oliver, the editor of the Edmonton *Bulletin,* was elected to represent Edmonton, but the centre of gravity of the prairies' population was slipping ever farther to the south. By 1884 over two thousand pioneers had reached Alberta and, now that the Canadian Pacific Railway had crossed the prairies and provided a means of getting their stock to market, most of them had come to try their luck at ranching.

Never in Canada's history has there been an era so romantic as that of the early ranching days in Alberta's foothills. Begotten of English dams by American fathers and suckled on the grasses of the glorious chinook belt, ranching grew to be a way of life never duplicated in any other time or area. Sired by the great cowboy era in the western states, it inherited its language and its trappings from its father. Out of Britain's Victorian era—a mother, who, crossing the ocean (bringing her culture, her money and often her cattle with her), embraced the magnificence of the chinook belt and then insisted on operating a ranche (with an *e*) —this hybrid filled a lusty span of twenty years of Alberta's history— and Alberta's exclusively.

With such parentage, ranching in Alberta was a far cry from its cousin south of the border. From its father it learned the care of the stock, the distinctive dress and the lingo. But its mother's traditions infused it with a distinct spirit and it became a happy synthesis of the codes of Victorian England's upper class with those of the Great Plains frontier. As Dr. L. G. Thomas has said, "the body is American but the spirit is English." With their ranch homes decorated like English country houses, formal hunts with their etiquette straight from England, polo playing, and formal dress for dinner, British cattlemen preserved the amenities. Bringing to their area a welcome atmosphere of gracious living which now after nearly a century still sets the chinook belt apart as a distinct region, they played dramatic parts. And never in Canada's history have actors played on such a magnificent stage as the foothills belt or against such a majestic backdrop as Alberta's mountains.

The starting point of commercial ranching in the area was the year 1881, the year Crowfoot brought his hungry band back to Fort Macleod. That year times were good, cattle prices were rising and, above all, the CPR, so long bound up in political problems, broke free and started across the prairies. That year too the government of Canada opened the flood gates and made it possible for one man or one company to lease up to one hundred thousand acres of crown lands at a yearly rental of one cent per acre. And soon many a man and many a company came forward to start a ranch.

While for a few years a number of owners had grazed sizeable herds, Senator M. H. Cochrane, a man of long experience in raising and breeding cattle in Quebec, became the first of the large-scale ranchers. In May 1881 he incorporated a company with a capital of $500,000, secured a lease of one hundred thousand acres west of Fort Calgary, and the Cochrane Ranche Company Limited, which was to suffer a history of failure and tragedy, but which finally enjoyed success, was on its way. After two or three almost disastrous years at Cochrane, the senator moved the scene of the ranch operation to a lease between the Oldman and the Waterton rivers where reward attended his efforts.

Ranching on that scale was a risky business and one which not only called for experienced men but for extensive financial resources. Fortunately neither men nor money were lacking and within two or three years of 1881 several large ranches, backed by capital from eastern Canada, Britain and the United States, lent their colour and their legends to the history of the chinook belt. By 1884 the Department of the Interior at Ottawa reported that forty-seven ranches, large and small, had leased 1,785,690 acres in the area. A year later, an additional million acres were leased. Not all of these followed through but some of those which went on to success were the Oxley, the North-West Cattle Company, the Walrond, Quorn, Maunsell and the Cypress Cattle Company.

A History of Alberta

Another interesting ranch was the MCC owned by the Military Colonization Company and organized and operated by Major-General T. Bland Strange. It was located on good range along the Bow River, but, being practically next door to Crowfoot's Blackfoot reserve, suffered its share of cattle mysteriously going astray. The Cypress Cattle Company, located south of Medicine Hat, is indicative of the fact that ranching was not confined to the foothills country but spread out far to the east. Other ranchers took up leases around Medicine Hat: James F. Sanderson, the Hargraves, Mitchells and Samuel Porter and his three sons and son-in-law, John Hawke, whose grandchild became the first white male to be born in Medicine Hat.

Since Fort Macleod found itself to be the commercial centre of the ranching area, it grew much faster than the little village of Calgary. When, after July 1882, ex-Mountie C. E. D. Wood's *Macleod Gazette* became the second newspaper to be published in Alberta, the world began hearing more about the wind-swept town in the heart of the grasslands.

About the same time the *Gazette* started, Kamoose Taylor aided the cause by launching the Macleod Hotel. And, under the circumstances, launched is undoubtedly the proper verb, for he notified one and all that: "The Bar in the Annex will be open day and night. All Day drinks, 50 cents each; Night drinks, $1.00 each. No Mixed Drinks will be served except in case of death in the family."

John D. Higinbotham, who in 1884 started Alberta's first drug store in Fort Macleod, has left us a good description of this hostelry with its rooms partitioned from each other by factory cotton. It was he who copied down the Macleod Hotel Rules and Regulations which Kamoose, in a moment of hilarity in keeping with the spirit of the place, posted on its bulletin board. While they are too long to reproduce in entirety, the following samples are worth passing on.

"Spiked boots and spurs must be removed at night before retiring.

"Towels changed weekly. Insect Powder for sale at the bar.

"Special Rates to 'Gospel Grinders' and the 'Gambling Perfesh.'

"A deposit must be made before towels, soap or candles can be carried to rooms. When boarders are leaving, a rebate will be made on all the candles or parts of candles not burned or eaten.

"No kicking regarding the quality or quantity of meals will be allowed; those who do not like the provender will get out, or be put out.

"Guests without baggage must sleep in the vacant lot, and board elsewhere until their baggage arrives.

"To attract attention of waiters or bell boys, shoot a hole through the door panel. Two shots for ice water, three for a deck of cards, and so on.

"All guests are requested to rise at 6 a.m. This is imperative as the sheets are needed for tablecloths."

But whether or not the guests were early risers or had to attract attention by shooting, one and all of them had one predominant topic of conversation—the progress of the CPR. In 1881 the voice of the hammer had begun to be heard in the prairies—the ring of the sledge spiking rails to ties. In Calgarians' ears it had a celestial peal but to Edmontonians who had counted so eagerly on its being built through their hamlet its sepulchral chime sounded the knell of their town's pre-eminence in Alberta.

In the south, however, the signs were more encouraging. In February 1881, with John A. Macdonald back in office, the government had come to grips with the railway problem and passed the act of Parliament which brought the CPR one step nearer reality. The CPR began actual construction, and by September 1881 was as far west as Brandon, Manitoba. Moreover, the railway's new management had decided to change the route of the line and to build it straight west across southern Saskatchewan, to run it up the valley of the Bow River and to force it through Hector's incredibly difficult Kicking Horse Pass. Instead of working its way north and west from Brandon, following generally the decades-old trail from Winnipeg to Fort Carlton and thence up the North Saskatchewan River through Battleford, the erstwhile capital of the western prairies, and finally through the fur traders' gently sloping Yellowhead Pass, it was run straight west through the cactus of the Palliser Triangle. The Dominion government, worrying about protecting the prairies' southern border from American invasion, had changed the route! Calgarians rejoiced.

Instead of a railway, Edmontonians had to get along with a stage coach line and Flatboat McLean took on a mail contract for Prince Albert, Battleford and Edmonton. At intervals of forty miles along the trail from Qu'Appelle to Humboldt and thence north to Prince Albert and west to Edmonton, he arranged for the erection of stage stations and stopping houses. Wagons especially built for the job and drawn by four horses hurried passengers, mail and express along the trail.

But the southern prairies woke up. The prairies which so recently had rumbled to the rush of the buffalo herds now felt a new rumble as graders, track-laying men and steam locomotives pushed the rusty new rails west. Now, thousands of men, sweating and straining, carousing and fighting, rushed the rails along. The work was all done by men and mule power—except for locomotives no real machines came into play. Horses and mules with crude graders and dump carts scored the sod, gouged out the larger cuts and piled up the larger fills. Men with hand shovels and wheelbarrows followed, heaving up the lesser grades while others carried the rails forward and dropped them where the men with sledge hammers could spike them down. For unlike later railways no mechanical track-layer eased their burden.

Young Canada's greatest accomplishment was on its way. And it was a magnificent accomplishment: the work of John A. Macdonald with his

Sketch showing the present-day
major railways.

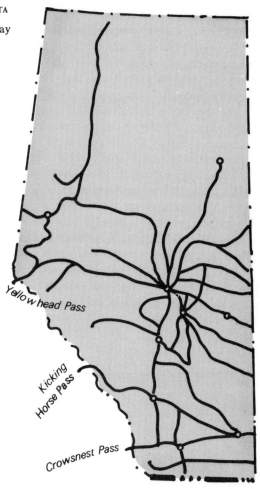

*Yellowhead Pass*

*Kicking Horse Pass*

*Crowsnest Pass*

persistence and political manoeuvring; the daring of George Stephen,
Donald Smith and Duncan McIntyre; the heavy hand of William Cornelius
Van Horne and his directing genius, and the stamina of the labouring men
who built it. Keeping up with the railway, settlers started to pour in to
the prairies—over 25,000 in 1881, about 100,000 in 1882—and the rush
was merely starting. In February 1883 immigration sheds were built at
Qu'Appelle to shelter the throngs of settlers. By March, Regina was incorporated; in May, Moose Jaw sought incorporation; in June, Swift
Current flashed into existence. And so it went—Medicine Hat, Gleichen
and Calgary, until by December the steel was laid 121 miles beyond
Calgary.

In its brisk canter across the prairies the CPR entered our Alberta a

Railroad and Rebellion 1881-1885

few miles north of the Mounties' Fort Walsh. From there on it worked out sidings where towns were later to spring up: Walsh, Irvine and Dunmore. At Dunmore the engineers faced the trickiest problem they had tackled for hundreds of miles—how to cross the broad South Saskatchewan which lay some six miles ahead and which involved a drop in elevation of some 250 feet.

By now they had ceased to marvel at the quaint names, such as Pile of Bones Creek and Moose Jaw, but here at Dunmore in an area replete with strange names they had to descend Bullshead Creek to its junction with Seven Persons Creek at a spot on the banks of the Saskatchewan known as *Saamis*, or the Medicine Hat—surely the most memorable of all names.

Its derivation is explained in as many ways as there are romantically inclined narrators. Some say it comes from the special hat which a brave had to give to mollify an angry chief whose prettiest, youngest wife he had seduced. Some give other stories involving maidens (always beautiful) either cast into the river or voluntarily sacrificing themselves. Souls more prosaic and probably closer to the truth maintain that during a fight with the Blackfoot a Cree medicine man lost his hat in the river. But no matter what its real meaning may have been, Medicine Hat is a unique gift from the Indians to our pioneer nomenclature.

When on June 10, 1883, the first locomotive reached The Hat, it was a town entirely of tents. After crossing the river on a temporary wooden bridge, the CPR set out to push its line over the next 180 miles of prairie. Over the flat, sparsely grassed prairie flecked with sage brush, with the great Sand Hills and the Rainy Hills as dim outlines on their left, the surveyors swept on. Leaving stakes to mark sidings that would eventually house cattle shipping pens, they hurried on until in sight of the Jumping Buffalo Hill, without giving the matter a passing thought, they began pounding their pegs into Crowfoot's reserve. There the chief and his associates, bristling with anger over this invasion of their land, bid fair to prevent further progress until Father Lacombe, hastily called as a peace-maker, rushed to prevent hostilities.

Eventually in sight of the mighty wall of the mountains to the west and on a straight stretch between the sidings bearing their names, the contracting firm of Langdon and Shepard established a record by laying five miles of track in one day. Whereas the first locomotive had reached Medicine Hat on June 10, the first train to whistle its way into Calgary did so two months later, on August 11—180 miles of track had been spiked down in two months.

Then, leaving Calgarians to uncork champagne, light bonfires and ring bells, Van Horne hurled his rails towards the mountains. But the going was rougher now; up the Bow River past the Cochrane Ranche, the Morley mission and old Bow Fort, unoccupied nearly fifty years.

Passing between Mount Rundle and Cascade Mountain as Sir George Simpson had over forty years earlier, the railway paused briefly by Tunnel Mountain through which the engineers had proposed at first to tunnel but later found a route around instead. A few miles up the Bow River, a spot beneath the ramparts of Castle Mountain aroused the prospecting instincts of many a labourer and since showings of silver rewarded their efforts, they stopped to create the town of Silver City. It mushroomed so quickly that the next year while the Dominion land surveyors were laying out Calgary's townsite, they were instructed to subdivide Silver City. Unfortunately, though it was one of Alberta's earliest towns, its boom broke and it quickly vanished. But the railroad builders swept on, scrambling over the Kicking Horse Pass, scaring goats atop Rogers Pass, starting the town of Revelstoke at the last crossing of the Columbia River. Some twenty-five miles further west, they laid out the station grounds at Craigellachie.

There, faraway in the Selkirk Mountains, Donald Smith drove the CPR's last spike in November of 1885. The impossible had been accomplished and now by means of this railway Canada really stretched from sea to sea. Now with the CPR the West must surely start to fill up. Now settlers had easy access to the rich lands of the West. Now the ranchers of southern Alberta could find a market for their cattle and a way to export them. Previously Calgary had been a mere way station on the trail from Edmonton to Macleod; it quickly set about changing that status.

For that August day when the locomotive rolled over the Elbow change was in the air. Calgarians, well over a hundred of them, realizing this, rejoiced. They were a forward looking band: George Jacques, Major James Walker, James Lougheed the lawyer, and others. Amongst them were some seventy-five Mounted Policemen, most of whom had recently been moved from Blackfoot Crossing and now occupied new and pretentious quarters built with lumber from Walker's mill. Rubbing shoulders with them was George Murdoch, then a harness-maker but soon to be Calgary's first mayor, and Dr. Henderson the town's first civilian physician, as well as T. B. Bradon, who, with the intention of starting a newspaper, had arrived a day ahead of the steel.

To add to the jubilation, some four hundred labourers, paid that very day, celebrated. As Bradon later recollected: "The whole day was a succession of sports and amusements of various kinds. There was a foot race of two hundred yards for five hundred dollars a side, and the outside betting ran away into the thousands. About $5,000 changed hands on the horse races. The saloons and billiard halls raked in the money by barrelfuls; the merchants drove a thriving trade, and the whole day was a continued round of excitement. . . . Whiskey flowed freely, and the night was made hideous with yelling, screaming and blasphemy." With an exuberance that is the envy of more straight-laced cities, an exuberance which over the decades Calgarians have frequently exhibited, they rejoiced. And well they may have for at that moment Calgary began its rapid transformation to a city. Previously it was what Bradon called "a row of tents on the bank of the Elbow which I was informed was Calgary. The tents were all either saloons or restaurants, and I got a very fair meal in the Far West Hotel. I asked about lodging, and was told that I could sleep on the floor in my blanket."

That day, celebrating no less and passing crystal goblets from hand to hand, another group of pioneers sat nearby in a private railway car as the guests of George Stephen, the president of the CPR. Amongst them were some of the great men who by their courage had brought this vast enterprise into being: Donald Smith, William Van Horne and R. B. Angus, along with the "black-robed voyageur" who had laboured so long in the West, Father Lacombe. To him the CPR owed much, but for him the recent unpleasant incident when the Blackfoot had stopped the surveyors could have become a serious one. On that occasion the CPR had hurried to the Oblate priest to ask him to intervene, and he too had hurried. Taking with him two hundred pounds of tea, some sugar, flour and tobacco, he conferred with the Blackfoot chiefs, first "opening his mouth" with the presentation of these gifts. Counting heavily on the respect in which they held him and using all his powers of persuasion, he won them over. Within a few hours he had smoothed the situation.

And now, amid many speeches and toasts, the directors conceived and carried out a unique way of showing their gratitude to the tireless priest. At the appointed moment they convened a directors' meeting and President Stephen rose and temporarily resigned his position. Then, to the black-robe's bewilderment, upon motion by R. B. Angus, a motion received with applause and unanimously carried, Father Lacombe was elected president of the CPR. Thus these men, as great in their way as he was in his, acknowledged their debt to the missionary; for an hour he remained the president of the CPR and for a lifetime they allowed him a free pass over their railway.

With a spirit no less courteous than theirs, he accepted the office and then in return mischievously nominated George Stephen to the rectorship of his Calgary St. Mary's parish. Amid more laughter and applause the ex-president accepted his new dignity as with a glance out the car window at the village he exclaimed "poor souls of Calgary, I pity you!"

But the poor souls of Calgary needed no pity. The city's first white child had been born on November 17, 1883—a boy who was named John Calgary Costello. Striking out in all directions Calgary's citizens were starting to seize the opportunities in front of them and to transform the town. Amongst the first to aid in its transformation was R. B. Bradon, who in association with A. M. Armour, set up his press (the first to reach Alberta by train) in a tent with a wooden floor and began publication of the *Calgary Herald—Mining and Ranche Advocate and General Advertiser* on August 31, 1883. Even though its first weekly papers had to be mailed from the Mounted Police post office, it was only a matter of days before James Bannerman became Calgary's first official postmaster and dispensed mail at his flour and feed store.

From then on Calgary grew apace. One of its first projects was to seek representation on the Northwest Territories Council which now sat at Regina, the new capital of the Territories. Doing so involved taking a census, which revealed Calgary's population to be 428, and that, combined with the people in the adjoining area, entitled the district to a representative. In short order Calgarians elected J. D. Geddes to take his seat beside Frank Oliver, the other Albertan who for a year had represented the Edmonton district. In August 1884, as well as beginning a campaign for a school, local enthusiasts organized the Calgary Agricultural Society. Then on November 17 the town of Calgary was incorporated, and at the subsequent election held within a few weeks George Murdoch was declared its first mayor. Bright and early in Boynton's Hall on the morning of December 4, the council held its first meeting and then in short order adjourned until eight P.M. when they met in the less frigid atmosphere of Beaudoin and Clarke's saloon. As the very hours passed, Calgary's prospects glowed a rosier red.

Thus rapidly Calgary began to fill out the mantle which the CPR had dropped over its shoulders, the mantle of being Alberta's foremost town. Fort Macleod in the south and Edmonton in the north became its outposts. Both of them, however, began taking steps to improve the old trails leading to Calgary and to organize stages to operate back and forth on regular schedules. Once the railway reached Calgary the freight for the far North came that distance by rail and then was hauled in wagons to Edmonton and transhipped along the Landing Trail which was reconstructed as far as the Athabasca River. From there, on account of the Grand Rapids, the freight had to go by scows from Athabasca Landing to Fort McMurray, where in 1883 the Hudson's Bay Company built the steamboat *Grahame* to ply from that point down to Fort Smith. Before long, in catering to the increased business in the far North, Edmonton found itself busier than ever.

As for the southern part of the province, the presence of the railway quickly decapitated the long established connections with Fort Benton, and from 1883 the Whoop-Up Trail began to decline in importance. Fort Macleod, however, continued to grow and to attract men of high calibre, such as a young man of great promise who came in 1884, a lawyer, F. W. G. Haultain. The town had its rivals and with every wagonload of

137

coal hauled across from Coal Banks thirty-five miles away came news of events threatening Fort Macleod's dominating position.

Sir Alexander Galt, a father of Confederation, had become interested in Nick Sheran's mine and had organized the North-Western Coal and Navigation Company. By December 1882, with William Lethbridge of England as president, E. T. Galt as manager and William Stafford as mine superintendent, the company had embarked upon large scale mining operations. All this had been made possible by the fact that the locomotives of the CPR, which were expected to reach Medicine Hat before long, would provide a market for the coal, and, moreover, would open up a way of hauling any coal which they did not burn to customers as far east as Winnipeg. Within a matter of weeks after the company began developing its mine and a large labour force moved to the site, the authorities set up a post office to serve them and called it Coalhurst.

One of the North-Western Coal Company's first problems was how to get the coal to the railway at Medicine Hat; sending it down the Bow River by steamer and barge seemed to be a likely solution. Accordingly the company constructed craft for this purpose, and in July 1883 the hull of the company's first steamer, 173 feet long, was completed and launched at Coal Banks and floated down to Medicine Hat. There the machinery, which had come from Pittsburgh by rail, was installed and in due course the new sternwheeler, named the *Baroness*, hauled some empty barges upstream to the mine.

As navigable streams, the stretches of the Oldman and the South Saskatchewan rivers between Lethbridge and Medicine Hat leave much to be desired, and for the remaining part of the season during which navigation was possible only two hundred tons of coal reached the railway. To remedy this situation, the company built a small sternwheeler, the *Alberta*, one hundred feet long, and a tugboat of thirty-five feet, the *Minnow*. When the 1884 navigation season opened, these three steamers and twenty-five barges were ready to haul coal downstream. Although the fleet delivered some ten thousand tons that summer, it was soon apparent that, because of the short season when the river was high enough to navigate (about a month), sending coal by water was an unreliable venture and the company cast about for other means of transport.

Coalhurst, the site of the mine, grew until by the beginning of 1885 it bid fair to rival Fort Macleod in size. By that time Edmonton, with its 125 white adults, and Calgary with over five hundred, together with the towns of Fort Macleod, Coalhurst and Medicine Hat, were the cardinal points of the framework of the future Alberta. As yet it had barely started to flesh out. A smattering of white people growing a few vegetables and milking a few cows occupied the various missions. Along the CPR at a few sidings, Gleichen, Canmore, Banff and Silver City, a handful of railway employees prodding with their picks tried to keep the recently laid rails

A History of Alberta

in approximate alignment. Along the trails at various places, later to be known as Wetaskiwin, Red Deer, High River, and others, a few optimists had come in to keep stopping places. Scattered here and there south of the Bow River from Medicine Hat to Morley, several ranchers were becoming bitter because starving Indians killed their cattle. In all of Alberta some five thousand white-skinned people had established a bridgehead.

Compared to these, there were a quarter as many Métis, mainly in the vicinity of the North Saskatchewan River, and probably eight thousand Indians scattered about the district of Alberta. One concentration of their reserves was clustered around Edmonton. Another grouping of two or three more straddled the Calgary–Edmonton Trail on either side of Ponoka, while not far from Calgary other reservations contained hundreds of plains Indians as disgruntled as their relations on the large reserves tributary to Fort Macleod and Lethbridge.

This, then, was the state of affairs during the early months of 1885 when for the first time white men and Métis began to look upon each other with suspicion. Trouble was in the air and, if it should come to open hostilities between Métis and whites, everyone wondered whose cause the Indians would espouse.

During the summer of 1884, at the invitation of the Métis of the Batoche area of Saskatchewan, Louis Riel had ridden north to stir their pot of bitterness—Louis Riel, variously regarded as the villain or the hero of the 1869 Red River Rebellion. Once more the monumental short-sightedness of the faraway Ottawa government had set alight the Métis' easily inflamed suspicions. Once more the questions of land rights and surveys had released the telltale smoke of rebelliousness and thereby revealed the presence of the deep-seated fire smouldering beneath the Métis' otherwise jocular countenances.

On the reserves, moreover, the Indians' dire economic plight was far worse than that of their mixed blood relatives. The once free plainsmen, forced to bend the knee to rough and often hostile political appointees of the Indian department, suffered from inadequate rations doled out haughtily and from provisions such as flour which was often inedible. For in that era, although the Ottawa civil service was composed of innumerable capable men, their hands were tied by political patronage of the worst kind and their policies were hampered by appointees whose main aim in life was to loll in political immunity and gorge at the public trough. Even on Crowfoot's reserve in January 1882 Indian resentment at their flagrant treatment nearly flared into open fisticuffs with the Indian department's employees. More and more Crowfoot turned an attentive ear to Big Bear and other Cree chiefs, including Poundmaker, his adopted son, who came reporting tales of Cree and Assiniboine unrest along the North Saskatchewan River.

Anticipating some of the thoughts fighting for ascendency in the chief's mind, Lieutenant-Governor Edgar Dewdney tried to offset some of them by taking Crowfoot and two or three other prominent Blackfoot chiefs on a railway trip to Winnipeg. There with his rock-hard face as immutable as ever, Crowfoot saw the brick houses, streets and multitudes in a white man's city, and for the first time realized that though he and his abused colleagues could easily wipe out the shack town villages of Alberta, it would avail them nothing in their conflict with the white man's might.

With the stupidity and incompetence of the Indian department employees angering him, with Poundmaker and other Crees inclining him towards turning on white men and finally Dewdney confronting him with a picture more striking than words, Crowfoot had a bad time. But in the showdown, which everyone knew was coming, no one, neither the white police whom he now regarded coolly, nor the Métis whom he found hard to tolerate, nor Big Bear and his Crees—none knew which way he would jump. Neither did he.

Then on March 27, 1885, the telegraph keys at Edmonton and Calgary tapped out the terse message: "Métis attacked at Duck Lake yesterday, ten police killed. Louis Riel and Gabriel Dumont victorious." Then in the northern hamlet the telegraph went dead. The North-West Rebellion had been touched off.

Fortunately its course was run far away in Saskatchewan and, except for the killings at Frog Lake near the Saskatchewan border, only its rumours disturbed Alberta's white people. Even at that its echoes stirred up lively reactions as Albertans took steps to defend themselves or to carry the war to the enemies' camp. The story of the North-West Rebellion has been told so often that there is no need to go into it in detail here. Its battles were fought in Saskatchewan and for our purpose we need only to study its interesting repercussions in Alberta.

Edmonton, so close to the Métis settlements at Lac Ste. Anne, St. Albert, Lac La Biche and the Salvais community, was very liable to attack. Fortunately the Roman Catholic and Methodist clergy exerted a restraining influence on most of the half-breeds in their bailiwicks, and on up to one thousand native warriors whose reserves were all within a day's march of the hamlet of 125 white souls. Calgary, even with several hundred Sarcee Indians on the reserve next door and well over a thousand more a mere fifty miles down the Bow River at Blackfoot Crossing, was in less danger and indeed contributed men to go to Edmonton's relief. Fort Macleod, feeling itself fairly safe, also contributed men who rode away in the direction of the forests of northern Alberta.

Edmonton had an uneasy time. For eight weeks it was in a position of defence; for six weeks Edmontonians lived in dread of rifle shots

A History of Alberta

roaring out from the bush which ringed the little settlement; for one week a state of panic prevailed.

During these weeks Frank Oliver's *Bulletin* tried to face up to the facts: "When the Indians around Edmonton will rise appears now to be only a question of days. What they will do in that case or what numbers they will be joined by is something which can be better decided after the event."

On Wednesday, April 8, Edmontonians decided to send to Calgary for help and from there to wire the authorities of the Northwest Territories and of Ottawa. James Mowatt, who volunteered to ride to Calgary, made a remarkable trip. All alone, but dropping in on the four or five settlers who lived along the trail, obtaining fresh horses from them and making his way through several Indian reserves, he delivered his message to General Strange, thirty-six hours after leaving Edmonton.

The day after Mowatt left Edmonton, S. B. Lucas came in from his farm on Bigstone Creek to say that the Indians had ordered him to get out. With him came the men from the mill at the Battle River. They, too, had been driven out when the Indians raided it and took all the provisions.

By this time most of the families in the Edmonton area had moved in to Fort Edmonton, Fort Saskatchewan or to the Roman Catholic mission at St. Albert for refuge. On Monday the 13th the Lac Ste. Anne Indians, headed by Chief Alexis, entered the Hudson's Bay store there and demanded some goods. Similar depredations took place at Beaverhills Lake and at the Salvais settlement on the Battle River.

On Saturday Frank Oliver, looking back over the week, declared: "That an unmistakable panic existed in Edmonton town and district on Saturday afternoon and Sunday last must be universally admitted as well as the fact now apparent that it was groundless. . . . The movement on Saturday and Sunday was a stampede into the fort and to St. Albert. . . . It is 15 days since we last heard from Battleford and the same since we heard from Saddle Lake. . . . Ten days have elapsed since our messenger went to Calgary and we have not heard." Edmontonians had been in such a panic that, according to the *Bulletin,* "The Literary Society did not meet this week."

But on Friday, April 17, too late to be reported in that issue of the paper, Reverend A. J. McLachlan came in from Victoria bearing the news of the massacre at Frog Lake two weeks earlier. At last the impenetrable wall of silence to the east had been broken. Through it had come the news that nine white men, two of them Roman Catholic priests, had been killed and mutilated and that the two white women there had been carried off as prisoners by Big Bear's band.

Frog Lake, a hamlet at the edge of the Unipauheos Indian Reserve some 130 miles east of Edmonton and astraddle the Winnipeg–Edmonton Trail, was close to the Saskatchewan border. By 1885, it had grown into a little centre of some ten or twelve houses scattered over the slope of the hill, rising from a charming little lake about a mile away from Frog Lake itself. About two miles west of the hamlet the government had built a saw- and grist-mill, which J. A. Gowanlock operated for the Indian department. Amongst the residents of this tiny post of civilization were W. B. Cameron of the Hudson's Bay Company's post, John Delaney, the farm instructor, two priests, Fathers Faford and Marchand, a detachment of six NWMP and two lonely white women, Mrs. Delaney and Mrs. Gowanlock.

While the Crees under Big Bear and Wandering Spirit raged nearby, Inspector Dickens, in charge of Fort Pitt, had sent a message to Frog Lake advising the whites to move into the protection of his fort. They declined, but suggested that the small police detachment should leave, because its presence might inflame the Indians to warfare. Indian Agent Quinn felt certain he could keep the warriors under control, and so the six policemen rode down the sandy trail and disappeared into the grove of poplars beyond the two lakes.

On April 2, the day before Good Friday, while the priests were holding service in their small church, a band of Crees under Wandering Spirit ransacked the Hudson's Bay Company store, entered the church, and disrupted the service. As the people left the building, pandemonium broke loose. Within a few minutes, nine men had been killed and mutilated, including the priests who tried to intercede with the Indians. The two women were taken prisoner along with Cameron, the Hudson's Bay Company's trader.

All was over in a few moments except the burning of the buildings. The Indians emptied them of supplies and then set fire to the village. All that remained were pieces of charcoal and ashes and a few tin cans in the old cellars.

Meanwhile at Calgary the news of the fighting at Duck Lake created considerable alarm. Even though Calgary had the protection of the railway, it nevertheless had to fear some five hundred Sarcee Indians at its back door and several times that many fifty miles down the river. Because a few days previously all but six of their Mounted Policemen had moved away for duty in Saskatchewan, Major Walker organized a home guard to patrol the town's outskirts.

At his ranch near Crowfoot's reserve, T. Bland Strange, a retired major-general, had been in touch with the minister of militia at Ottawa and had been authorized to raise a force which came to be known as the Alberta Field Force and also to take military command of the District of Alberta. In the Calgary area he had no difficulty mustering the men he needed. It was full of cowboys who would "as lief shoot as eat," as well as a fair sprinkling of ranchers who in the recent past had moved in British military circles. In fact, to Calgarians' annoyance, most of its home guard joined Strange's force. By April 15, however, when the first of his troops set out for Edmonton under Lieutenant Coryell, Calgary fairly buzzed with soldiers—young cowboys with the fuzz on their lips belying a valour which nothing could daunt, grave old colonels with moustaches, waxed or walrusy, eager to smell gunsmoke again, and young voltigeurs and carabiniers determined to uphold Quebec's name in the coming struggle. So many military units, homegrown or imported, concentrated in Calgary that it is hard to keep them all straight. Some of General Strange's men had originally joined up in one or other of the four troops of the Rocky Mountain Rangers which Major John Stewart had raised in the Pincher Creek–Fort Macleod area and then had been sent to Calgary to report to the general. One of these later formed much of Calgary's home guard, another made up a large part of Steele's Scouts, while the third became the Alberta Mounted Rifles.

Gathering at Calgary to form General Strange's Alberta Field Force and departing from there were the following units: Alberta Mounted Rifles—Major Hatton; Steele's Scouts—Sam Steele; 65th Carabiniers Mount Royal—Lieut.-Col. J. A. Ouimet; 92nd Winnipeg Light Infantry —Lieut.-Col. W. Osborne Smith; 9th Voltigeurs de Quebec, which arrived later under Lieut.-Col. Amyot.

In all, the force embraced some seven hundred men and, travelling in various groups, all (except three companies of the Winnipeg Light Infantry) started on their way to Edmonton on April 15, 20 and 23, hoping to catch up with Big Bear. With them went Fathers Lacombe and Scollen and Rev. John McDougall. Of the three companies of the Winnipeg Light Infantry, one each went to Gleichen and Fort Macleod and the other remained in Calgary.

The people of Fort Macleod and district, alarmed by what was going on in Saskatchewan, spent no time weeping or wailing. In short order their aggressive spirit brought into being Major John Stewart's Rocky Mountain Rangers. Naturally they consisted of cowboys, with such ranch owners and outstanding men as Dr. L. G. de Veber, Kootenai Brown, Lord Boyle, John Herron and George Ives. Some of them were sent to Calgary, and as we have noted, went north from there.

On March 28, 1885, the minister of militia had authorized Stewart, whose ranch bordered on the Blood Indian Reserve, to raise four troops of cavalry. At the time the Blood Indians were reported as being especially restless, and Fort Macleod residents, expecting trouble, braced themselves for it. So eager was the response to the call for men that the

143

first muster of some 114 troopers took place on April 15. About that time Kootenai Brown joined as a scout.

On April 29, after sixty men of the Winnipeg Light Infantry had arrived to protect the town, that part of the Rocky Mountain Rangers remaining in southern Alberta marched east to guard the telegraph line which was being built west from Medicine Hat. If they had hoped for the excitement of a major clash with the Indians, they were disappointed, because for the next three months they patrolled the border area south of the South Saskatchewan River without more than a fleeting shot at a fleeing Indian. With their headquarters in the new railway town of Medicine Hat, they patrolled a wide area. Then on July 8 the Rocky Mountain Rangers, tired and dusty after their long trip back to Fort Macleod, were paid off and discharged. Fort Macleod and its ranchers and rangers had measured up to their emergency.

Meanwhile, Crowfoot, like his fellow chiefs, Red Crow of the Bloods and Eagle Tail of the Piegans, all bitter over the unfair treatment the Indian agents continued to mete out to their people, became estranged from the Mounties. Day by day Crowfoot began to feel more and more sympathy for the Saskatchewan Crees, who kept sending emissaries to him—the Crees amongst whom his adopted son Poundmaker was a leader.

Crowfoot faced a difficult choice, that of a man who takes the middle road. As Hugh Dempsey says, he was neither as completely loyal as the Indian officials claimed, nor as secretly treacherous as the white settlers believed him to be. His personal sympathies were with the insurgents but he still liked and respected a few white men, Father Lacombe, Inspector Cecil Denny and Governor Dewdney. Furthermore, knowing the white man's strength, seeing the railway running past his reserve and remembering what he had seen of the multitudes in Winnipeg, he knew that while the Blackfoot Confederacy could kill hundreds of white people, in the end his own race would be quickly overwhelmed. Moreover, even if the Blackfoot were successful and did drive out the white people, who would then feed the Indians?

All the while various white leaders, feigning a belief in his loyalty, kept coming to toady to him. Alternating with them came pleading Cree messengers. Unfortunately for their cause, they became exasperated by his reluctance and, being less politically agile than the white men, threatened him, saying that as soon as they had rubbed out the whites, they would attack the Blackfoot. But they threatened the wrong man.

Hard on their heels, a week or so after the killings at Frog Lake, Inspector Denny, Governor Dewdney and Father Lacombe, having heard that the Crees had threatened Crowfoot, came to see him. They had come to tell him of the hundreds of troops which were even then pouring in by the railway and to explain that while this army was aimed solely at the insurgents and would not turn its guns on the Confederacy, it would if necessary protect the Blackfoot from any Cree onslaught. In these men's presence he took the step which committed him—he decided, and decided wisely, that loyalty to the queen would pay dividends, and publicly cast himself on the side of the government.

At that point he cleared all uncertainty from his mind—the uncertainty and the worry which, added to his failing health, had made him take the unheard of step of consulting a Calgary doctor. He was a sick man and for a month had been confined to his couch.

When at last he cast his lot on the white side, he was no longer an ardent young idealist dreaming impossible dreams. He was a practical politician, accepting a situation he did not like and setting a course which in the end would bring his people the better of two evils. If for their own purposes the white leaders, still unsure of his motives, proclaimed his loyalty from the housetops, let them. If his young men suspected him of cowardice and of truckling to the white men, let them. He was steering his people along a bitter road, but, under the circumstances, the only road.

While Crowfoot was fretting on his sickbed, the little town of Medicine Hat, about one hundred miles down the Bow, played its part in helping to quell the rebellion. Pulled up on the shore there for the winter were the North-Western Coal and Navigation Company's steamers, the *Baroness*, *Alberta* and *Minnow,* as well as the *Northcote*, and the military authorities decided to use them for transport purposes.

Due to the low water in the river, none of them was much of a success, but towards the close of the campaign they reached the battle theatre. General Middleton also used them for moving goods and men back and forth along the North Saskatchewan River and in this service in June 1885 both the *Baroness* and the *Alberta* went as far upstream as Edmonton, the first steamers to navigate from Medicine Hat to that town. Later on these two took homeward-bound troops down the main Saskatchewan to Lake Winnipeg where they embarked on lake steamers. Eventually these two boats returned to Medicine Hat.

Some of these troops had been units which in April had left Calgary to march to Edmonton. Strange's little army of horse, foot and guns made the difficult march over April's soggy soils and across brimful rivers and creeks in about ten days. One of his units, the 65th Mount Royal Regiment, took more time because its men had work to do. They were instructed to build and man three small blockhouses between Calgary and Edmonton which were to act as protection to the army's line of communication and as refuges in case the few settlers had to abandon their homes. These they duly built and named after some of the unit's officers, Forts Normandeau (Red Deer), Ostell (Ponoka), and Ethier, near Wetaskiwin.

Railroad and Rebellion 1881-1885

When Colonel Ouimet of the 65th Regiment established his head-quarters at Edmonton, he assigned some of his men to Fort Saskatchewan and went to St. Albert where he raised the St. Albert Mounted Rifles, which, under Captain Sam Cunningham, a prominent Métis, soon marched off to restore order at Lac La Biche. Moreover, looking suspiciously at the old Salvais settlement at Duhamel where Elzear Laboucane, a well-off Métis, was believed to be conspiring with Gabriel Dumont, he sent Captain L. J. Ethier there to lay down the law.

Meanwhile, General Strange's forces went down the Saskatchewan River, pausing at such places as Victoria, Saddle Creek and the mouth of Frog Lake Creek, whence they sent a few men to the charred remains of Frog Lake village. There they buried the dead which were lying where they had fallen some seven weeks earlier. By the time the general reached Fort Pitt on May 25, the Battle of Batoche nearly two weeks earlier had ended the Métis' hopes, and Louis Riel had given himself up. Gabriel Dumont, sincere and capable, having fought for his cause with courage and a skill surpassing that of his opponents, had slipped quietly through the hills and his enemies' patrols until he reached Montana.

At Battleford, the day after Strange's arrival at Fort Pitt, General Middleton had accepted the surrender of several Cree chiefs, including Poundmaker, the man who but for his leniency would have annihilated the force with which Colonel Otter had attacked his harmless camp.

Leaving the ruins of Fort Pitt, Strange's troops moved over to skirmish with Big Bear's Crees at Frenchman's Butte, and after a few days dislodged them. By that time General Middleton had come west and effected a junction with the Alberta Field Force and then, taking some of them with him, pursued Big Bear as far as Loon Lake. Strange's forces, notably Steele's Scouts, scoured the country as far north as the mission at Le Goff and the Beaver River looking for the fugitives. At that river they heard that several miles downstream at Lac des Isles in Saskatchewan the prisoners, including Mrs. Delaney and Mrs. Gowanlock, who had been held captive for sixty-two days, had been released. Finally, after seeing little fighting but considerable adventure and returning to the Saskatchewan River, the Alberta units of the Field Force embarked for Edmonton and home. The North-West Rebellion was over.

Now the ranchers in the south and the villagers in Calgary, Edmonton and Fort Macleod could relax and pursue their avocations in peace. Now all the plains Indians could see that Crowfoot's sagacity had saved them from making a terrible mistake—the mistake of choosing the losing side. Now Crowfoot, near the end of his course, could relax, even though he could not forgive the government for sentencing his beloved Poundmaker to a term in prison.

With Riel's death on the gallows at Regina on November 16, 1885, the chapter of the uprising officially closed. On the debit side, the rebellion upon which he had staked the peace of the West and the fate of the Métis had ended in failure. Unfortunately this failure, this rebellion which Ottawa's obtuseness had allowed to fester, had cost Canadians five million dollars in money and the more devastating cost of continuing for decades the rift in Canada's nationhood.

On the credit side, however, it had shown what those decades were to repeat, that Albertans found their country worth fighting for. Moreover, it had displayed to eastern troops what a fair land the West, and particularly Alberta, was.

# 10
# Slow But Definite Progress
# 1885-1900

When the fall of 1885 brushed Alberta with its beauty, it swept away the last traces of the North-West Rebellion. Turning the tamarack of the northern muskegs to yellow, the autumn scampered across the parklands to leave them aglow with gold and flew out over the short grass plains to paint the cherry leaves of the coulees red. Finally swinging west over the mixed grass prairies and bounding up the foothills it left them flaunting billows of aureate aspens far up towards the blue peaks.

And yet even though the rebellion had swept the last native obstacle off the prairies and onto reserves and though the CPR had finally opened the rich and beautiful province to easy access by white settlers, the last fifteen years of the century saw but a creeping influx of farmers. Two factors held back any rush of agriculturalists: the abundance of free land farther east in Manitoba and Saskatchewan and the long winter of the depression which, with little abatement, lowered like a fog over North America until in 1897 the Klondike's gold blew it away.

In spite of the fact that white folk were slow in coming—only an average of a thousand or so per year for the first five years after the rebellion and an average of two thousand annually during the following five years—Alberta's record in the building of railways, the arteries along which settlers flowed to seep out over the land, was more progressive. During this fifteen-year period some five hundred miles of railway came into being to wind along hillsides and to snake through curving valleys.

The clang of the CPR's spike-driving hammers had barely been cut off by the wall of the continental divide when fresh gangs came in to lay a coal railway 107 miles from Coal Banks to Dunmore station high up on the level prairies east of Medicine Hat. For the North-Western Coal and Navigation Company's *Baroness, Alberta* and *Minnow* had proven unable to haul the coal for which the CPR clamoured, and in 1885 the company set men to work winding its narrow gauge railway around the hillsides. Much to the company directors' satisfaction, it was completed by September 24, 1885, and then found itself exposed to the scorn of Polly, the gentleman who had formerly driven the stage along essentially the same route. Watching its diminutive cars wobbling and wiggling on their way to Dunmore, Polly dubbed the new railway the Turkey Trail, an apt name which stuck.

Despite Polly's scorn, the Turkey Trail performed so well that in 1890 the company laid another narrow gauge track to Coutts, and then continued it to Great Falls, Montana. However, it was not the only railroad to begin feeling its way into Alberta's fascinating nooks and meadows. For some time the CPR had been watching freight wagons pull out of Calgary along Alberta's axis north to Edmonton or south to Fort Macleod. Then in 1890, under the name of the Calgary–Edmonton Railroad, the CPR began to grade a line towards the North Saskatchewan River. To Edmontonians' anger it reached the south bank of the river and, instead of crossing it, started the rival town of South Edmonton into which the first train rolled on August 10, 1891. From then on the new town began to figure in Alberta's history, the town which Edmontonians in their huffiness declared had been born a mule, a creature with no pride of ancestry, which they hoped, like a mule, would have no prospect of posterity.

Then the CPR started building south to Fort Macleod, and on November 3, 1892, the first train reached the Oldman River to which sixteen years earlier Jerry Potts had guided the Mounties. That extension only whetted the CPR's appetite; looking upon southern Alberta and finding it full of promise it increased its railway network by leasing the old narrow gauge Turkey Trail and operating it from then on.

For indeed the southern part of the province was making good progress. This trend had been observable in the 1885 census figures of white and half-breed people: out of some 6,800 within the modern borders of Alberta (including the Medicine Hat area of Assiniboia), the northern part of the future province represented by Edmonton and its far-flung suburbs, such as Victoria and Lac La Biche, held only 2,900. The southern portion of the province held nearly sixty percent of the population.

In 1891, not counting some 9,000 Indians, the total white and Métis population of the area of the future Alberta was reckoned as 17,593. Edmonton and its surrounding district had 3,875 people, of whom Edmonton itself held 700. Calgary and the district from Red Deer south, including Medicine Hat, had more than three times as many, 13,718, of which the town of Calgary alone boasted 3,876. Obviously by that time the part of the future province from Red Deer south with eighty percent of the total population was the area on which the CPR should concentrate.

For the next few years that is exactly what it did. In 1897, following up its rosy prospects and its experience of operating the Turkey Trail, the CPR purchased that line and converted it to a standard gauge from Dunmore to Coal Banks, which was now known by its new name of Lethbridge. This new piece of the CPR line was to be but a stepping-stone towards an ambitious project the company had conceived of piercing the Rocky Mountains through the Crowsnest Pass.

On July 14, 1897, at Lethbridge, the first sod of the Crowsn.. Railway was turned and immediately the engineers faced the formidable task of getting their rails across the wide valley of the Oldman River. For the time being, they solved it by swinging their line upstream and while it clung like a goat to the side hills, they finally got it down to the river level not far from old Fort Whoop-Up. Then in another tortuous series of curves around crag and cutbank they brought it back up to the fairly level prairies west of Lethbridge and ran west to Fort Macleod. After connecting with the line from Calgary south, their rails continued up the Oldman River. At a point a couple of miles north of Pincher Creek the company built a siding called Pincher Station, but could never induce the well-established town to desert its choice, tree-shaded valley location for a site on the baldheaded prairie.

Even though the new railway was heading into the heart of mountainous British Columbia to haul shiny, metallic minerals, it was far from neglecting the shiny black coking coals of the Crowsnest Pass. When the railway actually reached the spot where as early as 1881 the NWMP had stationed a detachment, a man by the name of Willoughby took advantage of the hot springs in the pass to build a hotel and sanitorium. On November 15, 1898, the steel reached The Springs, otherwise known as the 10th Siding, and soon to be known as Blairmore.

Before long Blairmore found itself the centre of a coal mining area and by 1901 had 257 people, as businessmen, many of them from France, recognizing good coal when they saw it, began tunneling into the mountainsides and organizing communities that came to be called Lille, Bellevue, Hillcrest and Frank. Scores of men from Italy, the Ukraine, Poland, Scotland and Wales, and other places, came to pit their courage against the fearful hazards of the coal mines of the day.

Like all labouring men at the turn of the century, they worked under dangerous conditions and their employers paid scant heed to sanitation in their camps. Such lack of supervision and of hospital facilities, combined with the callousness and indifference with which the contractors treated these men and the downright dishonesty to which they resorted, form an unsavoury part of our heritage. Conditions on the Crowsnest Pass Railway were so bad that typhoid swept the construction camps and many men died. Fortunately when rumours of these circumstances began to leak out the aroused people and press of Canada clamoured for an investigation. As its outcome, the suffering and deaths amongst the construction workers, many of whom were new Alberta homesteaders fresh out from Europe, led to the government stepping in and demanding better treatment of labourers.

In any event, with the building of the Crowsnest Pass Railway additional mining began to increase coal's significant contribution to Alberta's economy and to the province's population. At the same time, enterprising men had begun sniffing around for other resources. Although their luck was not commensurate with their effort, they spent their own money (and any they could borrow) in a sporadic but mainly unsuccessful search for oil. Ever since 1718, when the Cree Indian named Swan had carried a sample of Alberta's tar sands to the traders at Hudson Bay, various explorers such as Mackenzie, Pond and Fidler had been tantalized by them but it was not until 1878 that the Dominion government sent its great geologist, George Dawson, to start a scientific assessment of this mysterious resource. Dawson's report put ideas into the Canadians' heads.

Probably the interest in oil would have remained in the background if in 1883 an unfortunate disappointment had not befallen a CPR crew drilling for water at what is now the siding of Alderson on the main line, some forty miles west of Medicine Hat. After drilling hundreds of feet without finding a trace of water, a flow of natural gas came gushing up the hole and stopped the crew's search. The men packed up their drills and departed, but other Albertans began scratching their heads, with the result that by 1890 the first commercial gas well in what is now Alberta was brought in to supply the new town of Medicine Hat, which as some years later Rudyard Kipling stated "had all Hell for a basement." Because of various delays, it was 1903 before the people of that town were cooking with gas.

Meanwhile, other venturesome souls filed petroleum claims along the Red Deer River near Tail Creek and, having filed, largely forgot them. Early surveyor A. P. Patrick, however, was of firmer faith. His application for a petroleum claim asserts that he staked it on June 29, 1889. Though it was to be a few years before he drilled there, he held this lease which was close to the modern highway going up from Waterton Lake to Cameron Lake. Undoubtedly Kootenai Brown, who seems to have been mildly interested in oil seepages, had helped to steer Patrick towards it.

Leaving the south for a few years the next oil plays took place north of Edmonton when in 1894 the Dominion government's geological survey sent a party to drill for oil at Athabasca Landing. By 1896, after being drilled intermittently for a year or so, this hole had reached a depth of 1,770 feet. The drillers had struck gas but not oil and the hole was abandoned. The next year at Pelican Rapids another hole was punched to a depth of eight hundred feet where it struck an uncontrollable flow of gas, which for the next twenty years was left to blow into the atmosphere. A similar well drilled across the river from George McDougall's old Victoria mission between 1897 and 1900 reached a depth of two thousand feet but struck nothing. Also disappointing was A. W. Dingman's well at Edmonton. Although drillers struck gas at Medicine Hat and along the

Athabasca River and although the vast wealth of the Athabasca Oil Sands pointed plainly to the possibility of Alberta being rich in oil reserves, little luck rewarded the pioneer drillers.

As a rule, however, those who chose to utilize Alberta's lumber resources, which needed no blind probing to locate, were amply rewarded. Following the few men who by 1880 were running small sawmills, lumbermen accustomed to operating on a large scale came to look at the timber along the CPR's proposed right-of-way west of Calgary. In 1886 one of these operators, the Eau Claire and Bow River Lumber Company Limited, built a mill in Calgary to saw logs rafted down from the Silver City and Kananaskis areas.

A sad disaster marred the company's first log drive when nine of the crew were swept over Kananaskis Falls. Taking in water each time it jumped the first and second falls, their boat dumped the men out at the third drop. Three of them escaped safely, but six were dashed against the rocks and killed.

The company operated its mill with a steam power plant, and incidental to that began to sell surplus electricity to some of the people of Calgary not already served by A. F. McMullan's small steam power plant, established about 1888. As the Eau Claire's load grew, the company was forced to turn to yet another of Alberta's resources and in 1893 put a small weir across the Bow River (near what was later to be the Louise Bridge) and started Alberta's first hydro-electric power plant. It was operated as a separate company called the Calgary Water Power Company Limited, but should not be confused with today's Calgary Power Limited, which has a different lineage.

Other large mills served the Edmonton and the Crowsnest Pass areas. Amongst those at Edmonton were the large operators, Moore and Macdowall, John Walter, and Fraser and Company. Then too, wherever settlers were edging their way into Alberta's forests some venturesome man was sure to erect a small sawmill, and as the years went by these mills, always situated further into the forests than the settlers, began eating their way into the vast stands of timber which covered northern Alberta. Just as a generation earlier white men had swept the buffalo off the prairies, now white men had started their attack on the forests. The actual trees they cut down were only a minor factor in their onslaught. Far more devastating were the fires they set accidentally or those which farmers, loathing the forests, set deliberately.

Fortunately a group of foresters and devoted federal civil servants who watched this happen began to press for conservation. In 1885 one of the Dominion government forestry men warned about "the increasing and wreckless waste of our forests. . . . The inevitable consequences of future neglect in this matter . . . will be, among other climatic changes,

A History of Alberta

drought varied by sudden and destructive floods, and a deterioration in the quality of the soil." His mind ran along somewhat parallel lines to those of the Northwest Territories legislators who in 1883 passed a near futile act prohibiting polluting streams.

Unfortunately some generations were to pass before matters of this nature could be pounded into the head of the man on the street and he too began to talk of conservation and pollution. One of the first results of men taking thought for the morrow was the setting aside of Banff, Canada's first national park. While its fascinating early story is too involved to detail here, some of its highlights are interesting.

One of the first men to think in terms of a nature reservation was none other than the great CPR builder Van Horne, who, under his paunchy, driving fist, concealed an artistic temperament. As a result of his idea, the Dominion government set aside an area of ten square miles as public property. Later in 1887 with William Pearce at their elbow the authorities enlarged the area to some twenty-six square miles. In 1892 a similar reservation of fifty square miles was established around Lake Louise. These then were the earliest moves in the direction of creating the great national parks which lie in Alberta's mountains. Needless to say they met with little favour amongst lumbermen.

While all this was going on, each of Alberta's budding cities, regarding itself as the West's future metropolis, made steady if slow progress. For some time after the North-West Rebellion, however, Edmonton, as certain of its long-time future as any, lay temporarily becalmed in its forest-fringed backwater, drawing its supplies north over the Calgary–Edmonton Trail. But such men as Frank Oliver, Matt McCauley and John Mc-Dougall the merchant, were not content to let Edmonton languish in its primitive fur-trade pattern. In 1889 they established the first board of trade west of Winnipeg. Then in 1891 Alex Taylor began operating a new marvel of the times, the first local electric lighting plant. By then, of course, Calgary, a much larger place, had enjoyed electric lighting for two or three years.

In February 1892 the hamlet of Edmonton was incorporated as a town which stretched over 2,168 acres on the north side of the river and embraced seven hundred people. Matt McCauley, the progressive citizen of eleven years' standing, was their unanimous choice for mayor. By this time a smattering of settlers had come in to try to clear and farm the adjacent forests and once more Edmonton started to grow. By the spring of 1894 the NWMP census taker counted 1,021 people in Edmonton, a large increase over the town's population at its incorporation. More and more of them found their livelihood in catering to incoming settlers.

Much of the town's business came from the North and, as they had done for a hundred years, Edmontonians always had an eye cocked in

Slow But Definite Progress 1885-1900

that direction. When in 1886 the steamboat *Wrigley* was built at Fort Smith and put into service from there down to the mouth of the Mackenzie, Edmontonians had a navigable route some 1,500 miles long running through the near and the far North. All of this route poured some tribute into Edmonton's lap. Moreover, before 1886, when Twelve-Foot Davis had started his string of trading posts along the Peace River, various missionaries had been testing the soils of that region.

One such missionary was Henry Lawrence who brought his family to the Anglican mission at Fort Vermilion in 1879. In due course, Lawrence developed an amazingly productive farm some miles west of the mission and one which has been cultivated continuously ever since. Not long afterwards, in 1887, the Reverend J. Gough Brick started his mission on the Shaftesbury Flats and then moved over to begin farming at Old Wive's Lake. In 1893 with some. wheat grown there, he exhibited at the Chicago World's Fair. A couple of years later, Peter Gunn and Charles Bremner purchased the Hudson's Bay Company's cattle ranch at Spirit River. As early as 1883, in a preliminary move to keep ahead of settlers, the Dominion land surveyors, William Ogilvie and W. T. Thompson, were sent to run meridian and base lines in the Peace River country.

Edmontonians, watching all these activities, felt themselves quite conversant with the problems and the prospects in all of the north country. Furthermore, they had always been interested in gold panning and were ever ready to go off on some gold rush or other. During the spring of 1897 they had a rush right in the town, for the *Bulletin* of April 15 reported: "Already the rush has commenced, and impatient miners and prospectors, local experts, wandering fortune seekers and businessmen not waiting for the ice to leave the river, have staked claims all along the banks from high to low water mark, all seeking to secure a share of the precious metal whose very name is a magnet to attract the millions. From the high river bank directly back of the business portion of the town can be seen far up and down the river innumerable stakes and pins set up there as soon as the frost had left the ground, staking off the newly located claims."

Less than three weeks later the news of the fabulous strike on Klondike Creek reached Edmonton and the world, and the Klondike Rush was on. Within weeks strangers from eastern Canada and the United States began stepping off the train at South Edmonton and asking for guidance and supplies to take them to the Klondike. They had looked at their atlases and seen that Edmonton was the end-of-steel nearest to the Klondike, and, disregarding the fact that from that outpost town the shortest distance to the gold fields was fifteen hundred miles and that the easier, longer water route down the Mackenzie River was 2,500 miles, they kept piling off the trains.

Of the thousands who poured into the Yukon during 1897 and 1898, all but about 1,500 chose the better route and sailed from west coast ports up the shoreline to Skagway and went inland from there. But the 1,500 chose to go by Edmonton, and for a brief period they came tumbling in, stayed to secure supplies, pack horses or both, and then went fumbling somewhat blindly north. They temporarily doubled the town's population, set it aflame with excitement and left some half a million extra dollars in Edmontonians' tills.

The Edmonton routes to the Klondike were perhaps the most difficult of any they could have chosen. Of the 1,500 who went that way, half chose the water route down the Mackenzie River, and some 565 of them reached the Yukon. The other half, using pack horses, set out to traverse fifteen hundred miles of muskeg and forest and of those about 160 got through, while, except for thirty-five who died of starvation or scurvy, the rest turned back. The Edmonton routes to the Klondike were dismal failures.

Whatever the Klondike Rush may or may not have done for Edmonton, it triggered a new worldwide era of good times. The discovery of gold in the northwest, along with that in South Africa, lifted the world and Canada out of the trough of depression and once more set its feet on the treadmill of progress. During the summer of 1897 when the Klondike Rush was at its height, all Britishers celebrated Queen Victoria's Diamond Jubilee. The old queen had reigned sixty years, the British Empire was at its zenith, and wherever English was spoken all was well. Canada began to feel the quickened pulse of that well-being spread across the West to the Pacific coast.

During the celebrations, Donald Smith, one-time fur trader and opponent of Louis Riel, and more recently a financier whose courage had gone far to push the CPR across the prairies, was raised to the peerage and became Lord Strathcona. When two years later, on April 29, 1899, South Edmonton obtained incorporation, its leaders chose to honour him by bestowing his name on their town of 1,156 people.

A few months later the Boer War broke out in South Africa, and when Canada decided to take a hand in the struggle, Lord Strathcona and the town named after him both played parts. The call of adventure or of duty incited many men who had served in the Alberta Field Force in the North-West Rebellion, as well as several younger Albertans, to volunteer for service in the cavalry units which were being formed. Colonel S. B. Steele, who in 1885 had led part of Strange's column, took command of the Canadian Mounted Rifles, which recruited many of its men from the ranching areas of southern Alberta and from Calgary, Edmonton and Strathcona. Within a matter of weeks the men left for South Africa.

The summer that the South African War broke out, all ignorant of the fact that they were entertaining a genius unawares, the good people of Strathcona allowed one of the great characters of the West's early days, Bob Edwards, to slip unlamented out of their town. Edwards, who eventually found in Calgary the environment in which his talent and his *Eye Opener* flourished, found little to like in either Strathcona or Edmonton.

At Strathcona he had started by publishing the *Strathcolic*, a name he soon changed to the *Alberta Sun*. The Edmonton environment proved a disappointment, and occasionally Bob returned to visit his friends in Wetaskiwin where "those who were not passing through the folding doors, were coming out, wiping off their chins." He liked Wetaskiwin but to him "Edmonton is but a snide place which gives everyone the blues." So, after a few months in its unbending atmosphere, Bob Edwards left the northern town to bring fame to the more congenial Calgary.

Prior to setting up shop in Strathcona, Bob had operated papers in Wetaskiwin and Leduc. He had come to Wetaskiwin in 1895 to observe life along the newly opened C & E Railway when that hamlet was known interchangeably as Wetaskiwin or the 16th Siding, or when, as he remarked somewhat later, it had a population of "287 souls plus three total abstainers." Like everyone else, however, he enjoyed the pioneer optimism along the new railway line where within a few years sidings became hamlets and villages and towns.

By 1901 when the census was taken, however, these communities made little significant contribution to Alberta's total. For instance, the populations of some of them were: Carstairs, 20; Didsbury, 112; Innisfail, 317; Lacombe, 499; Ponoka, 151; Olds, 218; Red Deer, 323; and Wetaskiwin, 550. The figures also indicate which land the earliest farmers along the line considered best and flocked to in preference to others. Because some of these new settlements looked to Edmonton as their distributing point and because the area for some thirty miles around it had been settled by that time, the population of Edmonton and Strathcona combined was 4,176, a vast increase over the seven hundred Edmonton had boasted at its incorporation nine years earlier.

Calgary, however, the crossroads of Alberta with a population of 4,392 in 1901 and the province's only city, was in a splendid position to take advantage of all the opportunities inherent in this land of rich resources. With such men as James Lougheed, G. C. King, A. E. Cross, W. R. Hull and R. C. Thomas, it was little wonder that it soon set its feet on the path to greatness. In 1885 its citizens had organized the Calgary Agricultural Society with James Walker as president and a year later the Society held its first exhibition.

In 1887 Calgary took some long steps forward by organizing some of its utility services: A. F. McMullan organized the Electric Light Company and built a generating plant; Alex Lucas drilled for natural gas but ended up with a dry hole, an experience which was to be all too common over the next half century, and the Bell Telephone Company bought out Colonel James Walker's system and took over the task of serving his forty-five customers. In 1889 the Agricultural Society purchased the ninety-four acres which became the exhibition grounds. The next year Calgarians organized their board of trade and chose P. J. Nolan as its secretary. Spurred on by that body, Calgary applied for incorporation and on September 16, 1892, became a city.

To the west Calgary drew nourishment from the aspiring village of Anthracite with its 167 people, and from the rugged community of Canmore with 450, both of them busily exploiting the excellent coal just outside the borders of the national park. Nearby the town of Banff, with a population of 271, was beginning to see an interesting future as the headquarters of the park. To the south along the old Whoop-Up Trail, Okotoks with 245 people and High River with 153, brought business to the growing city.

By 1901 old Fort Macleod was fighting a losing battle with its neighbour Lethbridge. When in 1892 the railway from Calgary reached the vicinity, Fort Macleod began to bustle with so much activity that that year it was incorporated as a town and elected John Cowdry, its earliest banker, as its mayor. At the same time, to add dignity to its stature, it dropped the Fort from its name and thenceforth called itself Macleod. By 1901 it boasted a population of 796. The fertile area south of it, however, had filled in with a very productive people, the Mormons, and their towns of Cardston, with 639 people, and Magrath with 425, also began to threaten Macleod's dominance of the southwest corner of the province.

But even they did not pose the same threat as the coal mining city, thirty-three miles away, which in 1885, in honour of one of its mine owners, had changed its name to Lethbridge. Immediately after that it began to assume all the trappings of a bustling centre. On November 27 of that year C. E. D. Wood and E. T. Saunders of the Macleod *Gazette* established the Lethbridge *News*. Like Calgary, the new centre in the chinook belt had a short gestation period and rose to considerable stature. In due course it was incorporated as a town and by 1901, shortly after the Crowsnest Pass Railway was built, it had a population of 2,072—nearly as many people as Edmonton.

Off to the east about a hundred miles, in what was then the District of Assiniboia and somewhat isolated from the rest of Alberta, the CPR divisional point of Medicine Hat made similar progress. Its economy was based upon the short grass ranching area which surrounded it on all sides for miles. One of its earliest businesses, of course, was a newspaper which first appeared in October 1885 when A. M. Armour, who had helped to start Calgary's first paper, got out the Medicine Hat *Times*. The next year the town's first official school district was set up. Other municipal organizations, however, were slow to get under way and it was not until May 1894 that an unofficial town council came into being. By 1901 the railway divisional point had a population of 1,570.

As the population of the Northwest Territories grew its political machinery struggled to keep pace with the people's needs and demands. When in 1885 an election sent some new men to the council session held at Regina, four members sat for Alberta: Samuel Cunningham of St. Albert, Viscount Boyle from Fort Macleod, I. G. Geddes of Calgary and Dr. H. C. Wilson, who had won the seat away from Frank Oliver.

By the time of the session of November 1886 Calgary had grown enough to be entitled to two members and that year H. S. Cayley and John D. Lauder represented it. Alberta now had five members out of the fourteen elected to the council. During 1887 Viscount Boyle resigned and the people at Fort Macleod elected F. W. G. Haultain, a young lawyer destined to loom large in the West's affairs.

During the 1886 session of the federal Parliament that body set up federal electoral districts in the Northwest Territories and provided for two senators from the West. Moreover, it changed the structure of the North-West Council which from 1888 was known as the North-West Territories Legislative Assembly. From it were to be selected four men who were to form an advisory council and in effect were a cabinet. This was an important step towards the attainment of fully responsible government.

By the time of the new assembly's first session it had twenty-two members, of which Alberta, including Medicine Hat which was still technically in the District of Assiniboia, had seven. Two came from Calgary (John Lineham and H. S. Cayley) and two lived in Edmonton (Frank Oliver and H. C. Wilson). Haultain once more represented Fort Macleod, while the two newcomers to the sessions were from the new electoral districts of Medicine Hat (Thomas Tweed) and Red Deer (Dr. R. G. Brett). Though many of them, including Frank Oliver, were good men, Haultain soon became the outstanding man in the group and during difficult times led in the disputes between the assembly and the governor backed by Ottawa.

The elections of 1891 sent twenty-six men to the assembly, of which nine came from Alberta, including Dr. R. G. Brett, who now represented Banff and its adjacent mining area, and C. A. Magrath from Lethbridge. That year Ottawa passed an act granting most of the things the North-West Territories Legislative Assembly wanted, and by a subsequent reshuffling the assembly was set up with Haultain as leader. Thenceforth he came to be considered premier of the Northwest Territories and under his leadership a second North-West Rebellion took place, this time quietly and with no shots fired. Two successive executive councils resigned over the issue of responsible government. As a result, the federal government extended the powers of the assembly in 1891, another step towards full responsible government.

The North-West Legislature, however, continued to press its demands and responsible government was achieved as a practical reality in 1893, although it was not formally conceded by Ottawa until 1897.

For the elections of 1894 and 1898 some readjustment of electoral districts took place to take into account the areas in which homesteaders were settling. As a result, starting in 1894 the new district of High River was created along with Victoria, which centred around George McDougall's old mission east of Edmonton. In 1898 R. B. Bennett, a young lawyer who had come west as a partner of James Lougheed, was elected as one of the Calgary members.

When in 1887 the Northwest Territories were represented for the first time in the federal House of Commons and were permitted to elect four members (one of whom was to represent the District of Alberta), it elected D. W. Davis, who had made his first appearance in the province as a whisky trader at Fort Whoop-Up. Being fundamentally a sound man, he remained in Alberta as an employee of the I. G. Baker Company and in due course proved himself to be an outstanding citizen.

When the next federal election came around in 1891 Davis was returned, having defeated James Reilly from Calgary. Frank Oliver, who was in the North-West Territories Assembly and was still managing his *Bulletin* in Edmonton, pitched into the fray on Reilly's side. To his great disappointment, Oliver had to record Davis's election. In doing so, however, his pen took a dig at the election practices of the times when abuses were common. He singled out the results at the poll at Woodpecker, a small mining village near modern Taber, by saying: "Woodpecker had 13 voters on the list and cast 51 Davis votes. None for Reilly."

By the time of the 1896 federal elections Frank Oliver had decided to step from the territorial field into federal politics and to seek the seat which Davis no longer wanted. He was elected with a clear majority over his two opponents and went to serve the West at Ottawa where he was eminently successful and made a major contribution.

While with a variety of machinations, anxious politicians pursued their ends, all of them exuded justifiable optimism about Alberta's future. In 1901 Edmonton, Strathcona, Calgary, Lethbridge and Medicine Hat, had a combined population of 12,210. Another 6,800 lived in towns, villages or hamlets, to bring the non-farm white population of the province to a total of some 19,000 as compared to perhaps 7,000 Indians and some 50,000 rural residents, mainly new settlers of recent arrival bent on farming. How they came and where they settled we will reserve for the following chapter. But by 1901 Alberta with its total population of 73,022 was ready to step into a future bright with rich resources and the promise of thousands of new settlers who in their homelands were already planning to plough the soil of the "Last Great West."

Alberta's era had dawned, its prospects were rosy.

Not so, however, were the prospects of the province's former owners —the 3,700 Indians on the large prairie reserves in the south of the province and the 2,400 more or less along the North Saskatchewan River, plus several hundred who still followed their primitive way of life north of the Athabasca River. They took no part and wanted no part in elections and could not see any virtue in the resources the white man snatched so eagerly. The Indians were well along the way to becoming Alberta's forgotten people.

For those north of the Athabasca River conditions had still changed very little from what they had been when Peter Pond and Peter Fidler had first descended the great river to Lake Athabasca. As a result, even by 1901 they had not yet experienced the full impact of the white man's presence and, because they lived very much as they had done for generations, had little cause to complain of the white interlopers who entered their territory, which as yet they had not ceded to the strangers.

When, however, the Klondikers came pouring through, they caused considerable unrest amongst the Cree and the Beaver Indians of the Peace River country. The gold-seekers, many of whom were American frontiersmen who still believed that the only good Indian was a dead one, acted towards the northern natives in accordance with that philosophy. The Hudson's Bay Company's traders, the missionaries and the Mounted Police, reported the Indians' indignation to the authorities at Ottawa. They also mentioned the decline in fur-bearing animals now that white trappers had been competing with the natives. Then, too, the Indians were aware that their southern relatives who had come under the provisions of previous treaties were receiving annual payments, relief food when necessary and other amenities. Consequently the Hudson's Bay Company and the Mounted Police urged Ottawa to hasten to do what they had done south of the Athabasca twenty years previously and sign a treaty with the Indians.

As a result, in May 1899, commissioners with two purposes in mind set out from Edmonton to conclude Treaty No. 8 with bands of Crees, Beavers, Slaves and Chipewyan Indians at such places as Lesser Slave Lake, Dunvegan, Fort Vermilion and Chipewyan, and to investigate and confirm the well-merited claims of the Métis to the lands they occupied in that general area. The commission to the Indians was headed by the Honourable David Laird, who had played a similar part in Treaty No. 7. That to the half-breeds was in charge of Major James Walker of Calgary, the former Mountie, who issued scrip to them, similar to that which their

An aerial view of the Old Women's Buffalo Jump (centre) looking southwest

Anthony Henday enters a Blackfoot camp, 1754. From a painting by Franklin Arbuckle.

Sir George Simpson, governor-in-chief of the Hudson's Bay Company territories

John Rowand, chief trader at Edmonton House between 1830 and 1854

John Palliser and Dr. James Hector

Rev. Father Lacombe

Rev. John McDougall

Blood Indians at Fort Whoop-Up in the early 1870s

Crowfoot, chief of the Blackfoot Indians

Lieut.-Col. James Macleod, NWMP

Fort Macleod, 1878

Crow Indians killed by Blackfoot in the Sweet Grass Hills

Fort Edmonton looking north across the river, 1879. The buildings on the skyline are those of the hamlet of Edmonton near Rev. George McDougall's church

Fort Calgary looking north, 1881

An 1884 passenger train at Calgary

Steamboats *Baroness* and *Minnow* at Medicine Hat, 1885

Big Bear's camp at Maple Creek, Saskatchewan, 1883. Two years later this chief was involved in the killings at Frog Lake

The Rocky Mountain Rangers, 1885; Kootenai Brown in the lead

Stagecoach on the Calgary–Edmonton highway, 1888

Steamboat *North West* at Edmonton, 1896

Drilling for oil at Victoria, Alberta (Pakan), 1898

Sarcee Indian camp in the 1890s with Calgary in the background

Blood Indian undergoing self-torture ritual, 1892

Ivan Lupul's thatched-roof house near Wostok, 1902

The Frank slide, Crowsnest Pass, taken shortly after the event

Bob Edwards of the Calgary *Eye Opener*

The first automobile brought into Alberta by W. E. Cochrane in the summer of 1903

Jasper Avenue, Edmonton, looking east, 1903

Frank Oliver

A prairie settler's sod house showing a pile of collected buffalo bones

Eighth Avenue and Centre Street in Calgary looking west, 1906

Colorado settlers arriving by special train in Bassano, 1914

Two steam tractors capable of breaking some thirty-eight acres of prairie sod a day, circa 1911

R. B. Bennett, later to become prime minister of Canada

Henry Wise Wood, leader of UFA

Lord Strathcona (right) and Lieut.-Gov. Bulyea, 1909

Dr. H. M. Tory, first president of the
University of Alberta

Guy Weadick, promoter of the Calgary
Stampede, 1912

The newly completed Alberta Legislative Building before old Fort Edmonton was demolished

relations farther south and east had already received. Essentially, scrip entitled each male adult to file a claim on 160 acres of land. Unfortunately the scrip was made negotiable and transferable and most of these people immediately sold their scrip for a pittance.

By the fall of 1899 most of the commissioners' tasks were completed and as a result all but a little corner of land northeast of Lac La Biche, and a worthless bit at that, passed from the Indians' hands to the Crown.

By this time the Indians farther south whose reserves had been established under Treaties No. 6 and No. 7 had been having a difficult time. With their former lands swept from under their feet, they suffered a psychological inertia which even the best of them could not overcome. The chiefs and some of the wiser men tried to get them to turn to an agricultural economy but with little success. Undernourished, vanquished and turning to liquor, the fatal panacea of the defeated, the victims of venereal disease and tuberculosis, they led a discouraging existence. While their relatives and children died all around them, the Indians stagnated and became the dispossessed, the forgotten people, the people which the rapid progress of civilization had passed by.

Even Crowfoot, the once rugged chief, watched the ravages of tuberculosis in his own home. On May 29, 1885, while General Strange's forces were still fighting the Crees at Frenchman's Butte, the dread disease swept away one of his daughters. That December another of his children died from it, to be followed five months later by one of his boys, and then a month later by another. By 1886, out of Crowfoot's several children, only two daughters and one boy remained, and one of the daughters was sickly and the boy was going blind. Tragedy similar to that in many another Indian lodge stalked the once great chief. Even his greatly beloved adopted son, Poundmaker, had died.

In the months preceding his death, in spite of being a far better man than the bulk of the enemies who had attacked his camp at the so-called battle of Cutknife Hill, Poundmaker had been sent to jail. At his trial, of course, no one pointed to the fact that he had avoided hostilities until Colonel Otter's forces had fired on his lodges and then after the troops had worked themselves into a helpless position, he had spared them by calling off his warriors. In spite of his reasonable appeal, he had been imprisoned.

At the trial, in his simple defence, he had said: "I am not guilty. A lot has been said against me that is untrue. . . . When my people and the whites met in battle, I saved the queen's men. . . . Everything I could do was to prevent bloodshed. Had I wanted war, I would not be here but on the prairie. You did not catch me. I gave myself up. You have me because I wanted peace. I cannot help myself, but I am still a man. You may do as you like with me. I am done."

But those who even tacitly allow themselves to substitute rebellion for reason have little cause to expect reason from their victors and Poundmaker had been hustled off to jail. There his tuberculosis had galloped towards its inevitable goal. Before it had got that far Governor Dewdney, acting partly on Crowfoot's urgent plea, had set him free and in May 1886 Poundmaker had come to visit the Blackfoot chief. By then he was a mere shadow of his former self, a coughing, hacking man, gaunt and grim.

Nevertheless, after relaxing for a few weeks in Crowfoot's lodge, he regained a little of his former vigour, and in July was able to attend the Sun Dance. There, the same dread disease which had recently carried away several of Crowfoot's children, finished its work; Poundmaker suffered a hemorrhage and died. There at Blackfoot Crossing, after proper funeral ceremonies, the remains of the great chief of the Crees were left to lie in the sun and to look out over the flowering prairies Poundmaker had known so well.

For Crowfoot, a man physically aged beyond his fifty-six years and coughing blood, the next years passed drearily. In November 1889 he went to visit the Sarcees near Calgary, and then on what he knew was to be his last earthly trip, travelling slowly past the scenes of so many former tribulations and triumphs, observing the new homes of white farmers and noting their cattle herds grazing where so recently he had hunted great masses of buffalo, he returned to Blackfoot Crossing. There, bedridden all winter, he awaited his end.

It came on April 25, 1890. And when the camp crier, spreading the news that all expected, announced his death, saying: "He is no more. No one like him will fill his place," the mourning Blackfoot knew that it was even so.

In a great coffin, partly covered by the hillside but partly exposed to the winds of the prairies, they left the great Crowfoot, the father of his people. Overlooking the river and Blackfoot Crossing's historic ground and the great grassy hills beyond, his body lay. But though his spirit set out on its long, lonely journey to the Great Sand Hills, the Indians' Valhalla, who could believe that it stayed there? Who, wandering reverently over the glowing parklands and the rolling prairies as Crowfoot had wandered, knowing every far-flung hill and greeting every winding coulee, does not feel that with him goes the spirit of the great chief— the last of the free Blackfoot chiefs—still watching over the land he loved, the magnificent land.

# 11
# Settlement
# 1891-1906

When in 1890 Crowfoot's spirit sought the silence of the Great Sand Hills, settlers had barely started to come to Alberta. The province's arable land, so vast—75,000 square miles of it—so empty and so beautiful, lay waiting for the next turn of fortune's wheel, waiting to grant its favours to all men who would match its richness with labour and devotion. Up and down this arable land for over six hundred miles north and south and across it for distances varying up to 250 miles a man might wander for weeks seeing no sign of men either red or white; seeing nothing but its wide, flowering meadows, its broad, smiling valleys and its alluring hilltops; seeing nothing but its tall grasses, its teeming bird life or its trickling streams. A wild, beautiful, untouched paradise.

But until times picked up it was to remain a paradise virtually untouched. The long winter of a decade of depression had laid its restraining hand over eastern Canada, the United States and Europe, and many a man dreaming of free land in the West feared to quit his familiar hearth. Alberta's time had not yet come. Much free land in the Dakotas was still available for homesteading and Americans sought new opportunities there. Furthermore, the few of the land-hungry who did come to the Canadian West found enough scope for their courage and their industry in millions of acres yet untouched in Manitoba and the nearby unspoiled parklands of eastern Saskatchewan. Alberta's dawn still had a few years to wait before about 1897 the sunrise of settlement displayed its many attractions to diverse peoples seeking freedom and free land.

Nevertheless, even before that dawn broke over the fruitful valleys of the St. Mary, Red Deer, Battle and North Saskatchewan rivers, a few small groups, from widely separated homelands, had come in to look, and having looked, hung on. Three of the earliest came fleeing persecution: Mormons, Germans from Russia and Austria, and sorely pressed Ukrainians from their ancestral lands in Galicia and Bukowina. Others not fleeing persecution came in the hope that the new land would give them greater scope for their talents—notably a large influx of Scandinavians, many of whom had spent a few years in Minnesota or the Dakotas or else came more or less directly from Europe. Similarly, in

163

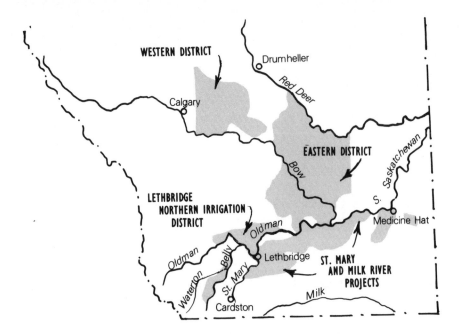

IRRIGATION FARMING IN SOUTHERN ALBERTA

Starting in 1878 and expanding sporadically ever since, a large area of southern Alberta has been made to blossom by a network of irrigation ditches.

---

1891 Father J. B. Morin's large colony of French went out to the Morin-ville area.

The first of these groups, a party of some forty Mormons, members of the Church of Jesus Christ of Latter Day Saints from Utah, was led by Charles Ora Card. In the fall of 1886, he and a couple of colleagues set out from Lethbridge in a democrat to spy out the land along the St. Mary River. On October 24, between the Belly and the St. Mary rivers, according to Card's diary, "while John W. Hendricks guarded camp, Bishop Zundell and myself went out into the prairie between the two rivers named and bowed before the Lord and dedicated and invoked the blessing of God upon the land and water, and asked His preservation of the same for the benefit of Israel, both white and red."

The next year Card led a group of some forty souls to the spot he had chosen. Accustomed to pioneering and to a ranching country, they knew what to expect as with their covered wagons, horses and cattle they worked their way north over the rolling terrain. On June 1, while Card was ranging ahead, the cavalcade heard him shouting and when they came up found him standing on one of the boundary cairns; "his bald head glistened in the sun." At last they had reached the border and stood and gave three cheers for Canada.

A History of Alberta

Two days later, with the Milk River Ridge off to the east of them and Chief Mountain west and south, they camped on Lee Creek. Next morning when they came out of their tents and found that six inches of snow had fallen during the night, one of the women in the party, addressing the leader and expressing her disappointment, said: "Brother Card, is this the kind of place you've brought us to?"

"Yes," he answered. "Isn't it beautiful?"

By July these resourceful pioneers had been joined by others of their faith and had established their headquarters' town of Cardston. By 1890 on the bare prairie lands sloping down from the Milk River Ridge they had started their first small scale set of irrigation canals and ditches. They, however, were not the first to practise irrigation in Alberta; they had been forestalled by John Quirk on his ranch at Sheep Creek. In 1878 he irrigated several hundred acres, and in 1879 John Glenn did the same on his ranch at Fish Creek. The Mormons, however, were the first to do so on a scale large enough to involve their immediate community.

In due course, so as to make full use of the irrigation works, Jesse Knight, a rich and philanthropic Mormon, supervised the ploughing of some three thousand acres around Raymond and also financed the first small sugar beet factory, which was opened in that town in 1903. Much of the Mormons' success is attributable to Knight who saw to it that when a project was planned it was carried out. On the ploughing, for instance, he assembled twelve teams which followed along behind each other turning over the prairie sod and preparing it for Alberta's first crop of sugar beets.

By 1901 some 3,200 Mormons had come to Alberta and were busily building their towns of Cardston (population 693) and Magrath (424) and converting their area into the paradise it has since become. When these industrious, purposeful and experienced people, backed by their church, came to Canada with determination and capital, they performed wonders in subduing the prairie. Alberta's earliest real dirt farmers, strengthened by their social organization, had found the province rewarding.

The second earliest group to turn to Alberta was a small band of Germans who in 1889 had been advised to try their luck on the dry, treeless plains at Dunmore near Medicine Hat and had been given all the land their hearts could desire—miles of it, ready to plough, and free of stick or stump. Like the Mormons, this small group, freighted with so much presage for Alberta's prosperity, were deeply religious but unlike them had no financial backing from their church. They were merely a part of a much larger group which had settled mainly in Saskatchewan and which had come fleeing financial persecution and injustices imposed on them by the government of Austria. Two or three generations earlier the Russian government had induced them to settle in the old Ukrainian province of Galicia, but after they were well established as farmers there and after that province had been taken over by Austria, their new governors made it advisable for them to move on to Canada, where they hoped to be free of persecution.

For two years at Dunmore, in a settlement they called Josefsberg after their former village in Galicia, they put in crops and gardens, but each time the drought of the area wilted everything they tried to grow. In this experience they were to be but the forerunners of untold thousands who, coming to the prairies from the more humid climates of eastern America or Europe, were to discover that all their former knowledge of farming in moister lands availed them little.

Nevertheless, in the spring of 1891, once they realized that the dry climate of Medicine Hat had wasted two of their precious years, they had courage enough to move in a body to the lands of greater rainfall around Edmonton. They chose homesteads in the dense virgin or burned over forests in the areas of rich soil at Stony Plain, Horse Hills and east of Fort Saskatchewan. There, thanks to their intense industry, they prospered.

The first of these venturesome colonists were but the forerunners of many more of their compatriots, and within three years several hundred other German settlers came in groups to homestead in the general area which had begun to look good to these earliest pioneers. In all, except for one colony which took up land west of Lacombe, some thirteen groups of Germans, some from Galicia and others, Moravians from Volynia, came to settle within a radius of thirty miles of Edmonton. Setting up areas which they named Hoffnungen (west of Leduc), Rosenthal (near Stony Plain), Josephsburg and Bruderheim, both near Fort Saskatchewan, Bruderfeld immediately south of Edmonton, as well as others at Rabbit Hill and near Wetaskiwin, Morinville, Beaver Lake and as far south as Lacombe, these valiant pioneers began hacking their way into the forest. Clearing enough land for a patch of oats, barley or vegetables, cutting slough hay on many of the natural meadows hitherto hidden in the forest, and throwing up a log shack roofed with sods, they settled in to their first experience of a bitter northern Alberta winter. Nearly everything they needed had to be produced from their lands and processed by their own hands.

And as more of their compatriots came following the surveyors' cutlines into the timber they too laid claim to 160 acres each along the banks of Whitemud and Blackmud creeks, west of the Peace Hills, or in the lower valley of Beaverhill Creek. Even the scantier timber near Gull and Sylvan lakes began to fall before their axes, while from lakes, little or large, an astonishing number of waterfowl of an amazing variety added a new and pleasant variation to their diet. Choosing building sites near a creek or on a rise overlooking a lake, these pioneers chopped trails ever farther back from the railway to connect one farmstead with another.

In March 1891, a month or two before the first German folk went out to Stony Plain, the first of Father Morin's French colonists passed through Edmonton. The convoy consisted of twelve wagons bringing sixty-five immigrants of all ages, who had detrained at Calgary and been met by willing Catholic colleagues who had come from St. Albert to bring them back to land which the good father had reserved for them there. These, of course, were only the advance guard of a much larger migration which, under the auspices of the church, came to settle: habitants from Quebec, fellow celebrants from France and Belgium, and repatriated French from Michigan coming once more under the protective cloak of the church. During the next several years they came flocking in to face up to the heavy forests of spruce which extended north from Edmonton. For these Canadiens were men of the forests, proficient axemen, proud of the well-mitred corners of the snugly fitting logs of which they built their homes. Year by year as they slashed new fields out of the timber they extended their parishes: Vegreville, sixty miles east of Edmonton; Beaumont, twenty miles south and Morinville; Villeneuve, Riviere Qui Barre, Legal, Vimy and Picardville. Year by year, living in the primitive simplicity of all pioneers, these laughter-loving, sociable people progressed up the scale of material living, cutting out roads, building schools and churches, and supplementing their larder with moose or deer or a bear which had been molesting their pigs. Before long their farmsteads and fields equalled those of some of their earliest compatriots, the people of the Lamoureux settlement, who, starting in 1872, had subdued the forest near the mouth of the Sturgeon River.

During the spring of 1892 a group of Anglo-Saxons who had turned their backs on the poor Ontario lands they had occupied, the Parry Sounders, arrived in a large contingent of 298 souls, of which sixty-six were grown men. With them they brought eighty-six horses and 170 head of cattle, thus showing themselves to be a well-equipped party of hardy, experienced pioneers. They chose land east of Edmonton, between present-day Bremner and Fort Saskatchewan and around the north and northeast flanks of the Beaver Hills near Lamont.

Having let their friends and relatives in the East know that they were well satisfied with sunny Alberta, these new colonists were soon followed by many others. Gradually they spread east beside the old Victoria Trail till by 1894 they had reached the vicinity of modern Lamont. By that time the number of Parry Sounders on land in the Edmonton region had reached 630.

Hard on the heels of these Ontario Anglo-Saxons, a group of rela-

167

tively well-off Norwegians from Minnesota and the Dakotas came along in their wagons and filed on land immediately north of the Parry Sounders in an area which later was called Limestone Lake. They formed one of the earliest Norse groups to reach Alberta. In 1892 and 1893 two other much more numerous Scandinavian colonies recruited largely from their European homelands and from more or less recent immigrants to the United States by C. A. Swanson, one of the Dominion's immigration agents, settled near Olds and east of Wetaskiwin. This last group took up most of the free land in an area of nearly three hundred square miles— some eight townships. Their new homesteads included heavily wooded land as well as some sparsely treed parkland generally in the large bend which the Battle River makes in running north from the Samson Indian Reserve, sweeping east past Gwynne to the vicinity of Camrose and then turning south to form Dried Meat Lake. The New Sweden and Malmo districts were some of the first lands to be occupied.

Like every other people, these new settlers embraced a variety of characters, ranging from some who could not read to well-educated leaders. Amongst them, for instance, was Olaf L. Save, who in his homeland had been a member of the Swedish parliament, and Charles H. Olin, who went on to become one of Alberta's early members of the legislative assembly.

Amongst them too was Karl Bjorkgren, who homesteaded north of Red Deer Lake near the site of the Blackfoot–Cree battle in which Crowfoot and Father Lacombe had figured so prominently twenty-seven years earlier. There, according to his daughter, Mrs. Elvira Backstrom, he built a "two-roomed house of poplar logs which he stood on end and pegged together with wooden pegs. It had a shingled roof. . . ."

Like all pioneers, the Bjorkgrens obtained much of their food by catching rabbits in pits concealed by brush, and by shooting the partridges which pattered over the leaves in the parkland bluffs, or potting the prairie chickens which roosted by the dozens in the trees bordering their small fields in the fall. Their furniture the settlers made from local poplar and the more painstaking of them used boards to form the platform of their beds instead of fashioning those of woven split willows. Their mattresses were big sacks stuffed with straw or slough grass. In the earlier days, as Mrs. Backstrom wrote, "often a whole bolt of calico was bought by one family and all the sewing was done by hand until a sewing machine could be acquired. On Sundays the mothers and the girls would come in dresses all alike and the boys would even have shirts from the same bolt of calico. Only the father was allowed to be individualistic. . . . Old clothing was used to its last shred; it was made over into the very common hand-me-downs. Mothers sheared, washed, carded, spun, and knitted mittens and socks for her own flock, her husband, and herself." Her father made many a seventy-mile trip to Edmonton to have his wheat ground into flour. Such then were the conditions the sturdy Scandinavians faced up to and enjoyed in their strenuous struggle which brought the area in which they settled to its present productive richness.

During the years 1893 to 1895 at least three other Scandinavian colonies came to throw in their lot with Alberta's thick timber in an area west of Stony Plain, at Bardo, north of Camrose, and along the Burnt Lake Trail, which they cleared through from Red Deer to Cygnet Lake.

In 1891, a few miles south of there but also along the Medicine River west of Innisfail, a small group of Icelanders chose a forested area to start their community of Markerville. With them came Stephansson Gudmundson Stephansson, a man perhaps better known in Norse countries today than in his adopted land, but nevertheless one of the few Canadian poets to be commemorated by a Canadian Historic Sites and Monuments Board cairn. Whenever he could take time off from farming, he spent long, happy hours in his log house writing the inspired poetry which ranks him as one of the great Icelandic bards. Like his compatriots, he cleared his land and helped to build up the rich farming community which during the passage of the next eighty years contributed so much to Alberta's mosaic.

To add to the colourful constituents which have blended to form the glowing tints of Alberta's fabric, the Norwegians who had settled in the Beaverhill Creek valley immediately north of the intermingling of German and Parry Sound homesteaders found still another element digging itself into the soil north of them—a Slavic element. By one of those curious coincidences which make history so fascinating, the arrival of these unique Ukrainians with their quaint customs and exotic costumes was linked directly to that of the first Germans who had preferred the mud of the Edmonton area to the dust of Medicine Hat. For Iwan Pylypow, one of the leaders of the Ukrainians, had gone to school in Galicia with John Krebs who had helped to lead his fellow Germans to the land east of Fort Saskatchewan. Indeed, accompanying Krebs and his fellows to Medicine Hat had been two Ukrainians who had intermarried with that group in the old land, Ludwig Kulak and Stefan Koroluk.

In any event, in 1891 the forerunners of the Ukrainian migration, Iwan Pylypow and Wasyl Eleniak, came to look over the possibilities of settling in Canada. The direct result of their trip was that the next year several of their compatriots filed on homesteads in the valley of Beaverhill Creek. Of even greater influence in starting the large Ukrainian migration to Canada was Dr. Josef Oleskow, the philanthropic professor who, starting in 1895, bent all his energies towards peopling Canada's prairies with his compatriots. Amongst the outstanding men who in the early

1890s took advantage of the leadership afforded by Pylypow and Dr. Oleskow are such great names as Mykhailo Melnyk, Mykhailo Pullishy, Nykola Tychkowski, Theodore Nemirsky, Stefan Shandro and Peter Svarich, all early pioneers.

They were the forerunners of thousands of their kin who, liking the wooded lands of the Saskatchewan valley, came to subdue and to love them. Ever onward they pressed, filling the valley of Beaverhill Creek, flowing over the flat lands around Beaverhill Lake and Whitford Lake, swarming over the rich lands of the Willingdon country, hewing their way into the forests along the south bank of the Saskatchewan River and hacking their way into the woods north of it. Over Eagletail Hill—the great ridge east of Cucumber Lake—they scrambled. The Snipe and the Snake hills scarcely slackened their stride. Neither did the stony, glaciated lands between the Vermilion River and the mighty Saskatchewan and around Plain Lake and Beauvallon, nor the sandy sites of Slawa Creek, nor even the long glacial gouges around Angle, Landon and Raft lakes. Until 1905 nothing could stop this influx of a people devoted to the soil and exulting in obtaining it free of monetary costs. They only stopped then because settlers of Anglo-Saxon stock had worked west from the Lloydminster Barr Colony and north from the new railway passing through Vermilion and had taken the land farther east.

By then a new Ukraine covering two thousand square miles had risen in a new land which, even if it had a harsh climate and even if it required the toil of every pioneer's whole life to subdue, nevertheless offered rewards and opportunities and above all, freedom. Like the influx of German, Norse, Anglo-Saxon or French folk, the Slavic migration was a success story.

Not so was the story of another group migration, a little Jewish band which during the summer of 1893 went to settle east of Red Deer. This pitiable troop, probably sponsored by the Young Men's Hebrew Benevolent Society of Montreal and probably with the active help of Sir Alexander Galt, who took a great interest in the plight of Russian Jews, was recruited in the slums of Chicago, brought west, and, along with a few axes, shovels and a team of horses, dumped into the inhospitable lands at the north end of Ghostpine Lake and left to farm or fail.

Although in places on the prairies some Jewish farming colonies prospered, this group, totally inexperienced, abysmally ignorant of forest or farming, failed. When winter came it found them eating snared rabbits and eking out an existence in cave-like holes they had dug into a hillside. By that time one of the team of horses entrusted to the rabbi's care had perished, leaving the little commune with only one horse. Some of the younger men had gone looking for work and eventually one who found temporary employment in Red Deer hurried back with a little cash, some

A History of Alberta

groceries and a .22 rifle, which would enable them all to obtain partridges to eat. Everyone rejoiced to see him, and along with the rabbi holding the remaining horse, shared in the welcome. In the excitement of passing the new gun from hand to hand, it went off and killed the horse.

What suffering these people endured that winter we can never know, but within a year the colony had dispersed as elsewhere its members found employment more in line with their capabilities. Undoubtedly few of their neighbours did much to help them ward off failure, for in the bitter intolerance of those days, more would be liable to lift a hand to smite than to help these Jewish people.

The arrival and settling of groups is easy to follow. Whether they were Germans who could not abide the dusty soils of the south and pulled out for the Edmonton area, or Mormons, who, looking at the dry soils, decided to add water and stir and stayed to transform the south, or whether they were Scandinavians, Parry Sounders or Ukrainians who headed for the tall timber, they were much easier to keep track of than the individual families who came pouring in. Actually these, mainly of Anglo-Saxon origin, who came wandering in laden with little more than cheerful optimism, were far more numerous than the group settlers of other ethnic backgrounds. Many of them settled on the southern prairies and began to crowd the ranchers, but most of them worked their way to the vacant lands adjacent to or even interspersed with the other groups.

All of them, groups or individuals, followed the railway which extended from Fort Macleod to Edmonton. In the south, before they began slicing up the sod and piling it up to form the walls and roofs of their first houses, they naturally went only as far from the railway as they needed to go. In the north, likewise gnawing their way into the timber and building their shacks with logs, they pushed back from the railway only as far as the nearest vacant quarter. For although it was a matter they soon forgot in their outcry at freight rates, they were doubly indebted to the railway; it provided them access to their new land, and, very often, it offered employment on construction crews, giving them the cash which enabled them to exist until their new quarters began producing.

During that time, however, several adventurous pioneers had been thrusting out branches from the trunk of Alberta's main axis. The southern ranch area, though not as populous as it was soon to become, had spread out over the country south of the Bow River from Medicine Hat to the mountains. Along the Red Deer River from Tail Creek west to modern Sundre a few hardy pioneers had homesteaded. Working out east of the railway at Didsbury and dropping down Rosebud Creek, a number of ranchers had sited their buildings along it and were pasturing their cattle on the adjacent grasslands. Soon they effected a junction with others pushing north from Gleichen.

Setting out in 1894 from Didsbury or Carstairs as well, but in a westerly direction, came one of Alberta's earliest Mennonites, Andrew Weber of Ontario, a lone individual who settled in the area to which a few years later many more of his faith came to homestead. The earliest Mennonite to file on land in Alberta, however, was Elias W. Bricker, who homesteaded in 1889 and who was also followed by more of his brethren.

Farther to the north, about 1891, another branch of settlement sprang up along the old trail from Lacombe station to the Métis settlements at Tail Creek and at the east end of Buffalo Lake. Into this paradise of rich soil and rolling scenery reminiscent of England's Cotswold country came some of the very people who could appreciate and cherish its beauty, some of the cultured folk of England. The first to settle far beyond the immediate environs of Lacombe were Walter Parlby, an Oxford graduate, and his brother. Soon these two were joined by others of similar background and interest and the community which was to embrace Clive, Tees, Alix and Lamerton had started on its way.

The two tenuous, topmost branches springing from Alberta's settlement tree spread out from Edmonton east along the old Winnipeg Trail and west along the Jasper Trail. For by this time a few ranchers were pushing east along the Vermilion River. Those purposeful pioneers who worked west from Edmonton along the Jasper Trail chose choice locations along the Sturgeon River as far as Lac Ste. Anne: the Taylors, the Beauprés and old Dan Noyes, the famous frontiersman. But even beyond them, far beyond in the valley at Jasper, in 1893 the genial old miner, Lewis Swift, set his heart on a homestead in the shadow of Pyramid Mountain. Moreover, a couple of years later John Gregg, one-time United States army scout, settled down at Prairie Creek near modern Hinton.

For the most part these early settlers had come to stay. A few indeed, looking in timorously, endured one winter in a frost-lined log shack and in the spring turned tail and ran back to a softer life. Many of the settlers who stayed were doomed to ultimate disappointment, but the vast majority stuck with their land and succeeded.

Alberta's tree was starting to thrive. With its roots firmly imbedded in the ranching area, its trunk reaching up through Calgary, Red Deer and Edmonton to its topmost twig at Morinville, it was well started. Then, as we have seen, thrusting branches out to Drumheller and Sundre, out towards Tail Creek, east along the Vermilion River and west towards Lac Ste. Anne, it had started to leaf out. Nevertheless it still needed careful nurturing, this tree which by 1895 had swelled Alberta's population to a mere 30,000.

And yet one of the colonies which had received the most careful nurturing—Father Lacombe's St. Paul des Métis settlement, officially opened on January 15, 1896—failed. Ever concerned with his Métis and anxious to remove them to what was then an area remote from the fleshpots of Alberta's growing white civilization, he obtained four townships of land and induced several Métis families to settle on its quarter-sections and to contemplate an agricultural way of life. In spite of the devotion of Father Adeodat Therien, who took charge of them, and of the establishment of a headquarters for them at his mission of St. Paul des Métis, settling and contemplating was about all that was done. Before many years most of the Métis had drifted away and eventually the land was taken over by a flourishing French colony.

In spite of that failure, all the conditions needed to nurture large-scale settlement in Alberta were on their way. By that time, like a favourable conjunction of planets, several events occurred which sent Alberta off into a veritable whirlwind of settlement. Hitherto, all its farmers had come in seeking a mere subsistence—a better existence than they had had in their old home—and some of them had not questioned the level of subsistence so long as they could find freedom and escape from tyranny. From about 1895 on, however, immigrants came in filled with the idea of farming and of exporting their produce. For two new conditions that were to be of vital importance to Alberta's arable soils had come into play—a market for wheat and new machinery to aid in the production and utilization of newly developed wheats which would withstand the prairies' frosts.

At this point great changes were also sweeping Europe and turning it, as well as the eastern United States, into an industrial society. In both these regions these changes were increasing the population, concentrating it into cities and necessitating the importation of food. A market was being established.

Today it is difficult to conceive of a time when the prairies were not exporting wheat. It was not until 1876, however, that the first export shipment of prairie wheat, 857¼ bushels of Red Fife, set off up the Red River on the sternwheeler *Minnesota,* bound for eastern Canada. To make up such a large shipment the very bottom of many a Winnipeg farmer's bin had to be scraped. Then it was not until 1884—a mere ten years before the time we are considering—that the first overseas shipment of wheat, 1,000 bushels of No. 1 Hard, went east by the CPR on its way to Britain. A market for Canadian wheat was now assured, and the recently built CPR could transport Alberta's grain to this market. The first condition had been met.

The second condition, acquiring the knowledge of how to farm these lands, came slowly. One element had been the development of Red Fife wheat, but even with it frosts claimed too much of the wheat crop. The steel-roller milling process was also part of this knowledge along with the invention of new ploughs, binders, and other machinery

173

which enabled the farmers to cope with the problem of large-scale farms. The combination of all these factors, and of other developments which in 1895 were yet to come, provided the know-how with which Alberta's vast soil resources yielded their riches.

Having met these conditions, two other factors came into play: the thousands of eager immigrants waiting in the wings, ready for their cue to come to Alberta, and the aroused immigration authorities at Ottawa, newly risen from their slumbers and refreshed with a resolve to populate the prairies. In 1897, just as the fever of the depression had begun to fade before the flush of the new gold supply and a new boom was in the bud, Sir Wilfrid Laurier, who had recently assumed the mantle of prime minister of Canada, appointed Clifford Sifton as his minister of the interior. Sifton, who put a world of intelligence and push into whatever he turned to do, thus had charge at one and the same time of Canada's land policy and its immigration policy. Affairs on the prairies were in for a decided upturn. Just at that time too, by a rare coincidence, the rapidly expanding United States found that at last its rush of immigrants had overtaken all the free lands in its west, and that its young folk or any newcomers seeking farm lands would have to look elsewhere. At this point, Sifton, determined to settle western Canada, provided the elsewhere.

Overhauling the homestead regulations, straightening the kinks in his department, and advertising extensively for settlers, he quickly set the tide of immigration rising. A year before, some sixteen thousand immigrants had come to Canada. During 1897, twice that many answered Sifton's call, and every year thereafter the tide rose higher. His policy was a single-minded drive to fill the West with immigrants from any country whence he could draw them. All the West, and especially Alberta, benefited by this policy, and before long its cities and towns were feeling the pleasant push of this new impetus. Of this push, northern Alberta got a large share, and within a few years, Edmonton began to grow at a rate it had hitherto never experienced.

At long last, Alberta's greatest resource, its soil, was on the point of being widely used. In the past its furs had been exploited, and a pittance of gold had been picked from its rivers, and to house and heat its few people who lived by furs or gold, some of its timber had been cut and its coal mined. Largely because its time had not come, land, Alberta's main resource, had been left relatively untouched.

Once its time came, once the iron was hot, Sifton struck, and his settlers came pouring in. In 1895 Alberta's population had been about 30,000. By 1901, two or three years after he got his forge heated, it had more than doubled to 73,022, of which eighty-four percent was classed as rural. But even then the immigration engine was merely

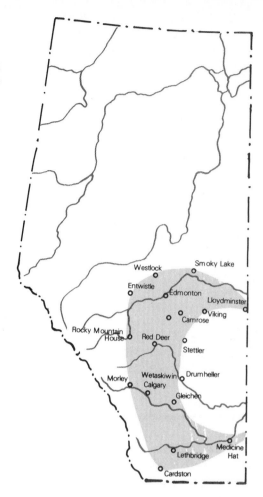

THE SETTLEMENT CRESCENT

By 1906 the bulk of homestead settlement was contained within this crescent-shaped area.

idling. As it picked up speed during the five years to 1906 the rush of settlers and of people flocking into the forests, mines and cities once more doubled the province's population.

During that interval when thousands of individual settlers flocked in to take up land, two interesting colonies, one small and the other large, one aristocratic old country French and the other run-of-mill old country English, came to add their bit of colour to Alberta's mosaic. The first, spearheaded by Armand Trochu in 1903 and including Count Paul de Baudrap and other military men, went into ranching ventures around what is now the town of Trochu. For some years the little colony progressed but in 1914, when France was invaded, every able-bodied man donned his old uniform and went to aid her in her distress. For all intents and purposes that marked the end of this interesting old country French settlement.

175

The other larger group, the Barr Colony, a most unique enterprise, was the immigration during 1903 of 1,964 people all in one batch from England to the district they soon named Lloydminster. Organized and led by the Reverend I. M. Barr, an Anglican, it took thirty railway cars to bring the group's baggage to Saskatoon. The newcomers' long overland trip to their homesteads, which were to be located in the vicinity of the spot where the Canadian Northern Railway survey crossed the 4th meridian, was the most trying part of their trip. At Saskatoon some of the colony's weaknesses began to show up and there it became evident that the Reverend Mr. Barr's enthusiasm had outrun his preparations for handling a large assortment of English people, very few of whom had any experience in farming but all of whom were free to complain and to voice the Britisher's right to free speech. Though evidently honest, he was a poor leader and within a few days he found his services rejected in favour of the Reverend George E. Lloyd, a man of strong character who thenceforth took command of the often obstreperous colonists, while Barr left for other pastures.

Aside from its organization the colony had another weakness in that though it had been recruited from several strata of English society and contained members of many diverse trades, almost none of its members had any experience in agricultural work. Most of the colonists had some money. Moreover, of gumption, courage and persistence in the face of adversity, all of them had full measure. But as bank clerks, tailors, millworkers and shopwalkers they lacked any conception of pioneering ways or conditions or of farming. This was a state of affairs common to most British immigrants of the homestead period, and in fact of northern European settlers in general. During Alberta's homestead era, while the authorities were eager to have British people settle on the prairies and while non-agricultural workers in Britain were clamouring to come out, the old country farming industry was in one of its rather rare profitable phases, so that men experienced in agriculture saw little to be gained by emigrating.

Nevertheless, leaving Saskatoon as soon as they could, over soft spring trails, the Barr colonists took two tedious weeks to battle the mud holes and the slush of new-fallen snow to reach the 4th meridian. There, smack on either side of this surveyor's abstraction, they started their headquarters' town, Lloydminster, and went out to face the inevitable consequence of inexperience with the Canadian West. Through it all, aided by the Reverend Lloyd's sane advice, they persisted and soon the productiveness of the Lloydminster area became a tribute both to Alberta's resources and to the courage and the adaptability of these one-time green settlers.

Only one of their mistakes remains to haunt their memories—

building their town on either side of the 4th meridian. Within two years that line became the boundary between the new provinces of Alberta and Saskatchewan. Its presence and the lack of thoughtfulness on the part of those who defined the boundary has split an otherwise thriving city down the middle and exposed its two parts to the vagaries of two far-off provincial legislatures.

With the advent of these two colonies and thousands of individual settlers, Alberta's population jumped to 185,412 by 1906. Calgary's had soared from 4,392 in 1901 to 13,573 in 1906, and the Edmonton–Strathcona combination, which had made a slightly more spectacular gain, had increased from 4,176 to 14,088. Each of the smaller but busy centres had increased proportionally: Medicine Hat to 3,020; Lethbridge to 2,936; and Wetaskiwin to 1,652. Running them a good race and mainly in the south part of the province were five towns of over one thousand people: Cardston, Raymond, Macleod, High River and Lacombe. Out of the province's 1906 population, thirty-one percent, or 58,000 lived in cities, towns or villages, leaving 127,000 on homesteads.

# 12
# The Move to Provincial Status in 1905

By restricting our attention to the earliest flood of settlers who by 1906 had increased the province's population to some 185,000, we have taken our eyes off many other developments which were going on at the same time. Because the area from Calgary south had been blessed with both the transcontinental CPR and the interprovincial railway through the Crowsnest Pass, the development of the south had proceeded more rapidly than that of the north. Of very great importance to the Alberta economy was the coal industry which in the main was then confined to a few regions in the southwest corner of the province, near Banff, along the Oldman River near Lethbridge, and in the Crowsnest Pass. Each year saw a marked advance in that industry's production. By 1903 the busiest coal mining area of them all was the Crowsnest Pass, where at intervals of a mile or so railway sidings and slack piles marred the one-time natural beauty of the valley.

At that time one of the most productive mines was at Frank, a town named after H. L. Frank, a wealthy man from Butte, Montana, who had brought his energy and capital to the area in 1901. For much of the year the imposing mass of Turtle Mountain towering above it on the south shaded the town which nestled on a little flat in the angle between Gold Creek and the Crowsnest River. Directly across Gold Creek several miners, avoiding the town's building restrictions, had scattered a dozen or so cabins. Across the Crowsnest River from them and the town, a gaping timber-framed hole indicated where for the last two or three years busy miners had been following a rich seam into the depths of Turtle Mountain.

On the evening of April 28, 1903, as the twenty men of the night shift carried their lunch buckets far along the galleries winding back into the mountain, all appeared normal. In due course, except for these men of the night shift and a wakeful freight train crew, every one of the town's five hundred souls, perhaps after planning what each would do on the morrow, settled down to another night's sleep.

For at least seventy-six, and undoubtedly a few more, there was to be no tomorrow. At 4:10 A.M. the disastrous Frank slide struck. A gigantic wedge of limestone 2,100 feet high, 3,000 feet wide and 500 feet thick let go its hold on the steep mountainside and crashed down on the sleeping valley. In a matter of no more than a hundred seconds the slide was over. Ninety million tons of rock, much of it in blocks as big as houses, had swept over part of the town, covered the railway track, buried the mine entrance, and killed at least seventy-six men, women and children.

The town proper had been left untouched, but the homes east of Gold Creek had been covered or crumpled. One of the living whose experience was the most remarkable of any of the survivors of the actual area where the slide struck was the baby Marian Leitch. Her parents and four brothers had been killed instantly; her two sisters, although pinned under the rubble, had suffered little more than bruises, but she was blown clear of the carnage. In the dusty dawn, as the rescuers probed the ruins, they could find no trace of baby Marian. Finally a neighbour woman, hearing her crying, came upon the child. Marian had been flung clear out of the top storey of the house and had landed in a pile of hay many yards from the debris that had once been her home.

Of the mine portal there was no trace. Its exterior works had been swept away and their site was buried under the talus slide down which at intervals great boulders continued to roll. The men in the mine, feeling the jar of the slide, soon found that their exit was crumpled and hopelessly blocked. With the practical miners' amazing coolness they felt that their only hope lay in digging a new way out of their dilemma. Realizing that one seam of untouched coal out-cropped higher up, they dug their way up the seam, and hours later their leader's pick broke into the open. A beam of sunlight dazzled him, but a rush of clean air bathed his face.

Their ordeal was not over, however, because erratic rocks still dribbled down the slope, making it impossible to escape that way. With excellent judgment the men began another tunnel through another thirty-six feet of clay and coal to a spot where they could see that a large embedded boulder would shield them from the dribbling rocks. There they emerged thirteen hours after many of their friends and some of their families below had been crushed.

There they stood and stared at a huge expanse of rock, lying like a giant fan half a mile wide, covering the area east of Gold Creek. Its last crazily skipping boulders had flung themselves as much as five hundred feet up the other side of the valley.

When news of the disaster reached Cranbrook, the CPR sent up a special rescue train, and soon police and officials from as far away as Calgary reached the scene. Amongst them were many a newspaper reporter and each with his profession's incurable penchant for exaggeration

The Move to Provincial Status in 1905

began sending out fantastic and fanciful reports. In all conscience the disaster was dramatic enough, but some of the drama they dreamed up to embellish the tragedy has continued to surround the event in a fog of misinformation.

Nevertheless, the Frank slide on that April morning in 1903 ranks as one of Canada's major natural disasters. Unfortunately it was to be but the prelude to a series of man-made catastrophies which for many a year blackened the history of the Crowsnest Pass mining area.

Not all Calgary journalists, however, were so irresponsible, for about this time Calgarians began hearing of the Bob Edwards who a few years before had left Strathcona to its fate. Early in 1902 when Bob started his *Eye Opener* in High River, he fell in love with the town and its ranching environment. As part of his opening announcement, he declared that "clothed in righteousness, a bland smile and lovely jag, the editor of this publication struck town two weeks ago. The management has decided on the name, 'Eye Opener' because few people will resist taking it. It will be run on a strictly moral basis at one dollar a year. If an immoral paper is the local preference, we can supply that too but it will cost $1.50."

Before long, with eager anticipation, everyone in the West looked forward to the *Eye Opener's* next instalment of the adventures of Bob's fictitious characters and their friends Hi Walker, Joe Seagram, Johnny Dewar and Benny Dikteen. While every one of his issues was interesting, his *Eye Opener* often reported an event fraught with significance, such as when on August 8, 1903, it told that "Billy Cochrane of High River has introduced the first automobile into Alberta. High River is the pioneer of progress. Okotoks still clings to the Red River cart."

By 1904 Bob Edwards had moved his paper to Calgary, and commented: "Picturesquely situated so as to be within easy reach of the brewery, Calgary extends right and left, north and south, up and down, in and out, expanding as she goes, swelling in her pride, puffing in her might, blowing in her majesty and revolving in eccentric orbits round a couple of dozen large bars which close promptly at 11:30 right or wrong." In announcing his move to Calgary he said that he had decided to start a paper under the "absurd title of Eye Opener. It is said that the editor has never drawn a sober breath in his life. . . . His rag will probably go bust inside of six months." Prophecy was not his forte, because the paper continued till his death, eighteen years later.

About the time of Bob's arrival in Calgary, that city watched the second car come to Alberta, John Prince's gasoline burning Rambler which competed for attention with Cochrane's Stanley Steamer. Edwards, thinking about these newfangled contraptions and hearing that J. S. Young, the editor of the *Herald*, had imported a McLaughlin and that up on Edmonton's Jasper Avenue in May 1904 J. H. Morris had displayed that city's first car, commented that "the first thing a man with a new automobile runs into is debt."

At that time Calgary, containing many a rich, far-seeing man and drawing sustenance from all the ranching regions, as well as from the busy mining areas of Banff and Crowsnest Pass, had outgrown Edmonton. Calgary could actually count some twelve thousand citizens, while the best Edmonton could do was produce 8,350. And if against Strathcona's wishes its citizens were added to the Edmonton tally, the lot would only have been a handful over ten thousand people.

In spite of that, Edmonton applied to the Northwest Territories legislature for the privilege of incorporation as a city. When on November 7, 1904, its new charter was proclaimed, it expanded its boundaries to take in an additional 2,400 acres. Like its rival, the northern city could boast of having its share of the latest fad, the newfangled cars, the half dozen of them in the province—those rattling contraptions with their rotating flywheels and their detonating cylinders. At the moment, however, they did not look like a likely bet and could never supercede the good old reliable horses who did all the light tripping and the heavy hauling.

As they had done for centuries, horses still remained the only practical motive power. Oxen, it was true, had made a long and honourable showing and homesteaders still used them by the thousands, but year by year they were on their way out, whereas, in this era of drays, buggies and lumber wagons, the number of horses continually increased. In a city such as Edmonton strings of twenty or thirty pack horses trotted or frisked about, hazed along by two or three hollering packers. Smart surreys flashed by, pulled by well-groomed check-reined horses, curried and combed to within an inch of their lives. Indians' democrats, with one or more wheels wobbling perilously, often dragged by derelict raw-shouldered skeletons, crept along. Buggies, oxcarts and carriages wound their way in and out of the traffic. Depending upon whether the previous week had enjoyed a dearth or a downpour of rain, cabbies whisking a fare along raised a cloud of dust or splattered pedestrians with mud or slush. Teams drawing covered wagons to the end of their sixteen-hundred-mile trip from Minnesota brought new settlers to stare at Jasper Avenue. Now and then a fire engine with its galloping team lurched and swayed around the corners.

But all these were merely the horses in motion. Others, either saddled or hitched to vehicles, were tied to sidewalk rings, posts or rails. Any vacant lot beside or behind any of the bigger stores was full of horses munching hay or merely waiting for their drivers to return. The market square contained other teams and wagons, and in front of the many livery barns a constant procession of horses stood to be hitched or unhitched. Stages, drawn by four horses, made scheduled trips along the Athabasca Trail, the North Victoria Trail, and between the city and many another embryo town not yet served by a railroad.

In the same way Calgary the cowtown, Lethbridge and Medicine Hat were also horse-drawn cities, possibly even more so for in addition to all their other traffic their streets were seldom lacking in cowboys. Usually these cowboys were busy working far back in the hills but on occasion they rode into Calgary on business or in search of a good time. Then they were prone to let off steam, gallop along the streets or indeed ride their horses into a store. At times they ended up in jail. At that, however, they left their impress on Calgary, more so than upon any other city.

And while they did, huge livery stables became part of the city's architecture. Moreover, within a horseshoe's pitch of any livery barn stood an unpretentious blacksmith's shop. There, with his bare, sweaty torso covered with grime and bulging with muscles, a cheerful smith repaired farm machinery, fixed vehicles, and shod horses. Closely related to the stable spacially and spiritually were the offices of the veterinarians, who found much to do in this horse-drawn world. Allied to the black-smith's shop also, and usually close by, were harness shops, for much of a city's industry centred around its mode of transportation. Many a shoemaker's shop catered to the needs of the town folk for smart shoes, and to lumbermen, miners, farmers or teamsters for heavier, thick-soled footwear.

A stroll along any one of the close-in side streets in Calgary, Edmonton, Lethbridge or Medicine Hat took one past a repetition of institutions all devoted to these important industries or services, while other businesses catered to the comfort, or at least the service, of this pioneer agricultural frontier. There were hotels of all grades, from clean, well-run establishments, to flop houses crawling with bed bugs. Each had its saloon with its brass rail and spittoons, long mirror and sawdust-strewn floor. Not far to seek were other houses run by the madams.

Vigorous indeed were Alberta's recently spawned cities in which the number of newcomers vastly exceeded old-timers of five years' standing, where nearly everybody was less than forty years old and where men far outnumbered women. Most of the stores, and many of the houses, used electricity for lighting only. In other residences coal oil supplied the lights. Hardware stores handled any petroleum products sold, but, except for a gallon or two of gasoline used in the few dry cleaning establishments, and a few jars of vaseline, coal oil for lighting and axle grease for wagon wheels formed the major contribution made by the oil industry. Small mines and a few sawmills used negligible quantities of lubricating oil, but as yet the oil age had not threatened the oats era.

Every city's builders were busy, some erecting steel frameworks, some building with brick, or in Calgary with local sandstone, and dozens throwing up wooden stores with false facades. The ra-tat-tatting of the riveters, the rasping of hand saws, and the banging of hammers kept up a continuous commotion, while the redolence of newly-sawn spruce lumber filled the air. In season, from the splendid stands of spruce timber far up among the foothills drained by the Bow River or the vast forests covering the watershed of the North Saskatchewan to mills at Calgary and Edmonton, drivers rode great log booms down the river. These log drives, long since gone from the rivers, brought many a lumberman out of the woods each spring to ride herd on the logs, anchor them to the pilings driven deep into the river's mud, and then head for the nearest saloon. And everyone, whether in Calgary or Edmonton, sniffed contentedly at the haze of wood smoke which rose from the industries down by its river or was wafted in from great forest fires burning perhaps fifty or a hundred miles back in the bush. Week after week, the afternoon sun descended as a red ball in the west as over the growing cities hung the aromatic pall of wood smoke, tinctured at times by the acidity of coal fires. If at times the exhaust fumes from one or more cars fouled the air, they were quickly diluted by the pervading pleasantness of wood smoke, or cut by the spicy savour of ammonia wafted from the piles behind every stable.

These then were the main cities of 1905, each bursting at the seams. Overflowing with newcomers, bubbling with energy, rejoicing in their horse-drawn might, rightly assured of their future, they were touched with the magic of a new land awakening and tinctured by the kindly medicinal mixture of mill smoke and manure.

Many of the newcomers from Europe had come because they were restless, underprivileged or idealistic. Most of them, complaining bitterly because of a lack of social progress in their homelands, had overlooked the value of the services, institutions and public works which they had enjoyed and until they came to the Canadian prairies many had failed to realize that as yet there were none of these in the homestead areas. Over the next two or three years they were to find that they themselves had to provide many of these: churches and schools, which they had taken for granted at home, and most of the works, such as roads and telephones. In their homelands they had looked to someone higher up to provide these facilities and here they looked to some government to supply them, often not realizing at first that they themselves were the government.

183

The Move to Provincial Status in 1905

Several idealistically inclined individuals with British socialistic backgrounds, many of them fiery of eye and of fluctuating practicality, came to add their contribution to the making of the prairies' personality. Teaming up with immigrants from the United States, recently members of such American organizations as the Society of Equity, the Farmers' Union, and the Non-Partisan League, all of them steeped in agrarian political revolt, they deluded themselves into believing that the mere passage of legislation would deliver the millennium. Vociferous and demanding, and soon collecting a following, they were hard taskmasters for any government to serve.

Many of their ideas and causes were good and helped to bring about reforms, but when shouting shibboleths they wandered from the agrarian fold into the economic field they put pressure on both the territorial and federal governments, which resulted in many a wasteful venture. Amongst these were many branch railway lines to which the legislators, driven by farm voters and drawn on by unscrupulous railway promoters, provided provincial guarantees.

Then too the farmers of the West quickly rebelled at an inevitable concomitant of the opening of the West, the colonial type of over-lordship exerted by the federal government and by eastern capital. With a distaste of anyone whom they regarded as not a producer, which soon grew into the belief that everyone who was not a cultivator was a crook, they fathered a political rift between East and West which endures to this day.

Farmers' organizations naturally started in Manitoba and Saskatchewan sooner than they did in Alberta. As early as 1883 farmers there, following similar previous moves in the United States, began to organize themselves to defend their interests from the overwhelming influence of the East. Though the CPR rails had barely been bedded down on their ties, the farmers complained of the "excessive charges of the railway monopoly" and of Canada's tariff policies. Some of them became so irate and spouted so much about armed revolt that mistakenly the instigators of Riel's North-West Rebellion felt that they had found an ally. During the next fifteen years prairie farmers leaned towards an importation from the United States, the Patrons of Industry, and calling their organization the Canadian Farmers' Alliance reiterated their dislike for tariffs, elevator companies and the CPR, and as a vindicative measure called for the construction of an impractical railway to Hudson Bay. Amongst other things, their efforts led to the passage of the Dominion Grain Act, which brought some of the reforms they desired.

In Alberta, farmers' movements started in the north shortly after 1879 when Edmonton held the first agricultural exhibition in the northwest and when its Agricultural Society, likewise the first organized in the Northwest Territories, came into being. By the time the Calgary–Edmonton Railroad reached Strathcona in 1891 the farm movement began to assume a more militant form with the appearance of the Patrons of Industry in the area. A parallel movement at Lacombe saw the birth of the Farmers' Association of Alberta, which by 1904 had several branches.

Less worrying to the territorial government but still an important part of Alberta's make-up were the early labour unions. The railwaymen and many of the miners had been members of unions before coming to the province and on their arrival began to protect themselves by banding together. The first union in Alberta was formed at Medicine Hat on January 6, 1887, when Cascade Lodge No. 342 of the Brotherhood of Locomotive Firemen was set up. It was soon followed in Medicine Hat by other lodges of the running trades, and in 1900 the first labour group to organize in Calgary was the railway carmen's local.

The coal miners were not far behind the railwaymen in forming unions, when in Lethbridge in 1901 they set up a local which a couple of years later was superseded by the United Mine Workers of America. Shortly thereafter other groups of miners came into the fold under the general supervision of such bodies as the American Federation of Labor, the Trades and Labor Congress and the Canadian Labor Congress. For a few years after 1906 the International Workers of the World, the IWW became a bitterly radical and largely unwelcome factor in Alberta's labour activity but quietened down with the onset of the war in 1914. By 1906 also, the United Mine Workers of America had taken a hand in Alberta affairs. Rather naturally most of the labour unrest was in the mining areas in which a long strike running from May 1 to November 20 directly affected some six thousand miners.

By 1906 most of the trades in the province had been organized. Even before the Great War the attitude of employers and of the government towards labour had undergone a marked change and the right of working men to organize had come to be recognized. Labour relations, in spite of occasional unwarranted strikes caused by jurisdictional disputes, had started along the path to better wages and working conditions.

But we are getting ahead of ourselves. Our last look at the West's political progress was in 1901 when the Northwest Territories had nearly attained fully responsible government, when Frank Oliver of Edmonton represented all 73,022 Albertans at Ottawa, and Clifford Sifton had shoved his immigration engine into high gear. At that time, of course, Alberta was merely a district of the Northwest Territories.

During the next three years the members of the North-West Territories Assembly kept up a clamour for provincial status, and when in

The Move to Provincial Status in 1905

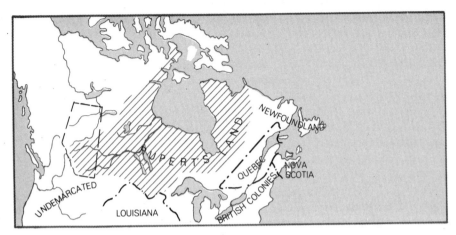

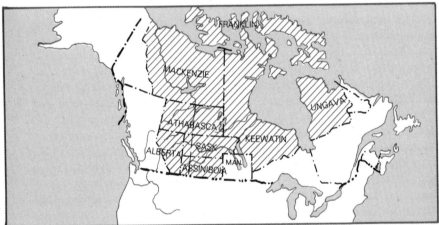

A History of Alberta

1904 Sir Wilfrid Laurier's government went to the country for another mandate, he promised to grant it. At the 1905 session, the House of Commons passed the Alberta Act and the Saskatchewan Act, creating the two new provinces. Under the Alberta Act the province took in all of the District of Alberta and about half of the District of Athabasca, as well as those portions of Saskatchewan and Assiniboia west of the 4th meridian. In this fashion the flourishing town of Medicine Hat, with its population of three thousand became part of Alberta. Poor Lloydminster, however, far to the north, found itself split up the middle with a portion in each province. Thenceforth, Alberta extended some 750 miles north and south from the 49th to the 60th parallel.

Westerners, although rejoicing on the whole, were disappointed in some of the provisions of the new acts. First of all, Haultain of the Macleod constituency, who was regarded as premier of the Northwest Territories, had advocated that only one large province be created instead of two. He and others also resisted the tendency of eastern politicians to impose party divisions along Liberal and Conservative lines on the new provinces and felt that governments on the prairies should not automatically follow established party lines. Moreover, he had fought to have the provinces granted ownership of their natural resources, land and minerals, but had failed, and his failure was to rankle in provincial hearts until some twenty-five years later when the federal government gave in and vested them in the provinces. In place of the revenue which its resources would have brought, each province was to receive an annual grant from the federal government which was to increase as their populations grew.

---

RUPERT'S LAND

In 1670 Charles II of England granted all the territory whose waters flowed into Hudson Bay to the Hudson's Bay Company. This territory was called Rupert's Land. In 1869 Rupert's Land and the Northwest Territory were ceded to the new Dominion of Canada.

NORTHWEST TERRITORIES 1898

In 1870, after Rupert's Land and the Northwest Territory were transferred to Canada, the province of Manitoba came into being with only a fraction of its present area. The vast lands of the new Northwest Territories were subdivided into districts whose boundaries shifted back and forth with the growth of Canada.

ALBERTA 1905

With the increase of settlers in the prairies, the population had grown to such a degree that both Saskatchewan and Alberta, made up of the former Districts of Alberta, Assiniboia, Athabasca and Saskatchewan, were granted provincial status.

The Move to Provincial Status in 1905

Equally irritating was the school question; such men as Bennett and Haultain led a fiery crusade against some of the clauses of the bills as drafted at Ottawa. The bills provided that minorities would have the right to establish their own schools, teach in their own language, and share in the public funds to maintain these schools, a matter to which most Albertans were opposed. Once more this vexing question led to battles polemical and political, and Prime Minister Laurier's difficulties in granting autonomy to the West were bedevilled by the rift between French and English and between Catholic and Protestant, a split in which the question of Roman Catholic separate schools loomed large. So strong were the emotions aroused that in February 1905 one of Laurier's ablest ministers, Clifford Sifton, the man who had accomplished wonders in settling the West and a man of passionate convictions, resigned. Yielding, Sir Wilfrid modified the offending clauses and the Alberta and Saskatchewan Acts were passed. The changes made with respect to education were to continue the system established by a Northwest Territories ordinance in 1901. This ordinance provided that the minority of the ratepayers in any district, whether Protestant or Roman Catholic, might establish a separate school and earmark their taxes for that school.

When Sifton resigned and Laurier appointed their member, Frank Oliver, as minister of the interior, Edmontonians began to prick up their ears. They had stuck by him when three times they had elected him to the North-West legislature at Regina and when for nine years they had kept him in Ottawa as Alberta's federal member. He had eaten of their bread and now he would butter it for them. Had he not written: "While the Saskatchewan runs downhill, while coal will burn or timber grow, or the seed produce after its kind, they [the people of Edmonton] ask no favours of anyone, but with their own hands will build up this country into the best province of the Dominion of Canada."

And in Ottawa when the chips were down, Frank Oliver aided them with their building. Ever at Laurier's elbow, he saw to it that clause nine of the Alberta Act declared: "Unless and until the Lieutenant-Governor in Council of the said province otherwise directs, by proclamation under the Great Seal, the seat of government of the said province shall be at Edmonton."

Once the act was through, all Edmontonians had to do was sweep in the pot. This they proceeded to do starting on September 1, 1905, the day Alberta became a province, the day Edmonton staged its first major celebration.

On the great day the weather was perfect, and mellow autumn sunshine lighted up Edmonton's magnificent valley. On the flats below Mc-Dougall Hill lay the half-mile race track, the grandstand, and other build-

A History of Alberta

ings of the new fair grounds. Among the poplars south of it shone the rows of white tents of more than two hundred officers and men of the Royal North West Mounted Police. Surrounded by the oval race track stood the white and blue ceremonial platform bedecked in red, white and blue bunting, with its purple crown. In the bright sunlight and the soft breeze, flags and pennants fluttered gaily. On the stand sat many of Canada's dignitaries, while thousands of Albertans, jostling good naturedly, stood and applauded.

At 11 A.M. Governor General Earl Grey and his party arrived in their glittering carriages and the military march past began. The governor general inspected the three squadrons of the RNWMP, consisting of 211 cavalry men and their four-gun battery, all commanded by Commissioner Perry. When the platform party took their places Mayor MacKenzie read an address to the governor general, who replied in a suitable speech. Then came Canada's great prime minister, Sir Wilfrid Laurier. Courtly of manner, with a finely chiseled face and an aureole of fluffy white hair framing his head, he rose to speak. All was hushed as he recalled his visit to the town eleven years previously. Noting the subsequent development and holding out radiant promise for the future, he said: "I see everywhere hope. I see everywhere calm resolution, courage, enthusiasm to face all difficulties, to settle all problems." He spoke to this people of many nations, urging them to be British subjects, to take their share in the life of this country, whether on the municipal, provincial or national level. "We do not anticipate, and we do not want, that any individuals should forget the land of their origin or their ancestors. Let them look to the past, but let them also look to the future; let them look to the land of their ancestors, but let them look also to the land of their children."

The commission appointing George Hedley Vicars Bulyea as lieutenant-governor was read. Then, promptly at high noon, to the accompaniment of gunfire from up the hill, and in the presence of twelve thousand people, the oath was read to Bulyea, he kissed the Bible, and Alberta had become a province.

At the same time, one of Strathcona's leading Liberal lawyers, A. C. Rutherford, had been named Alberta's premier and Calgarians knew that this appointment boded ill for Calgary's chance of becoming the capital city. For although Rutherford was not strictly an Edmontonian, he was nevertheless tarred with the Edmonton brush. He had been born in 1857 in Carleton County, Ontario, and for the decade ending 1895, after graduating from McGill University with a B.A. and a B.C.L., had engaged in law practice in Ottawa. Then he came to Strathcona and started an office there. In 1902 he had been elected to the North-West Territories Legislative Assembly.

Being a far-seeing man armed with the desire to do all he could for his adopted province, he chose the best men available for his appointed cabinet. Curiously enough, the best men all turned out to be Liberals. Assigning himself the posts of provincial treasurer and minister of education, he appointed C. W. Cross of Edmonton as attorney general. To W. H. Cushing of Calgary went the post of minister of public works, while W. T. Finlay of Medicine Hat assumed the duties of provincial secretary and minister of agriculture. Finally, to round out his cabinet, Rutherford appointed L. G. DeVeber of Lethbridge as minister without portfolio. In this way, Calgary and Edmonton and the other two cities in the new province were represented.

Having set up his temporary cabinet and taken steps to get some office space in Edmonton, and to begin transferring documents pertaining to Alberta affairs from Regina to Edmonton, Rutherford watched as Ottawa took up the task of dividing Alberta into constituencies. Out of these constituencies would come the MLA's who would have to make many decisions during the next four years. One of these decisions, Rutherford hoped, would ensure that Edmonton would remain the provincial capital. To him it was obvious that Edmonton, being near the geographical centre of the province, and having been the headquarters of this region for a century, should continue to be the capital of the area. But there were other opinions, and some advocated placing the capital at Red Deer, Calgary, and even Banff. Setting constituencies then was a job requiring care.

Primarily, they had to bear some relation to population, but because the sparsely settled area north of Edmonton was so far flung, the element of geography had to be taken into account. Eventually, Frank Oliver, as minister of the interior, announced the boundaries of the constituencies. They had been drawn with care; extreme Edmontonian care. Most of the twenty-five were drawn more or less as bands east and west across the province except around Edmonton where six of them practically touched the city, radiating out as the Calgary *Herald* said, "like the tentacles of an octopus."

"Gerrymander!" shouted Calgary, but as a weapon to combat Edmonton's chuckles, shouting availed them not at all.

Having tied up that situation, Rutherford called Alberta's first provincial election for November 9, 1905. In elections Albertans rarely do things by halves, and this first one was no exception. While in general the old-timers had hoped that their new government might be able to function on a non-partisan basis without being tied to either the Liberal or Conservative party, Frank Oliver had snuffed out any dreams they may have had in that direction and they had to vote for one or other of the regular parties.

When the results came in, Rutherford's Liberals had won twenty-three of the twenty-five seats. In Calgary, R. B. Bennett, the most capable and certainly the most vocal of the government's opponents, had been nosed out by twenty-five votes. Matt McCauley, Edmonton's first mayor, had been elected in the Vermilion constituency. Leaving out Red Deer in both cases, in the eleven southern constituencies 10,680 men had voted, while in the thirteen northern ones 9,393 votes had been cast. That round went to Edmonton.

But the whole business was to add to the legacy of Calgary–Conservative versus Edmonton–Liberal bitterness which for decades was to run through the fabric of Alberta's political life. In Calgary and the south generally there remained a strong feeling against the Liberals. Edmontonians and other northerners, still rankling because the CPR, the child of an earlier Conservative party, had turned its back on them and Edmonton's logical route to the coast and had run through Calgary, disliked that railway and all Conservatives. Edmonton Liberals rejoiced when in this first provincial election, even in Calgary, the hotbed of Conservatism and the homeland of the CPR, R. B. Bennett, a Conservative and worst still, a CPR lawyer, was defeated.

A mere couple of weeks after all the fun of the election which Edmontonians regarded as a win for their side, they had an excuse for another celebration. On November 24 Edmonton's own transcontinental railway, Mackenzie and Mann's Canadian Northern Railway, became a reality. At 10:30 that morning the track layer completed the line to the Edmonton station, and Mayor MacKenzie declared the afternoon a public holiday. That day, "in the presence of thousands of citizens of Edmonton and visitors from all parts of central Alberta, Hon. G. H. V. Bulyea . . . drove home with unerring blow the silver spike which held in place the first rail of the Canadian Northern Railway to reach the station in Edmonton." In the Queen's Hotel that evening at a banquet attended by two hundred guests, the city tendered its thanks to Donald Mann and to some of the visiting Mackenzies.

At long last Edmonton was on a transcontinental railroad, and now passengers going direct to Winnipeg could reach there after a trip of twenty-five hours. Though for the moment this railway stopped at Edmonton and was thus not yet a true transcontinental, it was destined to go west to Jasper and the coast. Moreover, at the moment it was welcome to anything Edmontonians had. The CPR on the other hand, the railway which twenty years earlier had spurned Edmonton and created Calgary, and which eight years later had not faced up to the task of bridging the Saskatchewan River but instead had set up Strathcona, would have had a dilligent search to find even one friend in Edmonton or a dozen in all of northern Alberta.

Now as far as Edmontonians were concerned they could get their own back at the CPR. Still, they had more important fish to fry. At three o'clock on March 15, 1906, Lieutenant-Governor Bulyea's carriage drew up in front of the freshly decorated Thistle Rink which had been transformed with flags, streamers and bunting. When with due ceremony he entered to open the first session of Alberta's new legislature he faced a large crowd. The recently elected members sat around in conventional fashion facing the dais, while behind them and on both sides four thousand visitors took up every available inch. After electing the member from Cochrane, C. W. Fisher, as Speaker, Governor Bulyea delivered the speech from the throne, which had been worded so as not to touch upon the subject that was in everybody's mind—was Edmonton to remain the capital of Alberta?

Bob Edwards of the *Eye Opener*, aware of the coming tussle over the capital and watching with a Calgarian's anxious eye, commented: "They take it for granted up in Edmonton that they are going to get the capital. This is not to be wondered at, since Calgary has not made the slightest effort in that direction. The citizens of Calgary are not a unit, the same as they are in Edmonton. Up there, there is constant evidence of union and community of interest. There are no inter-knocking societies. The business and professional men seem to be on excellent terms of camaraderie and the women are all on speaking terms and seldom snub each other. This is a wonderful showing."

Having got the ceremonies over, the new government, holding all subsequent sessions in the McKay Avenue School, got down to business. On March 21, J. T. Moore from Red Deer patted his party on the back by saying: "We are fortunate that the sceptre of power has been placed in the hands of the Liberal party." Though the twenty-three Liberals already knew that they were lucky, and smugly patted their pocketbooks, and though the two Conservative members were not listening anyway, everybody greeted his effort with applause. In his speech, moreover, Moore had averred that "if these walls could crumble so that we could look abroad and see the vast army that is headed for Alberta, the multitude of people for whom we will have to legislate, we would be able to appreciate the task that is before us here."

And there he had something. That was why the province had been created, and why these members held the sceptre of power. Alberta's agricultural hour had struck. Its almost unlimited soil lay waiting, machinery to work it was ready, suitable wheat was at hand, trains were ready to transport its progeny, and markets were clamouring for it. All that was needed was farmers, and by paddlewheeler, train, covered wagon and oxcart, they came rolling in.

At that time while homesteaders were expanding the area of settlement on all fronts, the recent completion of the CNR accounted for the fact that

A History of Alberta

the majority of them came heading for the areas around Edmonton. In the spring of 1906, according to Charles Sutter, Dominion immigration agent at Edmonton, daily arrivals had averaged between three hundred and five hundred. Newcomers overflowed the immigration building, filled the hotels and camped everywhere. The authorities opened new quarters at the exhibition grounds and a new immigration hall north of the CNR tracks. The agent spoke of a contingent of nine train loads of United States settlers all bound for the prairies that had recently started from Chicago. Most of these probably settled in Saskatchewan or in southern Alberta, for many of the United States immigrants coming with both experience and capital preferred prairie land similar to that they had known back home. Nevertheless, Mr. Harrison of the Edmonton land office had difficulty keeping up with the prospective settlers; some mornings a long lineup stood waiting outside his 100 Avenue office.

Since settlers were opening up the country, many promoters proposed to run railways out to serve them. Since by way of land grants given to railroad builders by various governments, many an astute businessman stood to make an immense profit, nearly everybody tried to secure a railway franchise. Securing it did no harm, and if, as sometimes happened, the promoter could follow through and build it, he obtained title to hundreds of thousands of acres. If he failed to build, here was a chance that he could sell the franchise at a profitable price to someone else. In any event, there was no harm in trying.

Throughout all the prairie provinces at that time, no one liked the CPR. Its freight rates appeared exorbitant, and the fact that the Canadian government had given it large grants of land rankled in the farmers' minds. While on both these counts the railway, with its attitude of "the public be damned," may have been riding roughshod over everyone, and therefore, was deserving of criticism, few of its critics stopped to realize that without the railway their farms would still have been virgin wilderness and the farmers would have no way to transport their products. They refused to consider the fact that without the railway nearly all of them could never have become prairie farmers but instead would still be labourers in Europe or eastern Canada. The CPR was a big corporation; in contradistinction to farmers, utterly unselfish all of them, all big corporations were soulless monsters; consequently, by legislation and regardless of its rights, the CPR must have its wings clipped.

Alberta's newly elected members fell into the same trap which over the years was to scar many another legislative body; not only did they use their power constructively but as well used it vindictively. One of their first moves and one which made them highly popular with their vengeful constituents was to pass an act taxing the railways' rights-of-way. The CPR took this to the courts, and with respect to taxing its main line, the act was found to be *ultra vires*, although its branch lines could be taxed.

And yet almost in the same breath and certainly in the same session, the legislators who had voted vindictively against one railway opened their arms wide to several other proposed railways. On the one hand, as was only natural, they wanted railways to run everywhere, but, on the other, they apparently felt that they should carry freight for practically nothing. On April 9 the legislature approved applications for five Alberta railway charters and did the very thing for which they had so often criticized Ottawa—they helped the railways get started by guaranteeing their securities on a most generous scale. But they took care to keep the CPR's snout out of their trough.

All the while, though it was pressing heavily on every member's mind, all of them had shied away from the momentous question of which city should become Alberta's permanent capital. Under the Alberta Act Edmonton was to be the capital until the legislature decided otherwise. Finally, in the House the Honourable Mr. Cushing rose and at the close of a long and a good speech, during which he said: "Calgary has been and is now the largest business centre in the province and will continue to be," he moved that the capital be transferred to Calgary. Once his motion was seconded, Moore moved an amendment, stating that the capital certainly should be moved, but only for half the distance which the Honourable Mr. Cushing advocated, and should therefore come to rest in Red Deer. No one seconded his amendment, so C. Hiebert, Alberta's first Mennonite member, tried his luck with an amendment advocating that Banff should be the capital. But likewise he could find no seconder.

By this time the afternoon and much of the evening had slipped by before Cushing's motion was put to a vote. The members representing the southern constituencies voted in favour, but that left the other two-thirds to vote against it. That also left Edmonton as the capital of the province. Cushing had done his best, and now the tension was over.

While the recently elected MLA's were busily planning Alberta's future, G. Carriveau, an Edmonton dealer who had sold a car, "a 29 Horse power, four seated affair," to W. H. White in Calgary, made the first recorded car trip between the two cities. According to the Edmonton *Bulletin* of March 2, 1906, "The party left Edmonton on Saturday morning at ten and arrived in Calgary at seven on Sunday evening, staying in Red Deer over Saturday night. From Lacombe to Red Deer, 20 miles, the car made the trip in 34 minutes. During the trip, 20 gallons of gasoline were used and one gallon of lubricating oil."

Indeed, one of the earliest matters to be considered by the legislature was cars, how to control them and how to turn these weird contraptions into a source of revenue. All the evidence pointed to the fact that it was full time to clamp down on them, for besides the half dozen cars already in Edmonton, the *Journal* of January 17 announced the arrival of a shipment of Buicks in the city. These were said to be capable of speeds up to 40 miles an hour, had a 22-29 horsepower engine, and cost $1,800.

Accordingly on April 23, 1906, Mr. J. R. Boyle, the member for Sturgeon, moved "an Act to Regulate the Speed and Operation of Motor Vehicles on Highways." This act provided that the owner of a vehicle must "register with the Provincial Secretary and take out a permit. He is given a number and a license and is requested at all times to carry the number exposed and to carry lights at night, bearing the number on the glass. . . ."

Proper legal speeds varied. They were to be "twenty miles per hour in the country, except when passing from the rear vehicles drawn by horses, when it is required that the speed be cut down to ten miles an hour. When meeting a rig, the speed limit is five miles an hour." If, however, the animal was frightened and got out of control, the car driver was to stop. In a city, town or incorporated village, the speed was to be 10 m.p.h., and everywhere, unless he could prove that he had taken all reasonable precautions, a motorist was liable for damages if he frightened a horse.

From this point on, the House rushed through the rest of its business, and on May 9, before proroguing, passed acts incorporating the cities of Medicine Hat, Lethbridge and Wetaskiwin and another to enable the creation of an Alberta university.

# 13
# The Last Arable Lands Settled 1906-1914

In 1906 a university was a far-flung fancy and cars a distant dream to most settlers. The realities were the pioneering hardships of the moment as they sought to scratch subsistence out of the prairie soil or clear a garden patch in the forest. And even as each newcomer claimed a quarter-section and lit a campfire to cook his first meal on his homestead, other immigrants on their way to land beyond stopped to rest their oxen and to ask directions.

Sifton's immigration policy, now stirred by Frank Oliver, had changed into high gear. During the five years after 1906 it brought about another doubling of Alberta's population so that by 1911 over 374,000 people had come to call the province home. After that immigrants continued to pour in at a rate of over forty thousand per year until in 1914 World War I dried up the flow. By then, however, Alberta's population was approaching 470,000, of whom two-thirds were farmers. During the two decades from 1895 to 1914 when the value of Alberta's rich soil resource had come to be realized and exploited, the province's population had increased by 440,000, a numeral increase not to be duplicated until some three decades later when its oil and gas resources came to be discovered and used.

But perhaps instead of stuffing our statistical maw too fast we should discuss rural settlement in smaller bites and chew it a little more carefully. By 1906 the bulk of the homesteaded area lay on the map of Alberta like a huge crescent facing east, with its back towards the mountains and one tip at Lloydminster and the other at Medicine Hat. From Lloydminster its outer circumference (coming perilously close to the region of marginal, arable lands) curved up to Smoky Lake, swung around by Westlock and bent farther around until at Entwistle its back was a straight line running south through Rocky Mountain House and Morley, whence curving with the foothills it continued to Cardston and headed for Medicine Hat. Its inner circumference starting near Lloydminster curved fairly symmetrically through Viking, Stettler and Gleichen to Medicine Hat, all the while facing towards the open grasslands into which a few intrepid ranchers had driven their herds but from which the earliest settlers had shied away.

A History of Alberta

By that time prospective farmers had pushed well into the timber west of the Calgary–Edmonton Railway and north and west from Edmonton into the fascinating, heavily forested valleys of the Paddle and the Pembina rivers and were well on their way towards the mighty Athabasca. To the east of Edmonton into the lands now served by Mackenzie and Mann's Canadian Northern Railway settlers had followed down the winding Vermilion River, seeking new homes around lovely Birch Lake, spreading out to Grizzly Bear Coulee, and skirting around the northern flank of the Blackfoot Hills. A mere five years earlier all the land east of the French colony of Vegreville had been empty except for a handful of Métis here and there and an occasional rancher who, finding a choice hay flat and a sheltered building site, had turned his cattle loose on the miles of adjacent unpastured uplands. These ranches, however, were just isolated establishments strung along some creek, pasturing their herds on the abundant grass all about; at no period did they cover the eastern prairies and parklands as completely as the ranches south of the Red Deer River where one owner's rangeland abutted another's.

In anticipation of a new railway running from Saskatoon to Edmonton the homesteaders flocked into the Vermilion River valley. Except for the group settlers such as the Ukrainians, who year after year were spreading farther east towards Myrnam, all the other homesteaders came in as individuals or small family bands, or even a little cluster of friends. As soon as they got their bearings and organized post offices, they named them after some prominent individual, or more often, in homesickness, for some town or village in the East or Europe or the United States, from whence they had come.

The Barr colonists of 1903 had also settled as near to the line of the newly surveyed Canadian Northern Railway as possible. For that line was the promise that was to make their homesteading tenable; once its route was determined, the adjacent lands became desirable. Not only would its construction provide work and ready cash for the settlers, but the railway itself would make it possible to ship their produce to market.

And yet as the CPR had already found out, and the Canadian Northern was to find out soon enough, the railway, the big corporation without whose very existence their farms would have been untenable, quickly became anathema to the farmers. The trait in human nature that feared bigness, the trait that came to light as a query as to whether or not they were being overcharged for freight and after endless ill-informed discussion became a certainty in their minds, led them to venting an often misplaced animosity on the railways. Westerners soon came to curse them.

But about 1900 when rumours of a second transcontinental railway had begun to float through the prairies, everyone, merchants and homesteaders alike, welcomed Messrs. Mackenzie and Mann as deliverers from the evil they imagined that the CPR was inflicting on them. For these two dreamers, both with experience in building railroads and rare genius for financing, had fought their way into the select circle of moneyed men, and now hoped to dip into the overflowing pot of gold available to railroad builders. Before long Canada was to hear much of the magicians William Mackenzie and Donald Mann, contractors, railroaders and capitalists extraordinary. Before long, out of small beginnings, they organized this new transcontinental, the Canadian Northern Railway, pointed it towards the Yellowhead Pass, financed it with Dominion government subsidies of some sixty-five million dollars and government guaranteed bonds of $245 million, and sent surveyors swarming all over western Canada. As they pounded the stakes along a line from Battleford to Lloydminster and on to Edmonton the pioneers in the Vermilion valley applauded, and those homesteaders who flocked to the land beyond them tried to get as close as possible to that line of stakes. For settlement followed the railway or the prospect of a railway.

But it was not only the Canadian Northern Railway that was looking to the ultimate profits to be made from homesteaders and not only the Vermilion valley that began to interest railroaders. By 1906 the CPR was building lines east out of both Wetaskiwin and Lacombe to tap the wealth of the parklands between its Calgary–Edmonton line and the Saskatchewan border. Although both of these railway lines were to take three or four years to complete, they pointed the way for settlers to follow onto the prairies and served notice on the isolated ranchers along the Battle River and in the Neutral Hills that their days of unrestricted free pasture were numbered. Prior to 1906 both railways and settlers had avoided the baldheaded prairie east of Stettler and east and north of the Red Deer River.

The grasslands south of that river and particularly along the Bow River, however, were beginning to hear the swish of the settlers' scythe as a fresh wave of German immigrants began to test their luck in all the area tributary to Medicine Hat—the area which their compatriots of 1889 vintage had spurned. As they tightened the barbed wire on their fences they brought down on their heads the ranchers' heartfelt curses.

By 1906 the Dominion land agent at Lethbridge was exulting that settlers had started to homestead the lands in his district. Moreover, he rejoiced at their calibre, for unlike most of the immigrants to the more northerly parts of the province, these newcomers came mainly from the prairie areas of the United States. Besides knowing what to expect of their new lands and having considerable experience in dry land farming, they came with a great deal of money. Moving in by covered wagon caravans, bringing horses, stock and cash, they soon followed these with steam tractors. Having land that needed no clearing, they were able to set to work and break up their areas. Industrious, experienced and fairly well financed, they were to mark a new era in Alberta's agricultural history.

By this time Lethbridge with its active coal mine, an affluent irrigated area lying south of it, and with scores of American homesteaders taking up land in its bailiwick, found itself basking in prosperity and rolling in cash. While new homesteaders in the Edmonton area were forced to count and hoard pennies, the people of Lethbridge scorned the copper coins, as their spokesman, the editor of the Lethbridge *Herald*, pointed out in September 1906: "A man, likely an Easterner, bought 120 coppers for 65 cents last week and tried to get Postmaster Higinbotham to accept them at full value, but as coppers don't circulate here, the Postmaster wouldn't take them. The speculator doesn't know what to do with his investment now. He had better wait until his next trip east and take them along to have a good time in Ontario."

Meanwhile, the Mormons in the Magrath country continued to put more land under the ditch. When in 1904 the Canadian Northwest Irrigation Company amalgamated with the Alberta Railway and Irrigation Company, which had been organized by Sir Alexander Galt and C. A. Magrath, the irrigated fields spread. In 1906, after Senator Cochrane had died, the Cochrane Ranche decided to sell out and dispose of its 106,500 acres to the Mormon church for a figure running into millions of dollars.

While the Mormons were prospering, the large ranchers were beginning to have their problems. By the turn of the century their heyday had passed and the days of the small homesteader, who came in and claimed much of the pasture land and the springs which the large operators needed, had arrived. While ranching was to be, and continued to be, of major importance to southern Alberta and remained a profitable business, the owners had to reduce their tremendous herds to fit the land left to them. Moreover, the homesteaders' barbed wire dealt them a deadly blow. Allying itself with the notorious winter of 1906–1907, it played its part in putting an end to the ranchmen's golden era.

All over the West that terrible winter (the first Alberta winter for some 26,000 immigrants who had arrived the previous summer) dealt the newcomers such a devastating blow that several died by freezing or of exposure and the next spring all of the weak-hearted who survived left for climates less harsh. It was a very long winter of record snowfall, exceptionally low temperatures and blinding blizzards and it bankrupted many a stockman.

Time after time through its dark, dreary days, a succession of storms, always from the northwest, swept over the prairies, which during the summer had been such lush grasslands. Now during the short days and

The Last Arable Lands Settled 1906-1914

long nights what had been pastures became a series of drifts ever shifting and ever seething as blizzards sifted fresh snow across them. The cattle, some from pastures along the Red Deer River and ever with their backs to the wind, snatched a bit of grass here and there as they drifted before the storms. Staggering along, cold, hungry and benumbed, with ears and tails frozen, they drifted south and east till tumbling into some drift-filled creek the beasts were too weak to struggle out. Equally deadly was the barbed wire of the homesteaders' or the railways' fences; the unreasoning cattle, sometimes in bunches of a hundred, piled up against them and could go no farther. Chilled and famished, they froze where they stood or had fallen. Ed Kelly, a CPR locomotive engineer long since retired, recalls as one of his most clear-cut memories the long line of dead cattle several feet deep which that spring lay against the railway fence near Bowell station west of Medicine Hat—cattle who would never return to their home pastures perhaps fifty miles northwest along the Red Deer River.

That winter the ranchers suffered terrific losses, but until the spring roundup no one could know how large his loss had been. With the completion of that roundup—the one which because of both the hard winter and the circumscribing homesteaders Katherine Hughes, an early Alberta author, called the last great roundup—their hopes that most of their cattle might be found alive far to the south across the open range faded. Thousands of cattle were found and driven back home, but an equal or greater number were left to lie in creek bottoms or against the fiendish wire.

One small-scale though much beloved rancher who did not live to see the devastating winter of 1906–07 was John Ware, a Negro who was born a slave in South Carolina. After the American Civil War he had made his way to Texas and the ranching country and there he had come to excel as a cowboy. Eventually he moved to Alberta and in 1891, with his wife and small children, he laid claim to a small range acreage far up Sheep Creek west of Turner Valley. Then in 1903, to expand his holding, he moved to a location near the Red Deer River north of modern Brooks and started grazing his herds. Unfortunately, two years later this sterling character, good neighbour and splendid horseman died instantly when his horse stumbled and rolled on him. With his passing went one of the institutions of the range country—one of the most honoured of the cattlemen.

During the following winter the recent immigrants to Alberta's prairies and parklands huddled in sod houses, or log cabins and suffered. Coming from lands where every month in the year they could see green grass and where once in a while the village pond froze deeply enough to slide on, the winter of 1906–07 caught them by surprise. But after enduring the snow-covered ground from October until well into May when the last drifts melted and having thereby proved themselves to be a match for the land, they stood ready the next winter to help a fresh batch of newcomers. Once again in 1907, and indeed for all the years until 1914, more immigrants from the moister green lands of Europe or from the drier Dakotas, continued to press in. Many came to fill the remaining empty spaces within Alberta's crescent of settlement or to purchase Hudson's Bay Company or CPR lands, while others crept cautiously into the parched prairies farther east.

Amongst these were two East Indians whose surnames were Singh and who in 1908 filed on land south of Gough Lake near modern Byemoor. When after a few months' residence one of them died, his compatriot found it difficult to observe their time-honoured custom of cremating his remains. Being far out at the very edge of the parklands' sparsely spread growth of twisty poplar, his neighbours of all nationalities rallied around and with some difficulty gathered enough of the stunted trees from their several quarters to maintain a funeral pyre.

Even in that area, however, the railway companies, finding Alberta filling up so rapidly, began competing in running lines through its choicer valleys. For by 1907 there were three railway companies, and each of them, flourishing on land grants and subsidies, scattered surveyors all over the land. Of greatest interest to Albertans in those days was the Grand Trunk Pacific Railway, which even as its competitor's silver spike was quivering in the tie at Edmonton in 1905 was clawing its way into the prairies from the east, rushing to reach that city.

Using homesteaders to throw up the best roadbed ever built in Alberta, the Grand Trunk Pacific came hurrying through the sand hills from Saskatchewan before farmers had time to settle near its right-of-way. For lack of settlers in that region, its builders invented names for its stations and selected them in alphabetical order—Artland, Butze, Chauvin and Dunn. Sweeping on to cross the Battle River on an impressive trestle, it continued its canter westward, still dropping alphabetical names: Hawkins, Irma, Jarrow and Kinsella. Then it swung around the bottom of Beaverhill Lake, cut its way through the Beaver Hills and reached Edmonton in August 1909.

Edmonton now had two transcontinental railways, the new Grand Trunk Pacific and its rival, the Canadian Northern Railway. And both of them, flying in the face of providence, laid duplicate sets of rails a stone's throw apart along the old Jasper Trail. Finally, about 1915, each reached the Pacific Ocean, out of breath, out of cash, and with a thousand miles of mountain railway that found little freight to carry. Their competition did not stop there, however; in the meantime they had looked longingly at Alberta's parklands and had begun to thrust feeder lines into them.

One of the first of these feeders, a Canadian Northern line, had sent its surveyors north into the forests through Father Morin's French colony, where in 1906 its rails reached Morinville. From there, heading into the Redwater River valley and in the sand hills near Clyde, crossing the height of land between the Saskatchewan River and the Athabasca watersheds, it set out down the Tawatinaw valley to follow the homesteaders to Athabasca Landing—the head of steamboat navigation to the Arctic.

Following this railway and the two transcontinentals which had run west of Edmonton came parties of Negroes from the United States who settled in little groups at such places as Junkins (modern Wildwood) and far back in the forest at Amber Valley. In these new lands they added to Alberta's amazing mosaic and like many of the pioneers' children some still farm these lands far removed from the warmth of the southern states.

Starting about 1912 all three companies commenced weaving a network of rail lines in the heartland of the province, the large elliptical area between Edmonton and Macleod. Many of them took care to pass over farming lands underlain by coal and a host of coal mining towns sprang up in the wheat fields or range lands. To name but a few, there were Big Valley, Drumheller, Sheerness and Alix. Some of the rail lines, such as that to Nordegg and the Coal Branch lines in the Cadomin and Mountain Park regions, were built for the sole purpose of hauling coal.

And because these railways ran north into the timber along the Athabasca or crisscrossed each other like the strings of a snowshoe all over the rest of the province, vacant land became accessible. In spite of heavy immigration there was land for everyone.

Some, of course, was land that should have been left to grow cactus, but while the railways were expanding, settlers continued to flock in. Before 1914 the empty space in Alberta's map, the space east of the crescent of 1906, the area which was later to be called the Special area, was also homesteaded. Into it where neither tree nor bush stood closer than the faraway skyline, settlers carried their ploughs. These they needed to slice the dry turf into blocks for their sod houses, but as for axes, they should have left them in their native lands; of trees for shelter or firewood there was none. Their very fuel had to be imported. To lend some semblance of their moist and leafy native lands they planted caragana hedges, and, gathering stones, arranged them in borderlines around their shacks. Caragana bushes and rock borders, however, do not provide fuel, and fuel in the form of coal which had to be hauled in. Up north in the parklands and the timber, the homesteaders, having to fight back the forest foot by foot, envied the prairie dwellers who could plough the empty grasslands without any clearing. But when winter with its biting blasts howled around the snug log shacks they peeked out of their small windows watching it fearlessly and then turned to throw another stick of their abundant wood on the fire.

So it was that the railways, standing ready to carry away trainloads of the prairie farmers' wheat, provided strings of cars to haul in their coal. As the homesteaders said: "They've got you coming and going." And indeed they had; at least so did the CPR and the Canadian Northern Railway. The Grand Trunk Pacific, like the others, had exploited Alberta's timber resources and its coal regions, but unlike them had shied away from the treeless plains.

While, however, the other two railways could carry coal to the arid areas and hopefully could haul wheat from them, they could not haul water, and without it the pioneers could not grow wheat. Once in a while, enough to tantalize everyone, it rained on the arid areas. Once in a while, they got five bushels to the acre, a pittance, and one year out of eight or ten, they had a rainy season, but on the whole the settlers on the dry plains faced failure unless by some financial miracle the land could be irrigated. For one reason or another it was impractical to irrigate much of it, but for some of the lands south of the Red Deer River the CPR accomplished the miracle of delivering water.

The CPR, with a soft spot in its heart for southern Alberta, a soft spot which on the whole was to bring it costly losses, set out to make the arid lands blossom with alfalfa, vegetables, sugar beets and dairy cattle.

By 1903, mainly as a result of Mormon effort, some 480 miles of canals and ditches had been constructed and were said to be capable of watering thousands of acres. The Mormons, the practical exponents of irrigation, continued and expanded their successful application of water to the parched soils until in 1912 the CPR, taking over the Alberta Railway and Irrigation interests, enlarged the main canal and gave the whole project a shot in the arm.

While all this had been going on in the Lethbridge area, the CPR had been looking at the more northerly lands along its main line. As a result, it decided to irrigate much of the land between Medicine Hat and Calgary in an area some fifty miles wide by 125 miles long. Dividing this great area into three regions, the company started digging its first ditches in what is called the Western Section. Taking its water from the Bow River at Calgary, it ran its main canal east to its reservoir at Chestermere Lake and then carried water even as far east as Crowfoot Creek in the area north of the Blackfoot reserve. This extensive system was completed in 1911 when the company had laid out some 2,500 miles of canals and ditches.

Then, starting about 1910, under the name of the Eastern Irrigation District, the company turned its attention to the more easterly division of its lands. Building its impressive dam on the Bow River near the east end of the Blackfoot reserve brought the town of Bassano into the limelight to the extent that it began to advertise itself as the best in the West by a damsite. According to the plans, the scheme was to irrigate some 200,000 acres by means of about two thousand miles of canals and ditches, and before long these began to reach out to points over fifty miles away in several generally easterly directions. For canals worked to the northeast towards Gem and Rosemary and to the southeast to use the reservoir of Lake Newell, and went on to the Brooks area. To reach Tilley still farther east the canal crossed a valley east of Brooks by means of the big concrete flume visible from the modern trans-Canada highway and then passed under the railway tracks.

While the CPR company was digging these ditches and running these canals, most of the arable land in Alberta south of the Athabasca River and as far east as Lac La Biche and thence south of the Beaver River had been taken up. A few interstices here and there remained but generally one continuous band of land stretching from that line to Alberta's south, east and west boundaries had been spoken for. North of that line the non-arable land began and except for one outstanding area stretched continuously north. That exception was the faraway Peace River country, a large arable area of some ten million acres, separated from the good soils of the more southerly part of the province by a minimum of two hundred miles of muskeg, sand hills or other forbidding terrain.

Around its old fur trading posts and missions agriculture of a sort had been practised for decades, but before the turn of the century hardly anyone had gone into the area with the intention of farming. Shortly after that time a few dedicated pioneers seeking the seclusion of far-off places began to move in and to stir its sod. Except for farming associated with missionary activity, one of the first of these was Alex Monkman, who in 1903 while working for the well-known northern traders Jim Cornwall and Fletcher Bredin at Cutbank Lake, had put in a small crop and thus became the first farmer on what the voyageurs had called the *grande prairie*. Others, Jim McCreight and Ralph Dyer, Bill Grant and Jim Meade, H. B. Clifford, A. M. Bezanson, J. E. Germain and J. Sexsmith, soon worked their way in. Moreover, north of the Peace River, but somewhat later, a similar sprinkling of pioneers scattered themselves about the generally open country from Peace River Crossing to the old Waterhole near modern Fairview and began to recognize the area's agricultural excellence.

It was to be about 1908, however, before many prospective homesteaders arriving at Edmonton began to face up to the rigorous 350-mile trip from there through muskeg and forest to Peace River Crossing and the extra trek of 125 miles around by Dunvegan to the *grande prairie*. Some tried the trip during the summer when after taking the 100-mile trail to Athabasca Landing they could go by steamboat up the Athabasca to Mirror Landing. Thence, after making a small portage, they could catch another steamer to Sawridge at the east end of Lesser Slave Lake and across the eighty-mile lake to Grouard at its western end. From there a ninety-mile wagon road took them to Peace River Crossing. Most of them, however, chose to make the trip during the winter with their own oxen or horses.

Up to 1911 a steady stream of homeseekers taking this long route by Lesser Slave Lake made the Peace River country their goal. Loading their furniture, their families and their pigs into sleigh, caboose or wagon and tying a cow or two behind, the pioneers set out on their long trip. At that time Grouard, which had a census population of 447, was the headquarters of the Peace River country, while the hamlets of Mirror Landing and Sawridge, which today are mere names on old maps, had become important villages.

One very important group under the patronage of Rev. Father Giroux went out to look on the lands west of Stinking Lake and found them fair. In April 1912 Donat Forgues, Oville Pilon and Alphonse Gariepy, the three precursors of the colony, led the way to be followed in May by many families. Within a few days after inspecting the heavily timbered land they gathered to participate while Father Giroux held a service and erected a cross upon which they all wrote their names. In due course they decided to name their new community in honour of Father Falher and before long had expanded to an adjacent area which they called Giroux-ville.

By that time, however, the settlers in the *grande prairie*, seeking a shorter route to the outside world, had begun looking south towards the recently built transcontinental, the GTP. By July 1910 it was running trains as far west as Edson and the Grande Prairie people, realizing that the line lay a mere 250 miles away, put pressure on the Alberta government to slash a trail through the timber, corduroy the worst spots and put ferries across the Athabasca and the Baptiste rivers. By assigning that task to a capable young engineer, A. H. McQuarrie, the government brought the famous Edson–Grande Prairie Trail into being. Although because of the moiety of money spent it was an execrable trail and although it meant 250 miles of mud, muskeg and mosquitoes, hundreds used it during its four years of active life.

By the end of that time another railway, one aimed at the agricultural resources of the Peace River country and at the hundreds of miles of saw timber through which it wound its tracks, the Edmonton, Dunvegan and British Columbia Railway had made a good start. Nicknamed the Exceedingly Dangerous and Badly Constructed, it reached the Athabasca River in 1914 at Mirror Landing, then a village of substance but shortly doomed to disappear physically as well as nominally when its site was moved across the river and its name changed to the much less mellifluous one of Smith. Month after month with its ties dunking in the muskeg,

The Last Arable Lands Settled 1906-1914

the railway wound its way along the eighty miles of Lesser Slave Lake until leaving its west end, bypassing the old town of Grouard and building a new one called High Prairie some ten miles distant, it reached Peace River Crossing in 1916. Two years earlier, however, World War I had broken out and the rush of settlement to Alberta and to the Peace River country had slackened off.

By 1914 a band of homesteaders had formed a thin line of settlement on the richer soils of the vast Peace River country, a great expanse of territory looking on the map like a reclining S which stretched two hundred miles from end to end. When the war broke out the Peace River country had a population of about eight thousand, in which Grande Prairie, its main town, the home of some three hundred pioneers, was basking in rosy prospects. Grouard, however, which for over a decade had been the headquarters of the Peace River country, watched sadly while its population, which at its zenith had passed the one thousand mark, dispersed to newer centres on the railway.

Once settlers had laid claim to the best of the Peace River country's soils, the end of Alberta's better arable land was in sight. Much more homesteading remained to be done but it was to consist of moving back into the poorer grey-wooded soils and onto much land that should never have been homesteaded. During the two decades to 1914, however, Alberta had witnessed an amazing influx of settlers. From 1895 to 1914 its population had grown by 440,000, from 30,000 to some 470,000. In the future, as others of its rich resources came to be utilized, the province was to witness far more prosperous times, but nothing in all its history so far can compare with the thrilling years when the first farming pioneers flocked in to occupy an area of arable soil twice as large as England and three times the size of Scotland.

Out of the province's 1914 population of 470,000 citizens sixty-two percent were farmers, while the rest had come in to work in mines, mills and in the cities and growing towns. And what a wondrous mixture of people had come to the new province. Nearly half of the newcomers, 226,000, had been born in Canada, while 83,000 had come from Britain or her colonies to make over 300,000 of mainly British backgrounds. From the United States had come a most important mixture of 86,000 Anglo-Saxon or Norse American citizens, many of them with capital, while from mainland Europe 67,000 assorted Scandinavians, Germans, Hollanders and Ukrainians, as well as a few French, had come in to claim the virgin soils. To leaven the mixture further a few Icelanders and Jews, some Mennonites, many Scotch and Welsh, a few Finns, several Italians, and an occasional Chinese, had thrown in their lot with the new province.

The newcomers represented several religious faiths, of which Roman

Catholic formed sixteen percent, or 75,000. The far greater number of Protestants included 85,000 Presbyterians, 72,000 Methodists, 71,000 Anglicans, 50,000 Lutherans, with the rest made up of seven other faiths including the Jewish and Mennonite. But no matter from what ethnic stock they sprang or what faith inspired them, they found themselves more or less cheek by jowl with others of different backgrounds who worshipped in different ways. Perhaps of far more importance for their future citizenship was the fact that they faced a similar harsh climate, similar hardships and a similar need to build up an acceptable society in this new land whose official language was English.

It took a few years—in some cases many years—before nearly all of them, Slav or Swede, Italian or Irishman, came to realize that the new land, not because of its virtue but because of its sheer perversity, had wrought great changes in them. There had come to be less difference between an Alberta Finlander and an Alberta Hollander than between a Usona Finn and his faraway reindeer herding folk, or between a Neerlandia Hollander and his remote dam-watching Dutch relatives.

So with all the institutions and services which this newly arrived polyglot population had to bring into being by its united effort, roads, schools, cemeteries and municipalities—all of them helped to bind the settlers to each other and to their new land. Moreover, hauling their grain to the same elevator over roads they had built themselves, tying their teams in the same market square which the municipality they had set up taxed them to maintain, encouraging their young folk to play on the same baseball teams or mingling together at sports days or picnics at sports grounds they had jointly levelled and furnished—all these things began to give them a new and a common outlook.

With a spider's web of some 3,600 miles of railways covering the province for the four hundred miles from the Athabasca River to the 49th parallel, with thousands of miles of irrigation canals and ditches and some two thousand schools they had built or financed themselves, and with the Indians, only six thousand of them now, virtually tucked away out of sight, Alberta had entered a new era. For that whole distance north and south and from Lloydminster in the east to Edson 250 miles off to the west, golden fields of wheat scattered here and there covered the plains and hillsides over which Crowfoot, Maskepatoon and Poundmaker had hunted. In the fall, under the bluest of big skies, binders banged as they cast out sheaves and steam threshers roared as they poured amber wheat into grain wagons ready to rumble along the winding dirt roads to tall elevators sited on who knew what recent Cree–Blackfoot battleground.

That early, however (in 1914), Alberta's mixture of men from many lands had merely started the fusion which later years were to work. The vast prairies and the endless sky widened each settler's outlook until he came to regard himself and his neighbours as new men far more broad-minded than were their compatriots in the old world, which had somehow come to seem slightly musty and somewhat decadent. And yet, as Dr. George Hardy has so well said: "by the constant and curious contradiction of frontier life, the West was also the home of a puritanism and religious fundamentalism more rabid than Ontario's smugness or Quebec's medievalism."

# 14
# Boom Times
# 1906-1914

With homesteaders flocking in and towns and cities growing at such a rapid rate, Alberta's newly organized government faced many a problem. Not only did it have to provide all the framework of legislation to which new towns, villages and rural municipalities could cling, but with sixty-eight percent of the province's population being recently arrived farmers, much of the government's concern had to be directed towards promoting their interest and meeting their demands. Roads, bridges and ferries were high on the bill of fare and an organization had to be set up to supply those facilities over the length and breadth of the large and ever-expanding settled areas of the province. Schools had to be brought into being, long distance telephone lines to be built, while at the same time every settled township clamoured for a railway line. Public works of all sorts had to be provided on what at the time was correctly regarded as being a stupendous scale.

So in 1906, with an occasional glance at labour and one eye cocked at farmers, Alberta's newly elected legislature set about the colossal task of assisting with the development of its far-flung multi-resourced province. One of the legislature's first jobs was to "protect" the public from the monopoly of the Bell Telephone Company. When the government tried to buy out that company's holdings in the province but could not come to satisfactory terms, it set up the Alberta Government Telephone Company and, raising the first of many loans, began building trunk lines from Calgary to Edmonton and east to Lloydminster. Before many years the publicly-owned telephone system, one of the most productive sources of debt and deficit in provincial history, was to involve it in serious difficulties.

Turning their attention to railways, the legislators plunged into the venture of guaranteeing the securities of branch lines. By 1909, pursuing a policy very popular at the time, they had guaranteed over twenty-five million dollars for Canadian Northern Railway, GTP and Alberta and Great Waterways Railway Company lines involving 1,761 miles.

By that time the cabinet began to prepare for the election which it had called for March 22, 1909, and the politicians of both the Liberal and Conservative parties called the first of their major conventions. In doing so and in spite of Albertans' long-standing apathy, or distaste for the traditional party politics, they continued the eastern imposition of Liberal and Conservative parties on the province.

In their respective conventions, as was to be expected in an agricultural province, many of the delegates were farmers, and naturally, the politicians serving such a rich arable area paid heed to what the farmers wanted. By this time many Alberta farmers had begun to support the American Society of Equity with its idea of controlled marketing and soon were at cross-purposes with the Territorial Grain Growers Association, an import from Saskatchewan which at the time had a branch in Strathcona. After Alberta became a province, the grain growers' group was organized on a provincial basis and called itself the Alberta Farmers' Association but found itself in competition with the local Society of Equity.

Then at a great convention held in Edmonton in January 1909 the two bodies joined forces under the stirring name of The United Farmers of Alberta, "Our Motto Equity." The organization had a membership of some five thousand. The meeting elected James Bower as president and Rice Sheppard as vice-president, and adopted as its official organ the *Grain Growers' Guide,* the publication of the Saskatchewan and Manitoba farmer-owned Grain Growers' Grain Company. This, the greatest agricultural journal ever published in western Canada, was a probing and prodding weekly which combined a diet of lean facts with layers of juicy, fat propaganda. With its perhaps crude but appealing cartoons, it soon came to occupy a place in prairie farm homes a little higher than T. Eaton's famous mail order catalogue but still a little lower than the family Bible.

Having accomplished all this, the United Farmers' delegates accepted an invitation which Premier A. C. Rutherford, the Liberal with a shrewd eye on his taskmasters, had extended to attend the opening of the provincial legislature. By one of the many ironies of Alberta's history this was the same UFA which in shining armour a dozen years later toppled the Liberals from provincial office into the supine position in which, after fifty years, they still lie. Nevertheless, when the election of 1909 took place, Premier Rutherford's sane government, combined with his appealing policy with respect to the spread of railway lines, swept his party back into power to the tune of thirty-seven Liberals out of forty-one elected members.

One of the opposition members, however, was R. B. Bennett, the Conservative from Calgary, who put an end to the hitherto placid administration of the province's affairs by letting loose a tirade against suspected graft in connection with the Alberta and Great Waterways Railway. Rutherford's government had signed an agreement with G. W. Clarke, a promoter from Kansas City, to construct the railway. The opposition discovered that in the course of creating subsidiary companies and shuffling bonds, the House of Morgan in New York had sold the proposed railway's bonds at a ten percent profit, which amounted to $740,000, and concluded that certain cabinet ministers had participated in this profit. A good many members of the legislature, who apparently thought that the Morgans were in the bond business for others and not for themselves, were influenced by these insinuations.

Within a day or so after the legislature met on February 10, 1910, hints of trouble were in the air. Ministers of various portfolios resigned, were placated and withdrew their resignations. Premier Rutherford was accused of double dealing. The most bitter debate that had rocked the walls of the legislature up to that time ensued. To keep the fur flying, R. B. Bennett, leader of the opposition, spoke for five consecutive hours. When the vote was called, the government was sustained by a majority of twenty-three to fifteen, with several of its own members voting against it and splitting the party.

As a result of this upheaval, cabinet ministers once more resigned, were reappointed, or refused to be reappointed, and precipitated other resignations along the lines of "I will not stay if he does." After appointing a royal commission to look over the evidence of his alleged graft, Rutherford resigned, and A. L. Sifton took on the job of premier. To Rutherford's honour it should be remembered that, while the judicial committee censured the government for some of its arrangements and actions and for its woeful inexperience, it completely exonerated him.

In spite of having opened a can of worms in connection with the AGW, the government, now headed by Sifton, continued the policy of guaranteeing more bonds for more railways. No member dared question the need for more rail lines or to wonder about a region's ability to pay for them. And so the legislature moved continuously towards the railway crisis which was to embarrass the Liberal regime in its closing years. By the end of 1911 the government had taken under its wing securities totalling forty-four million dollars for a total of 3,074 miles of line. It was noticeable, however, that the CPR did not share in this largesse. Fortunately for Albertans the onset of the First World War kept many of the lines from being built, and happily for the province's coffers the Canadian Northern Railway and the GTP lines went bankrupt and were taken over by the Dominion government as the Canadian National Railway. In this way a heavy burden of interest charges was transferred from the province to the much broader federal shoulders.

One of the most important pieces of legislation enacted during the 1913 session was that which assisted the incorporation of the Alberta Farmers' Co-operative Elevator Company Limited. Under this act, which exuded suspicion of private grain companies, the government was empowered to advance up to eighty-five percent of the cost of building or buying elevators. With this help the farming industry, by far the most important in the province at the time, was able to set out on its long and successful career of owning grain handling facilities which a decade or so later reached its climax in the Alberta Wheat Pool.

During the next few years the government kept busy passing measures affecting cooperative associations, schools and municipalities and generally concerned itself with keeping pace with an Alberta starting to stretch its skin to accommodate and help its immigrants. Though after the lapse of a couple of generations the process of absorbing them was to yield rich results, nevertheless at times they proved strenuous grist for the province's digestive mill.

For this heterogeneous mass of immigrants worshipping at so many altars, speaking so many diverse languages and, for the most part, whether English-speaking or not, woefully ignorant of how to farm in this strange land (or indeed in any land) taxed the government's varied educational facilities to the utmost. Religion was no problem because each of the many shades of Christians set about to care for its own members in its own way and at their expense. Even that early Alberta was rapidly on the way to reaching the unique distinction of being home to far more sects and cults than any other province. Before long, dominating many a hilltop and lighting up many a valley, churches, erected by devoted hands, added to the charm of the countryside. Similarly, but with grants from the province, schools, two to a township, soon sprang up as an indication of how anxious all immigrants were to provide their children with more education than they had enjoyed.

School buildings, however, were only part of the educational process. Providing teachers was one of the most difficult tasks the Department of Education had to face. As was to be expected amongst a population composed largely of homesteaders, the general level of education was low; besides, there were very few individuals capable of teaching who would turn to that sort of life for a livelihood. Not only did the department have to import a large part of its teaching staff from the older cultures of the eastern provinces, but even then it had to lower its standards. Qualified teachers were hard to get and they could choose the schools at which they would teach. Few of them cared to throw in their lot with the homestead areas where, amongst other disadvantages, they had to board with one of the local families. Fewer still welcomed the prospect of teaching in "foreign" areas and crowding into a "foreigner's" one- or two-roomed house along with his family.

The result was that, with a few outstanding exceptions, the backwoods schools, and particularly the Ukrainian schools, were left with a poor assortment of teachers, often seedy old veterans of the schoolmasters' trade who filled in for a few months now and then, or young university students from the East who came out for a brief period during their summer recesses.

To help cope with the language problems the Department of Education created a special branch which was to devote its efforts to helping the children of Scandinavian, German, Polish, Ukrainian and other immigrant families to become more proficient in the use of the English tongue. One of its outstanding moves in 1913 was to establish a "school for foreigners" in Vegreville. It was an attempt to provide a means by which a few of the more progressive youths, who either had had some education in the old country or else looked like good material, could take a crash course to upgrade their knowledge of English and the usual school subjects sufficiently to enable them to sit for the departmental examinations. Once they passed them, they were expected to go through normal school if they wished to teach. In addition, the school offered courses for those who wanted a quick drill in English and arithmetic, so that they could work in banks, stores or other business places.

But while formal schooling soon came to be taken for granted, the problems of educating homesteaders to farm in an efficient way in relation to the varied soils and to the climate so as to offer high grade produce were far more difficult. In fact, as problem after problem was solved, others came to take their place, and the process is still going on. Until recently, farmers, stubborn individualists all, were reluctant to listen to the scientists and the economists. To the farmers' credit it must be emphasized that at the start the scientists, equally ignorant of which farming practice to adopt but ever ready to discard ideas which did not work, often gave the men on the land a bum steer.

Both the federal and provincial governments devoted a great deal of effort by way of experimental stations, agricultural schools, support of creameries and butter factories, fairs and exhibitions, all aimed at upgrading the slipshod farming practices of the era.

If, however, neither the farmers nor the scientists knew anything about soil surveys, all of them were conscious of Alberta's short growing season. It and the weather, which no one could predict and which strangely enough not even the farmers could blame on the government, the railway companies, the grain trade or the financial interests, were constant topics of conversation. It was no wonder then that about this time both the scientists and the dirt farmers were watching the results Charles Saunders of the Dominion Experimental Farm at Ottawa was having with his new wheat which ripened several days earlier than Red Fife. By 1906 he had produced about a bushel of it; in 1907 and again the next year it was tested at Indian Head; in the spring of 1909, four hundred samples were distributed to western farmers to be tried. During the next couple of years

213

prairie grain growers clamoured for this miraculous Marquis wheat because at long last Saunders had developed a strain which could be grown successfully in the West. Not only was this a boost for the scientists, but it came as a great psychological boost for Alberta farmers. Hitherto, as George Simpson of the Hudson's Bay Company had asserted more than half a century previously, Alberta and indeed all the prairies had been risky areas in which to grow wheat. Now most of the risk had been removed and Albertans began seeing unlimited possibilities even for the one-time marginal lands north of the North Saskatchewan River. And if science had succeeded in pushing the frost barrier farther north, what might not it and the farmers do in the future?

So in a jubilant mood on September 3, 1912, Alberta's legislators watched as the governor general, the Duke of Connaught, assisted by the duchess and a host of Dominion dignitaries, officially opened the province's majestic Legislative Building.

And yet, even then when the land booms were beginning to burst and the cooling breezes of a day of reckoning started sifting across the fields and factories and above all along the system of vastly overexpanded railways, some began to have second thoughts. All their actions, even though they had been inspired by the highest motives—had they been without flaw? Indeed had their politicians weakly yielding to popular pioneer pressures—had they served them well? Or had they too become a prey to unsound speculation in railways and telephone lines? And had they now and then dipped into the morass of political corruption—at times deeply? And—sobering thought—their politicians, really estimable men on the whole, had they been any more irresponsible than the public at large?

Viewing the matter dispassionately, the thinking few had begun to conclude that everyone in Alberta and everyone in Canada had been swept along beyond his depth in the inflated assessment they had all placed on the value of the West and its ability to yield the daydream riches for which they had all hoped. Speculation piled upon speculation had counted too heavily on the vast wealth the West was capable of contributing. Bankers, manufacturers, merchants, western farmers, investors and gamblers from one end of Canada to the other had shared the same fever. Most of them, from the humblest voter to the most embroiled politician, had shut their minds to the risks of the great gamble and with hands widespread for any passing graft, turned their eyes away. For the prime minister, the provincial premiers and the politicians were not alone to blame; they were but the servants of a public which condoned and permitted such practices—provided its individuals stood a chance of getting a cut at the booty.

More and more, Albertans began to look closely at their Liberal government and to wonder. Its members indeed had tried hard to serve them and to give them what they had wanted, and on the whole had done a fine job. Then during the last two or three years, once the growing farmers' organization had put a ring in the government's nose and could lead it about, the members had tried harder than ever. But even this guided government, composed in the main of honourable men—was it what Albertans wanted? Old-timers of fifteen years' standing could recall the days when men like Haultain had declared that party government had no place in the Territories. Then when in 1905 it had been imposed on them and the Liberals had assumed the governing role, they had accepted party politics reluctantly but with little demur. Had the government in Ottawa been Conservative and hence saddled Alberta with a Conservative government, it would have mattered little. One was as good as the other. And yet many a man wondered why a provincial government should be tied so closely to eastern political parties.

For in the space of a very few years the East, to whom Albertans had to turn for their markets, their machinery and their mortgages and from whose bankers they had received lectures on their improvidence—the East had rapidly become their *bête noire*. If you owe a man money, you begin to cool towards him; if you cannot pay him, you hate him. Then too, Alberta's crown lands and resources were not its own to play with, but were administered by Ottawa. At the time, that was probably fortunate for Alberta's future but no westerner could see it that way.

For the time being, however, when the provincial election of 1913 came, Albertans, even with all this on their minds, elected A. L. Sifton's Liberal government. The farmers, rapidly coming to regard both parties as evil, voted for the Liberals as the lesser of two evils. For that party had demonstrated that with the ring in its nose it had relinquished control over legislation to the farmers and would head where they pointed it.

The election was a bitter battle where dubious practices vied with political juggling and assorted shenanigans. Electors were bribed, ballot boxes lost or stuffed, and the candidates, with the hearty approval of most of the electors, dragged out all the tricks known to successful politicians of the day. It was little wonder then that the election was followed by a host of disputes and petitions to unseat certain members. In this election in the constituency of Whitford, Andrew Shandro became the first of Ukrainian stock to gain a seat in the legislature. His election was protested and after legal proceedings he was unseated.

But political chicanery erupted in several other areas and was perhaps most noticeable in Clearwater, a constituency that had been created solely for political juggling. In a vague band it stretched east and west across the province as a sort of no man's land between the lightly populated area of the Peace River country and the rest of Alberta and took in such widely-separated places as Fort McMurray, Lesser Slave Lake, the Swan Hills and Grande Cache. In the whole of the Clearwater riding there were only eighty voters. When the polls closed it turned out that 103 people had voted, and, of course, they had elected a Liberal. Various legal actions, counteractions, and judicial pronouncements followed, but none of them got at the mystery of how 103 persons had voted when there were only eighty people entitled to do so.

Regardless of that, the Liberal party found itself safely in the saddle looking forward to another term of office. Moreover, it could look back with satisfaction upon its accomplishments since the province had come into being. It could look back upon a period of unparalleled growth in all phases of which it had taken a hand with policies that at the time had seemed to be far-sighted and on the whole were so.

And for aiding materially in this miraculous transformation each of the members of the Liberal government could deservingly take credit. To them, of course, the miracle nearest at hand was that which they could see out the windows of the Legislative Building—Edmonton.

For all the while Edmonton had grown at an unprecedented rate and was destined to keep on growing. New subdivisions had flashed into being and new houses had sprung up everywhere. So much work had been going on that back in April 1906 the Carpenters and Joiners Union had threatened to strike unless their staggering demands were met. They wanted, and finally got, an eight-hour day, with a minimum daily wage of $3. At that time the city was paying 65¢ an hour for top quality stone-cutters and 25¢ an hour for common labourers.

During 1907 the city's population had continued its thirty percent per year increase as it began bracing itself to leap into the boom days which lay ahead. In June the Edmonton *Bulletin* estimated that two thousand people were living in tents and the paper was of the opinion that by fall that number would rise to five thousand. Across the river Strathcona shared in this influx of new citizens to the point where on March 15, 1907, it was incorporated as a city with a population of 3,500.

Meanwhile, Calgary, having been denied the seat of provincial government, had every reason to expect that in all fairness it would be granted the site of the university. Then, a mere three weeks after Strathcona's assumption of city status, Premier A. C. Rutherford, one of its outstanding citizens, announced that the university should be built in the new city. As might be expected, Calgarians were bitter in their denunciation of this blatant demonstration of the lengths to which politicians of the day would go.

The score so far was Edmonton 2, Calgary 0. The next game was played with buffalo. At that time, out of all the millions of these shaggy beasts which had once covered the American prairies and in their wild

A History of Alberta

freedom had once blackened Alberta's grassy hillsides perhaps a thousand in all were left on the whole continent. By a clever piece of forethought Canada had purchased the largest remaining herd from a Métis, Michel Pablo, in Montana, and planned to create a park in Alberta where they could be turned out to graze. Immediately the Edmonton–Calgary game began again. Seeking some sop from the government, this time from the Liberals at Ottawa, the daddy of the Liberal regime at Edmonton, Calgarians suggested that the buffalo park be established near their city, possibly between it and the Red Deer River at Three Hills. But, like the Indians who had beseeched the Manitou to preserve the buffalo, the Conservative Calgarians also prayed to the wrong gods. The best they could do was to watch as 475 bruised and bedraggled beasts passed through Calgary in box cars on their way to be deposited in a woody quagmire at Elk Island Park, near Edmonton's back door. There they were held over the winter until the Wainwright Buffalo Park was fenced and ready to receive them. In the spring, while a few were left at Elk Island Park, the rest were shipped to Wainwright. The score now was Edmonton 3, Calgary 0; Edmonton had won the series.

Out of two hundred businesses in Edmonton, eighty-two, or nearly half of them, were real estate agents, and many of the other businessmen were not averse to taking a turn at buying and selling lots. Moreover, with gold dredges busily turning over the river's gravels and with flour mills, lumber mills and brick yards employing hundreds of men, Edmonton was a busy city. Perhaps its largest industry was coal mining within its own and Strathcona's city limits and nearby at such places as Clover Bar, Namao and Big Island.

With so many coal mines it is perhaps easy to understand Edmonton's lethargy over natural gas. Various attempts to supply it with that commodity, including wells drilled within the city limits, an artificial gas company and a proposition by a corporation to drill in the Morinville area, were all turned down by the citizens.

These, of course, were the days when big corporations earned the reputation of high-handedness and crookedness which they have been trying to live down ever since. This was the era of unbridled competition, of wasteful duplication of facilities and of governments not grown up enough to regulate properly. This was also an age when nearly all politicians at nearly all levels expected to be bribed in one form or another, and usually were.

In any event, on the gas question Edmonton's burgesses voted themselves into a corner. They wanted gas, but on the one hand they were afraid that someone might make money out of supplying it; on the other, if the city supplied it, it might lose money. That left everyone sitting on the fence, some facing one way and some the other. But for a long time thereafter, no matter which way they faced, they could see no other promoter who would entrust his proposition to their vacillating votes.

Although the taxpayers had steered clear of commitments on gas service the calls for funds to finance other civic utilities and various public works were beginning to create problems. When in 1907 Edmonton's mill rate was increased from 10½ to 13½ the Edmonton *Journal* sagely remarked: "The increase of the total tax rate indicates a tendency which if continued, must be attended in the future by undesirable results."

As soon as he could Premier Rutherford, a McGill graduate who was a major force in promoting education in the province, began casting about for someone—naturally a McGill man—to assume the task of bringing Alberta's university into being. Fortunately, he hit upon Dr. Henry Marshall Tory and on January 1, 1908, gave him a clear hand to get the job under way.

Even then most Albertans thought that the university's creation was a foolish waste of money. On the whole, Albertans were men of muscle— with much of it in their heads. Frank Oliver, for instance, prescient in many other matters, could see little necessity for it. He is reported to have said: "We don't need any college here at all; if we did, it would be to turn out horse doctors."

The university's first classes were held on September 4, 1908, on the top floor of Strathcona's Queen Alexandra School, and about a month later its first convocation, a body of 364 graduates of British and Canadian universities resident in Alberta met in the Strathcona Opera House. It was to be 1912, of course, before the first class of students who had received all their training at the new institution graduated and when it did five of its eighteen members were women—another sign that times were changing.

On the score of change, on February 24, 1909, the *Journal* reported the first aeroplane flight ever to be made in Canada. That day, in Nova Scotia, John McCurdy flew his Silver Dart half a mile. Edmontonians were properly impressed, and for a few days everyone talked of this curious feat.

Edmonton, however, was not to be far behind Nova Scotia in seeing one of the earliest plane flights, for on September 7, 1909, Reginald Hunt, a local carpenter who had built his own plane, flew the craft for thirty-five minutes. It had taken him three years to assemble the parts and to build his machine and fashion its four-bladed propeller, of which he said: "I based my design on the fans that keep flies from sleeping in restaurants." The very next day, far away in England, Captain S. F. Cody, although not the first to fly there, achieved fame by staying aloft for sixty-three minutes in a factory-built plane. Reginald Hunt, however, had won through all by himself, but bad luck turned him to other interests. Next

A History of Alberta

year his hopes in the aeronautical line ended when, in preparing to perform at the exhibition, he crumpled his hard-won plane against a fence. It was to be another two years before, at the Calgary exhibition, Albertans saw their next heavier-than-air machine when Howard Levan thrilled the crowd with what he could do with his *Golden Flyer.*

Certainly everything else was changing. By 1912 Laurier's Liberal government had been defeated and Edmonton's great Frank Oliver, although re-elected, no longer sat as a member of the federal cabinet. Even in the face of that calamity Edmonton continued to grow. On February 1, 1912, it and Strathcona had been amalgamated into one big Edmonton. During the twelve-month period of that year over twenty thousand had come pouring in. On August 30, when the *Bulletin* had tried to tally up the number of newcomers, it found that despite the fact that the city council had thrown open the Granite Curling Club and some temporary school buildings as sleeping quarters for newcomers, 2,671 people were camped in tents on the river flats or around the fringes of the city. Some of these, indeed, had spilled over into the areas annexed that summer.

Even though Edmonton's city limits had been expanded so as to include over twenty-four square miles, it appeared that even that area was going to be too little to hold its burgeoning thousands. All over these miles new subdivisions were being surveyed or at least plotted on paper and even outside the city's boundary other areas were being divided and sold. Edmonton's land boom was reaching its zenith. During this, the land speculators' golden age, real estate offices reached a peak never dreamed of in earlier years. Along Jasper Avenue, 97 Street, 101 Street and Whyte Avenue, and in fact in nearly every hole or corner, these offices sprouted till by the end of 1912 Henderson's Directory counted thirty-two real estate brokers, 135 financial agencies, and 336 real estate agents. The city swarmed with them.

Though much of the real estate promotion was a mirage, the clatter of hammers and the whine of hand-saws was real enough as everywhere carpenters and bricklayers built the new city. All the while too, riveters, balancing precariously on the end of the great steel girders of the High Level Bridge, waited there while other sections were swung into place and until they could insert the white-hot rivets and whack good sturdy heads on them. Day after day the river valley and the town rang with the rata-ta-tat of riveting hammers.

As the year 1912 closed everyone felt confident that it had been a mere prelude to what was to come. Then, strangely enough, an epidemic of fires marked the early months of 1913—a bad sign. Someone realized that though Edmonton's streets were more crowded than usual a large part of their traffic consisted of unemployed men. To add to them came gangs of labourers reporting that the CNR contractors had laid them off.

Boom Times 1906-1914

Far out west, beyond Jasper, that railway, creaking its weary way through canyon and coulee, was slowing up, and it was rumoured that Mackenzie and Mann were in financial trouble. To the thoughtful, waiting for the boom to begin again in the spring, the large number of unemployed, Mackenzie and Mann's shaky position, and the epidemic of fires, were disturbing straws in the economic wind. By mid-summer 1913, the money markets were collapsing, and one of the major tremors that toppled them was the imminent bankruptcy of Mackenzie and Mann's CNR empire.

By January 1914 unemployed men flocked into Edmonton. The civic relief department reporting in mid-February advised that it was doing all it could for some four thousand unemployed, and amongst other assistance was finding work for some of them on city relief projects. To complicate matters further, a number of Industrial Workers of the World (IWW) organizers arrived in Edmonton and by marches and other agitation started to foment trouble. Dubbed the I Won't Works, this group was a militant labour faction which, because of its many real grievances and a few imaginary ones, had incited riots and bloodshed and had become a serious menace to law and order in the northwestern States. Usually led by Anglo-Saxons or Irishmen, it recruited a large following from the recent non-English-speaking immigrants. On Sunday, February 1, three hundred unemployed, headed by IWW leaders, paraded to two city churches. Coming at a time when graft and inefficiency had undermined the morale of the Edmonton police department, the IWW inspired troubles had an ominous ring.

Then in May 1914 Calgarians, always unpalatable to Edmontonians, became insufferable. In Turner Valley at five o'clock on May 14, Calgary's Dingman well came in. On May 16 the *Bulletin* said: "Calgary people have gone oil mad. Oil shares jumped from $12.50 to $200 each." Forty new oil companies were floated in a week, and down-at-the-heels real estate salesmen switched from town lots to oil stocks. Without bothering to lock their doors, a host of Edmonton's lot peddlers hurried off to Calgary. Others remained, however, and within three days of Dingman's discovery, one hundred new oil brokers' offices opened in Edmonton. On May 21 the *Bulletin*, after a careful survey, estimated that $100,000 of good Edmonton money had been spent on oil stocks the day before. On May 22 it declared that oil brokerage offices had opened all down Jasper Avenue between McDougall Avenue (100 Street) and 101 Street. One company had rented a stand in a Jasper Avenue lunch counter, and another had a temporary office in the front of an ice-cream parlour. Edmontonians, alas, were casting their money into these to buy worthless paper, whereas Calgarians actually had oil.

Calgary, the long-suffering Conservative cinderella, had come into her own. Overnight the faith and expenditure of its venturesome citizens had

A History of Alberta

borne fruit and Calgary had become an oil city. Now Edmonton could have its lethargic legislature, Strathcona its book-toting students, and Elk Island Park its bone-headed beasts. Calgary had oil.

Though all of a sudden the Dingman well had blown in and Calgary had awakened to believe itself rich, its oil had been the reward of long years of effort—effort unaided by any government. As early as 1903 the Calgary Gas Company Limited had been incorporated to produce artificial gas, and before long, through twenty-six miles of pipeline, served 1,800 customers in the heart of the city. Then in 1905, A. W. Dingman, after drilling an unsuccessful well or two, hit gas in east Calgary. This well was so satisfactory that for fifty years it continued to produce. By 1910 Dingman was supplying the Calgary Brewing Company's fuel requirements and soon extended his distribution system to serve natural gas to many customers in east Calgary.

While Dingman was thus engaged, a successful geologist and promoter, Eugene Coste, turned his attention to the area around Bow Island along the Oldman River, and in 1909 brought in some gas wells. In 1911 he was instrumental in incorporating the company which today everyone refers to as the Calgary Gas Company but which was ushered into the world with what must surely be a record in unwieldy and all-embracing appellation, Canadian Western Natural Gas, Light, Heat and Power Company Limited. Before long it bought out the Prairie Fuel Gas Company which had drilled at Brooks, Bassano and Bow Island, and in 1912 acquired both of Calgary's existing gas companies, the artificial one and the natural gas one. That year the company had completed the long 170-mile line from the Bow Island field to Calgary, and on August 1 turned that gas into the city mains. Not long after that, the company started to serve Lethbridge and the towns between it and Calgary.

Meanwhile and much nearer to Calgary, other daring men had begun to wonder about the seepages on Sheep Creek. In July 1911 Calgary's mayor, John Mitchell, and a party of councillors went out to a spot near today's Black Diamond and planted a sign reading "Staked for gas and petroleum by the City of Calgary." Filled with exuberance instead of experience, however, they failed to follow through and register their claim. About the same time, William S. Herron, a well-known rancher, also became interested in the Sheep Creek area and purchased the farm whereon the city fathers had stuck their stake. Then in 1912 he organized the Calgary Petroleum Products Limited (which later became Royalite Oil Company Limited), in which he easily enlisted a number of Calgarians whose names figure large in any of the city's halls of fame: A. W. Dingman, James A. Lougheed, A. E. Cross, I. K. Kerr, R. B. Bennett, William Pearce, T. J. S. Skinner, William Elder, and others.

Backed by such an aggregation of men ready to put their money where their mouths were, the company soon got rolling, and on January 25, 1913, spudded in the first of the three Dingman wells. On May 14, 1914, as we have already noted, at a depth of 2,700 feet, the third of these wells blew in with a daily flow of about four million cubic feet of wet gas saturated with a straw-coloured light oil.

News of the strike reached the city Thursday night and next morning every available car was pressed into service to take hundreds of excited Calgarians out to see the first successful well in the first major oil and gas field in the British Empire. Pouring the straw-coloured oil into their gas tanks, they rushed back to town, convinced that Calgary would become the greatest industrial city in Canada and certain that they would all become millionaires overnight.

A wild scramble for oil shares followed. Every day new companies sprouted and printing presses groaned with the volume of highly coloured share certificates. Every spare bit of space in every downtown store or office or restaurant was rented by energetic salesmen shoving shares of some new company over the temporary counter with one hand while with the other they raked in customers' dollars and cheques and threw them into wastepaper baskets behind them. Frantically their helpers wrote receipts for a crazy mob lined up waving money at them.

Calgarians had gone wild. The recently subsided land boom had bankrupted many a man, but hard on its heels came this new boom. Sure, they had been deceived by land, but now there could be no mistake, for this was the real thing. This was the path to quick and easy fortunes; this was oil.

So at the close of 1914 Calgarians were floating on rosy-tinted clouds perfumed with oil, and hundreds of Edmontonians, swallowing their pride and overlooking their long-standing feud, came down to soar with them.

Except for Calgary's luck, which had found it located near the Turner Valley field—almost the only one in the province shallow enough to be reached by the crude cable tool drilling equipment of the day—Calgary's experience since 1905 had been essentially the same as Edmonton's. Always keeping a jump of a few hundred people ahead of Edmonton, it had grown and spread in much the same way as its northern rival. Its paving programs, its waterworks, its council's problems and its grafting episodes, its hotels, its music, theatres and movies, its stone and brick buildings spreading along its main streets—all of them had been much the same as those in its sister city. But at last, after Liberal politicians had favoured Edmonton and cheated Calgary out of the capital, the buffalo and the university, the hand of providence had intervened on Calgary's behalf.

A stroll around either city's business section was an interesting experience. For as well as the predominant mixture of British peoples, many of the citizens were of German, Scandinavian or Slavic stock and there

A History of Alberta

were representatives from Belgium, Holland, Hungary, Greece and Italy, with a sprinkling of Chinese and a few Negroes from the United States. By 1910 both Calgary and Edmonton had many merchants of Jewish descent, who, seeing opportunities, came to apply their energy and ability to developing these young cities. By that time too, many of the Greeks had found an outlet for their talents in the restaurant business or in small grocery stores. They met brisk competition from the Chinese, who, starting with every handicap against them, soon established themselves in those fields and in laundries and market gardens.

And all of them had dabbled in the fantastic real estate booms which had provided Edmontonians and Calgarians, and to a lesser extent the people of Lethbridge and Medicine Hat, with years of excitement during 1910 and 1911 and sent them into a frenzy of speculation. Any man with ten dollars could get into the game and by buying a lot today and selling it tomorrow at double the price and then buying it back the next day at a redoubled price could enjoy all the fun of the fair. When the booms were all over, of course, few indeed were any richer, but all had enjoyed a year or so of reckless gambling.

Land values rose at a rate out of all proportion to the growth of the cities. For instance, one lot on the corner of Calgary's Seventh Avenue and Second Street West had sold for $150 in 1895 and ten years later had changed hands at $2,000 and then increased in value down the years till in 1912 it sold for $300,000. Similarly, in Edmonton in 1898 the 145-acre Hagmann estate had been purchased from the Hudson's Bay Company for $1,450, or ten dollars per acre. During 1912 it sold for $850,000, or $5,862 per acre.

Of course, in the midst of the welter of real estate offices on Calgary's Eighth Avenue or Edmonton's Jasper Avenue many a new, sturdy business block or hotel began to rise to lend a new look to each city's four- or five-storey skyline. None of these buildings, however, lent either city such an air of comfortable, quiet dignity as the northern city's GTP hotel, the luxurious Macdonald, or the cowtown's plush CPR Palliser Hotel, both of which were completed in 1914.

Calgary's character, however, had a few vastly significant elements which it reserved unto itself, elements all relating to its ranching past. One of these, an annual event which was to become world famous, was its Bull Sale which Calgarians had started in 1901. Another, along somewhat similar lines, had been the Dominion Exhibition of 1908 which Calgarians had convinced the authorities to hold in their city and which during six days had seen 89,435 people click through its turnstiles. While it was only a foretaste of what was later to become Calgary's great Stampede, it was also the occasion of an early balloon flight in Alberta. Unfortunately for that particular balloon it was its last flight, for in a high wind something went wrong, the bag burst and caught fire, injuring both the airmen.

During the years, Calgary's failure to obtain the provincial university in 1907 had continued to rankle, and in 1910 R. B. Bennett secured the passage of an act to incorporate a Calgary College. Assured of financial support from many a businessman, its prospects of becoming a physical fact were excellent until once more the provincial government got in the way by rather sensibly refusing to allow it to grant degrees. The embryo province had had enough difficulty bringing one university into being without having to divide its slender funds between two competing institutions. Since Calgary could not get a fully fledged university, the citizens rallied round and did the next best thing by setting up Mount Royal College in 1910 and making the Reverend Dr. George W. Kirby its principal—a college and a principal who were both to go down in the city's history.

It is strange that the legislators at Edmonton with their idea that the government should be expected to undertake or to guarantee any risky venture or to own any public utility, did not get in the way of Alberta's first significant hydro plant. It is not strange, however, that Calgary's R. B. Bennett became one of the organizers of Calgary Power Company Limited, which came into being on October 19, 1909. Two other famous Canadians who were associated with the venture were W. M. Aitken (later Lord Beaverbrook) and Herbert Holt. Like the directors of the CPR a couple of decades earlier, these men were involved in several enterprises in which they took varying risks in developing Alberta's resources. Because of their foresight and their ability, they were the means of employing hundreds of men in a growing list of industries which without their risks and their efforts would have been much slower to develop.

In any event, once it was organized, the Calgary Power Company Limited went right to work damming the Bow River at the Horseshoe Falls, some forty-five miles west of Calgary, and by May 21, 1911, its turbines, which eventually had a capacity of some 13,000 kilowatts, started generating. By that time the first 55,000-volt long-distance transmission line to be built in Alberta was ready to carry the power to Calgary. Because this hydro plant was designed and constructed by some of the best engineering talent in Canada, it has continued in service to the present.

If by 1912 Calgary was unique in having its power supplied by a major hydro plant and transmission line, it was also unique in a venture upon which it embarked the next year. In 1912 a wandering promoter, Guy Weadick, perceived that in Calgary he had found the three ingredients which if touched by his showman's magic would combine to make one of the world's greatest spectacles: a ranching environment, wealthy men deeply loyal to their background, and a populace steeped in the rich lore of their region. From this favourable conjunction was born the world-famous Calgary Stampede, which because it was indigenous both fed upon

Tom Three Persons, Blood Indian winner of the world's championship at the first Calgary Stampede in 1912

Edmonton Women's Canadian Club, 1912

Dingman well, Turner Valley, 1914

F. R. McCall, First World War flying ace

Wop May, First World War flying ace

R. Moorehouse hauling 1,144 bushels of wheat to the Vulcan elevators in 1922

Percy Page and the Commercial Grads

The depression's "Bennett Buggy"

William Aberhart speaking at a picnic in 1936; Ernest Manning on the right

A destitute depression family on their way through Edmonton, 1934

Strip and contour farming near Nobleford

# Alberta
# Premiers

A. C. Rutherford, 1905–1910

A. L. Sifton, 1910–1917

Charles Stewart, 1917–1921

Herbert Greenfield, 1921–1925

J. E. Brownlee, 1925–1934

R. G. Reid, 1934–1935

William Aberhart, 1935–1943

Ernest C. Manning, 1943–1968

Harry Strom, 1968–1971

Peter Lougheed, 1971–

# Alberta
# Lieutenant -
# Governors

G. H. V. Bulyea, 1905–1915

R. G. Brett, 1915–1925

Wm. Egbert, 1925–1931

W. L. Walsh, 1931–1936

P. C. H. Primrose, 1936–1937

J. C. Bowen, 1937–1950

J. J. Bowlen, 1950–1959

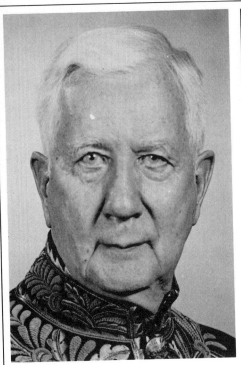

J. Percy Page, 1959–1966

J. W. Grant MacEwan, 1966–

Leduc Well No. 1, February 13, 1947

University of Lethbridge

University of Alberta viewed from the northwest

# Cities
# and
# Towns

Fort McMurray

Grande Cache

The heart of Calgary's downtown district

Edmonton's new skyline centering about the church built a century ago by Rev. G. McDougall

Medicine Hat

Lethbridge

Camrose

Grande Prairie

the city's loyalty and in turn nurtured it in a never ending circle which was to make Calgary and its Stampede known the world over. Of all Calgary's significant differences from other prairie cities, this was its most outstanding.

All that, of course, lay in the future when in 1912 Guy Weadick, the gifted cowboy showman, outlined his plans for a stampede and explained that it would take $100,000 to finance it. Almost overnight he had his guarantee put up by the big four: Archie McLean, Pat Burns, A. E. Cross and George Lane. When in September the great show came off, 250,000 people crowded through its gates the first day.

Perhaps the most memorable of the many exciting events was the bronco busting feat accomplished by Tom Three Persons, an Indian from the Blood Reserve. For not only did he ride Cyclone, the most feared bronco of the West to a standstill but won the riding championship. Rarely had the hundreds of Indians who stood amongst the thousands of spectators watched anything in this whole white man's world which gave them such grim satisfaction. Out of the scores of competitors, Tom Three Persons, a man of their own blood, had outranked all the white men.

Moreover, due to Weadick's showmanship and the Reverend John McDougall's interest in the native people, the first groups of Sarcees, Stoneys and Blackfoot to participate in the parade provided an opportunity for thousands of new immigrants to see their first Indians and to see them in the matchless decorated costumes which had been such a common sight to the real old-timers. Although the parade was to do the Indians little good, it did serve to remind the newcomers that the hillsides they farmed and the springs they fenced had recently belonged to this race of fine cavalrymen who also loved Alberta's far-flung parklands.

Tom Three Persons' victory and their participation in the parade gave the Indians' morale a temporary fillip. Moreover, the cash they collected came as a welcome boost to their resources. For tucked away out of sight on their reserves and living on meagre rations their morale could stand any help that came its way. Year after year, due to discouragement, tuberculosis and venereal disease, deaths amongst them had marched far ahead of births and on Crowfoot's old reserve, for instance, during the previous decade the population had decreased sixteen percent. The inrushing whites who had ploughed up their old homelands were increasing by the thousands, but the original people, once The People, had not only been banished to little pockets of their former empire but in the face of the white man's progress were slowly slipping away to the Great Sand Hills.

Utterly insensitive to that, Calgary, with its land boom, its Stampede and its recent oil strike, had taken on the characteristics which from there on would set it apart from its rivals. So too had the province of Alberta, which with its busy and prosperous population of 470,000 was thence-

225

forth a power to be reckoned with. From the standpoint of bustling cities, progressive towns, newly built railways reaching out to serve settlements spread all over its arable land, it was essentially the Alberta which we know today.

By 1914 by the judicious combination of the newcomers' eager efforts with untold millions poured in by often incautious investors, Alberta had achieved an outstanding record of progress. During that time the settlers had built two thousand schools to educate the children coming from their more than fifty thousand newly built homes. In 1914 they turned out 110 million dollars of agricultural produce which they hauled to market in wagons over perhaps thirty thousand miles of roads they had recently scratched out of the turf.

The farming population, which in 1906 had been 127,379, had sky-rocketed to some 300,000 by 1914. And now these farmers ploughed fields on quarters they owned, stretching five hundred miles north from the Sweet Grass Hills to the banks of the Peace River, and from the Barr colonists' unfortunate 4th meridian at Lloydminster 270 miles westerly to Edson. They, who with their slobbering oxen and their sweating horses had cultivated only 650,000 acres by 1906, could now drive their rattling binders over some 2,500,000 acres.

During that same era, with the assistance of outside capital, some 185,000 urban-oriented immigrants had built six cities ranging in population from 2,400 to 72,000. Having swallowed Strathcona, Edmonton's population, for instance, had grown from 14,088 in 1906 to 72,516 in 1914. During the same period, Calgary had grown from 13,573 to some 72,000; Lethbridge from 2,936 to over 9,000; Medicine Hat from 3,020 to over 9,000, and Wetaskiwin from 1,652 to 2,400, with Red Deer, which had been incorporated as a city in 1913, having 2,100.

Moreover, in 1906 there had been only forty-two towns and villages with a combined population of 20,647, whereas because of the impressive expansion of railway lines up to 1914, there was now 136 with a population of over 50,000. Furthermore, Albertans had brought 264 coal mines into being, and in 1914 these employed 8,000 men and produced 3,822,000 tons of coal. As well, they had set up scores of sawmills to slash, cut and buzz their way ever farther into the stately forests.

Even though in the fall of 1913 a recession had reduced the price of wheat to some eighty-seven cents per bushel (f.o.b. Winnipeg), everybody was cheerful. To threshing machines atop a thousand hills, loaded bundle wagons carried the heavy sheaves, while from other machines blowing straw down a thousand valleys the amber grain poured into bins. For much of the succeeding winter, with teams and sleighs, farm boys hauled the golden wealth to newly built red elevators in the rural towns sometimes forty miles distant. And even though most farm labour was done by horses, everybody was remarkably content; even better times, which would bring tractors and trucks, lay ahead.

Times were changing and Alberta was ready to enter a new era. When on January 21, 1914, all Alberta newspapers noted the death of the legendary Lord Strathcona, that event was but another mark in the dividing line between the long struggle of the past and the new era. The death of the old man, who long ago had been a Hudson's Bay Company employee and after rising in the company's service had played a major role in settling the Riel Rebellion, and who had finally gone on to organizing the CPR, came at the transitional point where pioneering had ended and was being succeeded by cultivation; where the rapid changes which were soon to overtake farming and to revolutionize life in the western cities that had grown up around his company's old trading posts were under way.

One of the changes was that on the western prairies immigrants from the United States, eastern Canada and Europe were busily creating a new society, one which from the very purity of their motives must surely be different and better than in the older lands. For in their own minds at least these new westerners knew themselves to be men of integrity and high principle whose worst fault might be a naive gullibility. As compared to the sordid greediness of which they accused easterners, that fault might indeed be felt to be a virtue. Many Albertans had broken away from decadent Europe, and, God willing, would soon put easterners to shame.

But whatever the vision of the future held by Albertans, so far the West had merely gotten away to a good start. So far it had not succeeded in cutting itself off from influences from the outside. For instance, according to the Edmonton and Calgary newspapers of December 1913, the tango had arrived in the United States, eastern Canada and Europe. It appeared that even though this terrible dance had been banned by the Vatican, Buckingham Palace and Ottawa's Rideau Hall, all the forces for good could not prevail and it was spreading. Fears were expressed that it would reach Alberta.

Moreover, in Germany, so the papers said, inventors had brought out lighter-than-air craft and the word zeppelin became familiar to everyone. It had some ominous aspects such as hovering overhead and seeing everything that was going on below, but the big powers, France, Germany and Britain, by some sort of high level agreement, had pulled its teeth, for they had made it illegal to drop things from it. Then too, Germany had built some very successful submarines, new and interesting devices, but here too the great powers had declared them illegal for war use.

Unfortunately for Albertans new forces were abroad in the world and in remote Europe had reached a point where they were soon to boil over. As soon as they should do so, Canada and even the innocent far West would also be scalded. The world which for so many decades had been in a state of relative peace was ready to explode.

On June 27, 1914, far away in a place called Sarajevo, capital of Bosnia in the remote Balkans, someone shot and killed Archduke Ferdinand, heir to the throne of Austro-Hungary. To Albertans this was a titillating bit of information to be tucked away in their minds until the next time someone mentioned Vienna or waltzes or beer gardens. To all Albertans nothing could have been of much less moment.

To the German war lords, however, who had long been waiting for *Der Tag* when they would break out their banners, that was the day— an assassination that might be fanned into the war they awaited so eagerly. All during July, Germany, blowing on the coals, alarmed the rest of Europe. Albertans, however, busy watching the sun ripen their rippling wheat fields, were too pleasurably occupied to give a second thought to this news from the faraway world. Even in the city of Edmonton it was only on July 30, 1914, that the Edmonton *Journal* made any front page comment on the possibility of war. On that same day Germany delivered an ultimatum to France and with its armies pointed at Paris, marched through Belgium. As suddenly, as surprisingly as that, World War I had started.

# 15
# The Great War Years and After 1914-1920

On August 4, 1914, like a hailstorm lashing out of the sky, World War I struck Canada. Albertans, farmers busily preparing for the harvest, or city dwellers plodding to their businesses and warehouses, had been too preoccupied to notice the massive build-up of black clouds over the green beauty of Europe's remote countryside.

When by newspaper or word of mouth the report spread from street to street in Calgary and Edmonton, and over a period of a week penetrated the pioneers' remoter valleys, it aroused mixed reactions. Instinctively the British-bred rose to the challenge of danger to their homeland. The republican Americans who some generations previous had turned their backs on Europe, found it hard to see why a war on that decadent continent should give them any concern. Moreover, in their opinion, if Germany conquered Britain, little would be lost. Feeling only slightly less indifferent towards England were many Canadians of two or three generations' standing. Since the Scandinavians' homelands were near neighbours of Germany they had some leanings towards the Prussian cause, and since many of them while sojourning in Minnesota or Dakota had been exposed to mid-west American hatred of England's institutions, they exhibited varying degrees of indifference or hostility to Britain. Finally, a small but vocal minority of German-bred felt, or openly expressed, sympathy for their fatherland.

With such emotions then, Albertans, nearly all recent immigrants, awoke to find themselves in an unexpected situation and some not too sure which side they wanted to be on. Little did they realize that the war was to mark a turning point in Alberta's economy, to affect them personally, and before it was over to unite them as Canadians.

Anxious for action, veterans of the South African War and former British regulars clamoured to enlist. Foremost amongst these were the men of the 19th Alberta Dragoons scattered here and there over the province. In less than three weeks this unit, 240 strong and made up largely of men from the cattle country, entrained from Edmonton for Valcartier Camp in Quebec. On August 7 the 10th Battalion was authorized and into it flocked most of the men of the 101st Edmonton Reserve Battalion, and three weeks later its 1,300 officers and men left Calgary for Valcartier Camp. So quickly did Alberta's British-born come forward to join the first units. Other regiments soon came into being. Before the war was over 45,136 men had enlisted in Alberta, forming twenty infantry battalions, four mounted regiments, three battalions of artillery and a field ambulance unit.

Of the infantry battalions only three maintained their identity in France: Calgary's 31st Battalion, Edmonton's 49th and Calgary's 50th. The others, raised somewhat later on, were sent to England for training and then were broken up to reinforce the three main battalions which went all through the four-year long war and came back as complete units.

As well as those already mentioned, other battalions mobilized mainly in Edmonton and Calgary but also in Medicine Hat, Lethbridge, Red Deer, Pincher Creek, Cardston, Macleod and Blairmore, went overseas: the 51st, 56th, 63rd, 66th, 82nd, 89th, 113th, 137th, 138th, 151st, 187th, 191st, 192nd, 194th, 202nd and 218th, as well as the 3rd, 12th and 13th Mounted Rifles. Of the supporting services Alberta supplied the 20th, 39th and 61st batteries of the Canadian Field Artillery, No. 2 Tunnelling Company and No. 8 Field Ambulance.

During the first three weeks of the war the German armies, a million strong, crumpled the Belgian forts and swaggered on into France. Even as the 19th Dragoons and the 10th Battalion were recruiting, 90,000 men of the British Expeditionary Forces with their 15,000 horses and 400 cannon, in a desperate effort to help their allies to stay the invincible Germans, were landing in France. Even as the 10th Battalion was entraining, the flower of the British regiments was being mowed down by the thousands at Mons. Fighting magnificently, countering cannon with raw courage and discipline, they hung on, backing up to the Aisne River and then to the Marne, and there they stopped the Germans. During those first disastrous weeks of the world's bloodiest war, when each day's news bulletins were worse than yesterday's, Albertans were jerked from a world where only profits, oil shares and land titles had counted, to an unreal world where armed might with its brutality and barbarity, brushing aside all resistance and putting aside all humanity, swept across the benign Belgian countryside. Every day's news was more bitter than the last. And each day more iron entered each Albertan's soul. By the time the Battle of the Marne had quietened down, Albertans were swarming to enlist.

Events moved quickly. Alberta's three main battalions, the 49th from Edmonton and the 31st and 50th from Calgary left Canada within months of the start of the war. By the end of 1914 all Anglo-Saxons, no matter how many generations they had been domiciled in Canada, also came rolling in to join up beside the English, Irish or Scottish-born who had been the first to enlist. To them too, the war had become a reality. Still neutral were the Swedes, Italians and the Americans, while pulled two ways between loyalty to their fatherland and to this new land were the Germanic peoples who found themselves in a most unenviable position. Their newspaper, the *Alberta Herold*, printed in German in Edmonton, was taking a strong pro-German stand. Even in November 1914, it came out with such gleeful articles and headlines as: "Ist Britischer Super-Dreadnought gesunken?" "Germans march again upon Warsaw," "Russians Entered into Trap and 23,000 Captured," and others. Early in 1915, just in time to avoid being forced to do so, the *Herold* ceased publication.

In February 1915, Lieut.-Colonel Jamieson's 19th Dragoons went into action in France. Now Albertans were really at war, hanging breathlessly on the news bulletins and the telegrams that started spelling out the names of those wounded or killed. North of Ypres on April 22, 1915, the Dragoons witnessed the first infamous gas attack, when the Canadians made a glorious name for themselves.

About the middle of May 1915, Calgary's fighting 31st and Edmonton's famous 49th sailed for England. There they endured the irksome delay of training, a delay occasioned by a factor most of them never understood—their lack of discipline. Coming from the untrammelled West their overflowing individual initiative, unparalleled daring and a zeal to come to grips, was only equalled by their lack of realization that discipline wins more battles than all the enthusiasm in the world.

In any event, both battalions arrived in France in September 1915 and immediately began to render a good account of themselves. By June 1916, Edmonton's 49th had endured its first major testing at the Battle of Mt. Sorrell where it lost fifty-two killed, 265 wounded and sixty-nine missing. Of the missing, most were dead, blown to bits by high explosives, or wounded and choked to death in the fearful mud of collapsed trenches, and were never found. Nearby were the Calgarians of the 31st, who also suffered grievously—thirty-three killed, 128 wounded and three missing. Then in September both of Alberta's battalions moved on to the Battle of Flers-Courcelette where they suffered equally appalling losses.

And so it went through the hell of battles now long forgotten while Calgary's 50th Battalion arrived in France in August 1916 and joined up with the other Alberta units in forming part of Canada's valiant army. Meanwhile, the Artillery Batteries, the Mounted Rifles and the men of the ambulance units played their heroic parts as Alberta men from Medicine Hat to the Peace River's Waterhole, or from the cattle ranches of the Pincher Creek country, or the fields of Paradise Valley did their bit, many of them never to return to the prairies and parklands.

Covered with lice, knee-deep in mud in trenches dug into the battlefields, they lived for weeks at a time, making occasional sorties across No Man's Land to strike at the enemy. At such times, wave after wave

The Great War Years and After 1914-1920

of men crossing this gap and crawling through barbed wire fell from machine-gun fire, while big guns booming very much farther away ripped up the earth and blew many a man to shreds. No wonder that since in the cesspool of mud and gore none of their comrades could ever find any identifiable part of their bodies, so many men were reported missing. For missing meant dead.

Back in Alberta as the casualty lists came out, the war began to come into focus. This was no lark which would soon be over, no shining crusade, but a bitter reality of death, crippling wounds and muddy trench warfare such as the world had never seen and in fact was never to see again. So far, except for the sheer guts and the grim resistance of the British, French, Belgian, Canadian and Australian troops, the Allies had nothing to exult over. The defence the French put up at Verdun had seriously weakened that nation. The British fronts at Ypres and on the Somme ended in costly stalemates. Italy too had made little progress. And so it went on other fronts, in the Middle East, and at sea. Only the massive Russian forces seemed to have made any headway. In the United States, President Wilson, still indecisive and apparently still unwilling to try to swing his people to the Allied side, listened while United States mothers sang "I did not raise my boy to be a soldier."

For better or for worse, the war imparted a new tempo to Alberta and wrenched the province and its people into new social and economic patterns. The year 1914 had started in a depression and that year, moreover, the farmers' crops were poor, but the war's needs quickly put money into circulation. The ideal, indeed heavy, rainfall of 1915 ensured a bountiful harvest. Wheat yielded 31.1 bushels to the acre, a phenomenal return never exceeded before or since. The acreage seeded to wheat increased amazingly and doubled from 1,371,100 acres in the spring of 1914 to 2,605,000 in 1916. Even the tremendous acreage of hitherto parched grassland extending east from Hanna and Castor—the region which was later to be known as the Special Areas—received unprecedented rainfall. Riches in the shape of overflowing granaries poured over this the most recently settled area of the province, the area which Palliser had written off as arid. Prosperity strode the streets of its new towns, Youngstown, Cereal, Chinook and Sibbald, or was garnered into dozens of newly built elevators at Throne, Consort or Monitor.

Moreover, from 1914 to 1916 the average prices paid for wheat rose from ninety-one cents per bushel to $1.33. Here and there even an occasional farmer bought a car, and Henry Ford's Model T's, durable yet simple in design and operation, began to bounce and chortle along country trails. On an unprecedented scale Alberta's rich resource of land had begun to pay off.

Prosperity, however, was not confined to the farming areas or to the

A History of Alberta

cities. Coal mines all over the province, busier than ever, boosted their production from 1,694,564 tons in 1911 to 4,648,604 in 1916. The older mining areas around Edmonton, Lethbridge, the Crowsnest Pass and Canmore doubled their output, while in the newer areas, the Coal Branch, Entwistle, Tofield, Camrose, Drumheller and Brazeau, new mines by the dozen came to contribute their share to Canada's fuel needs.

Even in the Crowsnest Pass, which as recently as June 1914 had experienced one of Canada's major disasters, courageous miners, casting nervous glances at the timbering of their tunnels and at the glow of their safety lamps, kept at their work. All too well they knew how hazardous their vocation was and that in coal mining accidents in Alberta alone from the inauguration of the province to the beginning of the war 375 men had been killed, most of them in the Crowsnest Pass. Of the total deaths, 220 had been in two fatal accidents in that area, but the rest, 155, was a large toll to be taken by miners' carelessness or by management's indifference. The two major disasters had both occurred within three miles of the Frank slide of 1903, one at Bellevue in 1910 where thirty-one men were killed, and the other at Hillcrest, which four years later took a far heavier toll. Truly the Crowsnest Pass and the Frank area in particular were black spots in coal mining history.

On the morning of June 19, 1914, 235 men had gone to work in the Hillcrest mine, a mile down the valley from the scar of the Frank slide. One of them was Charles Elick, who eleven years earlier had been caught when that slide had sealed off the mine entrance. In compliance with the knowledge of the day and with the mining regulations, inspectors had made their usual rounds and found nothing to cause any worry. But at 9:30 a tremendous explosion shook the mine and it was followed by one or more blasts in quick succession.

Some spark, no one would ever know its origin, had ignited a pocket of gas and it in turn had sent the ever-present fine coal dust off into the two or three explosions heard by those outside. Of the men in the mine, 189 never even heard the explosion but were killed instantly by the blast, some of them horribly dismembered. For forty-eight hours rescue workers brought out the bodies and buried them in a common grave. One of the victims was Charles Elick. Of another, only one leg was found and buried. That sunny June morning had turned into one of the worst days in Canadian mining history.

In spite of that disaster, miners continued to trundle their trucks along the galleries of other mines, for the war effort kept demanding more coal. Once the war had started and the output of mines and farms soared, more and more money began to flow across merchants' counters. As farm boys hauled the season's crops to the elevators, the country towns and villages prospered as never before. The stores brightened up, new one-storey cottage banks began to open their doors, and empty lots on a town's main street sprouted out with new bakeries, new barbershops, poolrooms, an occasional optometrist's shop, and even dental offices.

With increasing injections of war-oriented money, prospects in Alberta's cities began to assume a more hopeful look. During the optimism of the boom days, Edmonton and Calgary had each been greatly over-expanded and, although it had taken some time for the chilly winds of the depression of 1913 to blow them back down to earth, it had done so. Once their building booms collapsed craftsmen and labourers moved away—some seeking other employment and others going out to the country to farm. Edmonton's 1914 population, for instance, had been 72,516 but by 1916 it had dropped to 53,846, while Calgary, starting with a slightly higher figure than its rival, dropped back to 56,514. By 1916 Lethbridge, not aspiring so high, had actually increased slightly to 9,436, while Medicine Hat, having started into its industrial stride with flour-milling and with potteries, brick and glass works either within its limits or out at nearby Redcliff, had increased from 5,608 to 9,272, to run neck and neck with Lethbridge. From 1911 to 1916, Alberta's population as a whole increased by twenty-five percent to 496,525, but this was a result of increasing immigration up to 1914 of people who came to farm.

Edmonton and Calgary's great booms were now mere memories—memories tinged with the tincture of that morning after taste when the investors found their lots in the boom-time subdivisions not only unusable and unsaleable but eating their heads off in taxes. The result was that they allowed the land to revert to these cities for taxes. So, from time to time during 1915 and 1916 the Edmonton *Journal* and the Calgary *Herald* carried multi-page spreads listing the tax sale lots to be disposed of at the next public auction—lots many of which no one was to take off the cities' hands for thirty years.

Once the war started the influx of immigrants had been throttled back to a trickle. Furthermore, the money that had been poured out so lavishly to build branch railway lines all over the province had stopped pouring and now, to the province's discomfort, its investors were looking for a return on their investment. Practically the only railway construction capital still coming in was balancing itself precariously on the E.D. & B.C. Railway's muskeg-ballasted right-of-way, winding its way through black spruce forest to reach Peace River town and Grande Prairie in 1916. The much touted Canadian Northern Railway and the Grand Trunk Pacific, which Edmontonians had welcomed so warmly, had blasted their separate lines through mountains and canyons to the Pacific and had become transcontinentals, only to find that very few people had really wanted them after all, and that fewer still were willing to ride on the trains or to load their boxcars with paying freight.

A History of Alberta

By 1916 both railways were bankrupt. Their promoters, having enjoyed years of interesting work and having put by fortunes for a rainy day, sat back to enjoy their wealth. Their investors, who had put money into their securities, found that the rainy days were here indeed, and stood by helplessly while their lithographically perfect bonds dissolved into worthless paper. The politicians who had pocketed all the loot that came their way and in return had granted the promoters millions of acres of the country's finest lands, kept their mouths shut and looked away. The governments, both provincial and federal, which had been guided by the politicians' greed and the promoters' guile, had to conduct salvage operations, assume debts and defunct roadbeds and rolling stock, and out of the mess disgorged the Canadian National Railway. Only the CPR, from which the Alberta government had averted its face, continued with its policy of business as usual.

On the score of natural gas, Albertans likewise fared poorly. Due to other matters on its promoters' minds and to a lack of development capital, Calgary's Turner Valley failed to make any contribution to the city's growth. The towns of Vegreville and Castor and others, filled with the optimism of the boom days, drilled wells in 1913, struck gas and laid expensive distribution systems. Unfortunately, while the lives of their wells were numbered in weeks, the thousands of dollars of bonded debt which these towns assumed to pay for drilling them took twenty long years to repay. Even Edmonton's gas aspirations dragged because in spite of the fact that the promoters struck abundant gas in their Viking field little came of it during the war.

In these and many other ways the war years brought everyone down to earth. Furthermore, to all those who had unthinkingly believed that the new world, and particularly the free West, was somehow removed from the realm of human frailty and that somehow or other it had developed a breed of superior beings, the war came as an eye-opener. Neither the new world nor the new West could live in monastic seclusion. Moreover, none of its saintliness had rubbed off on the mass of mankind. After all, the world was a sinful place and a theatre where the full play of the human emotions of love, hatred, suspicion, greed and ambition went on regardless of wishful thinking; not even quiet little backwaters such as Alberta could remain insulated from it. Having tasted all this disillusionment, Americans and Canadians including Albertans had to recast their thinking. The world of the previous decades, of the great open spaces, was indeed a thing of the past. From here on, even Albertans would have to live in a changing world and to learn to become part of it.

One of the changes came in 1915 when the provincial government, intent on beautifying the grounds of the new Legislative Building, set a gang of men to tearing down the relatively sound buildings of Fort Edmonton. This indeed was breaking with the past with a vengeance. The old fort, successor to a series of forts all of which had looked down on the broad Saskatchewan River for over a hundred years, had been sacrificed to progress.

Another of the changes swept away two of the greatest figures of the early West. Father Lacombe and the Reverend John McDougall, men whom Grant MacEwan has called "fellow bishops in the Cathedral of the Great Outdoors," outlived the old fort by a mere year. On December 12, 1916, at the home for Indian children which he had founded, the great Catholic priest passed to his reward. A little over a month later, on January 15, 1917, John McDougall, the devoted Methodist who had given all fifty-five years of his adult life to Alberta, died in Calgary within a few miles of where, forty-one years earlier, he had found his missionary father's frozen body.

Great indeed had been these two missionaries, Father Lacombe and John McDougall, differing in their sacraments but united in serving their God and dealing out mercy and goodwill to the Indians. Their deaths left two more marks on the boundary line between the pioneer era and the troubled times of World War I.

But another and a different mark was to emphasize a transition in Alberta's history—the death of the saloon. Across nearly all of Canada, eager reformers, lacking in understanding of human nature but overflowing with zeal, had gradually pressed their case until during the war years most provinces clamped down various laws prohibiting the manufacture and sale of spirituous liquors. In 1915, Alberta, caught in the tide raised by emerging women's organizations, including the recently convened farm women, the temperance and other Protestant church groups, as well as the UFA, fell into the trap.

Fundamentalist Alberta, largely rural, egged on by an increasingly powerful United Farmers of Alberta, came to believe that if only the government would abdicate its power and common sense, defer to pressure groups and legislate for it, the province could enter into the millennium. It appeared that not only could the government guarantee railways into every remote corner and lay steel to the promised land but that by passing an act calling for prohibition, it could indeed create a liquor-free paradise.

Experience proved the law to be a mistake. Legislation alone could not remove the age-old thirst from parched throats, and succeeded only in replacing the sociability of a friendly drink with furtive trips to the blind pig. In the country, stills operated in the safety of the bush. In the cities, a vast network of blind pigs, usually in the poorer sections of town and often associated with brothels, sprang up to set the law at

A History of Alberta

naught and to vex loyal policemen, who should have been put to more useful tasks.

Against this background, Katherine Stinson, the amazing twenty-year-old aviatrix, astounded Edmonton and Calgary's exhibition crowds with her incredible daring as she looped and dived, spiralled and plummeted her Curtiss biplane. Her visits in 1916 and in two subsequent years allowed thousands of gaping Albertans to see one of their first aeroplanes. Even though the war news recorded the progress the Royal Air Force was making with its new reconnaissance planes, and even though letters began to tell of sons or friends switching from the army to the air force to fly these flimsy machines, few Albertans had ever seen one.

But though Pegasus-like, machines could fly through the air, horses still held the agricultural front and did practically all the cities' hauling. Nevertheless, the gasoline barrel was beginning its battle with the oat bucket and the horse's reign was being challenged. In 1913 in all of Alberta, there had been only 3,773 cars, and now three years later, 9,707 of them were putting around, getting in the horses' way and cluttering up streets and trails. Civilians had begun to realize their value. And they were real values too, especially the Model T Fords, the Tin Lizzies. Now and then they broke down, but when they did repairs were largely inexpensive: an axle shaft cost $1.90, a front axle installed, $12. Any fender cost $4. A whole new radiator, however, was costly at $15, while a complete engine block set one back $25. On farms and in cities, cars were beginning to sneer at the old lumber wagon.

Indeed the life of the western world was changing and at a rate never witnessed before. Ordinary women began to share in the changed era when the war released them from the rigidities of 19th-century traditions and from slope-shouldered, shapeless dresses they began to puff out their skirts and to shorten them. Women were on the march. In April 1916 the Alberta legislature, egged on by such stalwart citizens as Nellie McClung, Louise McKinney, Henrietta Muir Edwards and Mrs. Irene Parlby, who were to go on to greatness, won for women the right to vote in elections. Later that year in Edmonton, Mrs. Emily Murphy, the author, was made a police magistrate.

Women were able to exercise their new-found franchise in the June 1917 provincial election which was marked by two interesting items. One was the appearance of Non-Partisan League candidates—a farm-oriented political movement which elected two members. The other was the election of the first two women to any British or Canadian assembly—one, Nursing Sister Roberta McAdams (one of the two armed services representatives), and Mrs. L. C. McKinney, representing the Non-Partisan League in the Claresholm constituency. After the election A. L. Sifton, whose Liberals had been given another mandate, resigned to join the Union government at Ottawa, and Charles Stewart took his place as premier of Alberta.

Meanwhile great changes had also taken place in the United States and in 1917 the Americans entered the war on the Allied side. This action immediately gave direction to a large number of Albertans of Anglo-Saxon stock who had emigrated from the isolationist mid-continental United States and to many immigrants of Germanic and Norse extraction, all of whom felt that they could now aid in the war effort with a clear conscience.

An interesting side effect of the Americans' entry to the war brought the first Hutterian Brethren to Alberta. A sect of Germanic stock composed of good-living, God-fearing people who chose to live in self-contained communities, the Brethren had left Europe partly because of their resistance to military service and had settled as farmers in the general vicinity of the Dakotas. When the United States got into the war and they were called upon to undergo military service, many of them moved to Canada, which in its desire for immigrants promised to exempt them from such service. As a result, the first Hutterite colonies came to settle in southern Alberta where, as far as Canadians would allow them to do so, they went about their own business in their own quiet way.

While back home their relatives and friends were making these changes, Alberta's three main infantry battalions, the 31st, 49th and 50th, were playing valiant roles in this seemingly endless war. By April 1917 all three were in the midst of the Battle of Vimy Ridge, a successful though costly struggle by all four Canadian divisions to capture the Ridge.

By this time, after more than three years of desperate fighting, the German forces were weakening. In mid-summer 1918 victory for the Allies appeared to be in sight, and by fall, after moving quickly over the fields of France, mopping up small groups of Germans and pursuing others, Canada's armies celebrated the end of hostilities. November 11, 1918, had arrived. With it came emotional exhaustion, memories of four years of hell and horror, hardihood and heroism, and the prospects of a peaceful return to Canada.

In the fall of 1918, however, even before the troops returned, a strange malady, the Spanish flu, startled the world. The first Alberta cases occurred in Calgary on October 4 and its onslaught was so rapid that by October 18 all schools, churches and theatres in the province were closed and public meetings banned. Typical of the experiences in the larger centres are those of the capital city where, although Edmontonians were taking every precaution, the flu struck them suddenly on October 19 when forty-one cases were reported. Three days later that figure had risen to 127. By October 26, 695 cases were known, and when on October 30 two thousand cases had been reported in the city, Edmonton's death toll had risen to forty-four. By November 4 it stood at 120, and twenty-nine more died the next day, while November 6 recorded the highest mortality on any one day—fifty-four. By November 11, Armistice Day, the death toll stood at 262, but the number of new cases was falling off.

This dread disease killed swiftly. Many it spared; some it smote lightly and they lived. Others, mainly the young adults, the vigorous providers and the young mothers, it cut off. One day the victim complained of lassitude and a headache. Next morning he was delirious, and, if he had been marked by the flu as one of its victims, he died before another sunrise. Whole families came down with it, and though it was rarely fatal to all of them, in some cases it did claim mother, father and children.

Over the whole province some 30,000 had caught the disease, and before the end of the year one in every ten had died, a total of 3,259. As the new year came in, a chastened and prayerful Alberta bowed its head in thankfulness that the affliction had passed on.

By that time many Alberta boys had returned from the European holocaust to their farms, hamlets or cities. Albertans everywhere rendered thanks for those of their 45,136 enlisted men who were on their way back or were already home—even though wounded physically or mentally—and remembered sadly those thousands who would never come back.

And yet though the bombing and the barbed wire were becoming mere memories of the past, the war's legacy was to go rolling down the years, and the world, Canada and Alberta were never to return to the placid years of the homestead days. Inevitably, war is a solvent which unsticks past certainties and leaves them in fragments to be put together in a new fashion. This war was to be no exception and even Albertans began to experience the changes that followed in its wake. The returned men, trying to get their ideas back into a peacetime focus, had had a hard time. Their adjustment was made more difficult because of the change in outlook all Albertans had experienced—changes on the political, social, economic and labour fronts.

For one thing, Alberta, like the rest of Canada, was seething in a hornet's nest of labour unrest as the workers, never too well paid, watched the bare-faced graft practised by the war profiteers. Behind the unrest too stood the old IWW organization which became the progenitor of the OBU, the One Big Union, which, when it was launched in Calgary in March 1919, brought with it fear of a Canada-wide revolution. The celebrated Winnipeg strike of 1919 was but one of its manifestations, while in Edmonton the publication of the *Soviet* and a general strike were others.

The Great War Years and After 1914-1920

About this time labour candidates became more prominent in civic councils and many contributed their share towards bettering conditions. Two of the province's well-known and respected labour mayors, Joe Clarke in Edmonton and Andy Davison in Calgary, entered political life about this time.

The labour troubles in Edmonton and Calgary placed a heavy burden on the recently organized Alberta Provincial Police. When Alberta had been created, the Mounties had added the task of enforcing provincial laws to their decades-old Dominion government responsibilities. As the years had gone by they had risen to new challenges and had experienced many changes including the alteration of their official name. When they had been created they had been known as the North West Mounted Police. In 1904 they were honoured by being permitted to be called the Royal North West Mounted Police, and in 1920 became known as the Royal Canadian Mounted Police.

Before that time, however, their load had been lightened when the province reluctantly organized its own Alberta Provincial Police. The new body came into existence on March 1, 1916, when a board, made up of two former Mounties, Colonel G. E. Saunders and Colonel P. C. H. Primrose, along with the deputy attorney-general, A. G. Browning, took over supervision of the provincial organization. Many old-time Albertans considered this move a slight to the Mounties, and the APP, while performing its duties well, never became popular.

It came into being at a bad time. Some forty years earlier the Mounties had been called into existence to combat American whisky traders and now during the war the new police force found itself battling with another generation of whisky traders. This time the law-breakers, travelling in the highest powered cars of the day, carried tons of liquor along what was essentially the old Whoop-Up Trail. But this time they carried booze south and before swinging back onto the Whoop-Up Trail in Montana drove their loads across the line at Whisky Gap.

For by the middle of the war everything had gone topsy-turvey. Prohibition had lowered over the continent, and most of Canada's provinces, succumbing to some form of it, found that they had stepped from the frying pan of a few drunks into the fire of bootlegging and its concomitant ills. When in 1919 the United States, by its disastrous Volstead Act, went dry, Canada became a smuggler's paradise and a tremendous new Canadian industry came into being to ensure that parched Americans would still quench their thirst. The activities of smugglers spared no province as liquor, manufactured in a Canada which was largely legally dry and in which Canadians were not supposed to drink their own liquor, made its way across the four-thousand-mile United States border.

In Alberta the old Whoop-Up Trail assumed a new significance as enough liquor to irrigate hundreds of its adjoining prairie grassland acres slipped south along it to alleviate Montana's thirst. By ill luck, just as Alberta's new provincial police force was getting on its feet, it found itself deluged by this flow of liquor chugging south in tightly side-curtained McLaughlin Specials, Marmons and Hudson Super Sixes. The new whisky traders were abroad but this time they were debauching the thirsty white men of Montana. Under the circumstances, the new police did a creditable job.

The Crowsnest Pass also came in for its share of bootlegging as sleek cars passing back and forth between Blairmore and Fernie headed into Idaho. The pass, however, really flashed into prominence when in September 1922, during a liquor-running venture, Emilio Picariello, a hotel operator and the kingpin of the racket, but nevertheless a man otherwise well liked in the area, killed a policeman. In due course, after one of Alberta's more sensational criminal trials, he and his accomplice, Florence Lassandro, were hanged.

Nothing contributed more to the breakdown of law than prohibition whether in the United States or Canada.

When, therefore, the soldiers came back from the war they found this new prohibition problem at its height to add to the other changes that had come over Alberta—labour troubles and votes for women. All of them, however, were in the mood to share in Calgary's reorganized 1919 Stampede. As a result of many factors, particularly the effect of the war, the great Stampede of 1912 had never been repeated. Once more Calgarians asked Guy Weadick to run the show, which as a celebration of victory in the war and a dedication to the new era just ushered in, was another triumph for Calgarians' showmanship.

With record breaking wheat crops ripening all over southern Alberta and high prices prevailing for cattle, that area and Calgary, its hand-maiden, were on their way to make a showing in this new era. It was true that Alberta's single oil field, Turner Valley, had marked time during the war, but its prospects too were bright. Other indications of prosperity in the south were the discovery of a gas field at Chin Coulee in 1918 and a drilling program at Foremost which appeared favourable and which as it turned out was to prove successful in 1920.

Conditions in the south had also encouraged the Southern Alberta Land Company to start developing the large tract it owned west of Medicine Hat, and in 1919 it began to build works to supply water to the area. Starting at its Carseland Dam on the Bow River some thirty miles east of Calgary, it ran its main canal south and east past Queenstown into Lake McGregor and thence southeast to Enchant, Retlaw and Vauxhall. Then, heading still farther east the canal crossed the Bow

River by means of a siphon and headed for the Suffield country. There, finally, the last of the water which had been taken out of the Bow River over a hundred airline miles west was to spread out over land some fifteen miles northwest of Medicine Hat.

To the provincial government's distress, this was not the only irrigation project afoot in the drier area, where two or three others near Lethbridge, unable to interest any commercial corporation, turned to the federal or provincial authorities for help. What is today a very lush area, the Lethbridge Northern Irrigation District, whose canals spread out north across the Oldman River to the Picture Butte and Iron Springs area, had a long and difficult gestation. Finally the scheme fell into the lap of Premier Stewart, and during 1921 the Alberta government guaranteed all the district's bonds.

Due to various factors this scheme went on to success, while many others clamoured for provincial help and unfortunately some went ahead to plunge themselves and the government into a morass of debt. For whenever an irrigation scheme was proposed it became an obsession with all the local merchants and with the politicians who were—and still are—rarely loath to invest government money in their areas whether or not soil or climatic conditions make the project viable, or indeed whether or not the farmers in the area are amenable.

In the area along the Oldman River in southern Alberta, where conditions are such that sugar beets can be grown, most of the irrigation schemes were successful. The Knight sugar factory built a couple of decades earlier had only operated a few years, but by 1925 conditions were such that at Raymond a large, modern sugar factory was built which before long was taken over by Canadian Sugar Factories Ltd. Because sugar beets could be grown in the area, Lethbridge profited greatly and in 1920 was well on its way to becoming a bustling city. Postwar prosperity had marked much of southern Alberta for its own.

In northern Alberta too every indication pointed to a good future. The E.D. & B.C., with its main line from Edmonton to McLennan and with its branches forking out from there to Peace River Crossing and to Grande Prairie, had at last made the Peace River country accessible to all. Its growth, however, was not rapid, escalating from a population of 3,360 in 1911 to 10,875 in 1916, and to 18,539 by 1921. Furthermore, the AGW, the railway which for so long had bedevilled the provincial cabinet, was nearing navigable water on the Athabasca and the town of Waterways was springing up close to old Fort McMurray. By means of the railway the old hurdle of the Grand Rapids would soon be circumvented, and before long goods for the far North could go by rail to Waterways and thence down the Athabasca, Slave and Mackenzie rivers.

Moreover, at Peace River Crossing E.D. & B.C. locomotives, puffing back and forth in the yards beside the mighty Peace, could now transfer their loads to a line of steamboats which ascended the river for 250 miles to the mountains at Hudson's Hope and descended about the same distance to Vermilion Chutes. From there a short portage connected them with the line of steamers heading for the Mackenzie River. The far North, so long the isolated preserve of fur traders, was beginning to come into its own.

Now that the AGW gave access to the Athabasca oil sands at Fort McMurray, the government took the first steps towards investigating this tremendously rich resource by creating the Alberta Research Council. One of the council's first moves was to hire a young scientist, Karl Clark, who arrived in Alberta in September 1920 and started looking for methods of utilizing the sands, thereby embarking upon a lifetime's work which before his death decades later achieved success.

All of this was welcome news to Edmonton, which for a century had been the gateway to the North. The enhanced opportunities down the far-flung waterways were all grist for its mill. Along with the greatly increased output of farms tributary to that city, this new business began to stir the blood in its veins and to increase the traffic of its streets. It began to look as if the boosters who had greatly expanded both Edmonton and Calgary ten years previously had been right in their assessment of these cities' prospects.

For a while though Edmontonians and Calgarians had wondered. Their populations were still below what they had been just before the war—Calgary with 63,305 in 1921 and Edmonton with 58,821. And yet a new factor was beginning to contribute to their problems—cars. By 1919 there were ten times as many of them driving up and down Jasper Avenue and Calgary's Eighth Avenue as there had been in 1913. In 1916 Alberta had 9,707 cars; in 1917, 20,624, and now in 1919 there were 34,000. These cars, Buicks, Hupmobiles, Hudson Sixes, Chevrolet 490s and Dodges, imparted a new activity to the streets.

Along with the new busyness had come some inflation and the cost of living had risen some fifty-eight percent since 1914. But if it cost more to live, everybody had more money to jingle, and 1919 was a far contrast from the depression five years earlier. Everyone was prosperous, and everyone expressed that affluence by a desire to live more abundantly. The spirit of change was in the air.

Even farmers were jubilant. The price of wheat had risen from ninety-one cents per bushel in the spring of 1914 to $2.31 by the spring of 1920, and in general good yields prevailed. The acres sown to wheat had tripled from 1,371,100 in 1914 to 4,074,500 in 1920.

So all over Alberta a spirit of postwar optimism prevailed. In the south, things were looking up; in the north, new railways and steam-boats were pushing the frontier back. In the farming areas, while the cultivators complained that they were not getting their share of the increasing prosperity, nevertheless, they had never seen better times. In fact, for everyone, except the provincial Liberal government, everything appeared rosy.

The government, however, was beginning to reap some of the harvest it had sown in railways, telephones, irrigation and in yielding so readily to the farmers' demands and now was beginning to wonder how to pay its debts and yet keep its extended system of telephone lines from falling down due to having set aside no depreciation fund for them. When the government could no longer distribute largesse the farmers began to increase their pressure. For after all, of all Alberta's industry, farming was still far and away the most essential.

# 16
# The Roaring Twenties
# 1920-1929

Ushered in on the heels of the war, the new era of the twenties not only transformed Canada and the rest of the world but swept Alberta to new heights. All its resources, mines, forests, oil and natural gas, electric power, railways, the fledgeling air industry and farming, all shared in the impetus. Rum-running and bootlegging flourished as never before.

Towards the end of the decade the province's 250 coal mines scattered in scores of communities employed some twelve thousand men and in 1928 increased the output of fuel to over seven million tons. Sawmills ate their way farther back into Alberta's forests, in some cases building logging railroads to the timber—lines which after a few years' service would be taken up. Accompanying the sawmills, of course, and always present when farmers extended their operations, were forest fires. Every summer as hundreds of square miles of fires wrought their destruction the breezes wafted a haze of blue smoke as far south as Edmonton and at times to Calgary.

For many Albertans, however, the smell of smoke was not enough, and Calgarians especially, having previously sniffed the fumes of Turner Valley's oil, kept prodding the ground in that scenic valley. In January 1921, R. B. Bennett and others incorporated the Royalite Oil Company, a subsidiary of Imperial Oil Limited, and at the same time bought a controlling interest in the old Calgary Petroleum Products Company Limited. As a first move the new company built an absorption plant and compressor station near the Dingman well and laid a line which provided an alternate source of gas to Calgary. As its next move it embarked on a drilling program which ended in success for Royalite Well No. 4. When the bit had been forced several hundred feet deeper than the Dingman well had penetrated without result, the promoters in Calgary sent word out to Clarence Snyder, the head driller, to abandon the hole. These instructions arrived in the forenoon of October 14, 1924, after a new shift had taken over, but since the crew would have to be paid for the whole shift Snyder decided to keep on drilling until quitting time. That stint of drilling, ten feet more, made all the difference, for suddenly

245                                              The Roaring Twenties 1920-1929

that afternoon the bit released a tremendous flow of gas and oil. The gas blew the casing out of the well and for some days could not be controlled. Finally it caught fire. The resulting spectacular blaze took weeks to extinguish but the well, indicating that hitherto unsuspected rich reserves underlay the region, started a new boom which was to bring prosperity to Calgary and to Alberta.

Edmontonians, too, brightened up, and after years of shilly-shallying around, accepted an offer from Northwestern Utilities Limited to bring in gas from the Viking field. Once Edmontonians made up their minds, the company wasted little time, and built eighty miles of transmission line in eighty-eight working days. On the night of November 9, 1923, nine years and five days after the Viking discovery well had blown in, they turned on the gas.

Meanwhile southern Albertans, still speculating on Turner Valley, kept up their probing and in 1929, in a new section of the valley, Home No. 1 well came in as a prolific producer. The event touched off another of Calgary's oil booms. Elsewhere in the province, though the search for oil was less rewarding, two or three of the hundreds of hopefuls were now and then compensated by a few barrels of oil—enough to keep the ever sanguine oil-minded optimistic. In June 1925 a small field, but one destined to have a long life, was discovered near Wainwright. In 1927 and 1928 smaller, less successful wells were found at Skiff southeast of Lethbridge and at Dina near Lloydminster.

About the same time, a look at Alberta's growing towns inspired one of Canada's great men, G. A. Gaherty, to set about decorating the roadsides with a fringe of power lines to connect one town with another electrically. A young man who had already worked in British Columbia and served in the war, he came to Alberta to apply his tremendous engineering skill and economic insight to the operations of Calgary Power Limited. For decades it was to be his eye which saw possibilities no one else envisioned, his hand which through depression and war guided his company through economic shoals, and his brain which created the most efficiently run power organization in Canada. Acting on his inspiration, his company started buying small, poorly run plants as early as 1926 in Alberta's towns and villages and running transmission lines to connect them into a system which not only provided continuous service but materially reduced the power rates. Many of the town plants had been not only poorly designed and wastefully operated, but frequently had leaked illicit profits into some mayor's or councillor's pocket.

By 1929 Calgary Power Limited was building its Ghost River hydro plant and a transmission line which for decades was to be the backbone of Alberta's electrical system—the 132,000-volt line to Edmonton. In the same manner as Gaherty had done but on a much smaller scale,

E. W. Bowness of Canadian Utilities Limited also went around Alberta acquiring electrical properties and tying them together with transmission lines.

The Roaring Twenties also saw a considerable increase in railway mileage. Amongst others, the CNR built a line north of the North Saskatchewan River, through the Ukrainian area near Smoky Lake and the sand hills east of there until on October 28, 1920, it emerged at Father Lacombe's St. Paul des Métis. The CPR, not to be outdone, built a line south of that river and more or less along the old fur traders' South Victoria or Winnipeg Trail through Andrew, Two Hills, Marwayne and on to Lloydminster. Extensions were also made in the Peace River country when steel was laid westward to the vicinity of Fort Dunvegan, where the new town of Fairview was laid out two miles north of the homesteaders' old Waterhole. By 1929 the railway extended from Grande Prairie as far as Hythe, with the promise that before long it would run into British Columbia to create the town of Dawson Creek.

In the late twenties Herman Trelle of Wembley gave the Peace River country a tremendous boost when, starting in 1926, he won world-wide recognition by carrying off the Grand Championship for Hard Red Spring wheat three years in a row. By that time, however, all the really good land in the Peace River country had been claimed, although in large numbers sons of pioneers and other adventurous souls continued to file on much of the marginal land surrounding the good areas. Some indeed had begun looking at the enclave of black soil away up on the Battle River in what we now know as the Manning country, where within five years the communities of North Star and Notikewin came into being.

By 1924 the AGW Railway had finally reached the Athabasca River at Waterways. It helped Edmonton's northerly oriented businessmen to cut their costs and to increase their trade with the far North. With some fifty-four hundred miles of track in Alberta, the railway construction program was coming to an end.

Another form of transportation, however, the newly-born air industry, was just starting. Amongst Alberta's hundreds of daring young men was a remarkable group of youths who, having joined the army, were snapped up by the Royal Air Force and became pilots or air engineers. Of these war pilots, Edmonton could boast of "Wop" May, George Gorman, "Punch" Dickins and others, while Calgary had its Freddy McCall, whose name is proudly borne by that city's modern airport. Frederick Robert Gordon McCall, DSO, MC and Bar, DFC, was Canada's fourth-ranking war-time flying ace credited with having shot down thirty-seven enemy planes. At the end of the war he returned to Calgary and like so many other pilots took to barnstorming, that is, taking passengers up one at a time to give them a five- or ten-minute ride for five dollars.

247

Every Edmontonian, and indeed every Canadian, knew of Wop May and Roy Brown. Between the two they had made headlines when it was reported that they had shot down Germany's apparently invincible Red Knight, Baron von Richthofen, the most famous and the most feared enemy ace. On his first combat mission, Wop May had been attacked by Richthofen and then in the ensuing dogfight Brown had swooped and shot down the Red Knight. Both Brown, who stayed in the East after the war, and May went on to become fighters as deadly as the Baron had been, and when Wop returned to Edmonton wearing the ribbon of the DFC he had thirteen enemy planes to his credit.

In various ways these returned pilots set out to interest Albertans in the future they saw in aviation. Then late in 1920 the news of Imperial Oil Limited's discovery at Fort Norman electrified Albertans. Oil! A new oil field, a phenomenon as rare in Canada as a breathless politician. All Canadians pricked up their ears, but Edmontonians talked of nothing else. Though the new field was down the great Mackenzie River nearly a thousand miles away, Edmontonians had a prior claim to it; it was in their bailiwick—in Edmonton's Northland. The Imperial Oil Company, vitally concerned with following up its find, bought two old German all-metal Junkers, and hired George Gorman and Elmer Fullerton to fly them north.

During the next few years, Alberta was wafted into the air age, and Edmonton and Calgary, although making painfully slow progress towards building airfields, moved in that direction. Wop May, Freddy McCall, Vic Horner, Cy Becker and other wartime pilots began putting together commercial airlines and holding them together with courage and haywire. On December 10, 1928, a mail, express and passenger service got under way with a Western Canada Airways' plane landing regularly at Regina, Calgary and Edmonton.

Then Wop May and Vic Horner of Edmonton, by a feat of great heroism, gave a dramatic boost to Albertans' air-mindedness. On December 31, 1928, far off in the northern wilderness at Little Red River, near Fort Vermilion, diphtheria broke out. By dog team and telegraph the doctor at Fort Vermilion requested Edmonton to fly in a supply of antitoxin. In their rickety excuse for an aircraft the two pilots left Edmonton almost immediately in thirty-three degree below zero weather on their dangerous mission, involving hours of exposure in the cramped seats of their open cockpits. In three or four days, they returned to Edmonton to discover ten thousand citizens waiting to give them a hero's welcome.

The next spring (1929) James Richardson's Western Canada Airways of Winnipeg announced that with pilot Punch Dickins based at Fort McMurray, it was to start a regular air service between that point and

Fort Chipewyan, Fort Smith, Fort Resolution, Hay River and Forts Providence and Simpson. Extending his territory on July 1, 1929, Dickins set his plane down on the Mackenzie River at Aklavik. In a new fashion Edmonton's long and close association with the far North was beginning to pay off.

In a similar way Calgarians' long association with the cattle country led them to think it was time for another Stampede. Once more in 1923 they got Guy Weadick to put one on; it was such a success that they resolved that thenceforth they would make it an annual event.

Edmontonians, on the other hand, concentrated their acclaim on Alberta's world famous basketball team, the Grads—an Edmonton girls' team which as far back as 1914, under their amazing coach J. Percy Page, had won the Alberta championship and thereafter for over twenty-five years was to bring more fame to Alberta than any other organization or event. In 1924 the girls attended the Olympic Games in Paris and played in Munich, Strasbourg and many other cities, and won nearly every one of their games. Trained and disciplined by Page's genius, they won and won and won. All through the Roaring Twenties their victories were taken for granted and Alberta folk always turned out to adore and cheer the team. The fact that the Grads' fame focussed the limelight on their province was secondary. So, indeed, was its record of wins—a record unparalleled in the basketball world. After a twenty-five year history of 375 games played—international and national, competitive and exhibition—their victories totalled 355 games. What counted in what now must seem a remote era was its greater and more endearing record of clean play and good sportsmanship.

About this time too, in a wholly different but equally feminine field, five Albertans, led by Emily Murphy of Edmonton, established the fact that in Canada women were recognized as persons and as such could be called to the Senate. Doing so took quite a fight, one that went to the Supreme Court of Canada and then on to the Privy Council in England; on October 16, 1929, the latter decided that women were indeed persons. Aiding Emily Murphy were Irene Parlby, Louise McKinney, Nellie McClung and Henrietta Edwards. Some ten years later, in the lobby of the Canadian Senate, Prime Minister Mackenzie King unveiled a bronze tablet honouring these great Canadian women who pioneered women's rights in this country.

For news of all these eventful activities Albertans turned on their recently perfected radio sets to listen to the new stations brought into being by businessmen in 1922: CJCA in Edmonton and CFAC and CFCN in Calgary. That year, while leading citizens opened the new stations by speaking into a fantastic horn-shaped microphone, here and there in city or country, eager amateurs with cat's whiskers and crystal sets and with earphones clamped to their heads, actually heard them talking. As they sat hunched over and tense, and passed the earphones to other members of the family gathered in a tight knot around the crystal set, each in turn heard snatches of music and singing which by this new magic jumped the miles of empty air. A new miracle had come to entertain Albertans, a miracle with possibilities untold as yet.

Far out in the country, from the Cypress Hills to the Medicine Lodge Hills and from Lethbridge to Lloydminster, a farm family in each community listened, and next day over the rural telephone called up the neighbours to declare proudly that they had heard the broadcast. Away in the north, at Fort Vermilion, Fort Simpson and Fort Resolution, with bated breath, fur traders tickling their crystal sets with the whiskers listened to the new magic leaping over the leagues to bring them into instant contact with Edmonton—the first rent that was to cleave their ages-old curtain of isolation.

About the same time, a new form of entertainment commenced its decades of success—the Chautauqua. Starting in a small way, this American import appeared first in Lethbridge and other towns of southern Alberta during 1916 where it filled such a need that it rapidly spread all over the province and eventually across Canada. The Chautauqua was a travelling show which every summer spent a few days in scores of country towns and even in the cities. The tone of the performances was in the best moral taste as afternoon and evening they provided good entertainment with short plays, scientific addresses, outstanding speakers and musical groups. As an instance of their character, prairie people who flocked into the great tent heard such speakers as Vilhjalmur Stefansson, the renowned northern traveller, and Emmeline Pankhurst, the English suffragette. For years the arrival of the Chautauqua was the main event in any community and to it, mainly in Model T and Chevrolet 490 cars, rural people came rattling over the dirt roads of the day.

Cars were ever on the increase. In the cities and rural centres, garages had multiplied to keep pace with the rapidly increasing popularity of automobiles. At the close of the war, Alberta had a total of 29,250 cars. By 1926, the number had more than doubled to 65,101. Included in this provincial total were 4,362 trucks and 646 taxis, and their presence on city streets put a dent in the horse population to such an extent that here and there some of the old-time livery barns had either been torn down or remodelled into garages.

Indeed, all over the province Albertans were on the march and keeping in step was their university. In spite of the fact that university graduates were still scorned by practical men who had acquired their knowledge, however skimpy, the hard way, and who begrudged the taxes they spent on this educational frill, the institution continued to progress. By 1928, its enrolment had reached 1,560—a good showing for a first generation crop of pioneers.

All Albertans toiling on farms or in factories were determined that their children should not have to hoe the same hard row that had fallen to their lot, and the way to a better life led through the school gate. Regardless of the pioneers' privations, they spent money freely on schools and by 1929 their sacrifices, combined with the Department of Education's struggles, were beginning to pay off. By that time they had organized 3,242 school districts and had 164,850 children attending school. The educational road had been a long and a difficult one, but by that time the light of real accomplishment was beginning to shine on it, for 1,388 of these students were enrolled in Grade 12.

Schooling, however, was only one phase of the works which the pioneers of some twenty-five-years' standing had brought into being. By 1925 they had graded more than 59,000 miles of roads, and since starting their improvement program three years earlier, had gravelled 827 miles of them. By this time a few young men, having more gumption than guarantee that they would make expenses, had started providing bus service along most of the highways out of Calgary and Edmonton, using seven-passenger cars on roads gravelled or otherwise. And when in rainy weather they got stuck in a succession of mud holes, they could usually find a fallen telephone pole with which to pry out their car. For, except for the main lines, the once vaunted telephone system was in a woeful way and before long would soon have to be scrapped.

All of these interesting developments, bus lines, coal mines, power plants, oil wells and radios, however, were only one side of the picture of Alberta's development. The other side, the basic industry of farming, which had produced most of the province's wealth, had been making equally noteworthy progress. When the farmers were well fed the city folk waxed fat. Except for the dried-out region in the southeast corner of the province, the farming areas had changed remarkably as the homesteaders had converted the one-time homeland of Cree and Blackfoot into a land of beautiful and productive farms. Though worried some by a bit of a depression in 1921, they had pressed on to reap the rewards of their pioneering and had carried the agricultural industry to new heights.

Above all classes in Alberta, however, the farmers were in an anomalous and at times an unenviable position. They had come to a new land of freedom, a new paradise, only to find after years of effort that indeed they were still part of a world in which, as had always been the case, the more fortunate or the more ruthless exploited the less observant. And in Alberta, as on the prairies generally, in their eyes at least, they groaned under a system where an eastern oligarchy called all the shots and collected all the tribute. They were merely a part of a larger Canada which naturally was ruled by the more populous East to which they had to turn for both capital and markets. They had to borrow the one at the price demanded by the East and sell the other at whatever the East would pay.

The farmers were neither fish nor flesh, neither capitalists nor socialists, but a part of each, and therefore always of two minds and spitted on the horns of a dilemma from which for the next half century at least they were unable to free themselves. On the one hand they were independent capitalistic producers, proud of the title to their farm and, therefore, chary of any move that would undermine anyone's right to property. On the other hand (as they saw the situation) easterners who held the bulk of property rights in Canada continued to extract the last mite of levy from them. Under these conditions, obsessed by that belief and anxious to hasten the destruction of the competitive system, they soon came to rebel against eastern imperialism.

By organizing and exerting pressure on the provincial government they, the majority of electors, had cured some of their ills. One of their most effective leaders was the remarkable Henry Wise Wood, who in 1905, as a successful man with a growing family, had moved from Missouri to a farm near Carstairs. Eleven years later he became president of the United Farmers of Alberta, a position he held for fourteen years and to which as perhaps the most outstanding man ever to lead Alberta's farmers, he brought distinction. A tall man, with a lean look, a slow, resolute manner and a dry sense of humour, he was a voracious reader and a sound leader. Insisting at all times that though his organization must speak up forcibly, it must always weigh its pronouncements carefully and ever with an eye to justice, he became one of Alberta's great historical figures.

Under the guidance of his philosophy and that of William Irving, another political thinker, the UFA was to change the complexion of Alberta's politics. Wood, suffering under the constraints common to all the other independent commodity producers, created the political philosophy which later on became the ideal which inspired the UFA government. Combining homespun oratory with the ardent faith of a propagandist, he hammered out the theory which set his two classes of people, the competitive or plutocratic group (the bad guys) in violent conflict with the cooperative or democratic group (the good guys). With his strong belief that the few were exploiting the many and with his vision restricted to the farmers' point of view (forgetting that in Canada they were not the predominant class, and that, moreover, even Canada was only a small part of the world), he set out to bring about the downfall of the bad guys. By equating all virtues with the cooperatively minded and all vices with the competitive rogues, his theory provided a focus for all the yearnings and discontents of a hard working, relatively poor population of a puritan persuasion. Nevertheless, he refused to be a messiah leading his farm folk to the millennium over the next ridge but instead felt that the struggle would be a very gradual process with victory perhaps a couple of generations away.

When he took over as president of the UFA in 1916, he tried to keep that body from entering the political field directly, feeling that with the farmers' ring in its nose it was better to let the Liberal government bull batter down the defence of the powers of darkness than for the UFA to enter the arena themselves. Nevertheless, when in 1921 a minor recession pinched Alberta's economy, the farmers began to mutter. When the Liberal government, rapidly becoming financially harassed and realizing its inability to remake the world in the farmers' image increasingly failed to meet the farmers' expectations, the UFA members overruled Wood's opinion. Rather hurriedly they decided to enter the political lists against a government which at times had been accused of rampant corruption and which picked its civil servants by unabashed patronage.

So persuasive was Wood's philosophy and so quickly and thoroughly did the grass roots politicians in even the most remote communities respond to the opportunity that to the surprise of no one more than Wood, the election of June 17, 1921, was a smashing victory for the new UFA party. Thirty-nine of its members had been elected as compared to only fourteen Liberal, four Labour, three Independents and one Conservative.

At last the farmers as a party had risen constitutionally against the evil forces of competition. While the UFA government had a long, hard period ahead of it, and while it did not bring about the millennium, the Liberals were left hanging out their dry tongues. The long-time feeling of Albertans against party government—party government dominated by the East—had once more revealed itself, and this time in a decisive manner and in a manner which was to endure for decades.

Moreover, the feeling of resentment against the old line parties was similarly decisive in the 1921 federal elections when ten members of a new agrarian party, the Progressives, were elected along with two Labour men, leaving the Liberals and Conservatives to wonder why so many of their men had fared so badly. From then on until 1957 when John Diefenbaker's Conservatives swept the prairies, Alberta continued to elect federal members of splinter protest parties under varying names; UFA (1926, 1930) and Social Crediters in one guise or other from 1935 on. In the 1926 campaign, incidentally, the first Ukrainian-born federal member, Michael Luchkovich, was elected under the UFA banner.

Considerably surprised by its success in 1921, the provincial UFA party, a group as yet without a leader except for H. W. Wood, who preferring to govern from the sidelines, had not run in the election, had to gather its legs under it and find a leader. Wood refused the job. Many would have liked to see the UFA's able solicitor take on the task of being premier, but in its new enthusiasm it would have ill befitted the farmers' party to have truckled with its principles to the extent of having as a premier one of the competitive class—a lawyer. Then in casting about for an alternative, their eyes fell upon another of their leaders who had not run in the election, a persuasive orator with a booming voice and bulging girth—Herbert Greenfield, a successful dirt farmer from Westlock. In due course he was elected and formed the first of the UFA governments to which he was careful to appoint the lawyer, J. E. Brownlee as attorney-general.

If, however, in 1921 the millennium had arrived, its effects were not instantly noticeable. The competitive lion may indeed have lain down with the compassionate, cooperative lamb, but on Alberta's far-flung fields no immediate progeny began to disport itself. As ever, in spite of hailstorms and cloud bursts, the province's harvests continued to be garnered in, Alberta's bootleggers, who had never heeded competition anyway, continued their lucrative roles and Alberta bankers continued to weigh out their pound of flesh on the old-time scales.

Over the length and breadth of the province as a fresh wave of enthusiasm swept the farmers into a common cause, community halls—UFA halls—began making their appearance in the rural areas. Then to add to their well-being 1923 turned out to be a year of bumper crops and Alberta farmers' total wheat output was the largest up to that time: 145 million bushels, an average of twenty-eight bushels to the acre. Moreover, that same year saw the overthrow of prohibition. Ever since 1916, when by 58,000 votes in favour and only 37,000 against, Albertans had brought prohibition upon themselves, many had regretted it. Bootlegging with its associated ills had become so rampant by 1923 that, reflecting a major turnabout in sentiment, the legislature decided to permit the sale of liquor.

But even though nature smiled on the farmers and even though once more they could openly toast each other in a sociable drink, they were still suffering under the grain marketing system. For years they had been trying to improve it. At the United Farmers of Alberta convention in Calgary in 1913 they had laid the framework leading to the formation of the Alberta Farmers' Co-operative Elevator Company and by that fall had some fifty grain elevators in various stages of completion. In 1917 the United Grain Growers, a prairie-wide organization having much the same interests, amalgamated with this company and thenceforth the combination operated as the United Grain Growers Ltd. That year as a temporary war measure the Dominion government had set up a federal board to handle wheat sales and the farmers, feeling that this short circuited their old *bête noire*, the Winnipeg Grain Exchange, were satisfied with its operation. When, having satisfied its purpose, the board was disbanded in 1920

A History of Alberta

they began to look for a farm-owned means to accomplish much of what it had done.

Coincidentally or not, during the next two years the price of Alberta farmers' wheat had dropped by $1.54 per bushel to $0.77 and the agricultural economy was in sore straits. The federal government would not re-establish the wheat board, and finally, pushed as far as they would go, the farmers decided to set up their own marketing system in the shape of the Alberta Wheat Pool.

Towards that end, H. W. Wood's United Farmers of Alberta took the first vital move in July. Marshalling its forces, that organization with its hundreds of locals and a membership of 35,000, brought its massed strength to bear on the problem. On August 20 canvassers crisscrossed the farming acres in a whirlwind campaign, and such was the farmers' desire to help themselves that by September 5, 26,211 of them, representing forty-five percent of the wheat crop, had signed up. In this manner the wheat pool idea, certainly the farmers' greatest self-help venture came into being; first with Alberta Wheat Pool, which was to be followed the next year by the Saskatchewan and Manitoba pools. After some rapid foot work in making agreements with the United Grain Growers Company, getting financial backing from the Alberta government and encouragement from the rapidly rising politician R. B. Bennett, together with a fifteen million dollar line of credit from the Canadian Bankers' Association, the wheat pool opened its office in Calgary on October 29, 1923. The great Alberta Wheat Pool was in business.

For the farmers, the inception of the Pool and the successful 1925 crop marked a turning point. That year they had seeded over five million acres of wheat which had yielded well. Its price of $1.19 per bushel was fairly good, and, as a result, they had money to spend. On country trails cars became common. The trend to farm mechanization had also started. A few new-fangled combines made trial runs in the wheat fields, and that year 11,311 tractors put-putted their way across the fields.

To keep up with the trend, many a farmer mesmerized himself into buying out other farmers and doubling or redoubling the land he owned. With the aid of new machinery he could operate a larger farm, and acting on the belief that for him the sun would always shine, he plunged ahead recklessly, mortgaging all his assets and acquiring more chattels. Farmers' indebtedness to the banks and mortgage companies increased at an alarming rate.

During this time of fair prosperity the farmers had been too preoccupied to pay much attention to affairs on the political front. By 1925 they had scarcely observed that even after four years in office the UFA government had still failed in most of the plans for farmer-class government which Henry Wise Wood had envisaged. They had not even recognized

The Roaring Twenties 1920-1929

that by that time indeed their better MLA's, beginning to wise up to the realities of operating cabinet government, had been forced to accept many of the facts of life which they had sworn to circumvent. Moreover, they acquiesced when in November 1925 the members of the cabinet switched leaders and chose their attorney-general, J. E. Brownlee as premier. Brownlee was a real leader—but a lawyer!

Brownlee, practically the only businessman on the government side of the House and a man of rare firmness, intelligence and integrity, was an excellent choice. That he led them along the only practical course— away from the sort of government dictated to by local constituency hotheads and social dreamers—and toward a government much the same as that of any other party where the cabinet was supreme, few farmers noticed. When the 1926 election rolled around and they realized that their party had cleaned out many a musty political stable and had achieved many things the farmers wanted, they voted it back into office.

During the same revival of prosperity, beginning about 1925, many movements which had long been in the wings began to come forward. In various ways the efforts of the labour leaders had been successful in bringing about better working conditions, higher wages and more say in the industrial world. Since the end of the war too, in the same Alberta milieu, the province's penchant for religious nonconformity—paralleling its political peculiarities—began to flesh out as a bewildering complexity of evangelical organizations. Exclusive of the more traditional churches, well over forty new cults and sects had sprung up over the years and the number was to go on increasing in the future until no province in Canada had nearly such a commanding array.

One of the earliest of these was the Seventh Day Adventists, which as far back as 1909 had opened a bible school at Lacombe. Other groups quickly followed, most of them operating schools of sorts, some of them like the Prairie Bible Institute which opened a major school in Three Hills in 1922 and developed into a strong missionary organization. Before long some of these sects seized upon radio broadcasting as an ideal means of proselyting. Most of these evangelical groups attempted to recover the original and unadulterated bases of Christianity from which, so they charged, the regular churches had long since departed. Times of rapid social change seem to lead to the emergence of new sects which in the main aim their appeals at economically marginal segments of the population. And these were times of rapid social change.

One such evangelist was a Calgary school principal named William Aberhart. In the fall of 1925 he began broadcasting over Station CFCN, and within a couple of years his doctrine had proved so appealing that he had a widespread audience which listened regularly every Sunday to his two-hour "Radio Sunday School" program.

During 1926 when Aberhart's broadcasts were reaching even the most remote valleys of the province, the dry land dirt farmers were continuing to forsake parts of the south. For in the whole of the southeast quarter of the province that type of farming had proved a failure and people were pulling up stakes and either turning to some other occupation or else moving farther north. One of the areas most heavily hit had been the region east of Castor and Hanna which a few years earlier had looked so promising. By 1927 some six thousand farms in that region had been abandoned.

A mere decade earlier most of their homesteaders had streamed out over these plains when that region had been the land of promise. There on the bleak prairies where their only fuel was hauled from the mines at Castor or Sheerness and where no twig or tree stopped the pinpoints of light shining across miles of snowdrifts from their windows, they settled down to a hard existence. Harsh it may have been but prosperous they were soon to be as from dawn to dusk men turned over the miles of prairie sod, while women and children, in a pathetic attempt to lessen the starkness of the endless miles, planted gardens and hedges around their sod houses. And during the years 1913 to 1917 prosperity poured over the land as copious rains fell and the boundless acres of golden fields rippling in the breeze yielded abundantly. Bushels per acre? Eighteen in 1913, nine in 1914, forty in 1915, and twenty-nine and eighteen in the next two years. This indeed was the way to farm, here indeed was the promised land, and the wartime wheat prices ranging up to $1.94 per bushel wreathed the pioneers' windblown wrinkles in smiles.

In wagons and sleighs, tens of thousands of bushels wound along the prairie coulees to Pemukan and Altario, to Stanmore and Sunnynook. Back over the slippery grades luxuries for the farm wife or lumber for a commodious new house slid along, guided home by the light of the windows.

But then the smiles of the gods turned to a pitiless stare that baked the parched soil and burned off the wheat's first hopeful shoots, and from 1918 to 1922 showed that the land should have remained unploughed, remained for the hardy native grasses which alone could withstand the dry area's harshness. All the profits of the few good years were eaten up in mortgages on idle, rusting machinery which had no crop to cut. One by one the pioneers pulled out, slowly at first, but with increasing urgency as sadder and wiser they sought new farms in the forested lands of northern Alberta. Behind them, caragana hedges, grown whiskery with neglect, lived on untrimmed, and antelope snuffed at what had once been a line of whitewashed rocks, or at the stark skeleton of an abandoned binder.

Loading all their chattels into one or two wagons, hundreds of dry land farmers set out from the Palliser Triangle, a family or two at a time, for the wetter woodlands of the two provinces. Many of them found new homesteads north of the North Saskatchewan River and scores passed through Edmonton, some of them to take the long, lonesome trail for another four hundred miles to the Peace River country. En route they met many disgruntled northern families returning from that area. Strangely enough, in spite of the fact that some settlers had moved in from the dried-out areas, the population of the Peace River country actually declined. Some years of frosts about the end of the war had discouraged several of the new homesteaders there.

By the fall of 1929, in spite of the movement out of the dried-out regions, the area in farms in Alberta had increased from 29 million in 1921 to 35 million acres, and much of the increase was in the north. The area under cultivation likewise rose from 11.7 million to over 16 million acres, while the acreage seeded to wheat rose rapidly year by year from less than 5,000,000 in 1921 to 7,451,000 in the spring of 1929. In the province as a whole, the years 1927 and 1928, however, were the halcyon years, with each producing yields of 171 million bushels, records which were only to be equalled or exceeded in two subsequent years. Even though the price per bushel had dropped to 98 cents in 1927, the farmers' income from wheat reached a figure not to be exceeded for eighteen years. With such relative prosperity, mechanization of farms continued apace. The number of combines increased to 2,523, the number of tractors doubled, while the number of horses declined further. By this time, most farmers had a car or a light delivery truck. During the same period the total number of farmers in Alberta reached a high of some 95,000 and was nearing its all-time record. But the number of horses slaving away on the land or in the cities had started to decline, having reached its maximum of 806,000 in 1921. From then on, gradually at first, old dobbin's duties were to be increasingly taken over by machines, cars, trucks and tractors.

While Alberta farmers were enjoying some of their rare years of well earned prosperity, and while the city folk were egging them on, Canada and the world were revelling in one of the greatest binges in history. Everything was rosy; the world was at peace, the Empire had never been more solid, Charles Lindbergh had flown the Atlantic, and in New York, Chicago, Toronto and Montreal, the stock exchanges were buzzing with buyers. In Canada, factories worked overtime.

So, all over Alberta, except in the dried-out region, what with good crops, some oil and a new approach to the North, times were good, the war was long since over and there would never be another one. Wars were now inconceivable and the interest of the man in the street lay in other directions. For one thing, the movie industry had come out with an innovation. In the fall of 1927 city folk swarmed to see and hear Al Jolson in the *The Jazz Singer*, their first talking picture.

The Roaring Twenties in reaching into Alberta, had begun to brighten up its cities. One indication of this was the introduction of neon lights which added an encouraging cheeriness to their streets. The province's progress is best reflected in the 1931 census figures which revealed that Alberta had grown to a population of 732,000, an increase of nineteen percent during the previous decade. Calgary had grown to 83,761, far above the number of people it had had even in 1913 and also well above its northern rival, which could only scrape together 79,197 people. Lethbridge and Medicine Hat had also grown, having populations of 13,489 and 10,300 respectively, and so had all the towns and villages.

Moreover, most of the larger towns shared in the good times and being gradually connected to a network of power lines enabled their citizens to buy refrigerators and to switch over to the new alternating current radios which operated without the old cumbersome batteries. Even some new towns had come into existence; Grimshaw and Beaverlodge in the Peace River country, Willingdon and Marwayne, and several others, including the exciting oil towns of Black Diamond, Turner Valley and Little Chicago, whence anyone could see the tremendous flares of Hell's Half Acre which night and day for years burned up the waste gas from adjacent oil wells.

More and more farmers cranked up their Model T cars and rattled off over the improving roads towards the cities. Some indeed, the venturesome ones, tried their luck as far as Banff, which had become a beautiful town ready to cater to tourists of all sorts. Some adventurers, taking along crowbars and shovels, axes and logging chains, made the exhausting trip over the remains of the old CNR grade to Jasper National Park which had been created in 1907. In 1929 some fifty cars reached Jasper from Edmonton.

But though the province's roads were open in summertime, winter's snows left them fit only for horse-drawn sleighs. It was then that the train came into its own. Usually on time, winding its way up this valley or that, through forests or snaking around the treeless prairie coulees, daily or twice a week, the sociable train connected each of the over nine hundred railway depots to the outside world. At each station, watching for its plume of smoke trailing far over the countryside, a little crowd always gathered, waiting to welcome friends, to see who got on or off, or merely for the sheer sociability of train time. Whistling for the crossing beyond the hill, swinging around the last curve the train, with ringing bell and waving engineer, coasted to a stop. Pausing for five minutes, it unloaded groceries for the stores, mail sacks for the post office and beer kegs for the hotel. It brought the romance of far-off coral reefs, bananas from tropical lands, tea from China and salmon from Prince Rupert.

Then, puffing vigorously, it set off again to make the hills echo with its rumble, to hold the momentary attention of a wandering coyote or to acknowledge the watchful wave of some farm wife isolated but for the companionable train. As it left, each member of the station's cheery throng sauntered back past the civic pump to return to their busy or monotonous round until once more train time came—and all was well with the world.

Now that women were persons, now that cars abounded and the pall of prohibition had been lifted, now that neon lights imparted a festive glow to Eighth Avenue and to Jasper Avenue, now that prosperity reigned on every hand, a new era had dawned.

By the fall of 1929 Alberta had come into its inheritance.

# 17
# Funny Money
# 1929-1940

In October 1929, the world's train of prosperity jumped the track. All nations and governments, all capitalists and cultivators had flouted the law of supply and demand. Finally it had struck back, first with a few light taps and then the knockout of October 29.

By Christmas of that year Albertans began to feel the depression's impact. Farm prices fell, unemployed walked the streets, something called a scarcity of money—something ascribed to malign influences—cut purchasing power and paralyzed everyone's will. Almost immediately every Albertan had to tighten his belt; without warning the Great Depression had descended.

It hit even Premier Brownlee's UFA government, which, sorely pressed to pay the interest on its own and its predecessor's mortgages, had also found it necessary to rescue the Alberta Wheat Pool from a depression produced dilemma. Like so many other businesses, large or small, the Pool got caught with its guard down. Anticipating that its business would go on in a normal fashion it had paid the farmers much more for the 1929 crop than subsequently it could sell it for. Like all other businesses the Pool faced bankruptcy, but since the wheat-growing industry was so vital to the province, the government had to avert its failure by guaranteeing several million dollars of its bank overdraft.

Rescuing the Wheat Pool stood him in good stead when in June 1930 Premier Brownlee called another election. If he had any qualms over the fact that nine years earlier the farmers had hoped that their government would be a mere tool in their hands to which their locals could dictate and that he of all men had been instrumental in shifting the relative positions so that the cabinet dictated to the locals, he never let them show. His government was returned with a handsome, if somewhat reduced, majority.

One of its next acts was to arrange with the RCMP to resume policing the province and then to disband the Alberta Provincial Police. Far more important than that, however, was the government's success in prevailing upon Ottawa to remove a long-standing sore point and to return Alberta's natural resources to provincial control—something all Albertans had wanted since Haultain's days. In 1931 Brownlee's government, burdened with a load of debt, facing the fearsome depression and finding itself more or less powerless, nevertheless, had struck one effective blow at Ottawa.

By then, of course, the federal old line parties were having their own problems. In July 1930 the resurgent Conservatives led by Calgary's R. B. Bennett had defeated Mackenzie King's Liberal government. Bennett, stumping the country, had advocated policies designed to defeat the depression and the voters had turned over the hopeless task to him. Even then in his home province only four of his party had been elected. That, however, was a better showing than the Liberals had made. Once more Alberta, the recalcitrant province, had turned its back on the two eastern parties and stubbornly elected nine UFA federal members to the House of Commons.

In Alberta, however, and very soon after the provincial election, the farmers began to realize that the UFA government had not fulfilled their dreams. Various preachers, filling and rocking the airwaves with their fundamentalist Christian gospel, steadily gathered a large following in the one Canadian province which was the most fertile field for evangelical prophets. If they did nothing to raise the province's intellectual level, at least they carried comfort to doubting hearts. Albertans and, indeed, all westerners, were beginning to look for new gods.

And none of the many evangelical types enjoyed such a listening audience as William Aberhart, a sincere man, who, by a tempting mixture of religion and entertainment, spurred on the whole Canadian fundamentalist movement. Appealing on the one hand to the more distressed in the cities who were beginning to question middle-class motives and values and on the other to backwoods farmers harbouring resentments against city folk and city ways, he soon began to lash out at the economic system. And the deeper the depression the more ground he covered until, flaying the big shots, he veered from Bible prophecy to blasting the economic system and the scarcity of money. There he had something, there he touched the nerve that swept all amateur experts on the money problem into his camp.

For everything had gone wrong with the monetary system. Values on the stock markets had slumped nearly out of sight. International Nickel shares, which had sold at $72.50, fell to $4.50; Abitibi, from $57 to $1, and so on. In the cities men walked the streets looking for jobs, or stood in long lines at the employment offices, or moved over to lengthen the bread lines or those leading to the soup kitchens. During 1931, in Edmonton alone, 14,573 out of a population of 79,197 drew direct relief. Of some 18,000 city families, 2,601 were on relief. During 1932, 17,815 men and 2,785 women signed applications for work.

Casual labourers were the first to feel the pinch and to go on relief. Then the semi-skilled began losing their jobs and next the skilled carpenters, bricklayers and other workers. Soon they too were living off the weekly dole of food, then clothing and finally rent money. Many thousands, however, too proud to go on relief, held out through months of unemployment till, having exhausted their last resource, they were forced to give in. Eventually everyone's reluctance to seek relief was followed by a passive acceptance. In many cases individuals passed on to the third and final phase, that of demanding all they dreamed they should have.

By December 1932, the price of No. 1 wheat at Winnipeg had dropped to thirty-eight cents, which, when translated to the elevator meant about twenty cents per bushel to the Alberta farmer. The farmers, getting no money for their produce, had to default on their mortgages, and through poverty, debt and worry, steered a bitter course. Many a homesteader, who in good times had been lured by the city's bright lights, returned broke to his few acres in the country and increased the number of farmers dividing up an already hopelessly low income. By 1936, the number of farmers had risen seven percent, to bring the total to 99,732—a record never exceeded.

The province had found that even ownership of its own resources was a hollow victory if nobody could develop them. With rich soil which could grow almost unlimited wheat, forests which could produce enough lumber to house every Canadian family and mines with enough coal to heat all of the continent, and with men eager to work these resources, the system could not put them at the tasks they wanted. Few could get work. Many were hungry and more were cold, because no one could unlock the riddle of what Aberhart was to call correctly, poverty in the midst of plenty.

With no money to buy fuel so cars could take them to town or so that their tractors could pull their ploughs, mowers and binders, farmers fell back on horses. Lifting the motor out of their useless car, attaching a tongue and double-trees to it and dispensing with the windshield, they hitched the body behind a team of oat-burners. Their horseless carriages had failed them, but so long as they could grow enough feed for their team, they could get about. Their Chevrolet cars and their Ford Phaetons had been turned into what, in a derisive reference to the one-time Albertan who was now prime minister of Canada, they called Bennett Buggies.

By 1936 the depression was reaching its lowest point. Out of ten million Canadians, one and a half million were on relief and economic conditions had never been worse; prices had fallen, crops had failed, and every country and city merchant was at or near the end of his tether. Rumours spread in Alberta of people wearing gunny sacks, which was true (and to some extent had always been true), and of farmers reduced to eating gophers. But the wildest rumours falling on the ear of despair have a ring of truth.

On top of Albertan's other troubles, their creditors, the banks, mortgage and machine companies, themselves nearly insolvent and blindly unaware of how close they were to touching the match to the explosive of revolution, bore down on them. Conditioned by years of farm-movement-sponsored but dimly understood monetary reform propaganda, the disgruntled farmers, looking for some tangible cause for all their misery, focussed their hatred on the banks and loan companies. And marching beside them were their city cousins. The time was ripe for the appearance of any eccentric panacea.

William Aberhart found it when in 1932 for the first time he read one of Major Douglas's books on Social Credit. As the head of his Calgary Prophetic Bible Institute he was then nearing the peak of his career as a preacher. Immediately he shifted from Bible prophecy, at which he was an acknowledged master, to the field of economics, in which he was the blindest apprentice, and with his new theory set out to lead the world into the promised land. Shifting from Ecclesiastes to economics and waving his new-found banner, he charged into the fray.

Brandishing his Social Credit theory, Aberhart had not only won over the depressed folk of the cities but also the UFA locals. In the spring of 1934 Premier Brownlee invited William Aberhart and Major Douglas to present their views before the legislature's Committee of the Whole. Since the MLA's could make nothing of Douglas's theory, which Stephen Leacock once called "certain profundities of British fog impossible for most people to understand which in sunny Alberta, by force of prayer, turned into Social Credit," they refused to be taken in by it. When, exercising a mixture of conservatism and honesty, the provincial cabinet refused to embrace the new gospel, its one-time supporters in the locals turned their backs on Brownlee and his government.

Alberta farmers, independent producers selling in a collapsed world market, heavily in debt and having a long-standing disposition to turn to quick monetary cures, were a well-tilled field for Social Credit. With its cutting denunciation of existing society, its epochal vision of a new order in which to its credit the development of the individual was to be the highest good, the theory could not fail to appeal. Moreover, its remarkable similarities with evangelical religious doctrines opened the gates even wider.

Then to fan the flames of growing distaste for the provincial government, rumours of cabinet members involved in scandals of a matrimonial nature began to spread over the province. The strait-laced populace, worrying about depressed conditions, had little mercy to spare for their premier or their representatives who had taken time off from attempting to ease the economic situation to partake of amorous activities. Before the affair was over one of Alberta's best premiers resigned. On July 10, 1934, R. G. Reid, a long-time cabinet minister and a man highly respected, assumed the premier's office and began to gird the party's loins for an electoral contest with the new messiah.

Henry Wise Wood had hoped to transform the world within two generations, but here was Major Douglas ready to accomplish that task in five years and his newest enthusiastic apostle promising to cut that time span to eighteen months. Laying his head on the block with that policy in December 1934, Aberhart announced that the Social Credit party would contest the next election.

His exposition of monetary reform—of Social Credit, the final flowering of their long-held monetary views—filled the farmers with a clear conviction. His theory, made obtuse by such terms as "cultural heritage," "monetization of national resources," "control of credit," "fountain-pen money," "just price" and "basic dividends," was difficult if not impossible to understand. But by these terms Aberhart's magic had reduced his theory to a few stereotypes of low intellectual but high emotional content which made them ideal for proselytizing.

But no one really needed to understand—Aberhart told his followers not to concern themselves with details but to follow. One had only to believe. Slogans such as "political liberty with economic security," and "the struggle of the powers of light against the powers of darkness," made it easy to believe. Then when he announced that his proposed government would pay a basic dividend of $25 a month to everybody, who could resist his appeal? Some, a handful, of Aberhart's followers may not have taken this too seriously, but school teachers, the poorer farmers, the almost bankrupt small businessmen, and the working class generally, were completely sold on the government's ability to pay this money and to pay it more or less immediately after the election. Once the Social Credit government came to power, no one need fear high interest rates, unemployment and mortgages; suffering from crop failure would be a thing of the past, while the standard of living would soar.

Many Albertans touched the hem of his garments in absolute belief in the righteousness of the cause Aberhart espoused so sincerely and so emphatically. Many others who followed his banner may have been dubious about the $25 per month but felt that Aberhart and Douglas offered some positive hope of doing something while the other parties offered nothing. Any of the more astute or economically literate who professed doubt about Social Credit theories were immediately classed as enemies to whom the faithful should turn a deaf ear. The people were seized by a mass hysteria which has rarely come to the surface on this continent and one which forms a dire warning for the future of what depths despair can plunge even those with a long-established democratic tradition. Mob psychology had taken over to an extent almost unbelievable in what everyone hitherto had believed was an informed electorate.

It was no wonder then that on election day in August 1935 a record number turned out. Whereas at the previous election 182,000 had voted, this time 302,000 came out to cast their ballots. That night when the boxes were opened, an astounding fifty-six Social Crediters, not one of whom had any previous legislative experience, had been elected, along with five Liberals and two Conservatives. Not a single UFA man had made the grade.

This election completed Alberta's second wave of revolt against the old parties and eastern Canada; the first in 1921 had been accomplished by farmers only, this one was also supported by small town businessmen and by a large percentage of city folk as well. For the second time within fifteen years the virtuous had voted for the millennium. For the second time the voters had panted for pie in the sky; for the second time they had elected a government which would, they hoped, transmute their dreams into reality and do what the people back home in the locals wanted. For the second time they were doomed to be disappointed.

For with all his glib tongue and his sincerity Aberhart had unwittingly fooled them. And himself.

Nevertheless, although he probably failed to realize it, his entry into politics had acted as a safety valve which had averted violence. By the time a couple more years had gone by and all but the most devoted might suspect that Social Credit could not work, times had improved, and having worked off their fever, the faithful had cooled off enough that they no longer felt like taking the law into their own hands.

By 1935, of course, for most Albertans the pit of the depression caused by the diseased economic situation had passed. Not so the depression caused by drought, for it was only beginning. As many of the homesteaders on the lands extending east from Brooks had found out a decade earlier, that area should never have been settled by small scale dry-land farmers. In 1911 some 2,400 families had lived in it, but by 1926 that number had been reduced to 1,500. Then with incentives provided by the provincial government's Re-settlement Scheme farmers continued to flee until by 1930 only five hundred people—not farm families—were left cringing as the hot winds swept across the shadeless prairies.

North of the Red Deer River a similar migration had carried farmers out of the Youngstown–Alsask area. For in the whole of the Palliser Triangle all of the dry-land farmers' climatic foes had begun to mount a combined campaign. By 1934 they struck: the first year of the grasshopper plague, then only in its opening stages, infested a mere 1,600 square miles; the black blizzard of mid-May when from Drumheller to Medicine Hat the unceasing wind swept away the top soil; the stepped-up frequency of devastating hailstorms commencing with the terror of July 12,

1934, when one storm extending from Carstairs to Stettler pounded the crops to a pulpy mass and was followed by others scattered all over southern Alberta. To add to the burden of financial disaster, all these plagues had been visited on the Palliser Triangle. And these visitations had merely begun, for indeed in a physical sense the Dirty Thirties had only started to strike.

Meanwhile, after wiring Major Douglas to hurry over from England, Aberhart selected his cabinet and took care to appoint his neophyte, Ernest C. Manning, as provincial secretary. At the age of twenty after coming in from a farm in Saskatchewan, he had assumed the office of secretary of the Calgary Prophetic Bible Institute and later managed the Social Credit electoral campaign. In appointing Manning, who at the age of twenty-six was the youngest cabinet minister in the British Empire, Aberhart built better than he knew.

Neither Aberhart, his exceedingly capable protegé, the men of his cabinet, nor the Social Credit members—none of them had ever sat in the legislature before. They were as green to the procedures of such a body as they were to the intricacies of the new Social Credit theory. They were a mixed bag, heavily salted with twelve farmers and ten school teachers, but containing small town merchants and men from assorted walks of life, including two physicians, three preachers (not all of evangelical faiths), and five lawyers. All of them except possibly the lawyers came from occupations whose strong points had never been economic literacy. Many of them turned out surprisingly well and were elected time and again, some of them still retaining their seats after the 1967 election. In 1935, for the first time, men born in Alberta had been elected to the legislature when five, including two of Ukrainian origin, won their seats. Alberta was growing up.

Aberhart's theories were impractical but his compassion for the underdog was sound. His methods were wrong, but his revolt brought results. A further quotation of Stephen Leacock's remarks is apropos: "Whatever may be in it [Social Credit] in Alberta it led to partial repudiation of public debt, and scaling down of mortgage interest, things done however, under other names, in Saskatchewan. . . ."

Now that he was premier of Alberta with a large majority in the legislature, Aberhart was faced with the task of performing what he had promised—implementing Social Credit. Now that he was sitting in the premier's chair, the simple solutions he had advocated so confidently suddenly appeared much more complex than he had anticipated. And as reality began to confront him the hostile newspapers began an I-told-you-so campaign. Every move he made, every word he said, and every prayer he uttered, was seized upon in an attempt to deride him.

Trying to spell out Social Credit theory into legislation that would hold water was difficult indeed, and most of the government's economic legislation was as leaky as a well-worn sock. During three or four sessions the legislature passed the Alberta Social Credit Measures Act, the Alberta Credit House Act, the Alberta Social Credit Act, and several more. But they were all *ultra vires* or quite rightly were disallowed by Ottawa.

Nearly all the newspapers in the province ridiculed Aberhart but the Calgary *Herald* and the Edmonton *Journal* became the objects of his most vituperative hatred: the *Herald*, his hometown paper, and the *Journal,* the one published in the capital city. The feud with the *Journal* was particularly vicious. The paper reviled Aberhart, and Aberhart vowed to fix the *Journal*. As tirade followed tirade, the government fired a salvo at all newspapers and called it The Accurate News and Information Act. The *Journal* exploded. This, an act designed to gag the press, set off a fresh tantrum. In due course, the legislation reached the Supreme Court, and it too was turned down.

Considering the state of the economy and the province's coffers, it was little wonder that in April 1936 the government defaulted on bonds totalling $3,200,000, and by legislation cut in half the interest rate on its outstanding bonds. Then, floundering along during June and July the government issued what it called prosperity certificates, and forced some road contractors and their employees to take these in payment for their services. They were scrip issued in denominations of $1 and $5, and on their backs were little squares to which any merchant who deigned to accept them as legal tender and who happened to have them in his hands on any Thursday stuck a stamp purchased from the Alberta government. In theory, these stamps were a tax, and by the time a year was up the various merchants through whose hands they had passed were supposed to have affixed enough stamps to equal the face value of the scrip. At the end of that year, whoever held them could turn them in, and, if they were properly stamped, could get back the original dollar value from the government. By December that year the government was asking its civil servants, and asking pretty peremptorily, to take half their pay in these prosperity certificates. This funny money was bound to fail, but a courageous citizen, Charles Grant, hastened its demise by legal action in the Supreme Court, where the certificates were adjudged not to be legal tender. Actually, the government only issued some $360,000 of them, and within a short time it redeemed $340,000. The rest were kept as souvenirs.

Every time the government failed in another of its faltering steps the *Journal* had a field day vilifying it and its funny money, and continued to revert to the fact that all told thirteen of the acts passed by Aberhart's government during its special sessions had been disallowed. While the editor was undoubtedly sound enough in his economics, his furor availed nothing. His fight for freedom of the press, however, was not only valid enough, but valiant too. For in due course the *Journal* received a Pulitzer Prize for "leadership in the defence of the freedom of the press in Alberta." This, a signal honour, was the first time the award had ever been made outside the United States.

Although Aberhart continued to bluster at the microphone, he may well have felt less boisterous at his premier's desk. Except for the election, nothing seemed to have gone just as he had planned—righting the economy, such a simple thing when he had been looking in from out of office, had turned out to have inherent difficulties never previously perceived. His followers, a little disappointed after the expiration of his eighteen months but still lulled by his outward optimism, began to admire him more and more. For now they realized just how blindly stubborn these fifty bigshots, the bankers' toadies and the lackeys of the financial interests had turned out to be and how for the moment at least they still had the upper hand. By 1937, however, some of the MLA's and even cabinet ministers, beginning to sense what was happening to Social Credit and to themselves and to the locals, were not so easily satisfied and started an insurgency which ran its course and failed. For of necessity Aberhart had been gathering more and more power into his own hands and into the hands of a select few. The insurgents could recall that once upon a time they, like the farmers of 1921, had hoped that their government would be a tool of the local branches. Somehow that hope had gone awry. The more thoughtful MLA's could see its erosion when the leaders of the movement had been forced to tell the rank and file not to think—just to believe and to leave the thinking to those higher up. And just as they had told the electors not to worry about details, the MLA's now found the cabinet telling them not to question but to follow. (At that time other movements in Italy and Germany, based equally on faith in their leadership, were coming into prominence.)

The leaders, Aberhart, Manning and others, were, of course, as far from understanding how to implement Social Credit theory as anybody else, but following their own advice to the electors, they placed their reliance on the experts—first of all on Douglas and his counsel, and when they could neither fathom nor follow it, then on other imported Social Credit magicians. The plain fact was that Social Credit would not work. They were caught between two stools. In a world which presented them with the alternatives of being capitalists or socialists they were neither. Their followers, being largely independent landed proprietary farmers or small property-owning merchants, could not swallow the whole hog of socialism but hoped to ride two horses. They favoured such a form of socialism as would curb the callous easterners but which at the same time would encourage capitalism on the part of honest westerners.

It could not be found. And on that fact their form of Social Credit foundered.

In spite of that and even the conscientious footwork of Ernest Manning, who was rapidly growing in prestige and in economic knowledge, and the labours of the sincere Aberhart, the years until the next election saw no implementation of the Social Credit theory. For what consolation it might give them, word came that in England Major Douglas was also failing in his mission. This was evident from his publications which of late had somehow laid the blame for a Social Creditless world on international plotters and had indicated that Douglas was off on a new tangent, battling a new enemy he had conjured up—international Jewry.

When on March 21, 1940, the election came along, the constituency conventions, finding that orders did not flow from them to the government but from it to them, lost some of the cream of their enthusiasm. Despite that, they and everyone else had to admit that aside from wasting everyone's time with his theories and enraging the editor of the Edmonton *Journal*, Aberhart had done little real harm, and in fact, using the good civil service which the UFA government had assembled, he had continued to carry on the affairs of the province. Moreover, in a fashion most forcible, he had thoroughly startled the easterners, including even Mackenzie King, and nothing but good for Alberta could come out of that. Then too, by 1940 the depression and drought were over and a second world war had come. Fewer people had time for politiking. When the election results were tallied up, Aberhart and his government were returned to power with a substantially reduced, but nevertheless, a working majority of thirty-six seats out of fifty-seven.

The Social Credit heaven, of course, was still far off and the voters were right back where they had been before they had elected the UFA government in 1921 or the Social Credit government in 1935; in fact just about where they would have been no matter which government they had elected. But that, of course, is people and politics—the same yesterday, and today, and for ever.

While during the five years between elections the Social Credit government had been struggling with its problems, both the drought and the depression had righted themselves. For later students both the baneful abuse of land and the baleful lack of understanding of monetary practices provided interesting lessons. But they, like our knowledge of Social Credit's performance, were the produce of hindsight. Back in 1935 there had been no hindsight about drought and dust; they were the dreary facts of a discouraging present.

To add to southern Alberta farmers' other troubles, even the climate had now turned against them. In clothes worn thin through years of depression they huddled by their scantily fed stoves and watched the snows drift over their Bennett Buggies, as the winter of 1935–36, one of the coldest on record with unprecedented snow and blizzards, settled over the land. And even more devastating was the hot summer of 1936, which for high temperatures broke all records for the previous thirty years. The winds redoubled their assault and dust filled the air, piled up under doors and seeped through window frames. The continuous hot, grit-laden winds withered the fields and for the first time the whole area from Lloydminster to Lethbridge produced a negligible crop. Then to destroy any vestigial plants which had sprouted in spite of the drought, grasshoppers had spread, infesting millions of acres and leaving little grain to receive the *coup de grâce* of a stepped up invasion of rust and sawflies. Even the fall of 1936 was dry and when 1937, the worst disaster year of all, came, it was as devoid of moisture as a mother-in-law's kiss.

The very mud in the one-time water holes dried and cracked into cakes. Large lakes went dry. Cattle were in a desperate position. In the whole of the Palliser Triangle six million acres of once cultivated fields drifted unchecked and totally out of control. Fences disappeared under drifts of soil and road allowances deeply buried in loose sand and soil became impassable stretches.

Then in the fall of 1937, when they were too late to do any real good, the rains came. At least they settled the dust, and miraculously the wind-tortured fields turned green—with the farmers' old enemy, Russian thistle. But at least they were green and the farmers, feasting their eyes on this new vegetation, cut their one-time adversary for feed. The fall of 1937 marked the end of the disaster years, and the next season brought better rains and once more in the stricken areas the few farmers who had fought their way through the long drought began to look toward better years. In southeastern Alberta alone, however, five thousand farmers had not waited for the rains but had left for the cities or for greener farms in the northern woods. So had many a businessman in the rapidly depopulating smaller prairie towns.

There were, moreover, other farmers who had not sat idly by waiting for the weather to change. Aided by the federal government and the persevering scientists at the agricultural experimental stations, they had fought back—fought drought and dust to develop a better method of farming what were after all the very rich soils of the Palliser Triangle. In 1935 one of the last efforts of Bennett's doomed Conservative government had created the Prairie Farm Rehabilitation Authority—PFRA— the saviour of the dried-out prairies. Under pressure from the farmers and from the Honourable James G. Gardiner, the minister of agriculture in the new Liberal government which succeeded Bennett's ill-starred regime, the PFRA worked wonders. Amongst its earlier moves it con-

271

structed small dams to provide watering places for cattle and later on, using the excellent calibre of agricultural scientists at Lethbridge and Swift Current and of other prairie experimental stations, it attacked the problem of soil drifting. Against difficulties which seemed insuperable, the farmers and the scientists achieved the impossible—they stopped soil drifting.

To a graduate of the University of Alberta (the institution which Frank Oliver had once castigated as necessary only to train horse doctors), L. B. Thomson, who was in charge of the Swift Current experimental station, and to W. L. Jacobson and A. E. Palmer of the Lethbridge station, belong much of the credit for the victory. For they and their overworked assistants aided by the practical know-how of the toughest of the hard-bitten farmers who had refused to forsake the Palliser Triangle, conquered the soil drifting problem. Using a new design of farm cultivator which left the trash of any stubble on top of the fields and "listing" the land into ridges at right angles to the direction of the wind, practising strip farming and sowing crested wheat grass, they turned the wasted miles of windblown soil back into farm land. Hundreds of farmers contributed to this campaign, but in the field of developing entirely new designs of cultivating machinery one man stands out above the others— Charles S. Noble of Nobleford, the village near Lethbridge that bears his name.

Born in Iowa, he had homesteaded in 1902 near Claresholm. In 1917 he acquired a farm spread over 30,000 acres east of Nobleford, and the next year, hiring eleven giant steam tractors, broke most of it. Unfortunately two or three moderately dry years bankrupted him. Recovering from that failure he continued to farm on a very large scale, all the while concentrating on the problems of dry land farming. By 1935 he had concluded that to prevent the dry lands from blowing, a particular type of large cultivator was needed with a peculiarly shaped blade which he fabricated. It proved so successful that before long he directed all his efforts towards manufacturing hundreds of them for sale to prairie farmers. Charles S. Noble and the Noble blade played a major part in conquering soil blowing.

With this and other inventions and the overall aid of PFRA, the farmers and scientists soon repaired the devastation of the Dirty Thirties and restored the Palliser Triangle to a successful farming area. Part of their victory came as a result of the appearance of more powerful rubber-tired tractors and other large machinery which enabled aggressive farmers —a mere fraction of those who had once homesteaded the dry lands— to till their fields on the large scale necessary for success.

# 18
# World War Again
# 1935-1946

In the areas of the province's economy unrelated to dust storms, many other things had been happening. During the depression years the few men who dared tempt providence by going further into debt to drill oil wells did indeed hit small pools of oil: in 1932 at Del Bonita in the region of the old Whoop-Up Trail; in 1933 at Kehoe, north of Lethbridge, and in 1936 R. A. (Bob) Brown startled the oil fraternity by cashing in on a hunch in Turner Valley.

On April 17, 1934, Bob watched the crew spud in his Royalties No. 1 well. Seven times during the next two years work had to be suspended for lack of money. Finally the crew replaced the old cable rig with a rotary drill and on June 16, 1936, at a depth of 6,838 feet and with a thunderous roar, a gusher of green oil hurtled high into the derrick. Bob Brown had been right, and Turner Valley had become a major oil field.

During the next five years two hundred more wells were drilled in the valley and only half a dozen of them turned out to be dry holes. Up till 1935 in all its history the field had produced 9,300,000 barrels of oil; by 1942 it had reached its peak productivity of ten million barrels a year. In the meantime, now that Alberta had a good oil field, the government revised existing legislation and created the Oil and Gas Conservation Board. Moreover, encouraged by Bob Brown's success, other gamblers started a fresh search for oil, which repaid some of them by finding a small pool northeast of Brooks, in the vicinity of the CPR's irrigation ditches. Others had their faith rewarded by a small field near Vermilion and by a more significant find on the lands of Lloydminster's Barr colonists. At last, to lend a hand in lubricating the province's economy, oil fields became a light flickering through the gloom of the drought and the clouds of dust.

So in a small way were the airfields. For even the depression could not delay indefinitely an industry so pregnant with possibilities. By 1931 the Dominion authorities had set up a chain of beacons, which, blinking and flashing through the nights, guided pilots from Winnipeg to Regina, Saskatoon, Calgary and Edmonton. They had little impact, however, on Calgary's or Edmonton's primitive landing strips. Their future lay in serving, however sporadically, their own immediate area and in looking to the far North. Gradually, the bush pilots, as they were beginning to be called, were expanding their knowledge of the North and devising new tricks and new equipment to cope with its rigours. One day in the fall of 1930 Punch Dickins, who had been flying north in connection with the Copper Rush to Great Bear Lake, returned to Edmonton to report that the far North was "full of aircraft." He had counted, he said, "seven machines at Fitzgerald, two at Fort Rae, six at Hunter Bay, and two at Coppermine. And as we flew from Coppermine to Hunter Bay we passed two more machines in the air."

At last the North with its mineralized pre-Cambrian rocks was coming into its own and aeroplanes were the keys which unlocked its widely dispersed vaults. Assisted by aircraft, more and more prospectors began their wanderings in the land of the muskox and caribou. By 1936, many of them had found gold veins, and Yellowknife, with its Consolidated Mining and Smelting, and Negus and its Giant properties, came into being. And as the years went by and northern mines developed, all of Alberta's pilots began heading their rickety planes into the far North and returning to unload gold or silver ingots at Edmonton's Blatchford Field.

Then in 1937, young Grant McConachie pioneered in a new direction toward Whitehorse and incorporated Yukon Southern Transport Ltd. On July 5 that year he took off from the Cooking Lake Seaplane Base on the first flight and made the trip in eleven hours. Little knowing how soon fate and war would follow in his wake, he led the way through canyons and over mountains to the Yukon. By this time, of course, planes were equipped with two-way radio, and the Dominion government had established ground radio and weather stations at Fort St. John, Fort Nelson and Lower Post.

Within a few years more hangars spread over Calgary's McCall Field and Edmonton's Blatchford Field, and Ottawa, finally aroused from its lethargy, provided money for better runways and more land to lengthen them. Within a year or so, Trans-Canada Airlines came into being, and regular passenger services gave Albertans commercial access to the rest of Canada. To what extent Ottawa was keeping an eye on Europe, and how far it was concerned solely with keeping up with the growing air industry in the United States, is hard to say, but for Alberta the modern air age had arrived.

By some miracle during the decade after 1931, despite its difficulties of drought, depression and funny money, Alberta's population kept increasing. During this period, while the ratio of rural people to city folk remained the same, all the cities grew slowly. Edmonton rose to 93,817, an increase of 14,000, but strangely enough Calgary only grew to 88,904, an increase of a mere 5,000. In spite of a lack of progress in many other directions Edmontonians were able to rejoice that their city ended the decade with 5,000 more people than its rival.

From Alberta's point of view, however, the disturbing thing about its population was that with 164,000 children being born during the decade and only 57,000 old folk dying, the province's population should have increased about 107,000, but it did not do so. Instead, its increase was a mere 64,000: the equivalent of 43,000 of the babies born had pulled out, presumably for parts more prosperous. Alberta was unable to support or, in other words, to find work for its natural increase. What price now all its famous farm land, its mines, timber and other resources?

And yet conditions all over the world were unsettled and once more events in Europe were casting shadows over Canada, and alert observers began to worry. When in 1938 Hitler took over Austria and the Sudetenland, General McNaughton, Canada's chief of staff, was asked to report on the state of the military stockpile. His report said: "Except as regards rifles and rifle ammunition, partial stocks of which were inherited from the Great War—there are none." All of his report was in the same vein and concluded with the wry statement: "About the only article of which stocks are held is horses. The composition of a modern land force will include very little horsed transport."

About a year later, on August 25, Germany and Russia signed their non-aggression pact. Then on September 1, Hitler's bombers and panzer columns started their quick clean-up of Poland. Within two days Britain was at war, and on Sunday, a week later, Canada declared war on Germany.

Alberta was at war again. This time, however, it was with a better understanding of what war was all about and with some readiness, though still woefully little, on Ottawa's part. On September 1, 1939, Ottawa placed its reserve regiments on a war footing and recruiting teams went out to all the larger centres in the province.

During the years of peace Alberta's regiments had been rearranged and transformed in many ways. Edmonton's old 49th Battalion had become the Loyal Edmonton Regiment; Calgary's fighting 10th was now known as the Calgary Highlanders, while its original 50th Battalion had become an armoured regiment (the 14th), popularly known as the Calgary Regiment. As in the first war, Alberta supplied various groups of artillery, engineers and ancillary services. During the winter the main units found themselves on the stormy Atlantic en route to Britain.

For many months following its outbreak the war had been surprisingly innocuous. Poland, of course, had been laid waste, but in France and Belgium opposing armies merely watched each other. In Britain the war was still unreal, while in Canada Mackenzie King, outstanding prime

World War Again 1935-1946

minister though he was, bobbed about timidly in a sea of uncertainty. Concerned with holding his ill-matched French and Anglo-Saxon team together and asserting Canada's independence, his heart was not in the war.

Then on May 10, 1940, the real war set in, for that morning the *Blitzkrieg* started and Hitler's armies crashed into Belgium and Holland. That day too, Britain, fed up with the unfortunate Neville Chamberlain, laid itself in Winston Churchill's hands. Immediately a new spirit swept the Allied world. By June 14 Hitler's armies had occupied Paris, and France fell out of the war. Invasion stared Britain in the face. Between the German armies and Allied defeat stood Winston Churchill. The Battle of Britain was about to begin. And the British, bearing its brunt and now in desperate straits, rallied around their inspired leader. Now the war was real—too real.

Though officially neutral the United States leaned heavily towards the Allied side, and during 1941 worked out its Lend-Lease Act, which provided inestimable help against Hitler. On December 7, 1941, when the Japanese attacked Pearl Harbour and brought the United States into the war, Alberta's soldiers were still carrying out exercises in Britain, practising new techniques and waiting. Meanwhile at Stalingrad the aroused Russians minced up Hitler's 6th Army, and in Africa the 8th British Army, working with the Australians and New Zealanders, harried Rommel's armies and captured some 225,000 enemy soldiers.

Aside from some Canadians taking a small part in a few minor skirmishes, the months slipped by until August 19, 1942, before any Canadian force got a real crack at the Germans, and that was in what has been called the majestic fiasco of Dieppe. There, under almost hopeless conditions, the Canadian 2nd Division and the 1st Army Tank Brigade, which included the Calgary Tanks, suffered their first taste of the realities of war. Of the total force of 6,100 men who assaulted the heavy fortifications frowning on the Dieppe beach nearly five thousand were Canadians and of these 3,367 were casualties, of whom nine hundred were killed and 1,946 captured. Of the Calgary Regiment's twenty-nine tanks, half never crawled up the beach, but those which got ashore rendered a good account of themselves. When the regiment's casualty list was published the dead had come from all over Alberta, but an especially heavy toll had been taken of the young men from the Stettler area where one company had been recruited.

At last, after three years of war, the Canadians had taken part in their first battle—an assault of major proportions. Many Albertans wondered why the Dieppe landing had been necessary, but although its losses were appalling, the raid was of definite military value and the experience gained in this amphibious assault contributed greatly to the success of the subsequent invasion.

A History of Alberta

The Canadians made another significant step in July 1943 when they joined General Montgomery's army in Sicily and Italy. This time the Loyal Edmonton Regiment and the Calgary Highlanders fought Germans and Italians and fought them well. The Second World War was so vastly different from the first that perhaps its only common denominators were wounds and death. Where for months in the mud of France the old 49th and Calgary's 10th had slogged it out in muddy trench warfare and a month's gains were counted in hundreds of yards, this new warfare was mobile. In four weeks in Sicily the Allied troops drove the overextended Germans two hundred miles. It was a war of tanks, trucks and transportation, of buses, bulldozers and Bailey bridges, of radio, anti-aircraft guns and massive fire power. In such a war the boys from the prairies, to whom machinery was second nature, were at their best. In such a war where electronics was called into play, the new generation, better educated and better technicians, found full scope for their civilian adaptiveness. In such a war which involved extensive manoeuvres, Albertans, accustomed to focussing on vast distances in their daily life, were at home.

During 1944, after taking Rome and Naples, the Allied forces started pressing towards Florence. On July 25, Benito Mussolini was captured. The Alberta troops soon found themselves in the thick of the heavy fighting for the Gothic Line and the Rimini Line. At the bitter battle of San Fortunato they distinguished themselves again on their way to Italy's east shore. Other battles followed until finally many of the Alberta boys had spent their sixth Christmas away from home at the seashore near Rimini.

In the spring of 1945, 230,000 of Hitler's troops, backing up towards the Alps surrendered in one day. By that time, however, most of Alberta's soldiers had been transferred to France and Holland where they pursued the broken remnants of the German armies. On May 1, Hitler committed suicide, and two days later the war with Germany was over.

But the war on land was only part of the combatant duty played by Alberta's men. Scores of young prairie boys went to sea. Far out on the cruel wintery Atlantic in Canada's one cruiser and scores of corvettes, destroyers, torpedo boats and mine sweepers, which the navy had bought, borrowed or built, the prairie lads escorted merchant ships along the life line to Britain. During the amazing exploit that was the Battle of the Atlantic, Canada's naval men, alert in the rumbling bellies of escort vessels, convoyed 25,000 merchant ships to Britain. In other sectors of the far-flung seas as well, and on the way to Sicily, Africa and Western Europe, Canadian and Alberta boys faced up to Germany's well-trained navy.

In the same way, Alberta's contribution to the air force was spread over many units which served in so many flying capacities and groupings and on so many fronts that it is impractical to follow the fliers in any detail. The prairies' clear skies made them an ideal place for training young airmen. Adjacent to dozens of Alberta's towns and villages stretching from the Oldman River to Grande Prairie thousands of men took their lessons in flying. Because many of the air heroes of the first war were still alive and taking part in the civilian air industry they had created for it, Alberta may well have been the most air-minded province in Canada. As well as that, due to the fact that the air force, even if it was the most dangerous of military services, was also the most glamorous, young Albertans joined it. Even though official lethargy on the part of Prime Minister Mackenzie King and his colleagues during the early months of the war made it difficult for Canadian boys to start training as fliers and delayed their entering the air force, once they had the opportunity, they leaped at the chance to get into the air. Before the war was over, nearly a quarter of a million Canadians were serving in either the R.C.A.F. or the R.A.F. and of the 18,000 air force men listed as casualties, 17,000 lost their lives!

Because for several years before the war the Canadian government had been indifferent towards its own air force, more young Canadians crossed the ocean to enlist in Britain's R.A.F. than could get into the R.C.A.F. Mackenzie King's view was that such a force was only needed "sufficient to look after the defence of the Dominion." Believing that with the United States on one flank and Britain on another a direct attack on Canada was most unlikely, he maintained but a token strength. For this reason, scores of Canadians and several eager young Albertans played their part in the world's defence as members of the British force.

Once Mackenzie King took the halter off Canada's air force and began to lavish money on it, however, Albertans flew and fought in all the far-flung theatres of war. Exhibiting courage, capability and daring in every way equal to that of their comrades from America, Australia, Britain or New Zealand, they served in the Battle of Britain as fighter or bomber crews, as intruder squadrons, army cooperation units, reconnaissance, or Coastal Command, or as ground staff on hundreds of airfields liable at a moment's notice to be bombed or machine-gunned.

In this war, however, it was not only men and machines that went overseas and to all the various fronts but also Canada's young women, who in various women's divisions strove mightily. For times had changed and women who for years had worked shoulder to shoulder with men in factory or office now marched off to war with them. During this war there were jobs for everyone and girls from even the most remote farm came to the cities to take the place of some man who had gone to fight. For women were not only fighting to liberate the world but were advancing along their own front towards liberating themselves.

Superimposed on all this activity, came a great influx of air force trainees from Britain, Norway and all the Allied countries to learn their risky craft of flying. One of the country's greatest offerings to the war effort was the magnificent part Canada played in the Commonwealth Air Training Plan, turning out 130,000 pilots, navigators or bombers. In Alberta, Calgary's Lincoln Park and its McCall Field, and many a supplementary field buzzed with activity. Edmonton's Blatchford Field, first of all transferred to Dominion jurisdiction and then transformed in a matter of months, became almost overnight the busiest airport on the continent.

For Edmonton had suddenly come into focus as a strategic centre in United States defence plans. Keeping an eye on the Japanese, who were suspected of keeping an eye on Alaska, the Americans resolved not to be caught napping. Accordingly, in 1940, Canada and the United States combined forces in the Permanent Joint Defence Board, and that brought a searching look at the old Klondikers' route to the Yukon. The Americans, needing a rapid way of building up Alaska's defences, resorted to a huge airlift operation. Any Alberta pilots who could still be diverted to other activities, pitched in to help in the operation which became known as the Northwest Staging Route. Airfields along Grant McConachie's civilian Yukon Southern route to Whitehorse had to be upgraded, and hundreds of United States servicemen came in to do it. At Edmonton's Blatchford Field new runways were also built and soon began to accommodate the endless stream of freighters, fighters and bombers which made their way to and from Alaska. On top of this, Canadian Pacific Airlines bought out Mackenzie Air Services and McConachie's Yukon Southern Transport, and started to enlarge their operations, all aimed at the Yukon and Alaska.

On December 7, 1941, far away in the Pacific Ocean at Pearl Harbour, the Japanese caught the Americans napping and destroyed their Pacific fleet. That did it. Now Americans were officially at war, and in a mighty leap they jumped to the defence of Alaska, and DC-3's began raining in on Blatchford Field. On one June day five hundred planes passed through it on their way to Alaska. Moreover, about the same time, Edmonton's airport played its part in the United States transfer of fifteen hundred P-39 Bell Airacobras lend-leased to Russia. For months all the unexpected air traffic kept Blatchford Field in a flurry. On September 23, 1943, the staff established what was thought to be a North American record when that day 860 planes passed through their hands. In rising to meet the emergency the airport turned in a superb performance.

Even so it was felt necessary to build a satellite airfield to relieve the pressure. The Americans selected a site at Namao, some ten miles

World War Again 1935-1946

north of Edmonton's post office, and after they had spent $7 million there that major field took its place in the scheme of things. Taking in 2,560 acres and having 7,000-foot runways, it was the largest airport on the continent, and as soon as it was ready it slipped into high gear, still ferrying lend-lease planes to Russia.

Then the Americans decided to build a highway to Alaska and to do it within a few months. The few old-timers still around who forty-four years earlier had travelled the trail to the Klondike with pack horses shook their heads in amazement. All of the many Albertans who in the ordinary course of their business lives had looked to the far North for part of their livelihood rejoiced that at long last communication with that far-off region would soon become easy. Edmonton, Alberta's leading city, had long and truthfully boasted of being the gateway to the North and now the Americans in one stride were to clear away any remaining barriers to that claim.

The Americans allowed no grass to grow to hinder their project. Bombs had rained on Pearl Harbour in December; on February 2, 1942, the United States engineers were called in to discuss the possibility of a road to Alaska; on February 14 they were told to build one. On March 9, five officers and 127 men of a quartermaster detachment detrained at Dawson Creek. For as well as 302 miles in Alaska, the United States had offered to build and maintain 1,221 miles of highway on Canadian soil.

Before long 10,000 troops, 7,000 pieces of rolling equipment, forty-one American and thirteen Canadian contractors, and 17,000 civilians were at work on the project. By August 1, 1942, 858 miles of highway had been located. By September 24 clearing crews, working from each end, met at a point 305 miles west of Fort Nelson, and four days later the first truck from Dawson Creek reached Whitehorse—1,030 miles, at an average speed of around 15 m.p.h. The first regular convoy along the new Alaska Highway reached Fairbanks on November 22. For this road previously considered an impossibility, had been pushed through 1,523 miles of the world's worst terrain in nine months. It had cost $139 million, and after the war was destined to be sold to Canada.

To serve Alaska the Americans decided that they needed oil from the Norman Wells field, so over mountains and muskeg they built the 500-mile-long Canol Pipeline to supply a refinery at Whitehorse. Second in interest only to the highway, this pipeline resurrected all the romance in Edmontonians' souls. It had all the elements that appealed to the many who for so long had looked to the North and dreamed of the day when its riches would be exploited.

The Alaska Highway was served by the E.D. & B.C. Railway which some thirty years earlier had crawled bravely over the muskegs to the Peace River country and now heavily overburdened performed admirably in getting material through to Dawson Creek. Construction of the Canol project used Alberta's other north-seeking railway, the old AGW which in 1910 had cost Rutherford his premiership. Along its route went trainloads of pipe, which at Waterways were taken in hand by river scows and floated for hundreds of miles down the Athabasca and Mackenzie rivers—the old waterways which, though remote from Edmonton, had for so long been a part of the city's route of communication with its great northland. The North in which so many Albertans had invested money, the North towards which they had pushed railways and in which they had developed a major system of water transportation was beginning to vindicate their long held hopes.

With all this activity directed towards Alaska the second of the three American invasions hit Alberta and concentrated in Edmonton. Although it created annoying problems, it was as welcome as the invasion forty years previously when thousands of Americans had come in to till Alberta's soil. Hundreds of United States personnel made their homes and headquarters in Edmonton and rented every bit of available office and living accommodation. The streets swarmed with American servicemen. As well as taking all the available accommodation, they were accused, probably with some semblance of truth, of taking over the beer parlours and cornering all available girls, as well as stripping the stores by sending shoes, fur coats and English china back home.

Trained by half a century of service club greeters and imbued with the almost pathological American desire to be friendly, the United States personnel leaned over backwards to maintain their welcome. Nevertheless, both they and the local citizens were relieved when together on May 8, 1945, they celebrated V-E Day (Victory in Europe). Within days of a momentous turning point in the world's history, the dropping of the first atomic bomb on Hiroshima, the Japanese surrendered and on August 15 Canadians celebrated V-J Day.

At last the war was really over.

Once more, after five long years, Albertans, both soldiers and civilians, turned back to the ways of peace. Everyone longed to pick up civilian life where it had left off five years earlier. But that ideal turned out to be impossible. Radar, atomic energy, electronics and jet engines had catapulted the world into a new era and the leisure and prosperity made possible by automation was just around the corner.

As a result of the first war the Federal government had learned a great deal, and in 1939 began applying controls and financial policies aimed at preventing prices, profits and wages from skyrocketing. By the end of the war the cost of living had risen only twenty percent. Moreover, as well as supplying military personnel, Canada found an invaluable role in manufacturing munitions and equipment. The United States, for a year or so technically neutral but otherwise pitching in on the Allied side, assisted Canada in many ways so as to keep the country's financial situation stable. With this assistance, Canada finally emerged from the struggle as a strong manufacturing nation which had spent $18 billion on the war, had paid its way, and was financially solvent.

Moreover, the country's tremendous war effort had raised its people's sights to new horizons. Canada had grown up, had become independent of Britain, and now and then even snarled at the United States. What few of its people realized was that from being the numerically dominant race in Canada the English were becoming a minority. Canadians, rejoicing that they had torn the reins of domination out of the hand which Britannia was not using to hold up her trident had not noticed that in the process the lines had caught on Uncle Sam's little finger.

Despite that, on their own accounts, Canadians had worked wonders. Prime Minister William Lyon Mackenzie King had performed miracles in driving the diverse horses of his Canadian chuckwagon team. Swinging them around bilingual barrels, steering them past spills on the track and sneaking them clear of collisions, he had finally brought them down the final stretch to an amazing victory.

In the process he had assembled one of the ablest Canadian cabinets of all time, and in this group the Honourable C. D. Howe had stood out head and shoulders above all others. For to Howe more than to any other one man, Canada could attribute her amazing growth in manufacturing and industrial progress. To others and to King himself, Canadians could attribute such forward looking social moves as old age pensions (before 1930), unemployment insurance (1940) and family allowances (1944).

Of course, Mackenzie King had been nudged towards all these moves by an assortment of maverick fringe parties, most of whom obtained much of their inspiration and support from the prairies, the home of farmers, fundamentalists and for a few brief years of the Ku Klux Klan. When, as a young man in 1921 he had become prime minister, King had faced a House in which farmers in the Progressive Party held sixty-five seats: twenty-four from Ontario, fifteen from Saskatchewan, twelve from Manitoba and ten from Alberta. In 1925 when he was in opposition, King had watched while the mavericks, almost wholly from the prairies but by then reduced to twenty-four, performed ineffectually. Then as prime minister, after the election of August 1926 when the dissidents, splitting their ranks into eleven UFA members from Alberta and nine Progressives from the other prairie provinces, were weakening, he had sat sizing them up. All the while alternately fawning on them and out-foxing them, he had destroyed the effectiveness of this little group of westerners who had come so naively to flaunt their virtues before the suspect hosts of the East.

A History of Alberta

In 1930 when R. B. Bennett, leading the Conservatives, drove King out of office at the beginning of the depression and thereby rendered him a lasting service, he had once more observed the mavericks, ten persistent UFA members from Alberta and half a dozen assorted others. When in 1935 W. L. Mackenzie King at the head of a tremendous Liberal following resumed the office of the prime minister, the farmers' candidates had disappeared as such and he had to accustom himself to a new band of eccentrics, Social Crediters, fifteen from the eighteen Alberta ridings and two from Saskatchewan. At the same time, however, there appeared a new and noticeable tribe called the Co-operative Commonwealth Federation led by a noteworthy ex-preacher, J. S. Woodsworth.

And over the years from all of them, representing as they did the protests of the poor, the labouring classes and the prairie farmers, King had gleaned new ideas which were to sprout in the social reforms his long regime brought into being. Whether he learned more from the saintly J. S. Woodsworth, one of the most outstanding men ever to sit in the House of Commons, or from Aberhart, the messiah of Alberta, is a moot question, but learn he did from both of them. Partly as a result of that learning the Canada and the Alberta which emerged after World War II were vastly different and vastly better places in which to live.

Back in the West Albertans with their unorthodox government were watching all these landmarks of progress. By the time Aberhart had won the 1940 election, some common sense picked up from the Dominion government and from its provincial civil servants had seeped into the cabinet's mind through the fissures which had allowed the escape of so much supercharged Social Credit. Energetic and studious Ernest Manning had been digging into the problems of practical government and dipping into the field of economics, and before long conservatism began to rub the rough edges off his former convictions. When the cabinet descended from the clouds of their Social Credit theory to attend to the everyday tasks of operating the province's business, the Social Credit party carried on the tradition of honest government established by its farm predecessors. Some cries of graft in the Highways Department began to be heard, but either they were never proven or they were glossed over.

Many of Aberhart's MLA's followed Douglas into anti-Semitism, but both the premier and Manning, men to whom religion meant something, refused to countenance this route of escape from their dilemma. Both of them found a better excuse for their failure in the fact that the Dominion government had disallowed their legislation and that until the forces of Social Credit could overwhelm it, they could do little but run a good provincial administration. Then, when by 1939 times had improved and their voters became less strident and everyone began to face up to the war effort, that effort gave Aberhart a good excuse for delaying the implementation of his theories and for substituting good administration for Social Credit.

In 1943 everyone came to realize that Aberhart was ill and in May the man who had led Albertans in their fight, died in a Vancouver hospital. Even by that time, remarkably few of his followers would admit that he had failed to lead them into the millennium. As a messiah he had led them and as a messiah they mourned him. A sincere man, an excellent teacher, a superb organizer and a tireless worker, he had left his stamp on Alberta, and on Canada.

But none of his theories, none of his preaching and none of his effects on the province equalled the legacy he left Albertans in his disciple and successor, Ernest C. Manning. Born September 20, 1908, on a wheat farm at Carnduff, Saskatchewan, the son of immigrant English parents, he had been enthralled by Aberhart's radio broadcasts and moved to Calgary to sit at his feet. Immediately the master had recognized his talents and rapidly promoted him to high office in his Prophetic Bible School. On September 3, 1935, after the election in which Manning had played such a prominent role, Aberhart made him provincial secretary and for the rest of his life relied heavily on Manning's outstanding ability—the same ability and conscientiousness which for the twenty-five years after his mentor's death was to provide Canada with one of its best, most conservative and most often re-elected provincial premiers.

By the time Manning assumed the office of premier on May 31, 1943, Albertans were in the midst of their war effort. Prosperity surrounded them and though they could see that even after a lapse of eight years the Social Credit theories had not been implemented, they were inclined to be patient and not to talk too much about it. If the more ardent Social Crediters in the locals had noticed the reversal of the anticipated chain of command, the more politic at least did not complain. With coins jingling in their pockets angelic chants chiming in the heavens seemed afar off.

Election after election Albertans continued to send Social Credit members to Ottawa, sixteen in 1935, ten in 1940 and thirteen in 1945. There they were an unnoticed flock and even though they detested genuine socialism, they were equated with all the other mavericks, including the New Democrats and the Socialists.

It was fear of the socialists in fact which was largely instrumental in re-electing Manning's government in August 1944. That year, by relying on his record of excellent administration and by attacking socialism, he skirted around dogmatic Social Credit. Whether or not the electors realized that he had done so, they voted for him anyway, and amongst their number were a host of businessmen who formerly had voted for more orthodox parties.

By that time the war was over and many a statesman, including

Manning and Mackenzie King, many a businessman and many an economist anxiously tried to peer into the future. Mackenzie King's cabinet ministers and his civil servants, in collaboration with the provincial governments, had all tried to prepare for the change to a peacetime economy, and on the whole had done a remarkably good job. Once wartime restrictions were removed, everyone expected prices to go up and inflation to get in its deadly blows. On the other hand, once wartime's feverish activity fell off, everyone expected the spectre of unemployment to have its way. Neither became a serious problem.

Except for an increase in the tempo of its social life, Alberta had actually changed very little since 1929. From 1939 when covered with dust and confusion the province had crawled out from under the Bennett Buggies of the depression, its population had increased less than ten thousand to 803,000 in 1946. Population changes had mainly meant a redistribution of people—a movement into the cities, which saw Edmonton increase by 19,000 to 113,000 and Calgary to 100,000. The shift away from the land had started and by 1946 the percentage of rural people had fallen to fifty-six percent. From many a remote valley eager young people had started their trek to the cities. Reluctantly the older folk, the original homesteaders, had followed. They, the pioneers who had devoted their lives to winning a farm from the forested wilderness and often had eked out a sparse but on the whole a happy living, boarded up their windows and sold out to a neighbour with regret but yet in anticipation of a few years of comfort in the city.

During the war the farmers had fared well and at its highest point their cash income had reached $338 million, but by 1946 it had dropped off to $280 million, and looked as if it might continue to drop. During the war too, the lumber industry had flourished and had reached a new high by producing 353 million board feet. So too the output of coal had increased until in 1946 it had reached its all-time high of 8,826,000 tons. Oil's performance, however, had not been spectacular; one or two trifling fields had been found at Tilley in 1942, Conrad in 1944 and Provost in 1946, but none of them had caused much excitement. Turner Valley, the only real field, had produced surprisingly well but by the end of the war was seen to be suffering from its high rate of production. Perhaps the most noticeable physical change in the province had been the improvement of highways, for by 1946 there were 531 miles of bituminous surface, along with 9,316 miles of gravelled roads, an increase of some 6,000 since the start of the war.

Actually then, Alberta had changed very little. The beauty of its magnificent farming areas, of course, had not dimmed. Neither had Albertans' distrust of easterners; they continued to send a rebel group of Social Credit members to the House of Commons. The provincial political front was still unchanged except that its strong government still nominally Social Credit had in reality cooled to a blue conservative cast. Moreover, it was worried about how to keep all Albertans and their children at work. The oil outlook was not promising, the demand for coal would undoubtedly fall off, and activity in its forested lands which had risen to cope with the war's demand for timber and lumber was bound to drop.

On the agricultural front the future was not bright. Most of the arable land had been settled. What was left was of a lower grade, remote from railways. Even though much land on existing farms could still be broken, the physical volume of agricultural production was expected to flatten out at a figure less than it had been during the war. The trend to more and better livestock and away from complete dependence on grain was good, but modern farms employed fewer people, and by 1946 the farm population had slipped to eighty-seven percent of what it had been in 1941. The rural areas were losing people to the cities.

Furthermore, Alberta's population was not increasing as it should be and had not been since 1931. Because its birth-rate was good and its death-rate moderate, the balance between the two—what statisticians called its natural increase—should have resulted in a growth in its population each year. Actually, even though on top of this there had been some immigration, the increase in population had been less than the natural increase—a clear indication that Alberta was dropping into a have not position where its young folk had to go elsewhere in order to make a living. Between 1936 and 1941, while the natural increase had been 52,000, some 29,000 had sailed for other shores. Then in the more recent period, out of a possible increase of 60,000, all but 7,000 had moved away! Economists studying the figures shook their heads. Merchants in Alberta's cities, probably not knowing of the figures but seeing what their cash registers were ringing up, wondered at their lack of progress.

Alberta's prospects were grey. The number of farmers was bound to decrease. No one seemed to want two of Alberta's well-known resources, its 25,000 million tons of mineable coal and its 171,000 square miles of forests. Alberta's great rivers slipped silently off to the sea. No one could foresee mills to turn or wheels to whirl with their several million horsepower of potential hydro power. Sealed into the Athabasca oil sands were at least 300 billion barrels of recoverable oil, but since no one needed them, no one had come forward with the magic millions of dollars that would liberate them. For decades up and down Alberta, venturesome drillers had probed the underlying rocks searching for oil and gas, but their riches continued to elude them. It appeared that Alberta's prospects had reached their zenith and were destined to decline.

# 19
# Oil Money
# 1947-1971

Albertans, however, had been born lucky. On February 13, 1947, seventeen miles southwest of Edmonton, a black smoke ring belched out of the flare line of Leduc Oil Well No. 1 and floated lazily into the wintry sky—a smoke signal of amazing portent, a signal that ushered in the province's oil era. Alberta had hit the jackpot.

The previous November Imperial Oil Limited's Vernon Hunter had spudded in Leduc No. 1. Early in February, with the bit down some five thousand feet, the well showed indications of oil, and, acting on a hunch, Hunter set February 13 as the date when company and government officials, nosey newspaper and radio reporters could come and witness the final proof of the well's success or failure.

By noon a crowd had gathered; by four o'clock the less hardy had shivered their way back to town; shortly afterwards the well started to rumble. Then with a roar it came in. As Vernon Hunter said after explaining that they switched the flowing oil to the flare line and lit the fire, "The most beautiful smoke ring you ever saw went floating skywards." Smack in the middle of that smoke ring sat Alberta's fairy godmother.

Leduc turned out to be a field of 1,278 wells, containing 200 million barrels of recoverable oil—a field twice the size of Turner Valley. Even in Texas this would have been a major oil field. With the Turner Valley field running down so quickly, just when Alberta's demand was rising rapidly, local refineries had been making desperate bids to import crude oil from the States. But even the Leduc field rapidly yielded priority to other large discoveries.

Just as fifty years earlier Alberta's rich soils had proven to be a paradise for thousands of farmers, the province's oil resources became a mecca for thousands of oil workers. Within the next twenty-four years Alberta's population doubled to some 1,600,000. Farming, with some slight assists from coal and lumber, had supported 800,000 people. Twenty-four years later, by 1971, petroleum products directly or indirectly supported almost as many more. For in that quarter century everything good (plus much that was bad) happened to Alberta.

## OIL FIELDS AND
## OIL PIPELINES

Diagram of the larger
oil lines which in
themselves constitute a
major transportation
accomplishment.

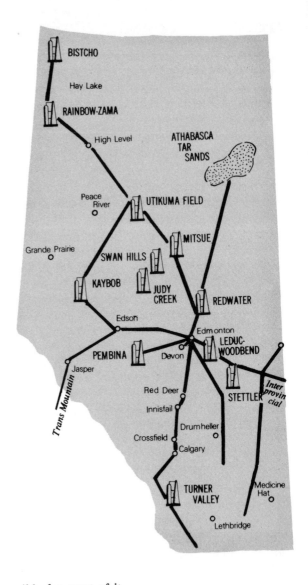

And oil was responsible for most of it.

Although several new towns sprang into being in the newly discovered oil fields, towns such as Devon, Redwater and Swan Hills, most of the oil-induced immigration concentrated in the cities. At the same time, there was a drastic shift of farm families to the urban centres. The effect of the resulting vast increase in population completely remodelled Calgary and Edmonton and had a major effect on Lethbridge, Medicine Hat, Camrose, Lloydminster and Red Deer. Practically all of Alberta's

A History of Alberta

larger towns, which for some fifty years had struggled along, also benefited in some measure from the new prosperity and increased in size and amenities. Much of their new prosperity came at the expense of nearby smaller towns and villages which, because of paved highways and everyone's new mobility, had to watch their trade vanish and their businesses close up when former customers passed them by on their way to the larger towns or even to the cities a hundred miles away.

These cities, however, basking in the wealth and welfare of a rich and growing Canada and perfumed with the scent of oil, soon found themselves physically and socially transformed. As a result of their doubled and redoubled riches and quadrupled population they obtained all the amenities of large urban centres: auditoriums and art galleries, museums and musical aggregations, larger and more luxurious schools, vastly expanded university campuses and many-storied, long-corridored hospitals—in short, all the trappings of a modern, costly and complicated civilization.

Not only had oil, both by means of its production and by means of the immense capital which had poured in from the United States, put chicken on every Albertan's table but it had saved every Canadian's bacon. During 1947, just when Canada was running into one of its most serious financial crises, Leduc No. 1 came to its aid. The very month that it blew in the governor of the Bank of Canada had declared that because Canada was selling so much to war-torn Europe on credit and at the same time running up vast deficits because of the luxuries Canadians were importing from the United States, stringent action would have to be taken to protect its foreign exchange position. Later in the year when D. C. Abbott, Canada's minister of finance, announced drastic measures to curb purchases and imports from the United States, he put his finger on the problem when he declared that Canadians had been living beyond their means. While on v-j Day, a couple of years earlier, Canada's foreign exchange reserves had been one and a half billion dollars, they were nearly exhausted by the end of 1947 during which Canadians had imported goods worth two billion dollars. The government was forced to take harsh measures to restrict Canadian buying of American luxuries and did so during the winter and spring of 1947–48, just when the Leduc field's Atlantic No. 3 burst into fiery prominence.

But before the restrictions had pinched Canadians for very long they got help from two widely separated natural resources: the Labrador iron mines and Alberta's oil fields. When American capitalists began putting up the billions of dollars necessary to develop these new riches, American money poured into Canada and almost overnight dissipated the worries over the country's foreign exchange position.

While of course the treatment—a large influx of American investment

Oil Money 1947-1971

—solved that problem temporarily (and indeed for a quarter of a century) it did not strike at the root of the disease, and it undoubtedly paved the way for more serious trouble in the future.

Canadians, however, shutting their eyes to the greater problem, rejoiced that once more they could easily buy American goods, resume touring in the United States as well as in Canada, purchase the "superior" U.S. radios and appliances south of the border and believe that they were sneaking them past the customs officers.

So much then for what petroleum—oil and gas—did for Alberta. Leaving the discovery and development of natural gas until later and confining our attention to oil only, the physical aspects of its production are fascinating. During the thirty years before Leduc No. 1 the oil industry had spent over $150 million on exploration, development and production and nearly all it had to show for the investment had been Turner Valley, a field having originally estimated reserves of 120 million barrels of oil. The next quarter century was to disclose nearly eight billion barrels of oil reserves in Alberta in scores of fields, of which fifteen were larger than Turner Valley. (One of them, Pembina, was fifteen times as large.)

Even at that, however, in 1946 alone the oil industry had spent $12 million in exploration and development activities. It had eleven geophysical rigs working in the province and nineteen drilling rigs, and bored fifty-four exploratory wells. Of these, three struck oil, five found gas, and forty-six were dry holes. Prospects were anything but encouraging.

Then early in 1947, within a couple of miles of the old fur traders' trail from Edmonton to Rocky Mountain House, the trail which almost a century earlier had seen so many gold prospectors coming and going, Leduc No. 1 roared in. Immediately, oil companies by the dozen set off on a wild scramble to track down other pools. Alberta's latest resource had come into its own.

To find today's fabulous underground reservoirs of wealth a new era of surveying was launched. It was to send the oil surveyors, the seismograph crews, into every valley and flat, every muskeg and hilltop, and to leave great bands of oil wells and later long strips of gas wells stretching over the province. Once, two hundred years earlier, the fur traders had come in to survey the province and, finding its first resources, bellowing buffalo in great droves and fur-bearing animals bobbing up behind every tree, had pronounced Alberta a rich land. Once, nearly a hundred years later, gold panners had come in to survey Alberta in their own fashion and after passing and repassing along the oil trail within a couple of miles of the future site of Leduc No. 1 had been disappointed and gone their ways entirely unaware of the oil riches a mile below their feet. Once, fifty years later still, the Dominion land surveyors had spread out over every square mile of Alberta's arable land and, finding it fertile, had left iron survey pegs sticking up all over it. Almost immediately these had guided farmers down the long, lonesome valleys and up the round, windy hilltops. In every corner of arable Alberta the farmers in general had been well content and had produced long trainloads of golden wealth. Then came this new breed of explorers poking into every creek and peering down every coulee.

These oil men were a different breed of surveyors—men with light trucks and drills that made holes but a few feet deep in which they could set off a charge of dynamite and with their mysterious electronic gadgets record how the shock wave from the explosion penetrated the various strata and was reflected back to the instrument. Along the good roads in the farming areas their movements were relatively straight forward, but as the years went by and they were asked to penetrate northern Alberta's forests and marshes, they sent bulldozers ahead to clear out a crude trail which their trucks could follow. After a few years, as one company's crew after another slashed these gashes out of the forest, all the hitherto silent forests became a crisscross of seismic lines. At last the white man had penetrated almost every square mile of the immense portion of remote, forested Alberta which interested him.

Eventually, setting off their dynamite, they had breasted the Clear Hills and the Caribou Mountains and swung west to the muskegs along the oxbowed Chinchaga River and near Hay and Zama lakes. Finally sweeping on north and west, following the sedimentary rocks past Bistcho Lake, some eight hundred miles north and west of Waterton Lakes, they continued their search into the Northwest Territories and passed out of Alberta. But when they were through they had an intimate knowledge of all the strata, folds and domes of the oil-bearing rocks, sometimes 8,000 feet below the surface. Albertans, buying and selling oil stocks and following the survey crews on their maps, learned of northland foothills, lakes and rivers of which they had never heard.

For months after the industry started its spate of drilling, most of the big plays were in the Edmonton area. By the end of 1947, in the Leduc field, Imperial Oil had brought in twenty-three wells, and within a fifty-mile radius of Edmonton dozens of other companies drilled frantically at hundreds of wildcat wells. Then on January 18, 1948, some fourteen miles west of Edmonton's post office, the first Woodbend well swooshed in, and that fall as Alberta's leaves were turning yellow, thirty miles north and east, the Redwater field came in. The fairy godmother, still astride her ring, circled Edmonton and strewed the farmers' fields with derricks, valves and oil tanks.

During 1948 in the Leduc–Woodbend area, companies drilled 147 wells. Five of them produced some gas and oil, eleven were dry, and 131 fairly spouted oil. None of these, however, made such a fuss about it as Atlantic No. 3, a mile away from Leduc No. 1. On March 8, 1948, it got out of control and blew out. Oil and gas gushed out, and, because they could not escape fast enough from the wellhead, formed craters in the surrounding cultivated soil and flowed off in streams to form pools. Atlantic's employees scurried about throwing up dikes to prevent the oil from spreading farther and laying pipes to conduct it away.

Six months later they still had not succeeded in bringing the wild well under control, and worse still, it caught fire. For days the blaze, visible at night for nearly a hundred miles, lured thousands of spectators from all over northern Alberta. The summer-long excitement culminated in the great pillar of fire and drew the eyes of the world to the province. Now everyone knew Alberta had an oil field.

But the Leduc–Woodbend field was just starting. By 1949 it had 363 producing wells, by 1951 it had eight hundred, and went on to reach its full development in 1954 with 1,278 wells. Similarly, by 1949, Redwater had 278 producers and reached its maximum of 926 three years later. And yet the Redwater field with 780 million barrels of estimated original recoverable oil and the Leduc–Woodbend field with 329 million barrels eventually turned out to be only Alberta's third largest and eighth largest fields respectively.

Albertans lived in a dream world. Their fairy godmother added rich prizes to her benefices and dotted the prairies and parklands with wells strewn from the 49th parallel to Cold Lake. Beyond Cold Lake, because the underlying sedimentary rocks were beginning to pinch out, the northern edge of the prolific fields angled off northwest to the Utikuma Lake and Red Earth fields and to Rainbow Lake and finally to the Zama field. There, where the northernmost find was a scant dozen miles short of the province's north boundary, it was 744 miles north of the 49th parallel. South of the line, angling northwest from Cold Lake, however, the fairy godmother unveiled scores of sizeable fields and some stupendous ones.

With some exceptions, such as the Crossfield and Innisfail areas, the oil play moved north as the years went by. Discoveries, of which we can only name a few, were made every year. In 1953 some seventy miles south and west of Edmonton the Pembina field, the granddaddy of all Alberta fields, came in and within a few years boasted approximately 1,700 wells and a recoverable of 1,732 million barrels of oil. Then of the major fields, the Swan Hills came in during 1957 (1,372 million recoverable barrels), Judy Creek in 1959 (487 million), Mitsue in 1964 (340 million), Rainbow in 1965 (317 million) and Zama in

1966. By 1970 Alberta had reserves of nearly eight billion barrels of oil.

In each of the major fields the various crews needed a town out of which they could operate. Even though the first two major oil fields, Leduc and Redwater, were relatively close to Edmonton, the companies nevertheless created the new towns of Devon and Redwater. Then, as the other fields came along in generally unsettled areas they set up towns such as Drayton Valley, Swan Hills, High Level and Rainbow Lake. All these towns were greatly assisted by a unique type of government financing.

Keeping an eye on all the oil drilling and associated activity was Alberta's Petroleum and Natural Gas Conservation Board, a body considered by many to be the most advanced and competent board of this nature on the continent. It had actually been set up about 1938 at the time of the resurgence of excitement in Turner Valley, and since its main job had been to ride herd on what was going on there, its office naturally came to be located in Calgary. As a result of Turner Valley also, Calgary became the headquarters for oil companies large and small. When, therefore, the Leduc field came into the limelight, it was only natural that the head offices of the oil companies already in Calgary should continue to operate out of there, and that the new oil companies, together with those organizations which served the industry, should also congregate in that city. Thus Calgary became the headquarters of the financial, geological and operating facets of the burgeoning industry.

Edmonton, however, being the geographic centre of a very large proportion of Alberta's significant oil fields, came in for its share of the oil-born prosperity that had to do with the actual drilling and servicing of the fields. While both Calgary and Edmonton, never forgetting their decades-old rivalry, each claimed to be Canada's oil capital, both of them grew amazingly as the thousands of men needed in the industry poured in.

The stupendous influx of capital and trained personnel, an influx both these growing cities welcomed, included thousands of professional and technical men. Once more Alberta experienced and welcomed an American invasion. During the first decade of the 20th century Americans with capital and experience had come in to farm Alberta's soils, during the Second World War they had poured in to push a highway through to Alaska, and now many of the men who had gone home after the war came back to take part in the development of Alberta's second major resource.

These mainly technically trained personnel not only turned their hands to discovering and producing oil but they faced up to the problem of how to get it to market. The obvious solution was to pipe it to Edmonton and to build refineries there. By August 1948, on Edmonton's eastern outskirts, the Imperial Oil Company began its refinery at Clover Bar. It had been the one the Americans had built at Whitehorse to handle the oil coming across the mountains in the Canol Pipeline from the Norman Wells, and Imperial Oil had dismantled it and trucked it down the Alaska Highway. By 1951 the British American Oil Company had completed its new refinery at Clover Bar, and in the same vicinity, a few months later, a similar McColl-Frontenac plant came on stream. Within three years Edmonton had become a major refining centre.

Out at the fields, after the drilling was over and the derricks came down, the land was dotted with oil pumps resembling prehistoric monsters in neatly fenced plots the size of a backyard garden, sixteen of them to a square mile, standing in the rich green or gold, or the silent snows of the farmers' fields. And night and day on each plot, bobbing up and down like so many hobbyhorses they kept up their regular beat, teetering up and down, up and down, to bring up the black riches from thousands of feet below. As fast as all of these could raise oil to the surface, new pipelines kept pushing it on to Edmonton. First of all was a short line from the Leduc–Woodbend field. Then, winding along underground and paralleling the old Victoria Trail, another line made its way to the refinery area. Then came others, from the Joarcam field, and through the muskegs from the fantastic Pembina field, and others.

But soon, even the new refineries could not handle all the oil and it had to be piped directly to eastern Canada. By December 1950 Inter-Provincial Pipe Line completed a 1,129-mile line to Lake Superior, most of it eighteen inches in diameter. Hard on its heels came 718 miles of twenty-four-inch pipe to the west coast—Trans-Mountain Pipe Line, taking the route the Overlanders of '62 had taken to Jasper and the Yellowhead Pass to tidewater. Before long, bringing their tribute from the southern section of the province, other lines were built to connect to the Inter-Provincial line. Moreover, as the northern fields began to produce, other lines were laid to carry their rich product south: a line from the Swan Hills, following the trail on which in 1898 so many hundreds of Klondikers had suffered; another from the Sturgeon Lake field, working its way south in the vicinity of the trail the Grande Prairie pioneers had once cursed so bitterly when they were bound north from Edson some forty years earlier. Year by year other lines were laid, heading through the pine forests, over hills and across such mighty rivers as the Peace and the Athabasca until finally oil was pumped to Edmonton from the Rainbow area by way of the Utikuma field north of Lesser Slave Lake, and the Mitsue field at the lake's eastern end—a distance of five hundred airline miles. In due course another line rippled through the foothills south to Pincher Creek and on to Montana and the United States' markets. And all of these constitute but a few of the major

Diagram of major gas
fields and gas pipelines
gathering from nearly all
parts of the province
and exporting across
three of its boundaries.

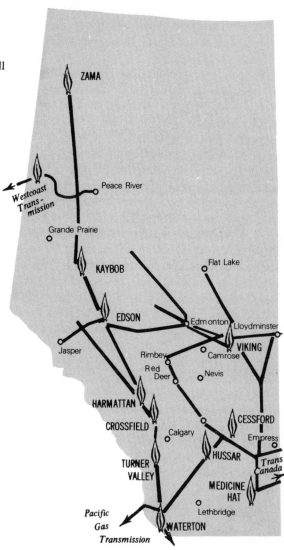

lines, for by 1970 the province had come to be covered by a network of over 31,000 miles of petroleum industry pipelines, nearly five times the total mileage of operating railway lines.

About two-thirds of these pipelines, however, transported gas; once the post-Leduc spate of drilling scattered oil rigs all over the province, it soon became apparent that another stupendous source of wealth was about to pour into Alberta's lap. Natural gas, long regarded in oil circles as a bothersome by-product, began to be recognized as an exportable commodity, and then it was sought for its own sake. Soon too it was discovered, and in tremendous quantities, and a new search sent drilling rigs and seismic crews and truckloads of drill-stem scurrying hither and yon across the province.

Of course, for years gas had been used to serve Calgary and Lethbridge from the Turner Valley field and Edmonton from the Viking field. Perhaps its earliest use had been by fur trade voyageurs who stopped at gas seepages along the Peace and Athabasca rivers to boil their kettles. But when in the course of drilling a water well at Langevin it had come to bother the drillers, they went away and forgot about it until the revived interest in gas came along in the fifties and they went back to have another look. In spite of sixty years of neglect, that field, renamed Alderson, became a fair producer. It was the Medicine Hat field, however, which surprised everyone. For half a century that city, having as Kipling said, "all Hell for a basement" had used it, and nibbled away at it by punching a shallow hole now and then for a fresh supply. No one suspected what tremendous reserves it had in its basement.

When, however, gas was needed for export and the drillers set out to see how much the field had, its immensity amazed everyone. It held over 2,000 billion cubic feet of gas, nearly three times as much as either Turner Valley or the Viking field. And yet it was only one of six such gigantic fields of which the Crossfield area with over 3,400 billion cubic feet led the procession. These huge fields were scattered all over the southern two-thirds of the province: Edson in the west with Kaybob some seventy miles north in the heart of the uninhabited timbered wilderness; the Harmattan pool in the rugged foothills west of Olds, and Waterton at the fringe of the mountains in Alberta's southwestern corner. Scattered all over the map between them, like the mud sprayed from a passing car on a pedestrian's pants, were over twenty-five other fields, each about the same size as Turner Valley, some of them associated with a major reservoir of oil and some not. Then to fill in the spaces between the major mud splatters the drillers found literally scores of smaller gas pockets, each significant in its own right. The Peace River country also had its quota of fields, which in due course sent their gas to Vancouver. By 1970 Albertans could gloat over reserves of 48,000 billion cubic feet of gas.

With gas practically popping out around the farmers' stooks and seeping into grizzly bears' dens hitherto undisturbed in Alberta's forests, great corporations came into being to gather it, deliver it to dozens of Alberta towns and pipe it to the continent's markets. The huge Alberta Gas Trunk Line was organized to gather the gas and to deliver it at the Saskatchewan border to Trans-Canada Pipe Lines for transport to Ontario markets, or to the British Columbia border for delivery to other companies, which in turn sent it to the Pacific coast and California. By 1971 Alberta Gas Trunk had constructed 3,493 miles of pipeline, most of it over twenty inches in diameter and some of it forty-two inches.

Forming a Y with its tips near Grande Prairie and in the Marten Hills and its arms each about 150 miles long, the northern portions of the system meet near Edson. Thence huge duplicate lines sweep south along the edge of the foothills and then diverge again to carry gas west through Crowsnest Pass and east across the Saskatchewan border near Empress, where about 1800 Peter Fidler had spent two exciting winters. And from all over—from Flat Lake, Cessford, Rimbey, Nevis, Waterton and many other fields, other collecting lines feed into the huge mains. For Alberta Gas Trunk is truly a gigantic venture.

Integral parts of the whole business of producing Alberta's tremendous output of petroleum are its many by-product plants. To make the oil and gas palatable for the continent's markets they had to be treated and scrubbed to take out some of the offensive sulphur and many other products. As a result, spotted here and there, from the haunts of the northern woodland caribou 750 miles south to the antelope pastures of the Sweet Grass Hills, scores of processing plants had to be fabricated and welded together—plants costing millions of dollars. Though costly, they soon started paying their way. During 1970, for instance, these plants, besides treating the oil and scrubbing the gas, turned out some twenty million barrels of propane, thirteen million of butane and some forty-three million barrels of "pentanes plus," as well as four million long tons of sulphur. These were only by-products of the 325 million barrels of oil and the 1,425 billion cubic feet of gas produced.

But all these riches came only from the conventional oil and gas fields. Until the last decade no one had the courage or could command the tremendous capital needed to begin actual production from the huge reserve of energy lying dormant in the Athabasca oil sands. Known to white men since 1719, reported in Peter Fidler's journals of 1791, these sands, located some two hundred miles north of Edmonton and underlying 23,000 square miles, contain over 300 billion barrels of marketable oil. In 1964 Great Canadian Oil Sands Limited, a subsidiary of Sun Oil Company, had the temerity to start investing $300 million in a plant to produce some 45,000 barrels of oil a day and pipe it to Edmonton. It takes big money to develop resources and big risks too, and sometimes big losses.

But the hundreds of millions of dollars—pennies from Alberta sources, a pittance from Canadian sources and a potful from the United States—invested in scrubbing plants, oil and gas pipelines and

297

refineries, was only part of the total capital spent by the oil industry as a whole. A host of subsidiary companies went into all the variety of new enterprises needed to service all aspects of oil and gas production. On top of them, petrochemical and fertilizer plants of all sorts began to be built in the vicinity of Edmonton and Calgary. The first petrochemical plant, of course, had been built by Cominco at Calgary during the Second World War to supply the raw material for explosives, but these new plants, such as the $70 million Canadian Chemical Company's plant near Edmonton and a dozen others, turned out plastics and other products needed by Canada's expanding peacetime economy.

Each of these plants, ranging from Medicine Hat to Edmonton, required scores or hundreds of employees to operate them and each was to foster a flock of smaller satellite factories. High on the list of new industries created to meet Alberta's increasing demands were steel rolling mills, pipe mills and cement plants. At last Alberta had some heavy industry.

To man these factories thousands immigrated to Alberta and found employment in its cities. Many others found work transporting oil equipment or servicing or repairing it. To them were added hosts of others required to build the thousands of miles of pipeline, the new factories large and small and new office buildings all indirectly linked to the oil industry. Other workers swelled the ranks of those providing financial or professional assistance to that industry, those retailing groceries and supplies to the thousands of new people, and all those employed by the enlarged government departments trying to gear up to cope with the new era. Finally, hundreds more found their livelihood in building homes, hotels, motels and apartments for the new temporary or permanent population.

In regard to population, while Canada grew from 12,292,000 to 21,377,000 (1971), Alberta grew from 803,000 to 1,600,000, an increase of one hundred percent as compared to Canada's growth of seventy-four percent. But far more significant was the increase in its per capita personal income, which in 1939 had been $340 and by 1969 was $2,915. Not only had Alberta's population doubled during the quarter century since Leduc No. 1 but on the average every one of this doubled population had about eight times as much money to spend as his counterpart at the beginning of the period.

During this great influx of workers and their families, metropolitan Edmonton had grown from 113,000 to 449,000, Calgary from 100,000 to 387,000, Lethbridge from 16,500 to 39,500 and Medicine Hat from 12,900 to 25,700. Furthermore, the other cities had shared in the growth; Wetaskiwin now had 6,450 people; Red Deer, 26,900; Lloydminster, 8,000; Camrose, 8,900 and Grande Prairie, 12,500.

Now, because during the quarter century since Leduc investors had spent nearly twelve billion dollars in exploration and development work related to the oil and gas industry, petroleum was predominant in the province's economy. In 1970 from a total of over 35,000 wells (including dry holes) drilled since 1946, 325 million barrels of oil gushed and 1,425 billion cubic feet of gas seethed, bringing with them the by-products, propane, butane, "pentanes plus" and sulphur. During that year the output of all these products had a market value of around a billion and a quarter dollars.

The influx of oil money not only enabled Alberta to hold her own in the new Canadian postwar era of prosperity but to march in front with the leaders. Undoubtedly the province could not have reached its present state of development as quickly without foreign capital and know-how. Looking back at the quarter century of oil development, however, today's Albertans are beginning to wonder if even more dividends could not have been obtained for their resources. But as in the case of the railways built sixty years ago, looking back is easier than yielding to the pressures of the moment.

In any event oil money brought with it increased population; just at a time when Alberta's economy needed exactly the type of assistance it could give, oil played the transitional role which enabled the province to overcome the lower and most difficult rungs on the ladder leading to success in the manufacturing realm. During the last two decades, with oil giving it a hoist, Alberta has broadened and diversified its manufacturing base.

Once its manufacturing role had been merely processing agricultural products but the quarter century to 1971 has changed that until now two-thirds of its factories are in fields not necessarily related to agriculture. Now, North American and even world markets look to Alberta for some of its manufactured production: pulp, nickel, chemicals, fertilizers, edible oils and plastics. Moreover, because of its solid resource base, coupled with tremendous stores of fossil energy (oil, eight billion barrels; gas, forty-eight billion MCF; oil sands, three hundred billion barrels and coal, twenty-five billion tons—in total, eighty-five percent of all Canada's fossil energy resources), Alberta's rate of development (for good or bad) exceeds that of all but a few of the world's regions. In an energy-hungry world, Alberta, possessing all these huge resources of energy, may well hope for a long future during which Canadians will turn increasingly to their Princess province not only for energy but as the location of major manufacturing plants.

All of these industries brought an increased demand for a rapidly diversifying agricultural production. By 1970 Alberta, the one-time forlorn farming province, found its prosperity firmly supported on four substantial bases: mining (including oil), construction, manufacturing and agriculture. Albertans, even those on remote farms, generally satisfied on the matters of food, clothing and housing, began reaching into the fields of luxuries and grasping at all the trappings of the wealthy.

Fortunately these trappings include appreciation and patronage of the arts. Alberta's cultural life suddenly found that the increased piles of folding dollars, combined with a rapid influx of immigrants from the music-steeped cities of Europe, allowed it to flourish as never before. Alongside the discovery of oil, came that of the arts: theatre, ballet, music, opera and painting, each found a new strata to tap and new heights to scale.

Any evening in the week each of Alberta's cities now offer spectators three or four choices of entertainment or cultural stimulation and in all these fields Edmonton and Calgary are particularly rich. Alberta's ethnic mixture has resulted in a colourful tapestry of the arts to which a dozen or so races have contributed, including the Scandinavians; the Ukrainians with their outstanding choirs, orchestral work and dancing; the Italians with their traditional love of and skill in music and the opera; the Jewish communities which so strongly support the province's cultural development, as well as many others. Religious and political differences naturally and fortunately remain in Alberta's mosaic of people, but in the arts they have been submerged in a tremendous contribution to the province's culture.

Fostering all these arts called for considerable subsidies in one form or another from both city and provincial purses. Although scarcely noticed by the general public, the money so expended probably brought more real value per dollar than many a million spent on material needs. Such financial help has brought into being the magnificent auditoriums in Calgary and Edmonton and lesser centres in smaller communities. It has built the enthralling Provincial Museum in Edmonton and the Banff School of Fine Arts, which from small beginnings in 1933 has developed to a world famous centre. New and striking libraries have been built to lay the written word before an increasingly interested populace. In 1970, for instance, the University of Alberta's library tallied up its one-millionth book.

But governments, municipal or provincial, each with assists from the Canada Council, were far from being alone in their aid to the arts. Oil and associated activities have made many Albertans rich and a fair number of them millionaires, and often these turned to expressing their gratitude by endowing various cultural activities and edifices. Though the public is perhaps slow to recognize the fact and some will never acknowledge it, businessmen in all walks of life make their donations and spend much of their time collecting for or fostering the amenities people enjoy. Desirable as it might be to name several of them, one in particular, Eric Harvie, by the magnitude of his contributions running into tens of millions of dollars and the direction his benefices took, stands out. His generosity created the Glenbow Foundation, an institution which needs no further elaboration than its name to be acclaimed for its excellence and its devotion to the preservation of all phases of western Canada's past. The Glenbow Foundation, housing its treasures and carrying out its work in Calgary, has been a significant factor in the province's cultural renaissance. More and more, Albertans, satiated with full bread baskets, are discovering that man cannot live by bread alone.

# 20
# Abounding Material Riches

Though oil was scarcely the Social Credit of which Aberhart had dreamed, it was nevertheless such a good substitute that his one-time followers lost their old-time fervor. With regard to oil, however, the provincial treasurer, ever a cool customer, never lost his. Starting in 1947 he looked down from his eyrie tower, pricked up his ears and during the next decade, by way of lease rentals, sales of royalties and indirect taxes, all of which sprang from the oil industry, plus various sundry taxes, set his hooks into $1,540 million. In 1946 he had collected $45 million in taxes, and owed some $145 million in various quarters. During 1956 he collected more than $250 million in taxes, and, instead of owing money, had some $250 million bulging out his vaults. By then Alberta was in fact debt free, in spite of having spent millions on roads, farm electrification, hospitals, schools and universities, and was still rolling in wealth. By 1970 from the oil industry alone the province had collected over three billion dollars. For Alberta's 1971 budget its petroleum resources were expected to produce over $210 million directly.

While the provincial government can take no credit for the presence of oil in the province, most believe it can take pride in the way it has administered the oil industry and the way in which it has handled the resulting revenues. With an integrity all too rare, Manning ruled his cabinet with a rod of which he was not sparing as soon as his keen perception detected any departure from the straight and narrow way.

In their dealings with the government the oil men were met with firmness and rare ability by the personnel of Alberta's Petroleum and Natural Gas Conservation Board. It made the rules as to spacing of wells, the interrelations of the companies and the rates at which they could produce from the fields. While the companies' individual interests often clashed with those of the board, that body stood firm and came to be one of the most highly respected regulatory authorities in Canada. Its scientific appraisal of all the elements involved and its carefully worked out judgments put the oil industry in Alberta on a sound basis, and on the one hand protected the investors and on the other guarded the public interest. Such is the worldwide acclaim accorded this board that

any history of Alberta should record the names of two of its successive and outstanding chairmen, Ian McKinnon (1948 to 1962) and George Govier who presides over that body at present under its new name, the Energy Resources Conservation Board.

In the eyes of oil men and businessmen in general the application of science to the regulation of the oil industry was only one of Alberta's attributes. Another was the stability of the province's long-time Social Credit government. After assuming office in 1943 Manning kept un-challengeable control for twenty-five years to mark a record for longevity in the premier's office unparalleled in the British Empire. When at last in December 1968, entirely of his own volition, he announced that he had served long enough, he resigned. Soon afterwards, by an ironic spin of fate's wheel, the Liberals in Ottawa appointed this one-time Social Crediter and small *c* conservative to the Senate.

During his long reign he had transformed himself from a radical— and by his adroit touch had converted most of his MLA's—to an ultra conservative stance. Once that happened, businessmen, appreciating stability and in a wholesomely large measure sharing Manning's belief in simple honesty, found a government which they could trust. Alberta became a mecca to which businessmen, whether their purses were lean or bulgy, could entrust their savings.

In 1968, with a nudge from Manning, the Social Credit Party chose Harry E. Strom, a farmer, as his successor. First elected in 1955, Strom held the portfolio of minister of agriculture from 1962 to 1968, and that of municipal affairs until his elevation of the premiership.

Strom's reign was short. Social Credit's long grip on the electorate was loosening and in the 1971 election the Progressive Conservatives swept his government out of office. When the votes were counted, out of seventy-four seats, the Social Crediters had won a third, the New Democratic Party had elected one member and the Conservatives had come to power with a handsome majority.

Heading the revived Conservative party was a dynamic young lawyer, Peter E. Lougheed, the grandson of Calgary's early Senator James Lougheed. Since his election to the provincial house in 1967 he had not only headed the official opposition, but had striven so mightily in reorganizing his party that for the first time in Alberta's history the Conservatives were able to form a government. Rather remarkably the voters in the southern part of the province elected the bulk of those Social Crediters who won their campaigns.

One of the former and present governments' policies, of course, has been to spend ever increasing amounts on the physical and social aspects of the province's life. The 1971 budget of $1.2 billion reached a new high in expenditures. It was nearly twice as much as the sum of all Alberta provincial budgets from 1905 to 1947, the year of the Leduc No. 1 smoke ring. That year it had been $34 million; that of 1971 was thirty-six times that sum and was equal to $750 for every man, woman and child in the province.

Over the years the province's health and hospital facilities had been upgraded beyond what could have been imagined twenty years earlier. After some argument with the federal government, Medicare had been introduced. Then out of the immense expenditure indicated in the 1971 budget, some forty million dollars were earmarked for social development, an area of life in which Alberta led the provincial parade. By a paradox, as the province's and the ordinary man's wealth increased, so did the number of the poor.

In one way or other a great deal of the welfare activity is directed towards the Métis, who have continued to experience difficulty in finding a place in the province's rapidly changing economy. In 1885 the Métis of the West had been given scrip entitling each male adult to claim 160 acres of land and for each of their children not then of age to claim an additional 240 acres. They had little ability to farm and less desire, and sold their claims to the land for a pittance.

For better or worse, in contradistinction to treaty Indians who under the Indian Act received various kinds of assistance, the Métis were considered as white men and were expected to fend for themselves. When on their behalf in 1896 Father Lacombe had secured a grant of land at what came to be called St. Paul des Métis and had tried to get some to settle down to farming, they disappointed the old missionary and his half-breed colony passed out of existence. Native experience and traditions ill-prepared the Métis for agricultural practices or managerial ability, which as many a small white farmer was to find is a main essential of farming. Moreover, mixed-bloods were expected to enjoy all the white man's privileges and obversely to assume his responsibilities. Unfortunately few privileges fell to their lot and they had few opportunities to shoulder responsibilities.

Scattered about in small settlements, mainly north of the North Saskatchewan River, they had watched anxiously while the province changed from a hunting and fishing economy to a land settled by farmers and while, year after year, trapping, on which they had depended so heavily, brought less and less income. All Albertans suffered during the Dirty Thirties but the Métis were reduced to such dire straits that the provincial government set up a commission to study their plight and to suggest remedies.

In 1939, as a result of its efforts, the government passed the Métis Betterment Act, which, although it has been revised from time to time, formed the basis of a new approach to their problem. One of its main

A History of Alberta

provisions set aside unsettled but marginally arable portions of the province for their exclusive use. Seven of these Métis colonies came into being, ranging from areas near Frog and Cold lakes to others near Lac La Biche and in the general High Prairie area, with the most northerly one and the one with the best land at Paddle Prairie, in the vicinity of Keg River. The title to these lands was to remain vested in the Crown, but any Métis family was to be allowed to settle on a portion of these colonies to all intents and purposes as if it possessed title.

Success was slow to shine on these settlements—slow and uncertain. Relatively few of Alberta's mixed-bloods took advantage of the colonies and moved to them. In spite of the fact that out of their total area of some one million and a quarter acres nearly 400,000 were considered capable of producing grain, the 2,800 Métis on them had broken only 12,000 acres by 1970. They were, however, pasturing some 1,665 cattle and over 1,000 horses.

If success measured in white men's terms has been slow, it has nevertheless been real. It is hard for societies to change their customs and beliefs rapidly but in the case of the Métis their interest in the amenities and the ways of the white world has been intensified and their opportunities for partaking of the phases they find beneficial have been enlarged. With government assistance, better homes, health and educational facilities have come into being and highways and electrical lines now reach their settlements. Cooperative ventures in logging and cattle raising have been started. In Métis circles and organizations, local leadership is developing.

The Métis' relations, Alberta's Indians, long the recipients of social assistance which in the past made their lot easier than that of their mixed-blood cousins, have also shared, even if meagrely, in Alberta and Canada's increased prosperity. Hindsight, which we all come by so readily indicates that Canada's policy with respect to its Indians has been sadly lacking. At the turn of the century, of course, that policy, which changed little over the decades, was slowly evolving and seemed the proper one. Like most policies set up in the context of their times by conscientious administrators, the Indian policy appears now to have had more failings than successes and to have done little to bridge the gulf of incomprehension between the dispirited red man and the hustling, profit-conscious white man. For half a century the one-time owners of all Alberta's riches remained on reserves, out of sight of the mainstream of the province's progress, hidden and forgotten. Their many attempts to emerge from their discouraging environment quickly met with disappointment, and rebuffed on every side many soon retired to the shell of their reserves to brood in despair.

For many long years while the natives south of the North Sas-

Abounding Material Riches

katchewan River half-heartedly scratched some of the soil on their reserves to grow grain and also grazed cattle on their circumscribed hills, the Indian population declined. Cattle raising was closest to the plains Indians' way of life, and in that field the Bloods, Piegans, Blackfoot and Stoneys achieved their greatest success. With varying success, all around the reserves as far north as the Athabasca River, white men were tilling the soil and making a fair living, but while successful farms were coming into existence alongside them, the Indians could not bring themselves to emulate the white pioneers. For the sudden transition to the modern world, made doubly difficult by the white man's indifference or open scorn, was beyond their unaided capabilities. And all the good intentions of the federal Indian department officials failed to bridge the frightful gap between the two worlds.

In spite of all these disabilities and about the time of World War I, due to slightly better economic conditions and vastly improved health conditions, the decline in Indian population stopped and the trend reversed. By the end of that war some 9,000 Indians lived in Alberta and by the end of World War II 13,000 Indian people had begun to look out of their reserves and to question the wisdom of the treatment that had been dealt them. Then in less than twenty years their numbers doubled until in 1970 some 29,000 Indians, fired with a determination to break the white man's stultifying hold, began to talk back. Even those Indians north of the Athabasca River, whose isolation from the mainstream of Alberta's development had left them fishing and trapping in the same lakes and the same forests and in the same fashion as their forefathers, began to question the white man's unproven superiority. Living under primitive, nomadic conditions, clustered about the end of some forest-locked lake trying to keep from starving when the wild fur crop failed or the world prices of pelts faltered, they too decided that their starvation in the midst of Canada's plenty must cease.

All this coincided with a new era during which Canadians, having become wealthy, began to consider the plight of the less fortunate and rediscovered the Indians. Some spent their time criticizing what had been done to the Indians, but others more alert to the course of human history wasted little time in recrimination but strove to end the discrimination practised against the native people. Turning to their governments they demanded that this be stopped. But both the government and the Indians, suddenly confronted with an outpouring of money designed to solve the problem, were at a loss when it came to setting up appropriate programs. For money alone could not buy the solution.

In these days of frozen dinners and instant porridge, when money is mistakenly thought to be the cure for any cancer, loans for this and that were made to Indian bands. New homes appeared on the reserves, water

A History of Alberta

supplies and toilets and electricity were provided, and new access roads were cut to the isolated northern reserves. But all these amenities, so long overdue, have only been a start in the right direction—a physical start.

On the physical level the Indians entered the decade of the 1970s much better off financially than most people realized. Out of the 1,600,000 acres of Alberta's reserves, most of which were arable, the native people had some 280,000 under cultivation and grazed 25,000 cattle. Various bands had participated directly in the oil boom with 125 producing wells on their property bringing in some $1,400,000 annually.

On the psychological side the Indians enunciated loudly some largely justified complaints. One obvious move was to stress education where their facilities, while continuously upgraded, were still sadly lacking.

Assuredly in this direction and along the route the Indians are taking in creating a host of organizations to challenge the white man's wisdom, to define native goals and to achieve parity in the white world, the Indians will bring about their own transformation. Recriminations are perhaps consoling; looking to the future, however, in which the Indians also must bear their share of the load, it is important that they define their goals in specifics and not generalities and show even more concrete evidence of helping themselves. The modern world is indeed a far cry from the nostalgic days of the glorious buffalo hunts, but they, like the halcyon days of the great British Empire, are gone forever.

Fortunately out of the turmoil of hazy ideologies and clamouring campaigns, capable Indian leaders are beginning to emerge. The future lies in their hands and in the hands of the inspiring leaders which the years will produce.

Paralleling the increased opportunities available in some small measure even to the Indian and Métis children, a similar and unprecedented upgrading has taken place in all other phases of Alberta's vast educational industry. For with new ideas and new sources of revenue, education too has come into its own. In the rural areas yellow buses on their way to consolidated schools drive past the sites of many an old one-roomed schoolhouse. In the cities, schools have multiplied and expanded into vast conglomerates fitted with swimming pools and all the lavish trimmings available to a wealthy people. It has become increasingly evident that the world bestows its richest material and spiritual prizes on the educated.

From the high schools thousands go on to the magnificent institutions of technology where, instead of having to import them from Europe and the United States, Albertans endeavour to produce their own highly skilled technicians. Other students crowd the three university campuses at Edmonton, Calgary and Lethbridge and the Banff School of Fine Arts.

By 1945 Calgarians who had rankled so long over being defrauded of their university in 1907 had raised their voices so threateningly that a branch of the University of Alberta was established there. Finally in 1966 Calgarians rejoiced when this branch institution was raised to the status of an autonomous campus and named the University of Calgary. Then in 1967 Lethbridge made good its claim for a similar institution.

By 1970 these institutions were sorely overtaxed with nearly 40,000 part-time and full-time students. Of the latter, Lethbridge could boast 1,261; Calgary, 7,962; and the University of Alberta at Edmonton, 17,354. In total, the three universities employed 1,774 full-time faculty members on their campuses, plus a host of part-time instructors, and granted 5,491 degrees, of which 171 were doctorates. Alberta, by ploughing much of its oil riches into education, is merely fertilizing the land so that it will produce the bountiful and as yet unperceived wealth of the future.

In addition to ploughing money into education, Albertans have continued expanding and improving their excellent highway system. Each year further miles of multi-lane highways have been built, new bridges erected, a bewildering array of overpasses and traffic exchanges introduced, more town and village streets paved and additional roads built to remote resources. By 1970, out of a total of some 86,000 miles of roads improved with public funds, 6,600 were considered as primary highways, and of these, 4,900 were paved. Several of these paved highways stretched east and west across the province and 700 miles of first-class pavement extended from the United States border to Manning. With the remaining 240 miles of the Mackenzie Highway between there and the boundary of the Northwest Territories capable of bearing the heaviest trucks, access can be had to the western half of Alberta's northland at sixty miles per hour.

Up the east side of the province the gravel highway to Fort McMurray, the Athabasca oil sands town, is in the process of paving. In the extreme western side of the province a relatively new highway has been built from Hinton to serve the 3,000 people in the recently established coal mining town of Grande Cache and continues to Grande Prairie. As well as these, other shorter road links connect all of the new coal mining or petroleum processing plants scattered here and there all over the area between the Athabasca River and the province's faraway northern boundary. For this expansion of the highway system into the former wilderness has made these new industries possible and they in turn bring in tax income which makes more highways possible.

Making constant use of this ever lengthening highway system in 1971, some 890,000 cars, trucks and buses have placed Albertans among the world's most mobile people. To such an extent is this so that railway passenger traffic is rapidly approaching the vanishing point. Cars, buses, trucks and pipelines have struck telling blows against the intricate network of 6,000 miles of railways for which early Albertans had clamoured. Indeed, several of the minor lines have been discontinued and, now that they are in competition with sixty-six hundred miles of Alberta's well finished primary highways, indications are that others will soon follow them into limbo.

And yet as other railroads were being abandoned, two new ones heading north to resources came into being. One of these, built in the early sixties, the Great Slave Lake Railway, parallels the Mackenzie Highway all the way from Peace River town to Hay River on Great Slave Lake. It carries its share of the freight for the far North and brings out long trains of lead and zinc concentrate from the Pine Point mine which the Klondikers of 1898 had discovered.

The other is the Alberta Resources Railway which was started during the later sixties as an essentially provincial government project. Originally it was to go as far north as Grande Cache to give access to that large field of rich coking coal. That far it was a sound venture.

Unfortunately the cabinet had learned nothing from the much earlier Liberal government's experience with the AGW Railway, nor from the relief of the UFA government when it got out of the railway business. Instead it bowed to popular pressure, this time from the Peace River country, and extended the line to Grande Prairie until the whole venture had cost some $96 million. For the first year or so of that northerly portion's operation, which was completed in 1969, a weekly, though generally empty, train rocked along its roller-coaster track. Following much the same route taken by Ignace Giasson and Tête Jaune the Iroquois 150 years earlier, its southbound trains ascended the Smoky River to Ignace's Grande Cache and then crossed over to strike the Athabasca River near the earlier Jasper House where it joined the CNR tracks.

But during its 1972 spring flood the Smoky River rose and ripped away thousands of feet of fill and hundreds of yards of track on the northerly portion of the new railroad, and trains no longer operate between Grande Prairie and Grande Cache. Estimates of the cost of the repairs and alterations necessary to put that portion of the line back into service run into many millions of dollars.

World demand for oil products (including the Athabasca oil sands and sulphur), pulp, paper and coal have splattered all of Alberta with large and sometimes huge industrial plants with a considerable concentration of them north of the Athabasca River in the area which but a few years ago was the remotest of wildernesses. Just as in previous generations world demand enabled the farmers to market their wheat and cattle, a new and highly industrialized and international world has now come calling on Alberta's nonagricultural resources. The impact of that demand for petroleum products has brought a prosperity to the province which

Abounding Material Riches

has tended to overshadow the very real contribution made by Alberta's other natural resources.

One of these is coal, which has had a checkered career. In the boom years of the twenties its annual production had been over seven million tons. Then during the depression it had fallen back to five million tons, only to regain its influence and to reach an all-time output of 8,826,000 tons during 1946. After that, by a coincidence, in the years following the discovery of the Leduc oil field the railways converted from coal-burning to oil-burning locomotives and a few years later to diesel engines; coal output came a cropper until by 1962 it touched bottom at slightly over two millions tons. But at that point two other major uses of coal were waiting in the wings. One was the export of extra fine coking coal to Japan, which brought the Grande Cache and the Luscar mines into production. The other was coal's increasing use in the production of thermal electric power. Between the two Alberta's annual coal production has risen to 6,600,000 tons and is well on its way to establishing new records.

The output of thermal electric power generated in new plants such as the great coal-burning installations on the Battle River, at Grande Cache and on the shores of Lake Wabamun has grown even more rapidly than the rest of Alberta's economy and for many years has had an annual increase of well over ten percent. The tremendous demand for power arising from all the new industries, coupled with that from a population of rich householders and from some 65,000 electrified farms, has not only necessitated the building of these immense plants but has made it imperative to string huge, new transmission lines up and down the province until now Alberta is covered with a web of interconnected power lines totalling 74,000 miles.

Accompanying the increased use of power, timber and coal and the exploration of our fossil fuels, employment has swept on to new heights, while the manufacturing industry's production has soared to new records. Paralleling its progress, the construction industry practically rebuilt the larger towns and cities. Over a span of a few years it revitalized Edmonton and Calgary. Scores of lofty office structures, including Calgary's spectacular Husky Tower and Edmonton's 35-storey Alberta Government Telephones Building changed the downtown areas beyond recognition. New hotels and a host of office buildings, towering an additional ten or twenty or more floors above the old seven- or eight-storey buildings, began to congest the downtown areas. Hard by in groups or scattered here and there in the vastly expanded new subdivisions, high-rise apartments arose to add variety to the cities' ever changing skyline.

New subdivisions by the dozens, new bridges and arterial roads and shopping malls came into being. Around each city's fringes fascinating new centres filled with shops, spread-eagled over expanses of once rich farming land, competed with their acres of displays of groceries, clothing and all the exotic merchandise sent by faraway world-wide producers eager to sell in this oil-nurtured Alberta.

Much of the older downtown Calgary and Edmonton disappeared, swallowed up by modern glass and stainless steel buildings. With their erection came a renaissance in the arts as better symphony orchestras came into being, new art galleries, new museums, new live theatre and a host of other amenities, including new restaurants and, wonder of wonders, not only public mixed drinking but liquor served with meals.

Two problems, however, worried the thoughtful. The first concerned the export of those raw resources which was paying for these fancy cities and for everyone's luxuries and was in truth an export of capital which a later generation may sorely need. The time is not yet economically right to process all these riches in Alberta, but by the time it becomes so they may well have been exhausted. The second problem, that of the degree of pollution, is relatively minor. Fortunately Alberta is not faced with extensive pollution and, having been warned in time, is taking steps to preserve its ecology and to keep its cities habitable.

Pollution is a problem that can be solved but depletion of resources can ultimately become a desperate situation. No matter how enormous our reserves appear, they are not inexhaustible. Fortunately two of Alberta's main resources are renewable: the forests which grow on 171,000 square miles of our less arable land, and the farmers' crops, which grow in the good soils.

While the cities are burdened with growing populations, the farmers, in spite of their problems, have benefited from the province's riches and are contributing increased production to that wealth. Although agriculture's net value of production has dropped to the bottom of the list of the four most important industries, nevertheless in 1969 it contributed some $620 million to Alberta's economy. Although since the Leduc smoke ring the number of farmers in the province has fallen from some 90,000 to below 65,000, they occupy some fifty million acres of land, of which they cultivate a little more than half. As due to consolidation of farms the rural population dribbled away to the cities, the size of the average holding increased from 460 acres in 1946 to around 700 acres in 1970. Whereas when the Leduc well came in the province's population was fifty-six percent rural, by 1970 that percentage had dropped to thirty.

In recognition of the shift of people to the urban areas, city folk protested vigorously against the injustice inherent in a situation where in effect during provincial elections one rural vote counterbalanced over four city votes. During the 1967 election in the rural riding of Dunvegan, for instance, 3,059 voters marked their ballots to elect one member, while in Calgary's most populous constituency it took 17,070 votes to achieve this same end. In 1967 Calgary and Edmonton together, having half of Alberta's total population, could elect only twenty members out of sixty-five. Finally, during 1969 the government set up a commission to affect a redistribution of electoral districts. While perfect representation by population is impossible to attain, the commission recommended that the province be divided into seventy-five electoral divisions of which it classed thirty-eight as urban and thirty-seven as rural. Edmonton and Calgary between them were to elect twenty-nine members to the legislature and for all practical purposes the long-time overwhelming electoral bias in favour of rural areas was eliminated.

But although the farmer's preponderant influence in provincial affairs has waned, his standard of living unquestionably has risen. During the last two decades many amenities have reached his modern picture-windowed house with its propane or natural gas heating and its electrically-operated farmyard equipment, and no longer need the farmer or his wife feel embarrassed in the presence of city cousins or envious of their conveniences. While some years are better than others, his livelihood is relatively secure. In general, as conditions have changed he has improved his practices to keep abreast of them. Today's large farm-operated feed lots, for instance, were unknown a couple of decades ago.

With commendable and sometimes quixotic audacity the farmer will tackle any problem and tilt at any adversary, imaginary or real. For decades he has challenged the railways and shivered his lance against the immutable monetary system and now by launching into a hail suppression program with the assistance of the provincial government's Alberta Research Council he is threatening Jove and shaking his fists at the very hail clouds which assail him. How successful this venture will be is not yet apparent.

While in essence the magnificent countryside of which his farmstead is so much a part and to which it adds so much has not changed, the methods of farming his particular part of it have changed and differ from those applied in another region. In the extreme south the ranching areas are much the same as they always were, but the experience of years has brought higher returns and fewer losses. In the cultivated south the fall-out from the Dirty Thirties is reflected in even more irrigation, the Taber sugar factory built in 1950, the striking St. Mary's reservoir and more canals, and the Rolling Hills Re-establishment area. Interspersed here and there are the huge strip-farmed fields often yellow with rapeseed where the Noble blade plays its part and where farmers once in the clutches of bankruptcy are now the lords of substantial estates. Farther north and east in the Palliser Triangle, where once hopeful but doomed homesteaders tore up the short grass sod, long scores across the land, occasionally passing a bristly, desiccated caragana hedge or a line of stones, show where irrigation ditches failed and where weathered and disillusioned wheat farmers walked away in disgust. Farther north still, extending from the Red Deer River to the Neutral Hills but within the Palliser Triangle, a hardy breed of folk look fondly over the rolling prairies. Spread sparsely over the land up through Chinook, Sedalia and Consort, the few, whom the Dirty Thirties could not break, till the dry lands with new large-scale equipment and graze their cattle on the heights and over the years have reaped riches.

Still farther north in the glowing parklands bounded on the north by the North Saskatchewan River, farmers of another type, confining their activities to fewer but richer acres, have also consolidated their holdings. Now, keeping pace with the great changes in agricultural methods, they mix grain farming with hogs and cattle and are grateful that seventy years ago their grandparents threw in their lot with a land so fair. Between the North Saskatchewan River and the Athabasca, where a few areas of exceptional fertility form patches and bays in a land otherwise roughened by glacial moraines, thousands of farmers who till the grey-wooded soil find their living less lucrative than that of their colleagues farther south. They too have found it advantageous to change to newer methods, to grow grasses and rape, to feed cattle, wait upon hundreds of hogs and to reduce their numbers but expand the acres left for the remainder. Along with rich farms the area contains many marginal operations which by the inexorable laws of economics and with the assistance of the federal government's Agricultural Rehabilitation Development Authority (ARDA) are slowly and reluctantly being abandoned and either absorbed by a more capable neighbour or allowed to revert to the forest out of which, with infinite labour, they were hewn. But for those hundreds of farmers who persist and succeed, this green land teeming with waterfowl and song birds, glowing with fireweed and tiger lilies and bathed in the balm of spring or steeped in the fragrance of autumn, has no peer in charm or contentment.

Although a line drawn east and west halfway between the borders of the United States and the Northwest Territories passes south of the town of Athabasca, the area south of that line is much smaller than that north of it. For many a weary mile north of that line, however, a traveller passes through various types of forest, all productive of pulp and saw timber and petroleum products but not arable. Then suddenly he enters the lush farming area of the well-known Peace River country. In general, as a band of varying width and wealth, it extends along the Peace River from British Columbia's Pouce Coupé Creek to Fort Vermilion, some four hundred river miles. This is the Peace River country with its fifteen million acres of arable land, of which perhaps five million are cultivated,

Abounding Material Riches

the country that carries farming so far north in Alberta. In its most northerly region, that from High Level to Fort Vermilion, the area which is served by the Mackenzie Highway and the Great Slave Lake Railway, contiguous farms of one or two square miles in extent spread over the arable soils in a wide band more than fifty miles long—excellent farms 660 miles north of the 49th parallel. Within twenty-five miles of being as far north as Port Churchill on Hudson Bay and within 125 miles of being as far north as the southern tip of glacier-covered Greenland, crops in this good farming area ripen in the fall sunshine. Twice as far north of the United States border as the most northerly farm in Saskatchewan and three times as far as Manitoba's most northerly farm, flax and oats sway in the summer breezes. And these Fort Vermilion farms are only a fraction of the agricultural land of the Peace River country.

But whether they were on the shady side of the Sweet Grass Hills or 660 miles north on the sunny side of Caribou Mountain, it was the farmer who first ferreted out each of the province's arable valleys and converted them to the fascinating far-flung Alberta we know. It was the farmer who for half a century carried Alberta's economic ball and who each year continues to lay a mighty harvest in the province's lap. In spite of Alberta's other riches, it is farming which preserves the character of our beautiful, bountiful province. And since farmers cultivate a resource renewable with each spring's rains and harvest it in each August's heat, they look to a long future.

Alberta, however, has other and very important resources. With its magnificent mountains, the widespread beauty of productive farm lands and the fascination of its remote but now easily accessible northern areas, it is becoming recognized as a tourist haven. But far exceeding in value any of its other resources is the yearly renewable crop of its students who in their thousands, enjoying unparalleled leisure earned for them by the struggles of the pioneers, flock through the schools and universities. In their hands, freed by Alberta's wealth to feel their way into the future, and in their brains, crammed with learning never available to any other generation, lies Alberta's greatest wealth, the wealth which inevitably will improve our very good present system and the wealth which will delve into and perceive physical and social resources of which we are yet unaware and develop them for the good of mankind. Moreover, they, the third and fourth generation fruit of Alberta's pioneers, are today's product of the province's rich mosaic of many ethnic stocks living in harmony in a progressive and fruitful land—a people closing each day in safety and contentment, sleeping through a peaceful night and arising with a zest for the challenges ahead.

And indeed there are challenges ahead. For they have come on the scene at a time when the more advanced of mankind have at last realized

A History of Alberta

that our technology and our pelf have brought us to a perilous fork in the road. There, one sign points to the short, easy, paved speedway leading to the dead end of material success; the other points to a new, dimly perceived path barely scratched out along jagged rocky ledges, through thorny thickets and across quaking bogs, but holding forth the promise that along it social values will supersede mercenary motives. To that path our young people, like ourselves, subscribe.

But now for the first time in all his long history man has the capability to choose his future. In opening up our province the pioneers of seventy-five years ago chose to follow a rough road and stuck with it until they set sunny Alberta on the highway to our modern material riches. Today's youth, having no less courage but infinitely more know-how, have the opportunity to choose their own rocky path of sacrifice and patience which, pursued quietly but persistently, could lead them and the world to witness the swiftest expansion of human well-being that has ever coloured men's dreams.

If they have the will, Alberta as always will give them the wherewithal.

## Historical Highlights

1716    William Stewart becomes first white man to travel in the Mackenzie watershed.

1719    Swan, the Cree, takes first sample of Athabasca tar sands to Hudson's Bay Company.

1730    Approximate date that Alberta Indians acquire horses and guns.

1754    First white man—Anthony Henday—arrives.

1778    Peter Pond crosses Methy Portage and builds the first white man's house in Alberta on the lower Athabasca River.

1782    Crees and Beavers make peace at Peace Point.

1786    A. N. McLeod builds the second house in Alberta at present-day Fort McMurray.

1787    Peter Pond was growing vegetables at his post.

1787    David Thompson's first view of Alberta.

1788    First Fort Chipewyan built.

1789    Alexander Mackenzie sets out from Chipewyan and reaches the Arctic Ocean.

1792    First fur trade post built on Saskatchewan River in Alberta.

1792    Peter Fidler on his famous trip to southern Alberta discovers coal.

1793    Alexander Mackenzie sets out from the junction of Peace and Smoky rivers and reaches the Pacific Ocean.

1795    First Edmonton House established.

1799    Rocky Mountain House built.

1805    Fort Dunvegan established.

1807    David Thompson crosses the mountains to reach Columbia River.

1811    David Thompson travels through Athabasca Pass on his way to the Columbia.

1812    First all white child born in Alberta.

1813    Hudson's Bay Company moved Edmonton House to its permanent location within the present city limits.

1821    Hudson's Bay Company and North-West Company amalgamate.

| 1822 | Hudson's Bay Company sends out the abortive Bow River Expedition. |
| 1823 | John Rowand takes charge of Edmonton House. |
| 1824 | First Alberta road cut from Edmonton to Fort Assiniboine— Edmonton thus became an important depot on the first trans-Canada highway to the coast. |
| 1832 | Hudson's Bay Company builds Piegan Post on Bow River. |
| 1833 | Cattle already domiciled at Edmonton. |
| 1838 | First missionaries—Blanchet and Demers—pass through. |
| 1840 | Rev. R. T. Rundle, Methodist, takes up residence at Edmonton. |
| 1841 | Hudson's Bay Company's Oregon-bound colonists pass through Edmonton. |
| 1842 | Rev. Father A. Thibault, Roman Catholic, comes to live at Edmonton. |
| 1843 | Rev. Father A. Thibault establishes Lac Ste. Anne mission. |
| 1852 | Rev. Father Lacombe arrives. |
| 1854 | John Rowand dies. |
| 1857 | Palliser Expedition arrives. |
| 1858 | Earliest gold panners reach Alberta. |
| 1859 | Three Grey Nuns arrive. |
| 1861 | Father Lacombe establishes St. Albert. |
| 1862 | Overlanders pass through on way to Cariboo goldfields. |
| 1862 | Brother Scollen starts a school. |
| 1862 | Arrival of Rev. George McDougall. |
| 1865 | Cree and Blackfoot battle near Red Deer Lake. |
| 1867 | Canadian Confederation. |
| 1868 | A. J. Snyder opens Methodist day school at Edmonton. |
| 1869 | Red River Rebellion. |
| 1869 | First whisky post—Whoop-Up—built. |
| 1869 | Crowfoot emerges as prominent leader. |
| 1869 | Maskepatoon killed. |
| 1870 | Alberta legally becomes part of Canada. |
| 1870 | Smallpox epidemic. |
| 1870 | Last Indian battles at Edmonton and Lethbridge. |
| 1872 | 49th parallel surveyed. |
| 1872 | Nick Sheran starts his mine at Coalbanks (Lethbridge). |
| 1873 | First Dominion land survey in Alberta. |
| 1874 | North West Mounted Police build Fort Macleod and arrive at Edmonton. |
| 1875 | First steamboat, the *Northcote*, reaches Edmonton. |
| 1875 | Mounted Police start Fort Calgary. |
| 1876 | Indian Treaty No. 6 signed. |
| 1876 | Sioux seek refuge in Canada. |

| 1876 | Frank Oliver arrives at Edmonton. |
| 1876 | Several ranchers around Fort Macleod. |
| 1877 | Treaty No. 7 signed with the Blackfoot. |
| 1878 | First official post office at Edmonton. |
| 1879 | Buffalo nearing vanishing point. |
| 1879 | Telegraph line extended into Edmonton. |
| 1879 | Edmonton's Agricultural Society formed. |
| 1880 | Edmonton *Bulletin* starts publishing. |
| 1882 | Maclead *Gazette* started. |
| 1882 | Northwest Territories divided into four districts, one of which was Alberta. |
| 1883 | Alberta elects first representative to Territorial Government. |
| 1883 | CPR reaches South Saskatchewan River at Medicine Hat and goes on to Calgary. |
| 1883 | First natural gas struck at Alderson. |
| 1883 | Calgary *Herald* started. |
| 1883 | Steamboat *Grahame* built to ply from Fort McMurray to Smith Rapids. |
| 1884 | Calgary incorporated as town. |
| 1884 | F. W. G. Haultain arrives at Fort Macleod. |
| 1885 | Calgary Agricultural Society organized. |
| 1885 | Northwest Rebellion. |
| 1885 | Narrow gauge railway, Lethbridge to Medicine Hat. |
| 1886 | Steamer *Wrigley* navigates down Mackenzie River. |
| 1887 | D. W. Davis becomes first federal member from Alberta. |
| 1887 | Town of Cardston started. |
| 1887 | First Alberta labour union. |
| 1887 | First electric service in Calgary. |
| 1888 | Northwest Territories Legislative Assembly established. |
| 1889 | Edmonton starts the first board of trade west of Winnipeg. |
| 1889 | Germans from Ukraine settle near Medicine Hat. |
| 1890 | Crowfoot dies. |
| 1891 | Calgary and Edmonton Railway completed. |
| 1891 | Father Morin's French colonists arrive. |
| 1891 | First Ukrainians look Alberta over. |
| 1891 | Start of significant farming settlement near Edmonton. |
| 1891 | Farmers begin to organize. |
| 1892 | Edmonton incorporated as a town. |
| 1892 | Calgary incorporated as a city. |
| 1892 | Parry Sound colonists arrive. |
| 1892 | Beginnings of group Scandinavian settlements. |
| 1894 | Drilling for oil at Athabasca Landing. |
| 1896 | Father Lacombe starts St. Paul des Métis colony. |

1897    Klondike Rush starts.
1897    Crowsnest Pass Railway started.
1899    Treaty No. 8 signed north of Athabasca River.
1903    Barr colonists arrive.
1903    Frank slide.
1903    Billy Cochrane brings first automobile to Alberta.
1903    Settlers start to trickle into Peace River country.
1904    Edmonton incorporated as a city.
1905    Province of Alberta created with Edmonton as temporary capital, and A. C. Rutherford becomes the first premier.
1905    CNR Transcontinental reaches Edmonton.
1906    Cities of Lethbridge, Medicine Hat and Wetaskiwin incorporated.
1907    Strathcona incorporated as a city.
1908    University of Alberta started in Strathcona.
1909    United Farmers of Alberta organized.
1909    First Alberta aeroplane flight.
1909    First samples of Marquis wheat distributed.
1910    A. L. Sifton becomes premier.
1911    CPR completes first major irrigation system.
1912    Edmonton and Strathcona amalgamate.
1912    Calgary's first Stampede.
1913    Alberta Farmers' Co-operative Elevator Company incorporated.
1913    First Ukrainian elected to legislature.
1914    Turner Valley's Dingman well comes in.
1914    Hillcrest mine disaster.
1914    Start of World War I.
1914    Viking gas field discovered.
1915    Imposition of prohibition.
1916    Alberta Provincial Police organized.
1916    Chautauqua started.
1916    E.D. & B.C. Railway reaches Peace River country and AGW Railway heads for Fort McMurray.
1916    Henry Wise Wood leads UFA.
1916    Franchise extended to women.
1916    Death of Father Lacombe.
1917    Death of Rev. John McDougall.
1917    First woman elected to legislature.
1917    Charles Stewart assumes premier's office.
1918    Armistice signed.
1918    Onset of Spanish Flu.
1918    Returned aviators start civil aeroplane companies.
1921    United Farmers of Alberta party sweeps Liberal government from office and makes H. Greenfield premier.

| 1922 | First radio station. |
|------|----------------------|
| 1923 | Prohibition rejected. |
| 1923 | Alberta Wheat Pool organized. |
| 1925 | Evangelist William Aberhart starts broadcasting. |
| 1925 | J. E. Brownlee succeeds Greenfield as UFA premier. |
| 1926 | Herman Trelle of Peace River country wins world wheat championships. |
| 1927 | First talking movies. |
| 1929 | Women recognized as "persons." |
| 1929 | Neon signs appear. |
| 1929 | Start of the Great Depression. |
| 1931 | Alberta Provincial Police disbanded. |
| 1931 | Alberta accomplishes return of its natural resources from Ottawa. |
| 1933 | Banff School of Fine Arts started. |
| 1934 | R. G. Reid succeeds premier Brownlee. |
| 1935 | Aberhart's Social Crediters sweep UFA out of office. |
| 1936 | Number of farmers reaches all-time peak, 99,732. |
| 1936 | Drought compounds problems of the Dirty Thirties. |
| 1939 | Start of World War II. |
| 1940 | Social Credit government re-elected. |
| 1942 | Americans build Alaska Highway. |
| 1943 | Premier Aberhart dies and is succeeded by E. C. Manning. |
| 1946 | Start of heavy drift from farms to city. |
| 1947 | Beginning of oil era—Leduc No. 1 Well. |
| 1948 | First of new oil refineries built. |
| 1950 | Inter-provincial pipe line completed to Ontario. |
| 1957 | First pulp mill started at Hinton. |
| 1961 | Alberta Gas Trunk company started. |
| 1964 | Northern Alberta Railways extended to Northwest Territories. |
| 1964 | Great Canadian Oil Sands start developing Athabasca oil sands. |
| 1966 | University of Calgary achieves autonomy. |
| 1966 | University of Lethbridge started. |
| 1968 | Premier Manning resigns after twenty-five years' service and is succeeded by Harry Strom. |
| 1969 | Alberta Resources Railway completed from Jasper Park to Grande Prairie. |
| 1971 | Social Credit regime is ended when Peter Lougheed leads a revivified Progressive Conservative Party to form Alberta's first Conservative government. |

## Picture Credits

Page *1*, top: Dr. R. G. Forbis, bottom: Franklin Arbuckle for the Hudson's Bay Company; page *2*, top left: Hudson's Bay Company, top right: Provincial Archives, Victoria, B.C., bottom: Alberta Provincial Library; page *3*, top left: Alberta Government Photographs, Ernest Brown Collection, top right and bottom: Glenbow-Alberta Institute; page *4*, Glenbow-Alberta Institute; page *5*, top: Glenbow-Alberta Institute, bottom: Geological Survey of Canada; page *6*, Glenbow-Alberta Institute; page *7*, top: Glenbow-Alberta Institute, bottom: Geological Survey of Canada; page *8*, top: Glenbow-Alberta Institute, bottom: Geological Survey of Canada and Glenbow-Alberta Institute; page *9*, top: Alberta Government Photographs, Ernest Brown Collection, bottom: Geological Survey of Canada; page *10* – page *11*, Glenbow-Alberta Institute; page *12*, top left and right: Glenbow-Alberta Institute, bottom: Provincial Museum and Archives, Ernest Brown Collection; page *13*, top left: Provincial Museum and Archives, Ernest Brown Collection, top right: Alberta Government Photographs, Ernest Brown Collection, bottom: Glenbow-Alberta Institute; page *14*, Glenbow-Alberta Institute; page *15*, top right and left: Glenbow-Alberta Institute, bottom: Alberta Government Photographs, Ernest Brown Collection; page *16*, top left: University of Alberta, top right: Glenbow-Alberta Institute, bottom: Alberta Government Photographs, Ernest Brown Collection; page *17,* Glenbow-Alberta Institute; page *18*, top: University of Alberta, bottom: Glenbow-Alberta Institute; page *19*, Glenbow-Alberta Institute; page *20*, top: Glenbow-Alberta Institute, bottom: Percy Page and McDermid Studios; page *21*, Glenbow-Alberta Institute; page *22*, top: Glenbow-Alberta Institute, bottom: Dominion Research Station, Lethbridge, and Neils Kloppenburg; page *23*, Glenbow-Alberta Institute; page *24*, top left: Provincial Museum and Archives, top right: Glenbow-Alberta Institute, bottom left: Glenbow-Alberta Institute, bottom right: R. G. Reid; page *25*, top left: Alberta Government Photographs, top right: E. C. Manning, bottom left: Alberta Government Photographs, bottom right: Peter E. Lougheed; page *26* – *27*, Provincial Museum and Archives; page *28*, top left: Provincial Museum and Archives, top right: Alberta Government Photographs; bottom: Provincial Museum and Archives; page *29*, top: University of Lethbridge, bottom: University of Alberta; page *30*, Alberta Government Photographs; page *31*, top: Alberta Government Photographs, middle: City of Edmonton, bottom: Freelance Photos Ltd.; page *32*, top: Lethbridge *Herald*, middle and bottom: Alberta Government Photographs.

# Index

Athabasca oil sands, 35, 152, 243, 297, 308
Athabasca Pass, 45, 46, 117
Athabasca: town of, 103, 242, 313
Atlantic Well No. 3, 289, 292
Attickashish, 26

Baker, I. G. Co., 93, 98, 121, 123, 125
Banff National Park, 153
Banff School of Fine Arts, 300, 307
Banff: town of, 16, 65, 66, 138, 153, 157, 158, 178, 190, 194, 259
Bannerman, James, 137
Bardo settlement, 169
*Baroness*: steamboat, 138, 145, 148
Barr Colony, 117, 176
Barr, Rev. I. M., 176
Bassano: town of, 203, 221
Batoche: battle of, 146
Battleford (Sask.), 21, 29, 30, 110, 119, 129, 132, 146, 198
Bayrock, Dr. L. A., 14
Bear's Paw, Chief, 108
Beauchamp, Jaques, 38
Beaulieu, Jacques, 38
Beaulieux, Francois, 38
Beaumont: hamlet of, 167
Beauvallon: village of, 170
Beaver Lake post office, 166
Beaverhill Creek, 166, 169
Beaverlodge: town of, 259
Becker, Cy, 248
Bell, H., 125
Bell Telephone Co., 209
Bellevue: village of, 150, 233
Bennett, R. B., 159, 188, 191, 210, 211, 221, 224, 245, 255, 262, 271, 283
Berger, Jacob, 54
Bezanson, A. M., 204
Big Bear, Chief, 92, 103, 139, 140, 141, 142, 143, 146
Big Swan, Chief, 91, 101
Bigstone Creek, 141
Big Valley: village of, 202
Birch Mountain, 39
Bird, James, 52, 61
Bird, Jamie Jock, 61
Bisson, Baptist, 38
Bjorkgren, Karl, 168

Black Diamond: village of, 221, 259
Blackfoot Crossing, 105, 122, 135, 140, 162
Blackmud Creek, 166
Blairmore: town of, 150, 230, 241
Blakiston, Thos., 75, 76
Blanchet, Fr. Francois, 64
Boat Encampment, 45
Bompas, Rev. W. C., 87
Bond (whisky trader), 100
Bonnyville: town of, 39
Bootlegging, 240
Bourassa, Rev. Fr., 69
Bourgeau, Eugene, 75
Bowell: hamlet of, 200
Bower, James, 210
Bow Island: town of, 221
Bowness, E.W., 247
Bow River Expedition, 51–55
Boyer, Chas., 38
Boyle, J. R., 195
Boyle, Lord, 143, 158
Bradon, T. B., 135, 136
Bragg Creek, 120
Brazeau: village of, 233
Bredin, Fletcher, 204
Bremner, Chas., 154
Bremner: village of, 167
Brett, Dr. R. G., 158
Brick, Rev. J. Gough, 154
Bricker, Elias W., 172
Brisbois, Insp. E. A., 119, 121
Brockett: hamlet of, 125
Brooks: town of, 200, 204, 221, 273
Brown, John George "Kootenai," 88, 124, 143, 144, 151
Brown, R. A. (Bob), 273
Brown, Roy, 248
Browning, A. G., 240
Brownlee, Premier J. E., 254, 256, 261, 264
Bruderfeld: post office, 166
Bruderheim: village of, 166
Buffalo: disappearance of, 111
Bull's Head, Chief, 108, 122, 123
Bullshead Creek, 134
Bulyea, G. H. V., 189, 191, 192
Bungo, Pierre, 53
Burns, Patrick, 225
Butze: hamlet of, 201
Byemoor: hamlet of, 201

Enchant: village of, 241
Entwistle: town of, 196, 233
Evans, Rev. James, 68
*Eye Opener*, 156, 180
Eyehill Creek, 18

Faford, Rev. Father, 142
Fairview: town of, 204, 247
Falher, Rev. Father, 205
Faraud, Rev. Father, 69, 87
Farmers' Assn. of Alberta, 185
Farmers' Union, 184
Fidler, Peter, 31–36, 39, 42, 51;
   discovers coal, 32
Finlay, John, 38
Finlay, W. T., 190
Fish Creek, 122, 127, 165
Fisher, C. W., 192
Fleming, Sandford A., 117, 118
Forbis, Dr. R. G., 15
Forgues, Donat, 205
Fort Macleod: incorporated, 157;
   town of, 123, 124, 128–131, 135,
   137–140, 143, 144, 149, 150, 157,
   171, 177, 230
Fort McMurray: town of, 216, 242,
   243, 248, 308
Fort Saskatchewan: town of, 42,
   166, 167, 169
Forts (Houses, Posts): Acton House,
   33, 42; Assiniboine, 55, 57, 60,
   61, 68, 85, 117; Astoria (Oregon),
   45; Augustus, 33, 39, 42, 43, 46,
   47, 52, 59; Benton (Montana),
   54, 62, 87, 88, 93–98, 123, 126,
   137; Boggy Hall, 33; Bow River
   (Piegan Post), 61; Brisbois. *See*
   Calgary; Buckingham House, 31,
   32, 42; Calgary (police). *See* Calgary; Carlton House, 75, 78, 79,
   103, 104, 118; Chesterfield House,
   34, 42, 46, 51, 53; Chipewyan, 14,
   36, 38, 42, 43, 48–50, 57, 58, 68,
   69, 80, 85, 87, 160, 249; Colville
   (Washington), 66; Cumberland
   House (Sask.), 34, 36, 68; de
   Tremble, 38; Dunvegan, 38, 42,
   48, 57, 58, 85, 86, 124, 204, 247;
   Edmonton House. *See* Edmonton;
   Elbow River (whisky), 94; Ellice,
   118; Ethier (military), 145; Fitz-
gerald, 274; Fork, 38, 39; Garry,
   65–69, 78–81, 85, 87, 98, 103;
   George, 31, 32, 39, 42, 47; Ghost
   River, 121; Greenwich House, 39;
   Jasper House, 57, 85, 309;
   Kanouse's Post (whisky), 94, 120;
   Kootenae House, 44; La Jonquière
   (Sask.), 26; Lesser Slave Lake
   Post, 85; Macleod (police), 99,
   111, 113, 117, 119, 123, 125–127,
   130, 138; Manchester House
   (Sask.), 31; McKenzie Post
   (Montana), 62, 63; McMurray,
   16, 35, 36, 39, 57, 137; Moose
   Lake, (Lac d'Orignal), 39; Nelson
   (B.C.), 274, 280; Nelson House
   (Alta.), 33; Normandeau (mili-
   tary), 145; Ostell (military), 145;
   Pembina House, 33; Piegan Post,
   61; Pitt (Sask.), 71, 87, 142, 146;
   Providence (N.W.T.), 249; Rae
   (N.W.T.), 274; Resolution
   (N.W.T.), 249, 250; Rocky
   Mountain House, 33, 42, 44, 54,
   57, 58, 61, 79, 85, 117, 119, 121;
   St. John (B.C.), 274; St. Louis
   (Sask.), 26, 29, 30; St. Mary's
   House, 49; Saleesh House (Mon-
   tana), 44; Saskatchewan (police),
   33, 118, 122, 127, 141; Shaw
   (Montana, American army), 89;
   Simpson (N.W.T.), 69, 87, 249,
   250; Slide-out (whisky), 93;
   Smith (N.W.T.), 137, 154, 249;
   Spitzee (whisky), 88; Standoff
   (whisky), 93, 98; Sturgeon Creek.
   *See* Fort Saskatchewan; Union
   (North Dakota), 61, 63; Van-
   couver (Washington), 64, 66;
   Vermilion (Peace River), 38, 42,
   48, 85, 87, 154, 160, 248, 250,
   313, 314; Victoria, 85; Walsh
   (police), 102, 104, 126, 134;
   Wedderburn, 48, 49; Whitemud
   House (Wabamun Creek), 33;
   Whoop-up (whisky), 88, 93, 94,
   98, 99, 124
Fourmand, Rev. Father, 120
Frank, H. L., 178
Frank slide, 178–180
Frank: village of, 150, 178, 233

Lethbridge Northern Irrigation
District, 242
Lethbridge, Wm., 138
Levan, Howard, 219
Lewis & Clark expedition, 50, 52
Lille: village of, 150
Limestone Lake settlement, 168
Lineham, John, 158
Little Chicago: hamlet of, 259
Little Pine, Chief, 92
Livingstone Range, 32
Livingstone, Sam, 88
Lloyd, Rev. George E., 176
Lloydminster: city of, 18, 117, 170,
176, 187, 196, 198, 207, 209, 226,
246–250, 271, 288, 298
Lodgepole: village of, 33, 44
Lougheed, Premier Peter E., 303
Lougheed, Senator James, 135, 156,
159, 221
Love, Timolean, 79, 80
Lower Post (B.C.), 274
Lucas, Alex, 156
Lucas, S. B., 141
Luchkovich, Michael, 253
Luscar Mine, 310
Lyndon Creek, 127

MacDonald, Big Donald, 46
MacDonald, John, 33
Macdonald, Prime Minister John A.,
82–84, 95, 96, 117, 119, 132
MacKay, Alex, 38
Mackenzie Air Services, 279
Mackenzie, Sir Alexander, 33–39,
43, 47, 50, 69
Mackenzie & Mann, 191, 220
Mackenzie Highway, 308, 309, 314
MacKenzie, Mayor K. W., 189, 191
Mackenzie, Roderick, 36
Mackenzie, Wm., 191, 198
Macleod *Gazette*, 131, 157
Macleod, Major J. F., 97–100, 121
McAdams, Roberta, 237
McCall, F. R. G., 247, 248
McCauley, Matt, 153, 191
McClung, Nellie, 237, 249
McConachie, Grant, 274, 279
McCreight, Jim, 204
McCurdy, John, 218

McDougall, David, 120, 121, 125
McDougall, Rev. George, 86, 92,
117, 120, 121
McDougall, George (fur trader),
68, 69
McDougall, Rev. John, 86, 92, 99,
101, 102, 120, 121, 125, 143,
225, 236
McDougall, John A. (merchant),
153
McFarland, Joe, 125
McGillivray, Duncan, 32
McGillivray, John, 48
McGillivray, Wm., 61
McIntyre, Duncan, 133
McKenzie, Donald, 52, 53
McKenzie, Kenneth, 54
McKinney, Louise, 237, 249
McKinnon, Ian, 302
McLachlan, Rev. A. J., 141
McLaurin, D. F., 79
McLean, Archie, 225
McLean, Flatboat, 132
McLennan: town of, 242
McLeod, A. N., 36, 38, 42
McMullan, A. F., 152, 156
McNaughton, General A. G. L., 275
McQuarrie, A. H., 205

Magrath, C. A., 158, 199
Magrath: town of, 157, 165, 199
Maidstone (Sask.), 31
Malmo settlement, 168
Manitoba Act, 84, 114
Manitoba: becomes province, 84
Mann, Donald, 191, 198
Manning, Premier Ernest C.,
267–270, 283–285, 302, 303
Manning: town of, 247, 308
Mannville: town of, 32
Marchand, Father F., 142
Markerville: hamlet of, 169
Marwayne: town of, 18, 247, 259
Maskepatoon, Chief, 86, 91
Massacre Butte, 90
May, "Wop", 247, 248
Meade, Jim, 204
Meadow Creek, 127
Medicine Hat: city of, 88, 124, 131,
138, 139, 144–151, 157–159, 165,
166, 171, 177, 182, 185, 187, 190,

Index

Shandro, Andrew, 215
Shandro, Stefan, 170
Shaw, Angus, 39
Sheep Creek, 127, 165, 200, 221
Sheerness: hamlet of, 202, 257
Shepard: hamlet of, 134
Sheppard, Rice, 210
Sheran, Nicholas, 126
Sibbald: hamlet of, 232
Sifton, Premier, A. L., 211, 215, 237
Sifton, Clifford, 174, 185, 188
Silver City, 135, 138, 152
Simpson, Sir George, 49–60, 65–74, 80, 81, 85; meets plains chiefs at Edmonton, 65; sends settlers to Oregon, 66
Sinclair, James, 66
Sinclair Pass, 66
Sitting Bull, Chief, 104, 105, 111, 113
Sitting-on-an-Eagle-Tail, Chief, 108
Skinner, T. J. S., 221
Slawa Creek, 170
Smallpox, 63, 91, 92
Smith: village of, 205
Smith, J. B., 125
Smith, Joseph, 30
Smoky Lake: town of, 43, 196, 247
Snyder, Clarence, 245
Society of Equity, 184, 210
Solomon, Mose, 93
South African War, 155
South Edmonton, 149, 154; incorporated, 155
Southern Alberta Land Co., 241
Spanish Flu, 238
Special Areas, 202, 232
Spirit River: town of, 154
Stafford, Wm., 138
Stanmore: hamlet of, 257
Steele, Col. Sam B., 118
Steinhauer, Rev. Henry B., 86
Stephansson, S. Gudmundson, 169
Stephen, George, 133, 136
Stettler: town of, 26, 32, 103, 196, 198, 267
Stewart, Premier Chas., 238, 242
Stewart, Major John, 143
Stewart, Wm., 35
Stinson, Katherine, 237
Stony Plain: town of, 166, 169

Strange, Major General T. Bland, 131, 141–143
Strathcona: city of, 156, 159, 180, 181, 185, 189, 191, 210, 216, 217, 221; incorporation, 155
Strathcona, Lord (Donald A. Smith), 84, 133–136, 155, 227
Strom, Premier Harry, 303
Suffield: village of, 242
Sun Oil Co., 297
Sundre: town of, 171, 172
Sunnynook: hamlet of, 257
Sutter, Chas., 193
Svarich, Peter, 170
Swan Hills: town of, 288, 293
Swanson, C. A., 168
Swift, Lewis, 172
Swift Current (Sask.), 103, 272

Taber: town of, 13, 159, 312
Taché, Bishop A. A., 69
Tail Creek settlement, 88, 92, 122, 151, 171, 172
Taylor, Alex, 153
Taylor, Kamoose, 124, 131
Tees: village of, 172
Territorial Grain Growers' Assn., 210
Tête Jaune, the Iroquois, 309
The Pas (Man.), 30, 103
The Swan, Cree trader, 35, 36
Therien, Rev. Father Adeadot, 173
Thibault, Rev. Father A., 65, 68, 78
Thomas, R. C., 156
Thomas, the Iroquois, 46
Thompson, David, 10, 20, 23, 24, 31, 39, 43, 46, 50, 52
Thompson, W. T., 154
Thomson, L. B , 272
Three Forks (Montana), 52
Three Hills Creek, 32
Three Hills: town of, 217, 256
Three Persons, Tom, 225
Three Suns, Chief, 90, 91, 100
Three Swans, Chief, 64
Throne: hamlet of, 232
Tissier, Rev. Father, 86
Tobacco Plains, 23
Todd, Dr. Wm., 49
Tofield: town of, 233
Tomison, Wm., 33

A History of Alberta